W9-CTW-167

UNITED STATES

City to City Atlas

For the Traveling Professional

© Copyright 1991 by Creative Sales Corporation, 1350 Michael Drive, Suite B, Wood Dale, Illinois 60191. All material contained within this publication is copyrighted by Creative Sales Corporation and all rights are reserved. Reproduction of this information in whole or in part without the express written permission of Creative Sales Corporation is prohibited. ISBN 0-933162-45-6.

American Map
Part of the Langenscheidt Publishing Group

Contents

State, City Center, Vicinity & Weigh Scale Maps

(* denotes detailed city center map)

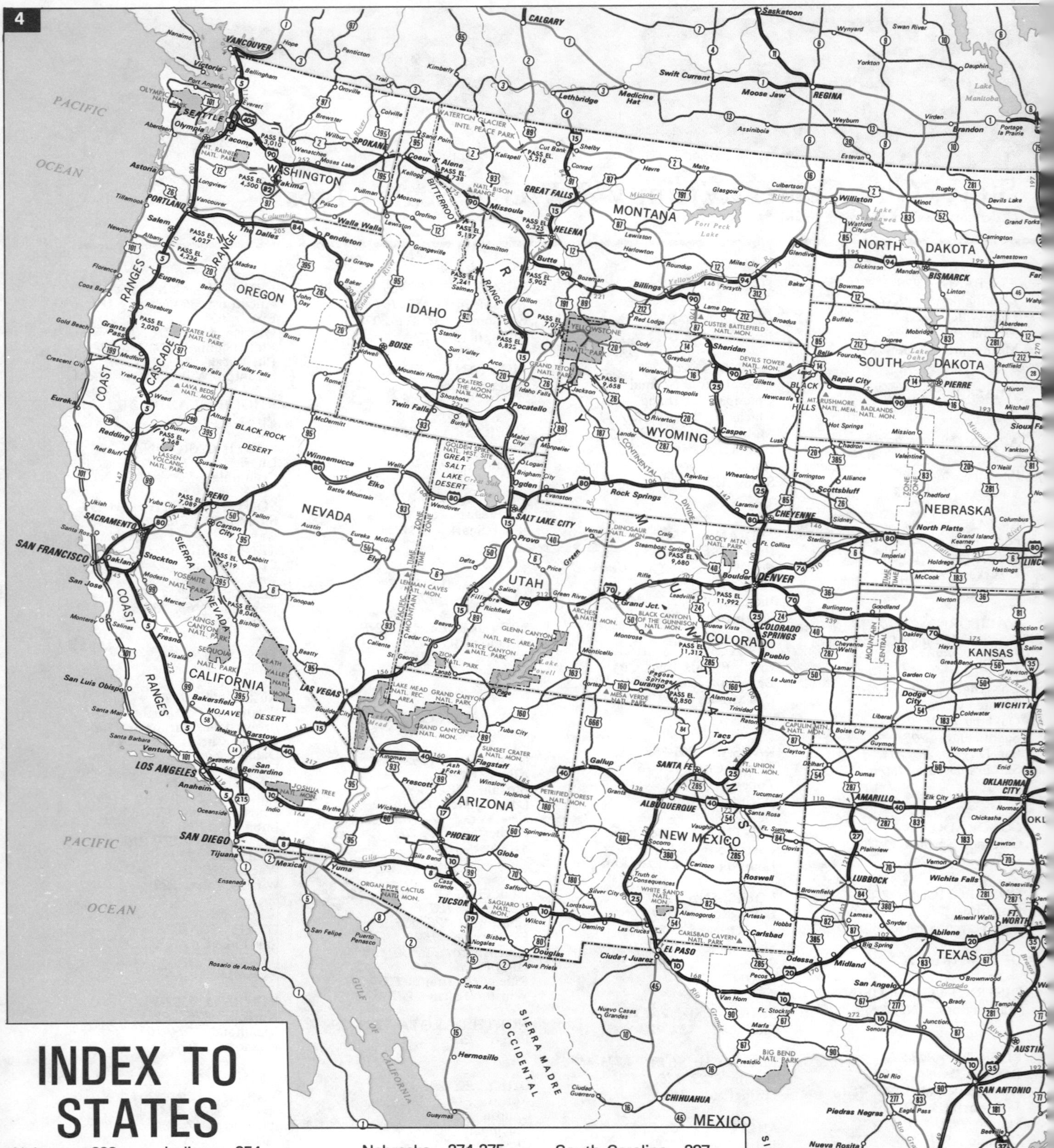

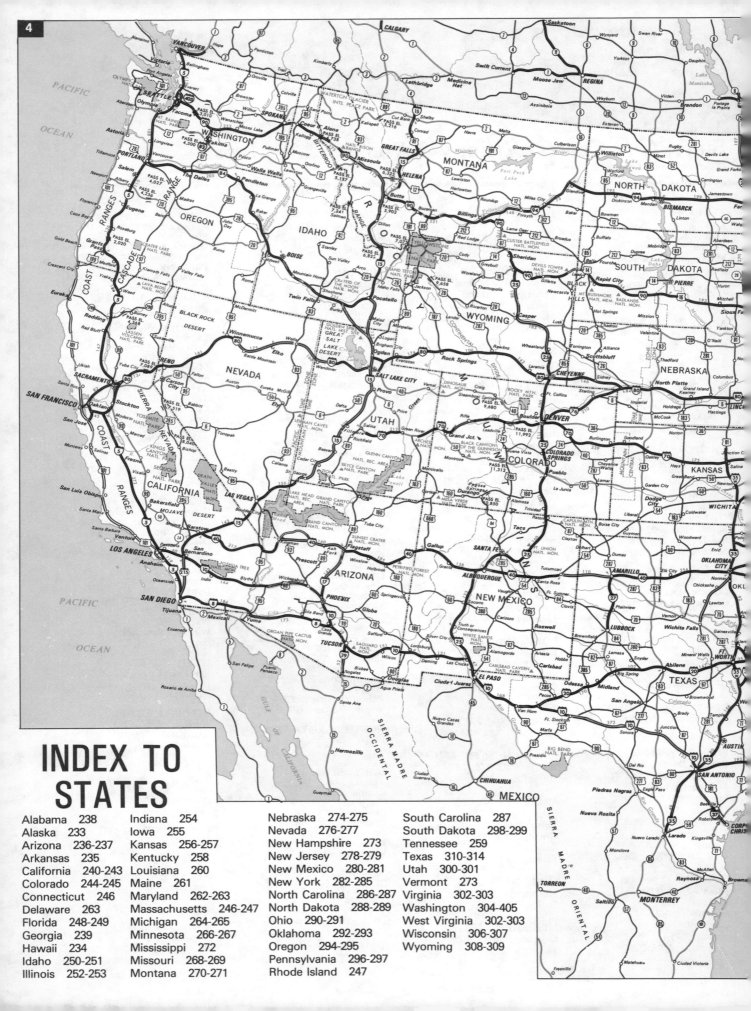

INDEX TO STATES

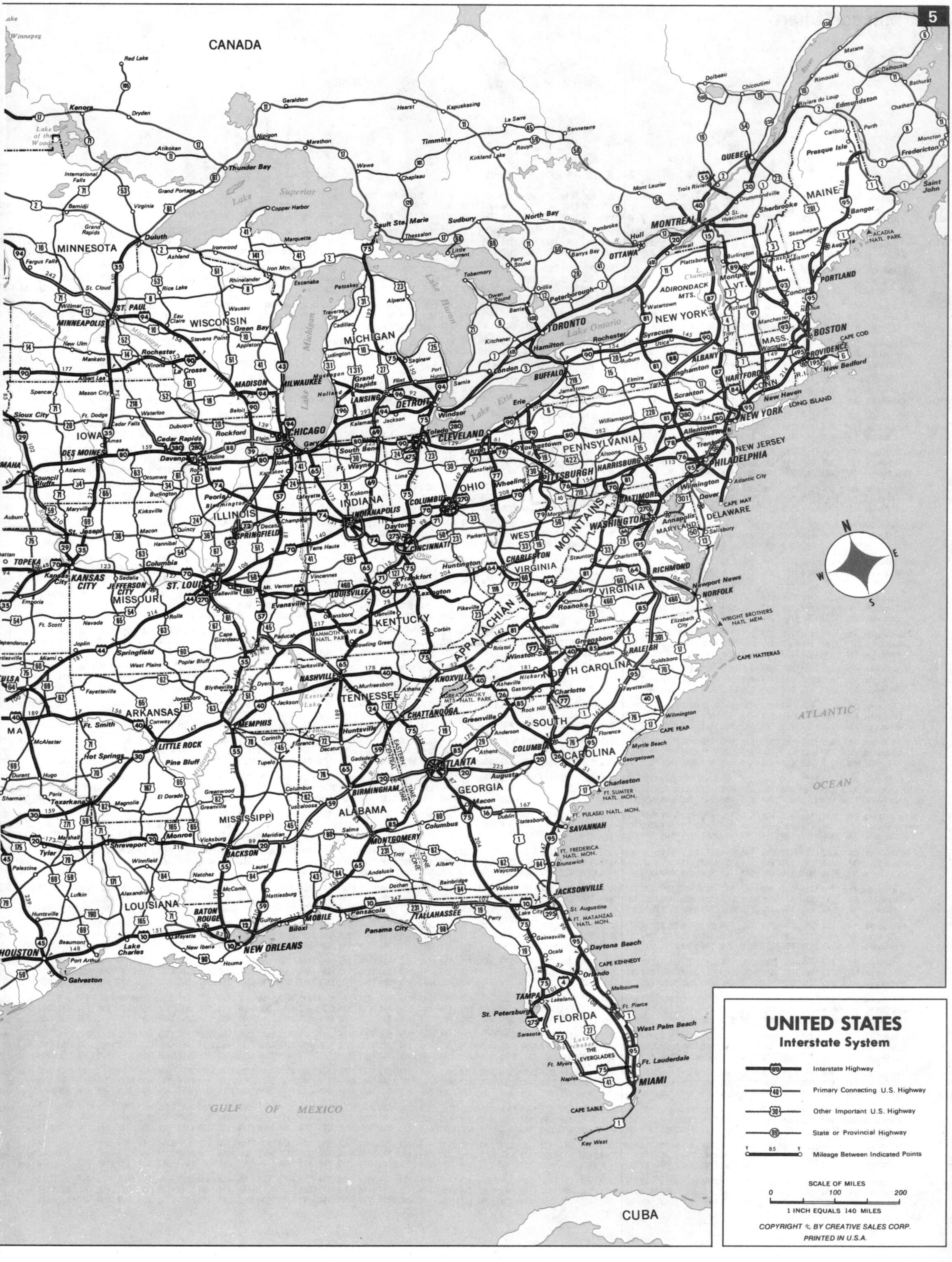
UNITED STATES
Interstate System
Interstate Highway
Primary Connecting U.S. Highway
Other Important U.S. Highway
State or Provincial Highway
Mileage Between Indicated Points
SCALE OF MILES
0
100
200
1 INCH EQUALS 140 MILES
COPYRIGHT ©, BY CREATIVE SALES CORP.
PRINTED IN U.S.A.
CANADA
MINNESOTA
WISCONSIN
MICHIGAN
IOWA
ILLINOIS
INDIANA
OHIO
PENNSYLVANIA
NEW YORK
VT.
N.H.
MAINE
MASS.
CONN.
R.I.
NEW JERSEY
DELAWARE
MARYLAND
WEST VIRGINIA
VIRGINIA
KENTUCKY
TENNESSEE
NORTH CAROLINA
SOUTH CAROLINA
GEORGIA
ALABAMA
MISSISSIPPI
LOUISIANA
ARKANSAS
MISSOURI
FLORIDA
APPALACHIAN MOUNTAINS
ADIRONDACK MTS.
GREAT SMOKY MTS. NATL. PARK
MAMMOTH CAVE NATL. PARK
ACADIA NATL. PARK
THE EVERGLADES
Lake Superior
Lake Michigan
Lake Huron
Lake Erie
Lake Ontario
Lake of the Woods
Lake Okeechobee
ATLANTIC OCEAN
GULF OF MEXICO
CUBA
CAPE COD
LONG ISLAND
CAPE MAY
CAPE HATTERAS
CAPE FEAR
CAPE KENNEDY
CAPE SABLE
WRIGHT BROTHERS NATL. MEM.
FT. SUMTER NATL. MON.
FT. PULASKI NATL. MON.
FT. FREDERICA NATL. MON.
FT. MATANZAS NATL. MON.
EASTERN TIME ZONE
CENTRAL TIME ZONE
N
E
S
W
Thunder Bay
Duluth
St. Paul
Minneapolis
Madison
Milwaukee
Chicago
Des Moines
Omaha
Kansas City
Topeka
St. Louis
Springfield
Indianapolis
Detroit
Lansing
Toledo
Cleveland
Columbus
Cincinnati
Louisville
Frankfort
Pittsburgh
Harrisburg
Philadelphia
Buffalo
Rochester
Syracuse
Albany
Hartford
Providence
Boston
Portland
New York
Baltimore
Washington
Richmond
Norfolk
Charleston
Raleigh
Charlotte
Columbia
Atlanta
Chattanooga
Knoxville
Nashville
Memphis
Little Rock
Birmingham
Montgomery
Jackson
Shreveport
Baton Rouge
New Orleans
Mobile
Tallahassee
Jacksonville
Savannah
Orlando
Tampa
St. Petersburg
Miami
Key West
Houston
Galveston
Tulsa
Toronto
Hamilton
Ottawa
Montreal
Quebec
Sault Ste Marie
Sudbury
North Bay
Timmins
Fredericton
Saint John
Bangor
Augusta

Mileage Chart

	Albany, NY	Albuquerque, NM	Amarillo,TX	Atlanta, GA	Austin, TX	Baltimore, MD	Billings, MT	Birmingham, AL	Boise, ID	Boston, MA	Brownsville, TX	Buffalo, NY	Charleston, SC	Charleston, WV	Charlotte, NC	Chicago, IL	Cincinnati, OH	Cleveland, OH	Columbia, SC	Columbus, OH
Albany, NY	0	2125	1825	1007	1882	332	2073	1112	2601	170	2007	292	932	639	795	795	729	496	823	657
Albuquerque, NM	2125	0	300	1387	716	1881	1022	1260	970	2214	988	1801	1695	1583	1628	1346	1394	1606	1598	1468
Amarillo, TX	1825	300	0	1087	485	1581	1037	965	1235	1914	784	1501	1517	1304	1338	1046	1094	1306	1298	1168
Atlanta, GA	1007	1387	1087	0	884	669	1804	160	2252	1068	1175	912	300	495	251	695	438	692	211	543
Austin, TX	1882	716	485	884	0	1550	1449	793	1716	1930	331	1566	1247	1251	1237	1100	1127	1371	1095	1233
Baltimore, MD	332	1881	1581	669	1550	0	1875	804	2416	409	1825	352	567	339	430	697	510	355	513	405
Billings, MT	2073	1022	1037	1804	1449	1875	0	1759	586	2232	1771	1857	2222	1762	2027	1214	1479	1662	2075	1654
Birmingham, AL	1112	1260	965	160	793	804	1759	0	2101	1267	1065	941	460	539	411	669	468	722	359	584
Boise, ID	2601	970	1235	2252	1716	2416	586	2101	0	2794	1921	2271	2503	2246	2408	1777	1983	2058	2289	2069
Boston, MA	170	2214	1914	1068	1930	409	2232	1267	2794	0	2255	454	989	728	828	965	875	632	928	738
Brownsville, TX	2007	988	784	1175	331	1825	1909	1065	1921	2255	0	1865	1500	1479	1426	1430	1426	1670	1360	1533
Buffalo, NY	292	1801	1501	912	1566	352	1857	941	2271	454	1865	0	947	430	666	543	438	195	822	333
Charleston, SC	932	1695	1517	300	1247	567	2222	460	2503	989	1500	947	0	479	203	912	628	750	113	670
Charleston, WV	639	1583	1304	495	1251	339	1762	539	2246	728	1479	430	479	0	276	469	178	284	376	156
Charlotte, NC	795	1628	1338	251	1237	430	2027	411	2408	828	1426	666	203	276	0	738	446	543	100	453
Chicago, IL	795	1346	1046	695	1100	697	1214	669	1777	965	1430	543	912	469	738	0	291	348	794	340
Cincinnati, OH	729	1394	1094	438	1127	510	1479	468	1983	875	1426	438	628	178	446	291	0	249	502	105
Cleveland, OH	496	1606	1306	692	1371	355	1662	722	2058	632	1670	195	750	284	543	348	249	0	627	138
Columbia, SC	823	1598	1298	211	1095	513	2075	359	2289	928	1360	822	113	376	100	794	502	627	0	513
Columbus, OH	657	1469	1168	543	1233	405	1654	584	2069	738	1533	333	670	156	453	340	105	138	513	0
Dallas, TX	1679	673	363	805	203	1347	1395	637	1610	1727	526	1363	1164	1134	1054	932	924	1168	1032	1030
Daytona Beach, FL	1209	1716	1467	446	1158	876	2173	505	2576	1257	1353	1069	351	726	469	1096	883	952	381	901
Denver, CO	1853	446	454	1401	1009	1692	579	1370	870	1953	1251	1602	1743	1377	1548	1037	1199	1407	1616	1270
Des Moines, IA	1193	1013	806	924	897	997	959	838	1402	1305	1184	867	1185	761	1029	357	583	672	1126	657
Detroit, MI	690	1537	1289	726	1330	511	1579	721	2020	795	1694	366	874	371	607	284	260	171	745	195
El Paso, TX	2327	267	508	1453	583	1997	1274	1304	1241	2376	806	2011	1729	1672	1710	1435	1372	1716	1668	1540
Fargo, ND	1463	1314	999	1364	1333	1339	625	1311	1245	1625	1601	1185	1557	1126	1414	649	940	997	1446	989
Fort Lauderdale, FL	1435	1953	1670	681	1326	1036	2466	764	2820	1492	1542	1400	586	1004	721	1348	1086	1232	622	1126
Fort Wayne, IN	705	1410	1109	612	1200	550	1405	610	1871	847	1455	381	740	284	602	159	184	219	671	150
Fort Worth, TX	1682	632	344	837	192	1379	1406	702	1598	1761	518	1395	1116	1056	1061	945	956	1200	1057	1062
Grand Rapids, MI	710	1491	1191	749	1288	624	1396	739	1917	908	1585	419	959	457	791	178	357	284	858	311
Greensboro, NC	661	1677	1377	348	1281	346	1958	493	2408	739	1480	641	271	227	89	729	458	486	188	381
Hartford	106	2084	1822	969	1867	308	2169	1058	2652	105	2044	397	867	662	763	875	746	339	836	641
Houston, TX	1825	870	608	816	162	1409	1639	676	1854	1878	357	1492	1027	1246	1053	1160	1053	1297	1066	1159
Indianapolis, IN	836	1289	989	543	1111	584	1400	497	1890	933	1427	512	743	328	551	186	105	317	625	179
Jackson, MS	1320	1087	787	397	519	1006	1743	251	2091	1395	991	1119	702	790	640	762	680	924	610	786
Jacksonville, FL	1111	1678	1378	329	1057	770	2227	472	2579	1167	1264	1068	248	676	413	999	786	908	290	850
Kansas City, MO	1279	811	552	810	680	1078	1078	724	1476	1435	1008	1007	1135	777	940	543	591	803	1025	665
Knoxville, TN	836	1407	1107	204	1051	503	1723	255	2022	871	1320	671	368	284	219	537	246	489	267	351
Las Vegas, NV	2609	576	876	1947	1297	2408	1060	1822	662	2765	1573	2254	2247	2119	2173	1749	1921	2059	2162	1995
Lincoln, NE	1386	837	596	1013	851	1192	836	953	1205	1500	1216	1057	1287	960	1151	527	802	867	1199	776
Little Rock, AK	1370	883	607	540	520	1207	1439	394	1781	1472	819	1046	814	707	743	675	608	851	759	713
Los Angeles, CA	2911	823	1095	2197	1410	2676	1254	2067	837	2993	1678	2587	2521	2394	2617	1989	2164	2392	2426	2254
Louisville, KY	868	1332	1041	421	1022	608	1550	373	1908	976	1321	543	608	258	438	300	105	349	494	211
Memphis, TN	1232	1021	721	397	658	900	1557	239	1833	1379	957	908	689	653	604	551	469	713	612	575
Miami, FL	1439	1994	1694	665	1338	1095	2710	788	2860	1516	1580	1524	630	1046	745	1338	1086	1264	658	1210
Milwaukee, WI	933	1443	1143	784	1203	794	1143	766	1777	1078	1530	640	1032	566	835	92	388	445	891	448
Minneapolis, MN	1215	1256	1062	1105	1120	1105	812	1088	1488	1362	1456	948	1316	874	1143	405	696	753	1276	753
Mobile, AL	1322	1265	965	340	656	990	1854	269	2343	1379	851	1184	607	825	575	908	745	989	555	834
Montgomery, AL	1178	1345	1042	164	804	833	1836	93	2346	1232	1041	1076	464	632	405	762	561	815	379	707
Nashville, TN	993	1232	932	243	869	688	1640	195	2059	1062	1168	722	576	458	399	474	283	527	458	389
New Orleans, LA	1453	1187	875	493	535	1136	1820	352	2191	1526	730	1273	727	891	721	925	820	1078	701	940
New York City, NY	146	1995	1695	855	1728	201	1926	1019	2571	203	2002	390	786	524	625	794	628	446	715	551
Norfolk, VA	505	1905	1632	551	1403	237	2098	711	2551	660	1735	569	454	369	341	851	681	493	412	559
Oakland, CA	2982	1134	1430	2488	1786	2864	1218	2321	671	3124	2034	2745	2788	2600	2755	2098	2317	2498	2703	2391
Oklahoma City, OK	1523	559	267	863	414	1322	1168	701	1451	1659	680	1242	1176	1031	1069	804	835	1047	1091	909
Omaha, NE	1308	905	754	989	847	1143	904	904	1274	1443	1249	1005	1303	899	1135	464	721	824	1283	795
Orlando, FL	1249	1751	1451	446	1142	917	2277	545	2695	1297	2034	1306	401	814	559	1127	892	1046	440	997
Philadelphia, PA	251	1922	1622	766	1630	97	2051	880	2488	327	1954	397	688	517	522	757	559	430	627	460
Phoenix, AZ	2512	446	746	1810	1030	2311	1220	1700	1022	2644	1289	2269	2222	2045	2061	1776	1808	2045	2025	1907
Pittsburgh, PA	471	1654	1354	712	1412	245	1681	778	2203	584	1713	219	778	211	504	470	291	128	572	186
Portland, Or	2869	1378	1636	2763	2059	2765	867	2571	439	3149	2468	2677	2952	2615	2757	2140	2474	2416	2972	2478
Providence, RI	178	2156	1856	1027	1898	356	2238	1189	2701	41	2222	454	956	699	785	924	790	600	888	713
Raleigh, NC	656	1759	1459	397	1355	324	2273	557	2560	713	1506	721	300	297	162	802	540	559	215	453
Reno, NV	2763	1056	1345	2411	1775	2562	1021	2363	404	2871	2068	2433	2765	2407	2570	1897	2221	2238	2626	2295
Richmond, VA	482	1833	1533	527	1463	155	1655	699	2594	544	1646	552	462	251	280	341	356	583	390	498
Rochester,NY	219	1857	1557	1015	1623	300	1922	965	2352	381	1891	81	871	495	689	608	502	268	789	397
Saint Louis, MO	1028	1054	754	588	806	827	1381	539	1727	1184	1216	747	884	544	689	292	340	552	737	414
Saint Paul, MN	1215	1362	1062	1105	1120	1095	812	1118	1398	892	1565	948	1316	870	1143	405	696	753	1320	745
Salt Lake City, UT	2290	621	1324	1900	1341	2051	579	1825	349	2417	1775	1922	2254	1896	2059	1386	1710	1727	2115	1711
San Antonio, TX	1986	684	530	965	81	1646	1600	895	1709	2052	300	1638	1371	1419	1272	1208	1208	1443	1180	1305
San Diego, CA	2855	787	1078	2174	1313	2714	1309	2034	1010	2992	1574	2613	2505	2402	2423	2335	2193	2334	2389	2277
San Francisco, CA	2966	1135	1396	2511	1776	2765	1239	2371	595	3133	2044	2403	2923	2616	2756	2108	2329	2408	2738	2461
Seattle, WA	2855	1500	1805	2656	2157	2685	815	2475	524	2961	2521	2531	2960	2748	2765	2043	2334	2336	2971	2408
Shreveport, LA	1599	868	568	624	340	1229	1691	474	1912	1618	644	1265	945	899	885	916	826	1070	833	592
Spokane, WA	2652	1346	1563	2367	1981	2417	541	2469	369	2693	2359	2263	2700	2503	2505	1775	2066	2068	2572	2115
Tallahassee, FL	1249	1508	1208	268	899	932	2306	302	2512	1312	1094	1155	364	868	559	957	706	949	408	828
Tampa, FL	1281	1759	1459	476	1150	949	2143	553	2763	1329	1345	1346	479	903	584	1143	908	1091	497	1013
Toledo, OH	633	1526	1220	641	1315	454	1557	673	2020	742	1622	309	973	284	533	243	203	114	683	138
Tuscon, AZ	2442	486	656	1785	908	2246	1342	1621	1144	2571	1176	2166	2100	2039	1913	1711	1750	1971	2080	1833
Tulsa, OK	1409	674	336	803	462	1208	1293	636	2020	1532	835	1128	1103	941	989	673	721	933	1018	795
Washington, DC	378	1864	1564	630	1509	41	2006	781	2441	430	1787	429	559	299	334	697	478	341	498	418
West Palm Beach, FL	1396	1938	1638	632	1329	1046	2736	702	2942	1426	1524	1443	568	982	673	1289	1063	1192	586	1146
Youngstown, OH	462	1632	1346	719	1368	298	1632	738	2090	568	1695	190	709	251	502	413	275	74	561	170

	Dallas, TX	Daytona Beach, FL	Denver, CO	Des Moines, IA	Detroit, MI	El Paso, TX	Fargo, ND	Fort Lauderdale, FL	Fort Wayne, IN	Fort Worth, TX	Grand Rapids, MI	Greensboro, NC	Hartford, CT	Houston, TX	Indianapolis, IN	Jackson, MS	Jacksonville, FL	Kansas City, MO	Knoxville, TN	Las Vegas, NV	Lincoln, NE	Little Rock, AK
Albany, NY	1679	1209	1853	1193	690	2327	1463	1403	705	1682	710	661	106	1825	836	1320	1111	1279	836	2609	1336	1370
Albuquerque, NM	673	1716	446	1013	1537	267	1314	1953	1410	632	1491	1677	2084	870	1289	1087	1678	811	1407	576	837	883
Amarillo, TX	363	1467	454	806	1289	508	999	1670	1109	344	1191	1377	1822	608	989	787	1378	552	1107	876	596	607
Atlanta, GA	805	446	1401	924	726	1453	1364	681	612	837	749	348	969	816	543	397	329	810	204	1947	1013	540
Austin, TX	203	1158	1009	897	1330	583	1333	1326	1200	192	1288	1281	1867	162	1111	519	1057	680	1051	1297	851	520
Baltimore, MD	1347	876	1692	997	511	1997	1339	1036	550	1379	624	346	308	1409	584	1006	770	1078	503	2408	1192	1037
Billings, MT	1395	2173	579	959	1579	1284	625	2466	1405	1406	1396	1958	2169	1739	1400	1743	2227	1078	1723	1060	836	1439
Birmingham, AL	637	505	1370	838	721	1304	1311	764	610	702	739	493	1058	676	497	251	472	724	255	1822	953	394
Boise, ID	1610	2576	870	1402	2020	1241	1245	2820	1871	1598	1917	2408	2652	1854	1890	2091	2579	1476	2022	662	1205	1781
Boston, MA	1727	1257	1953	1305	795	2376	1623	1492	847	1761	908	739	105	1878	933	1395	1167	1435	871	2765	1500	1472
Brownsville, TX	526	1353	1251	1184	1694	806	1601	1542	1455	518	1585	1480	2094	357	1427	791	1264	1008	1320	1573	1216	819
Buffalo, NY	1363	1069	1602	867	366	2011	1185	1400	381	1395	419	641	397	1492	512	1119	1068	1007	671	2254	1057	1046
Charleston, SC	1164	351	1743	1185	874	1729	1557	586	740	1116	959	271	867	1027	743	702	248	1135	368	2247	1287	814
Charleston, WV	1134	726	1377	761	371	1672	1126	1004	284	1056	457	227	662	1246	328	790	676	777	284	2119	960	707
Charlotte, NC	1054	469	1548	1029	607	1710	1414	721	602	1061	791	89	763	1053	551	640	413	940	219	2173	1151	743
Chicago, IL	932	1096	1037	357	284	1435	649	1348	159	945	178	729	875	1160	186	762	999	543	537	1749	527	675
Cincinnati, OH	924	861	1199	583	260	1472	940	1086	184	956	357	458	746	1053	105	680	786	591	246	1921	715	608
Cleveland, OH	1168	952	1407	672	171	1716	997	1232	211	1200	284	486	539	1297	317	924	908	803	489	2059	867	851
Columbia, SC	1032	381	1616	1126	745	1668	1446	622	671	1057	858	188	836	1066	625	610	290	1025	267	2162	1199	759
Columbus, OH	1030	901	1270	657	195	1540	989	1126	150	1062	311	381	641	1159	179	786	850	665	351	1995	776	713
Dallas, TX	0	1123	806	714	1203	648	1131	1097	1030	33	1110	1122	1664	243	908	422	1005	511	820	1249	648	317
Daytona Beach, FL	1123	0	1823	1329	1103	1728	1714	227	1006	1126	1143	551	1138	952	880	688	97	1209	603	2316	1401	904
Denver, CO	806	1823	0	695	1321	705	915	2067	1186	773	1201	1621	1988	1060	1091	1246	1779	608	1341	743	507	992
Des Moines, IA	714	1329	695	0	600	1114	475	1581	516	747	502	1028	1283	930	478	846	1270	203	821	1399	203	562
Detroit, MI	1203	1103	1321	600	0	1701	922	1346	170	1240	162	567	701	1304	293	923	1046	791	506	2011	819	850
El Paso, TX	648	1728	705	1114	1701	0	1460	1869	1573	609	1554	1783	2263	743	1460	1070	1626	915	1488	722	946	960
Fargo, ND	1131	1714	915	475	922	1460	0	2007	808	1072	827	1412	1531	1334	835	1335	1704	609	1195	1535	451	1091
Fort Lauderdale, FL	1097	227	2067	1581	1346	1869	2007	0	1271	1129	1342	786	1403	1191	1232	883	332	1459	860	2530	1670	1184
Fort Wayne, IN	1030	1006	1186	516	170	1573	808	1271	0	1053	172	551	768	1176	122	784	929	648	430	1878	686	711
Fort Worth, TX	33	1126	773	747	1236	609	1072	1129	1053	0	1121	1154	1696	264	912	446	1037	513	853	1203	648	349
Grand Rapids, MI	1110	1143	1201	502	162	1554	827	1342	172	1121	0	707	794	1196	263	957	1071	638	573	1889	699	799
Greensboro, NC	1122	551	1621	1028	567	1783	1412	786	551	1154	707	0	650	1167	563	770	483	1013	283	2237	1202	778
Hartford	1664	1138	1988	1283	701	2263	1531	1403	768	1696	794	650	0	1773	805	1306	1071	1297	841	2675	1378	1344
Houston, TX	243	952	1060	930	1304	743	1334	1191	1176	264	1196	1167	1773	0	1041	406	891	754	922	1468	892	446
Indianapolis, IN	908	980	1091	478	293	1460	835	1232	122	912	263	563	805	1041	0	681	867	486	351	1816	673	608
Jackson, MS	422	688	1246	846	923	1070	1335	883	784	446	957	770	1306	406	681	0	591	716	506	1650	874	251
Jacksonville, FL	1005	97	1779	1270	1046	1626	1704	332	929	1037	1071	483	1071	891	867	591	0	1110	555	2238	1321	843
Kansas City, MO	511	1209	608	203	791	916	609	1459	648	513	638	1013	1297	754	486	716	1110	0	752	1345	211	409
Knoxville, TN	820	603	1341	821	506	1488	1195	860	430	872	573	283	841	922	351	506	555	752	0	1983	944	523
Las Vegas, NV	1249	2316	743	1399	2011	722	1535	2530	1878	1203	1889	2237	2675	1468	1816	1650	2238	1345	1983	0	1224	1483
Lincoln, NE	648	1401	507	203	819	946	451	1670	686	648	699	1202	1378	892	673	874	1321	211	944	1224	0	616
Little Rock, AK	317	904	992	562	850	960	1091	1184	711	349	799	778	1344	446	608	251	843	409	523	1483	616	0
Los Angeles, CA	1401	2407	1009	1654	2270	818	1844	2704	2137	1361	2148	2478	2829	1581	2075	1880	2402	1589	2201	275	1476	1678
Louisville, KY	819	801	1127	591	365	1467	949	1078	222	851	373	462	867	948	129	575	729	519	246	1861	730	502
Memphis, TN	455	749	1151	599	712	1103	1224	989	592	487	690	640	1209	584	470	211	697	470	385	1581	647	138
Miami, FL	1321	259	2131	1582	1386	1958	1986	24	1326	1353	1356	810	1427	1207	1208	907	356	1475	859	2570	1673	1208
Milwaukee, WI	1013	1180	1070	365	389	1528	576	1443	256	1059	275	826	948	1155	283	884	1067	568	643	1752	560	772
Minneapolis, MN	1013	1458	956	251	698	1520	244	1723	564	1001	583	1135	1257	1266	591	1123	1376	459	932	1630	409	881
Mobile, AL	592	502	1372	954	988	1236	1413	705	839	624	1006	681	1290	478	749	178	413	819	449	1841	1039	430
Montgomery, AL	677	458	1412	1311	814	1325	1521	671	686	701	819	512	1133	709	590	255	379	867	348	2015	975	470
Nashville, TN	666	639	1167	712	536	1314	1136	900	385	698	534	429	973	795	302	422	592	590	174	1792	770	349
New Orleans, LA	530	632	1323	978	1077	1127	1494	843	916	519	1071	810	1436	367	857	193	551	857	607	1800	1114	430
New York City, NY	1525	1054	1775	1070	620	2173	1450	1289	691	1557	706	561	101	1679	730	1192	957	1192	771	2520	1274	1235
Norfolk, VA	1359	702	1800	1202	711	1998	1581	964	709	1382	802	227	471	1362	669	948	632	1179	412	2534	1354	1025
Oakland, CA	1803	2831	1223	1742	2350	1194	1870	3041	2257	1723	2308	2809	2909	1957	2212	2270	2771	1799	2509	582	1604	1984
Oklahoma City, OK	211	1257	660	576	1030	708	989	1481	852	210	932	1118	1546	454	730	575	1181	373	847	1119	433	324
Omaha, NE	693	1402	559	146	726	1256	464	1604	634	634	640	1208	1321	949	616	914	1305	195	930	1249	57	690
Orlando, FL	1078	81	1896	1363	1143	1735	1826	208	1059	1110	1188	648	1208	964	989	697	138	1266	665	2311	1452	965
Philadelphia, PA	1427	914	1762	998	585	2075	1370	1127	604	1459	672	438	220	1581	624	1094	859	1134	646	2449	1260	1110
Phoenix, AZ	1013	2101	802	1497	2019	438	1791	2244	1831	983	1906	2099	2523	1110	1719	1500	2100	1277	1845	284	1236	1379
Pittsburgh, PA	1209	859	1475	770	304	1833	1112	1216	336	1241	397	438	486	1345	349	965	882	851	515	2181	965	899
Portland, Or	2051	3018	1283	1816	2368	1661	1484	3204	2299	2003	2251	2823	2877	2369	2335	2518	3042	1809	2550	991	1641	2270
Providence, RI	1695	1201	1961	1256	746	2335	1566	1459	799	1727	859	706	73	1849	892	1362	1127	1378	935	2683	1451	1395
Raleigh, NC	1152	559	1694	1123	643	1800	1485	794	603	1184	754	73	624	1233	635	815	486	1086	356	2319	1263	851
Reno, NV	1731	2758	1030	1606	2190	1183	1660	3008	2056	1608	2067	2591	2749	1932	2116	2143	2716	1606	2363	478	1411	1986
Richmond, VA	1313	713	1904	1293	609	2023	1481	946	635	1333	722	191	455	2291	907	946	693	1205	440	2406	1249	963
Rochester,NY	1420	1176	1637	932	424	2036	1249	1410	464	1452	499	600	324	1555	551	1183	1102	1062	710	2371	1135	1111
Saint Louis, MO	641	956	859	377	585	1238	872	1208	369	698	437	762	1030	835	251	495	859	251	497	1581	462	422
Saint Paul, MN	1013	1458	956	251	698	1541	244	1753	564	987	583	1138	1257	1266	591	1160	1376	459	951	1630	408	881
Salt Lake City, UT	1287	2283	519	1085	1679	892	1172	2578	1527	1184	1556	2059	2238	1460	1605	1742	2286	1095	1766	413	900	1054
San Antonio, TX	284	1175	975	1022	1500	576	1402	1378	1269	283	1353	1321	1965	203	1200	649	1086	795	1150	1273	916	592
San Diego, CA	1369	2418	1054	1760	2419	721	1934	2621	2189	1332	2269	2457	2944	1484	2067	1783	2329	1627	2269	349	1573	1743
San Francisco, CA	1865	2827	1233	1832	2360	1184	1886	3073	2304	1735	2318	2740	3019	1947	2224	2183	2781	1869	2549	592	1614	1994
Seattle, WA	2203	3070	1371	1889	2299	1775	1440	3882	2202	2071	2221	2773	2918	2498	2229	2585	3090	1884	2553	1209	1636	2320
Shreveport, LA	196	903	1112	827	1069	844	1229	1144	909	228	1018	937	1519	271	827	223	814	624	729	1468	727	219
Spokane, WA	1978	2811	1095	1556	2020	1686	1166	3014	1921	1978	1941	2503	2650	2222	1961	2205	2822	1727	2298	1119	1460	2092
Tallahassee, FL	835	259	1727	1216	957	1492	1598	462	871	867	1022	608	1223	721	818	421	170	1045	584	2068	1227	679
Tampa, FL	1086	141	1858	1460	1200	1743	1849	268	1092	1118	1219	673	1240	972	1069	672	195	1296	730	2319	1477	958
Toledo, OH	1112	1063	1272	567	65	1699	885	1289	105	1144	170	516	624	1249	243	876	989	717	449	1954	762	803
Tuscon, AZ	964	1999	835	1484	1938	316	1897	2271	1783	932	1856	2059	2433	1079	1668	1378	2010	1281	1755	389	1246	1257
Tulsa, OK	259	1156	714	471	916	788	972	1409	738	305	818	1037	1411	504	616	510	1167	283	782	1224	416	259
Washington, DC	1306	802	1654	1054	506	1954	1322	1062	531	1338	608	309	341	1220	551	965	730	1046	554	2376	1184	832
West Palm Beach, FL	1265	195	2157	1646	1305	1922	2028	41	1157	1297	1476	737	1339	1151	1176	851	284	1052	806	2498	1598	1101
Youngstown, OH	1193	986	1421	737	239	1804	1038	1219	275	1225	340	482	470	1322	341	949	958	843	521	2124	923	876

Los Angeles, CA	Louisville, KY	Memphis, TN	Miami, FL	Milwaukee, WI	Minneapolis, MN	Mobile, AL	Montgomery, AL	Nashville, TN	New Orleans, LA	New York City NY	Norfolk, VA	Oakland,CA	Oklahoma City, OK	Omaha, NE	Orlando, FL	Philadelphia, PA	Phoenix, AZ	Pittsburgh, PA	Portland, OR	Providence, RI	Raleigh, NC	Reno, NV	Richmond, VA	Rochester, NY	Saint Louis, MO	Saint Paul, MN	Salt Lake City, UT	San Antonio, TX	San Diego, CA	San Francisco, CA	Seattle, WA	Shreveport, LA	Spokane, WA	Tallahassee, FL	Tampa, FL	Toledo, OH	Tucson, AZ	Tulsa, OK	Washington, DC	West Palm Beach, FL	Youngstown, OH	
1	868	1232	1439	933	1215	1322	1178	993	1453	146	505	2982	1523	1308	1249	251	2512	471	2869	178	656	2763	482	219	1028	1215	2290	1986	2855	2966	2855	1599	2652	1249	1281	633	2442	1409	378	1396	462	Albany, NY
23	1332	1021	1994	1443	1256	1265	1345	1232	1187	1995	1905	1134	559	905	1751	1922	446	1654	1378	2156	1759	1056	1833	1857	1054	1362	621	684	787	1135	1500	868	1346	1508	1759	1526	486	674	1864	1938	1646	Albuquerque, NM
95	1041	721	1694	1143	1062	965	1045	932	875	1695	1632	1430	267	754	1451	1622	746	1354	1636	1856	1458	1345	1533	1557	754	1062	917	530	1078	1396	1805	568	1563	1208	1459	1220	656	336	1564	1638	1346	Amarillo, TX
37	421	397	665	784	1105	340	164	243	493	855	551	2488	863	989	446	766	1810	712	2763	1027	397	2411	527	1015	588	1105	1900	965	2174	2511	2656	624	2367	268	476	641	1785	803	630	632	719	Atlanta, GA
40	1022	658	1338	1203	1120	656	804	869	535	1728	1403	1786	414	847	1142	1630	1030	1412	2059	1898	1355	1775	1463	1623	806	1120	1341	81	1313	1776	2157	340	1981	899	1150	1315	908	462	1509	1329	1368	Austin, TX
76	608	900	1095	794	1105	990	833	688	1136	201	237	2864	1322	1143	917	97	2311	245	2765	356	324	2562	155	300	827	1095	2051	1646	2714	2765	2686	1229	2417	932	949	454	2246	1208	41	1046	298	Baltimore, MD
54	1550	1557	2710	1143	812	1854	1836	1640	1820	1926	2098	1218	1168	904	2277	2051	1220	1681	867	2238	2273	1021	1655	1922	1381	812	579	1600	1309	1239	815	1691	541	2306	2143	1557	1342	1293	2006	2736	1632	Billings, MT
37	373	239	788	766	1088	269	93	195	352	1019	711	2321	701	904	545	880	1700	778	2571	1189	557	2363	699	965	539	1118	1825	895	2034	2371	2475	474	2469	302	553	673	1621	636	781	702	738	Birmingham, AL
47	1908	1833	2860	1777	1488	2143	2346	2059	2191	2571	2551	671	1451	1274	2695	2498	1022	2203	439	2701	2560	404	2594	2352	1727	1398	349	1709	1010	595	524	1912	369	2512	2763	2020	1144	1582	2441	2492	2090	Boise, ID
93	976	1379	1516	1078	1362	1379	1232	1062	1525	203	560	3124	1659	1443	1297	327	2644	584	3149	41	713	2871	544	381	1184	892	2417	2052	2992	3133	2961	1618	2693	1312	1329	742	2571	1532	430	1426	568	Boston, MA
78	1321	957	1580	1530	1456	851	1041	1168	730	2002	1735	2034	680	1249	2034	1954	1289	1713	2468	2222	1506	2068	1646	1891	1216	1565	1609	300	1574	2044	2521	644	2359	1094	1345	1622	1176	835	1787	1524	1695	Brownsville, TX
37	543	908	1424	640	948	1184	1076	722	1273	390	569	2745	1242	1005	1306	397	2269	219	2677	454	721	2433	552	81	747	948	1922	1638	2613	2667	2531	1265	2263	1155	1346	309	2166	1128	429	1443	190	Buffalo, NY
1	608	689	630	1032	1316	607	464	576	727	787	454	2788	1176	1303	401	688	2222	778	2952	956	300	2765	462	871	884	1316	2254	1371	2505	2923	2960	945	2700	364	479	973	2100	1103	559	568	709	Charleston, SC
4	258	653	1046	566	874	825	632	458	891	524	369	2600	1031	899	814	517	2045	211	2615	699	297	2407	251	495	544	870	1896	1419	2402	2616	2748	899	2503	868	903	284	2039	941	299	982	251	Charleston, WV
7	438	592	604	835	1143	575	415	399	721	625	341	2755	1069	1135	559	522	2061	504	2757	785	162	2570	280	689	689	1143	2059	1272	2423	2756	2765	885	2505	559	584	583	1913	989	334	673	502	Charlotte, NC
9	300	551	1338	92	405	908	762	474	925	794	851	2098	804	454	1127	757	1776	470	2140	924	802	1897	341	608	292	405	1386	1208	2306	2108	2043	916	1775	957	1143	243	1711	673	697	1289	413	Chicago, IL
4	105	469	1086	388	696	712	561	283	810	628	601	2317	835	721	892	559	1808	291	2369	790	540	2201	503	502	340	696	1671	1208	2193	2329	2334	813	2066	706	908	203	1756	721	478	1051	275	Cincinnati, OH
2	349	713	1264	445	753	989	815	527	1078	446	493	2498	1047	824	1046	430	2045	128	2416	600	559	2238	583	268	552	753	1727	1443	2384	2408	2336	1070	2068	949	1091	114	1971	933	341	1192	74	Cleveland, OH
6	494	612	658	891	1276	555	379	458	701	715	412	2703	1091	1283	440	627	2025	572	2972	888	215	2626	390	789	737	1320	2115	1180	2389	2738	2971	833	2572	408	497	683	2080	1018	498	586	561	Columbia, SC
4	211	575	1210	448	753	834	707	389	940	551	559	2391	909	795	997	460	1907	186	2478	713	453	2295	498	397	414	745	1711	1305	2277	2461	2408	592	2115	828	1513	138	1833	795	418	1146	170	Columbus, OH
1	819	455	1321	1013	1013	592	677	666	530	1525	1359	1803	211	693	1078	1427	1013	1209	2059	1695	1152	1731	1313	1420	641	1013	1287	284	1369	1865	2203	196	1978	835	1086	1112	964	259	1306	1265	1193	Dallas, TX
7	801	749	259	1180	1458	502	458	639	632	1054	702	2831	1257	1402	81	914	2102	859	3018	1201	559	2758	713	1176	956	1458	2283	1175	2418	2827	3070	903	2811	259	141	1063	1999	1156	802	195	986	Daytona Beach, FL
9	1127	1151	2131	1070	956	1372	1412	1167	1323	1775	1800	1223	660	559	1896	1762	802	1475	1283	1961	1694	1030	1904	1637	859	956	519	975	1054	1233	1371	1112	1095	1727	1858	1272	835	714	1654	2157	1421	Denver, CO
4	591	599	1582	365	251	954	1131	712	978	1070	1202	1742	576	146	1363	1037	1479	770	1816	1256	1123	1406	1293	932	377	251	1085	1022	1760	1832	1889	827	1556	1216	1460	567	1484	471	1054	1646	737	Des Moines, IA
0	365	712	1386	389	698	988	814	536	1077	620	711	2350	1030	726	1143	585	2019	304	2368	746	643	2190	609	424	535	698	1679	1500	2419	2360	2299	1069	2020	957	1200	65	1938	916	506	1305	239	Detroit, MI
8	1467	1103	1958	1528	1520	1236	1325	1314	1127	2173	1998	1194	708	1256	1735	2073	438	1833	1661	2335	1800	1185	2023	2036	1238	1541	894	576	721	1184	1775	844	1686	1492	1743	1699	316	788	1954	1922	1804	El Paso, TX
4	949	1224	1987	576	244	1413	1525	1138	1521	1450	1581	1870	989	464	1826	1370	1791	1112	1484	1566	1485	1660	1481	1249	872	244	1172	1402	1934	1886	1440	1229	1166	1598	1849	885	1897	972	1322	2028	1038	Fargo, ND
4	1078	989	24	1443	1723	705	671	900	843	1289	964	3041	1481	1604	208	1127	2244	1216	3204	1459	794	3008	946	1410	1208	1753	2578	1378	2621	3073	3382	1144	3014	462	268	1289	2271	1409	1062	41	1219	Fort Lauderdale
7	222	592	1326	256	564	839	686	385	916	691	709	2257	852	634	1059	604	1831	336	2299	799	603	2056	635	464	369	564	1527	1269	2189	2304	2202	909	1921	871	1092	105	1783	738	531	1157	275	Fort Wayne, IN
1	851	487	1353	1059	1001	624	701	698	519	1557	1382	1723	210	634	1110	1459	983	1241	2003	1727	1184	1608	1333	1452	698	987	1184	283	1332	1735	2071	228	1978	867	1118	1144	932	305	1338	1297	1225	Fort Worth, TX
8	373	690	1356	275	583	1006	819	534	1071	706	802	2308	932	640	1188	672	1906	397	2251	859	754	2067	722	499	437	583	1556	1353	2269	2318	2221	1018	1941	1022	1219	170	1856	818	608	1476	340	Grand Rapids, MI
8	462	640	810	826	1135	681	512	429	810	561	227	2809	1118	1208	648	438	2099	438	2823	706	73	2591	191	600	762	1138	2059	1321	2457	2740	2773	937	2503	608	673	516	2059	1037	309	737	482	Greensboro, NC
9	867	1209	1427	948	1257	1290	1133	973	1436	101	471	2909	1546	1321	1208	220	2523	486	2877	73	624	2749	455	324	1030	1257	2238	1965	2944	3019	2918	1529	2656	1223	1240	624	2433	1411	341	1339	470	Hartford, CT
1	948	584	1207	1155	1266	478	709	795	367	1679	1362	1957	454	949	964	1581	1110	1345	2369	1849	1233	1932	2291	1555	835	1266	1460	203	1484	1947	2498	271	2222	721	972	1249	1079	504	1420	1151	1322	Houston, TX
5	129	470	1208	283	591	749	590	302	857	730	669	2212	730	616	989	624	1719	349	2335	892	635	2116	907	551	251	591	1605	1200	2067	2224	2229	827	1961	818	1069	243	668	616	551	1176	341	Indianapolis, IN
0	575	211	907	884	1123	178	255	422	193	1192	948	2270	575	914	697	1094	1500	965	2518	1362	815	2143	946	1183	495	1160	1742	649	1783	2183	2585	223	2205	421	672	876	1378	510	965	851	949	Jackson, MS
2	729	697	356	1067	1374	413	379	592	551	957	632	2771	1181	1305	138	859	2100	882	3030	1127	584	2716	693	1102	867	1374	2286	1086	2329	2781	3042	814	2822	170	195	989	2010	1167	730	284	958	Jacksonville, FL
9	519	470	1475	568	459	819	867	590	857	1192	1179	1799	373	195	1266	1134	1277	851	1809	1378	1086	1606	1205	1062	251	459	1095	795	1627	1869	1834	624	1727	1045	1296	717	1281	283	1052	144	843	Kansas City, MO
1	246	385	859	643	932	449	348	174	607	753	412	2509	847	930	665	646	1845	515	2550	951	356	2363	440	710	497	935	1766	1150	2269	2549	2553	729	2298	584	730	449	1755	782	554	806	521	Knoxville, TN
5	1861	1581	2570	1752	1630	1841	2015	1792	1800	2520	2534	582	1119	1249	2311	2449	284	2181	991	2683	2319	478	2406	2371	1581	1630	413	1273	349	592	1209	1468	1119	2068	2319	1954	389	1264	2376	2498	2124	Las Vegas, NV
6	730	647	1673	560	409	1039	975	770	1014	1274	1354	1604	433	57	1452	1260	1236	965	1641	1451	1263	1411	1249	1135	462	408	900	916	1573	1614	1636	727	1460	1227	1477	762	1246	416	1184	1598	923	Lincoln, NE
3	502	138	1208	772	881	430	470	349	430	1235	1025	1984	324	690	965	1110	1379	899	2270	1395	851	1986	963	1111	422	881	1054	592	1743	1994	2368	219	2092	679	958	803	1257	259	832	1101	876	Little Rock
0	2136	1816	2828	2238	1905	2013	2035	2027	1883	2790	2809	372	1354	1508	2585	2717	389	2449	989	2902	2554	511	2641	2400	1849	1905	672	1378	121	382	1159	1687	1406	2342	2578	2213	502	1459	2659	2772	2424	Los Angeles, CA
6	0	364	1102	397	705	626	466	178	729	707	607	2333	738	671	907	664	1782	381	2298	421	525	2132	686	608	290	705	1638	1103	2119	2388	2320	721	2075	664	915	300	1697	633	533	1094	373	Louisville, KY
6	364	0	1013	673	949	389	332	211	397	1095	876	2122	462	705	770	989	2948	795	2408	1257	712	2124	825	973	300	949	1613	730	1881	2132	2506	357	2230	527	778	665	1370	397	363	957	738	Memphis, TN
3	1102	1013	0	1435	1743	729	695	908	867	1313	988	3087	1524	1670	227	1215	2448	1248	3366	1483	818	3032	988	1435	1231	1743	2602	1402	2645	3097	3406	1130	3138	486	292	1293	2326	1483	1086	65	1264	Miami, FL
3	397	673	1435	0	332	981	859	571	1045	851	948	2171	884	503	1224	834	1873	567	2002	1021	899	1930	832	697	389	332	1419	1305	2109	2175	1970	1013	1702	1053	1240	332	1808	770	770	1386	510	Milwaukee, WI
3	705	949	1743	332	0	1227	1281	892	1346	1160	1337	2065	803	381	1673	1126	1848	868	1670	1322	1241	1776	1237	1005	628	1	1475	1265	1975	2075	1638	985	1370	1354	1589	641	1702	705	1078	1737	794	Minneapolis, MN
3	626	389	729	981	1227	0	176	462	146	1176	884	2351	786	1011	486	1078	1593	1050	2611	1346	738	2278	867	1273	673	1158	1903	697	1971	2361	2710	401	2342	243	494	940	1542	713	949	673	1005	Mobile, AL
5	466	332	695	859	1281	176	0	288	322	1010	715	2295	794	1037	452	930	1655	843	2632	1191	561	2456	792	1179	632	1281	1918	904	2127	2464	2838	478	2562	209	460	766	1633	765	794	639	831	Montgomery, AL
7	178	211	908	571	892	462	288	0	551	859	665	2374	673	735	689	761	1671	575	2376	1029	502	2189	614	770	323	892	1678	941	2092	2375	2384	669	2124	486	737	478	1581	608	632	875	543	Nashville, TN
	729	397	867	1045	1346	146	322	551	0	1322	1054	2317	681	1362	624	1224	1540	1078	2505	1492	876	2278	1114	1362	681	1346	1842	551	1824	2327	2574	309	2409	381	632	1005	1419	657	1095	811	1095	New Orleans, LA
	707	1095	1313	851	1160	1176	1010	859	1322	0	389	2876	1436	1208	1094	101	2425	381	2330	162	510	2635	366	320	941	1160	2124	1832	2773	2886	2837	1415	2569	1109	1126	556	2360	1331	252	1223	403	New York, NY
	607	876	988	948	1337	884	715	665	1054	389	0	2957	1349	1262	770	268	2393	365	2968	527	197	2789	98	535	927	1337	2262	1606	2669	2967	2975	1203	2700	802	827	592	2271	1234	190	916	438	Norfolk, VA
2	2333	2122	3087	2171	2065	2351	2295	2374	2317	2876	2957	0	1660	1596	2844	2913	744	2528	614	2974	2865	201	2988	2681	2003	2065	545	1734	493	9	777	2052	979	2601	2836	2293	878	1766	2772	3055	2463	Oakland, CA
	738	462	1524	884	803	786	794	673	681	1436	1349	1660	0	495	1281	1363	998	1095	1946	1597	1200	1662	1287	1298	495	803	1151	478	1345	1670	2044	389	1768	1038	1289	961	908	105	1305	1468	1087	Oklahoma City, OK
3	671	705	1670	503	381	1110	1037	735	1362	1208	1362	1596	495	0	1421	1200	1427	908	1605	1394	1281	1395	1400	1078	446	381	947	949	1641	1606	1679	729	1403	1241	1492	705	1400	401	1151	1671	875	Omaha, NE
5	907	770	227	1224	1673	486	452	689	624	1094	770	2844	1281	1421	0	1005	2205	1025	3123	1273	608	2789	776	1200	1030	1551	2359	1159	2402	2854	3163	920	2895	243	89	1086	2083	1240	876	194	1052	Orlando, FL
7	664	989	1215	834	1126	1078	930	761	1224	101	268	2913	1363	1200	1005	0	1025	292	2830	259	412	2627	252	324	868	1126	2209	1734	2911	2923	2780	1270	2512	1020	1037	502	2287	1249	133	1134	357	Philadelphia, PA
3	1782	1377	2448	1873	1848	1593	1655	1671	1540	2425	2393	744	998	1427	2205	1025	0	2084	1322	2586	2172	754	2285	2281	1484	1808	673	989	357	754	1492	1282	1386	1962	2213	1950	122	1103	2367	2392	2061	Phoenix, AZ
9	381	795	1248	567	868	1050	843	575	1078	381	365	2528	1095	908	1025	292	2084	0	2538	559	519	2335	333	284	600	868	1824	1468	2441	2538	2513	1087	2190	932	998	227	2021	981	219	1111	65	Pittsburgh, PA
5	2298	2408	3366	2002	1670	2611	2632	2376	2505	2330	2968	614	1946	1605	3123	2830	1322	2538	0	3000	2903	616	3012	2676	2068	1670	764	2168	1078	624	170	2255	365	2880	3131	2311	1483	1987	2846	3310	2481	Portland, OR
2	421	1257	1483	1021	1322	1346	1191	1029	1492	162	527	2974	1597	1394	1273	259	2586	559	3000	0	673	2814	511	381	1102	1322	2303	2002	2978	2984	2967	1585	2644	1288	1322	689	252	1483	397	1402	538	Providence, RI
4	525	713	818	899	1241	738	561	502	876	510	197	2865	1200	1281	608	412	2172	519	2903	673	0	2716	175	600	835	1241	2205	1427	2529	2797	2911	538	2651	624	657	584	2124	1103	283	754	535	Raleigh, NC
4	2132	2124	3032	1930	1776	2278	2456	2189	2278	2635	2789	201	1662	1395	2789	2627	754	2335	616	2814	2716	0	2803	2489	1881	1776	511	1768	535	211	810	1927	770	2546	2797	2133	867	1702	2579	2976	2303	Reno, NV
	686	825	988	832	1237	867	792	614	1114	366	98	2988	1287	1400	776	252	2285	333	3012	511	175	2803	0	455	976	1237	2324	1555	2643	2989	3029	1173	2761	794	827	630	2425	1222	114	924	662	Richmond, VA
	608	973	1435	697	1005	1273	1179	770	1362	320	535	2681	1298	1078	1200	324	2281	284	2676	381	600	2489	455	0	803	1005	1978	1686	2674	2691	2660	1361	2384	1208	1257	381	2222	1398	341	1346	265	Rochester, NY
3	290	300	1231	389	628	673	632	323	681	941	927	2003	495	446	1030	868	1484	600	2068	1102	835	1881	976	803	0	628	1370	916	1840	2075	2076	624	1881	795	1030	466	1419	381	795	1241	592	Saint Louis, MO
5	705	949	1743	332	1	1158	1281	892	1346	1160	1337	2065	803	381	1551	1126	1808	868	1670	1322	1241	1776	1237	1005	628	0	1475	1265	1975	2075	1638	985	1370	1354	1589	641	1702	705	1078	1737	794	Saint Paul, MN
3	1638	1613	2602	1419	1475	1903	1918	1678	1842	2124	2262	545	1151	947	2359	2209	673	1824	764	2303	2205	511	2324	1978	1370	1475	0	1447	762	714	851	1563	706	2116	2318	1715	795	1223	2141	2490	1805	Salt Lake City, UT
3	1103	730	1402	1305	1265	697	904	941	551	1832	1606	1734	478	949	1159	1734	989	1468	2168	2002	1427	1768	1555	1686	916	1265	1447	0	1274	1774	2255	474	2110	915	1151	1387	876	535	1605	1370	1477	San Antonio, TX
	2119	1881	2645	2109	1975	1971	2127	2092	1824	2773	2669	493	1345	1641	2402	2911	357	2441	1078	2978	2529	535	2643	2674	1840	1975	762	1274	0	527	1276	1565	1403	2213	2464	2604	405	1403	2733	2072	2456	San Diego, CA
2	2388	2132	3097	2175	2075	2361	2464	2375	2327	2886	2967	9	1670	1606	2854	2923	754	2538	624	2984	2797	211	2989	2691	2075	2075	714	1774	527	0	787	2061	852	2611	2846	2415	868	1776	2949	3065	2569	San Francisco, CA
2	2343	2506	3406	1970	1638	2710	2838	2384	2574	2837	2975	777	2044	1679	3163	2780	1492	2513	170	2967	2911	810	3029	2660	2076	1638	851	2255	1276	787	0	2335	274	2920	3155	2231	1573	2034	2684	3388	2456	Seattle, WA
	721	357	1130	1013	985	401	478	669	309	1415	1203	2052	389	729	920	1270	1282	1087	2255	1585	538	1927	1173	1361	624	985	1563	474	1565	2061	2335	0	2038	644	895	1099	1160	356	953	507	1081	Shreveport, LA
3	2075	2230	3138	1702	1370	2342	2562	2124	2409	2569	2700	979	1768	1403	2895	2512	1386	2190	365	2644	2651	770	2761	2384	1816	1370	706	2110	1403	852	274	2038	0	2652	2887	2100	1496	1727	2417	3196	2125	Spokane, WA
2	664	527	486	1053	1354	243	209	486	381	1109	802	2601	1038	1241	243	1020	1962	932	2880	1288	624	2546	794	1208	795	1354	2116	916	2213	2611	2920	644	2652	0	251	900	1840	955	891	430	1005	Tallahassee, FL
3	915	778	292	1240	1589	494	460	737	632	1126	827	2836	1289	1492	89	1037	2213	998	3131	1322	657	2797	827	1251	1030	1589	2318	1151	2464	2846	3155	895	2887	251	0	1143	2076	1182	908	219	1088	Tampa, FL
	300	665	1293	332	641	940	766	478	1005	556	592	2293	961	705	1086	502	1950	227	2311	689	584	2133	630	381	466	641	1715	1387	2604	2415	2231	1099	2100	900	1143	0	2051	867	438	1248	170	Toledo, OH
	1697	1370	2326	1808	1702	1542	1633	1581	1419	2360	2271	878	908	1400	2083	2287	122	2021	1483	252	2124	867	2425	2222	1419	1702	795	876	405	868	1573	1160	1496	1840	2076	2051	0	1038	2254	2270	2003	Tuscon, AZ
	633	397	1483	770	705	713	765	608	657	1331	1234	1766	105	401	1240	1249	1103	981	1987	1483	1103	1702	1222	1398	381	705	1223	535	1403	1776	2034	356	1727	955	1182	867	1038	0	1284	1167	964	Tulsa, OK
	533	363	1086	770	1078	949	796	632	1095	252	190	2772	1305	1151	876	133	2367	219	2846	397	283	2579	114	341	795	1078	2141	1605	2733	2949	2684	953	2417	891	908	438	2254	1284	0	1005	283	Washington, DC
	1094	957	65	1386	1737	673	639	875	811	1223	916	3055	1468	1671	194	1134	2392	1111	3310	1402	754	2976	924	1346	1241	1737	2490	1370	2072	3065	3388	507	3196	430	219	1248	2270	1167	1005	0	1167	West Palm Beach, FL
	373	738	1238	510	794	1005	831	543	1095	403	438	2463	1087	875	1052	357	2076	65	2481	527	535	2303	662	265	592	794	1877	1477	2432	2569	2456	1181	2125	1005	1088	170	2003	964	283	1167	0	Youngstown, OH

Telephone Area Code Time Zone

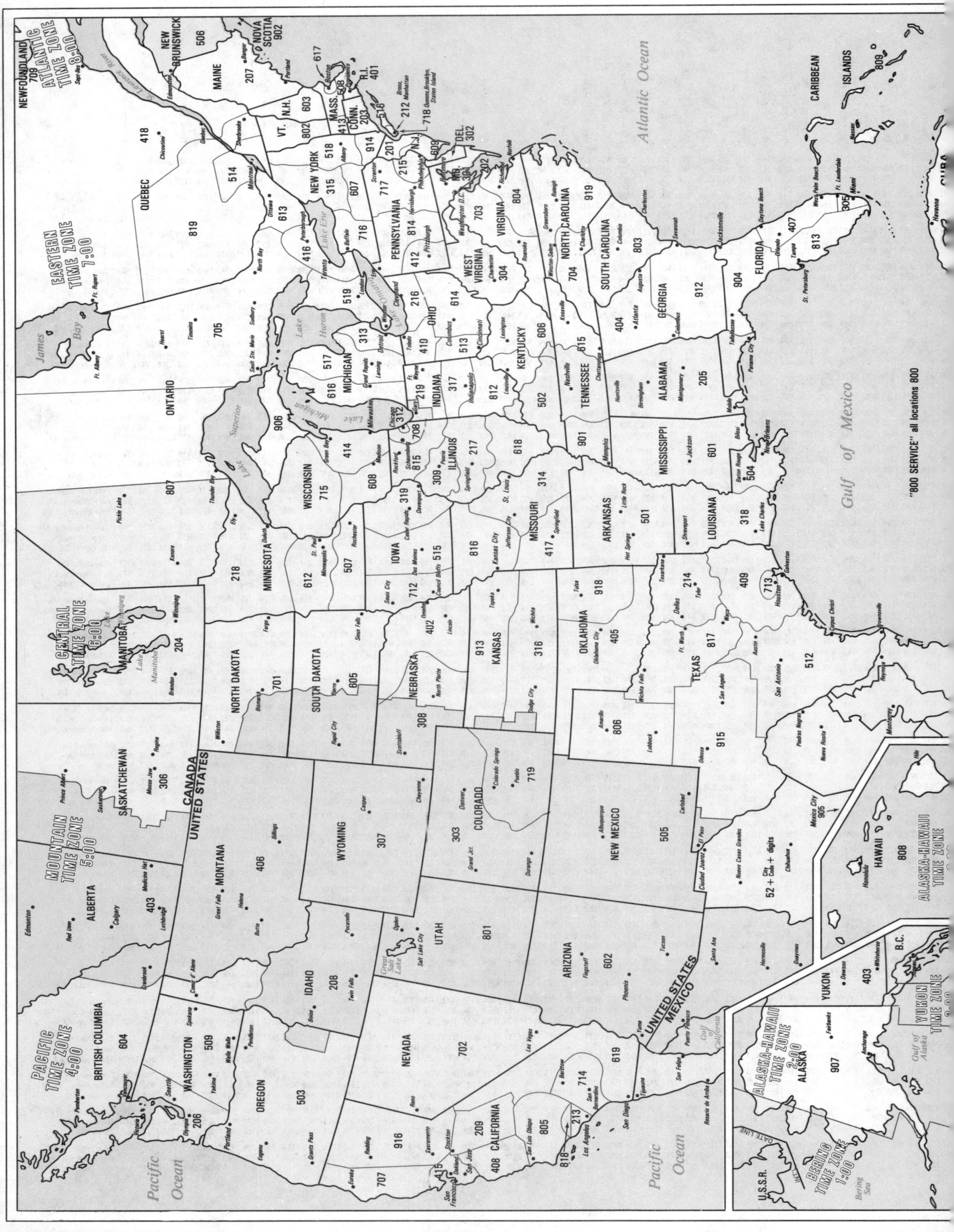

AREA CODES

ALABAMA

all locations	205

ALASKA

all locations	907

ARIZONA

all locations	602

ARKANSAS

all locations	501

CALIFORNIA

Bakersfield	805
Barstow	714
Encino	818
Eureka	707
Fresno	209
Los Angeles	213
Oakland	415
Orange	714
Redding	916
Sacramento	916
San Bernardino	714
San Diego	619
San Francisco	415
San Jose	415
San Louis Obispo	805
Stockton	209

CANADA

Chicoutimi, Quebec	418
Calgary, Alb.	403
Edmonton, Alb.	403
Edmunston, N.B.	506
London, Ont.	519
Montreal, Quebec	514
North Bay, Ont.	705
Ottawa, Ont.	613
Prince Albert, Sask.	306
Quebec, Quebec	418
Regina, Sask.	306
St. John's, Nfd.	709
Sudbury, Ont.	705
Sault Ste. Marie, Ont.	705
Thunder Bay, Ont.	807
Toronto, Ont.	416
Vancouver, B.C.	604
Winnipeg, Man.	204

COLORADO

Colorado Sprs.	719
Denver	303
Durango	303
Pueblo	719

CONNECTICUT

all locations	203

DELAWARE

all locations	302

DISTRICT OF COLUMBIA

Washington	202

FLORIDA

Avon Park	813
Daytona	407
Ft. Lauderdale	305
Ft. Myers	813
Jacksonville	904
Key West	305
Miami	305
Orlando	407
St. Petersburg	813
Tallahasse	904
Tampa	813
West Palm Beach	407
Winter Haven	813

GEORGIA

Atlanta	404
Augusta	404
Columbus	404
Rome	404
Savannah	912
Waycross	912

HAWAII

all locations	808

IDAHO

all locations	208

ILLINOIS

Aurora	708
Bloomington	309
Carbondale	618
Champaign	217
Chicago	312
Decatur	217
Elgin	708
Evanston	708
Highland Park	708
La Grange	708
La Salle	815
Lincoln	217
Mt. Vernon	618
Peoria	309
Rockford	815
Schaumburg	708
Springfield	217
Waukegan	708

INDIANA

Angola	219
Connersville	317
Elkhart	219
Evansville	812
Fort Wayne	219
Gary	219
Green Castle	317
Hammond	219
Indianapolis	317
Kokomo	317
Lafayette	317
Michigan City	219
Muncie	317
Richmond	317
South Bend	219
Terre Haute	812
Warsaw	219

IOWA

Cedar Rapids	319
Council Bluffs	712
Davenport	319
Des Moines	515
Dubuque	319
Mason City	515
Souix City	712

KANSAS

Dodge City	316
Ottawa	913
Topeka	913
Wichita	316

KENTUCKY

Ashland	606
Lexington	606
Louisville	502
Shelbyville	502
Winchester	606

LOUISIANA

Baton Rouge	504
Lake Charles	318
New Orleans	504
Shreveport	318

MAINE

all locations	207

MARYLAND

all locations	301

MASSACHUSETTS

Boston	617
Framingham	508
Plymouth	508
Springfield	413

MEXICO

Country
52 + city code + digits

MICHIGAN

Adrian	517
Ann Arbor	313
Battle Creek	616
Cadillac	616
Detroit	313
Escanaba	906
Flint	313
Grand Rapids	616
Jackson	517
Lansing	517
Kalamazoo	616
Monroe	313
Saginaw	517

MINNESOTA

Albert Lee	507
Duluth	218
Ely	218
Minneapolis	612
Rochester	507
St. Paul	612

MISSISSIPPI

all locations	601

MISSOURI

Jefferson City	314
Joplin	417
Kansas City	816
St. Joseph	816
St. Louis	314
Springfield	417

MONTANA

all locations	406

NEBRASKA

Lincoln	402
North Platte	308
Omaha	402
Scottsbluff	308

NEVADA

all locations	702

NEW HAMPSHIRE

all locations	603

NEW JERSEY

Atlantic City	609
Hackensack	201
Newark	201
Paterson	201
Trenton	609

NEW MEXICO

all locations	505

NEW YORK

Albany	518
Buffalo	716
Elmira	607
Greenwich	518
Manhatten & Bronx	212
Mt. Vernon	914
Niagara Falls	716
Poughkeepsie	914
Queens & Brooklyn	718
Rochester	716
Schenectady	518
Staten Island	718
Syracuse	315

NORTH CAROLINA

Charlotte	704
Greensboro	919
Greenville	919
Raleigh	919
Salisbury	704
Williamston	919
Winston-Salem	919

NORTH DAKOTA

all locations	701

OHIO

Akron	216
Canton	216
Cincinnati	513
Cleveland	216
Columbus	614
Dayton	513
Massillon	216
Niles	216
Salem	216
Toledo	419
Youngstown	216

OKLAHOMA

Muskogee	918
Oklahoma City	405
Tulsa	918

OREGON

all locations	503

PENNSYLVANIA

Allentown (Lehigh Co.)	215
Erie	814
Harrisburg	717
Hershey	717
Philadelphia	215
Pittsburgh	412
Reading	215
Scranton	717

PUERTO RICO

all locations	809

RHODE ISLAND

all locations	401

SOUTH CAROLINA

all locations	803

SOUTH DAKOTA

all locations	605

TENNESSEE

Chattanooga	615
Knoxville	615
Memphis	901
Nashville	615

TEXAS

Amarillo	806
Austin	512
Brownsville	512
Corpus Christi	512
Dallas	214
El Paso	915
Ft. Worth	817
Galveston	409
Houston	713
Lubbock	806
Odessa	915
San Angelo	915
San Antonio	512
Temple	817
Texarkana	214
Tyler	214
Waco	817
Wichita Falls	817

UTAH

all locations	801

VERMONT

all locations	802

VIRGIN ISLANDS

all locations	809

VIRGINIA

Charlottesville	804
Fredericksburg	703
Norfolk	804
Richmond	804
Roanoke	703

WASHINGTON

Olympia	206
Seattle	206
Spokane	509
Walla Walla	509
Yakima	509

WEST VIRGINIA

all locations	304

WISCONSIN

Beloit	608
Eau Claire	715
Green Bay	414
Madison	608
Milwaukee	414
Racine	414
Wausau	715

WYOMING

all locations	307

800 SERVICE

all locations	800

ALBERTA

Banff	J-4
Calgary	J-4
Camrose	H-5
Cardston	J-5
Drumheller	H-5
Edmonton	H-5
Edson	H-4
Fitzgerald	F-5
Fort Chipewyn	F-4
Ft. McMurray	G-5
Ft. Vermillion	F-4
Grande Centre	G-5
Grande Prairie	G-4
Habay	F-4
High Level	F-4
High River	J-4
Hinton	H-4
Jasper	H-4
Lethbridge	J-5
Medicine Hat	J-5
Peace Point	F-4
Peace River	G-4
Rainbow Lake	F-4
Red Deer	H-5
Rocky Mtn. House	H-4
Waterways	G-5
Wetaskiwin	H-4
Whitecourt	H-4

BRITISH COLUMBIA

Alert Bay	J-2
Atlin	F-2
Bella Coola	H-2
Campbell River	J-2
Cassiar	F-2
Courtnay	J-2
Cranbrook	J-4
Dawson Creek	G-3
Ft. Nelson	F-3
Ft. St. John	G-3
Hazelton	G-2
Kamloops	J-3
Kelowna	J-3
Kimberley	J-4
Kitimat	H-2
Masset	G-1
Nanaimo	J-2
Nelson	J-4
New Westminster	J-3
Ocean Falls	H-2
Penticton	J-4
Port Alberni	J-2
Port Alice	J-2
Powell River	J-3
Prince George	H-3
Prince Rupert	G-2
Quesnel	H-3
Revelstoke	J-4
Sandpit	H-1
Smithars	G-2
Stewart	G-2
Telegraph Creek	F-2
Trail	J-4
Ucluelet	J-2
Vancouver	J-3
Vernon	J-4
Victoria	J-3
Ware	G-3
Williams Lake	H-3

MANITOBA

Berens River	G-7
Brandon	H-7
Brochet	F-6
Churchill	F-7
Dauphin	H-7
Flin Flon	G-6
Gillam	F-7
Gods Lake	G-8
Grand Rapids	G-7
Island Lake	G-7
Lynn Lake	F-6
Norway House	G-7
Portage la Prairie	H-7
Selkirk	H-8
Snow Lake	G-7
S. Indian Lake	F-7
Swan River	H-7
The Pas	G-6
Thompson	G-7
Virden	J-7
Winnipeg	H-8

NEW BRUNSWICK

Bathurst	E-13
Campbellton	E-12
Chatam	E-13
Edmundston	F-12
Fredricton	F-13
Moncton	E-13
Newcastle	E-13
St. John	F-13
St. Stephen	F-13
Tracadie	E-13
Woodstock	F-13

NEWFOUNDLAND

Battle Harbour	C-13
Bonavista	C-14
Cartwright	C-12
Channel-Port aux Basques	D-14
Churchill Falls	D-12
Corner Brook	D-13
Gander	C-14

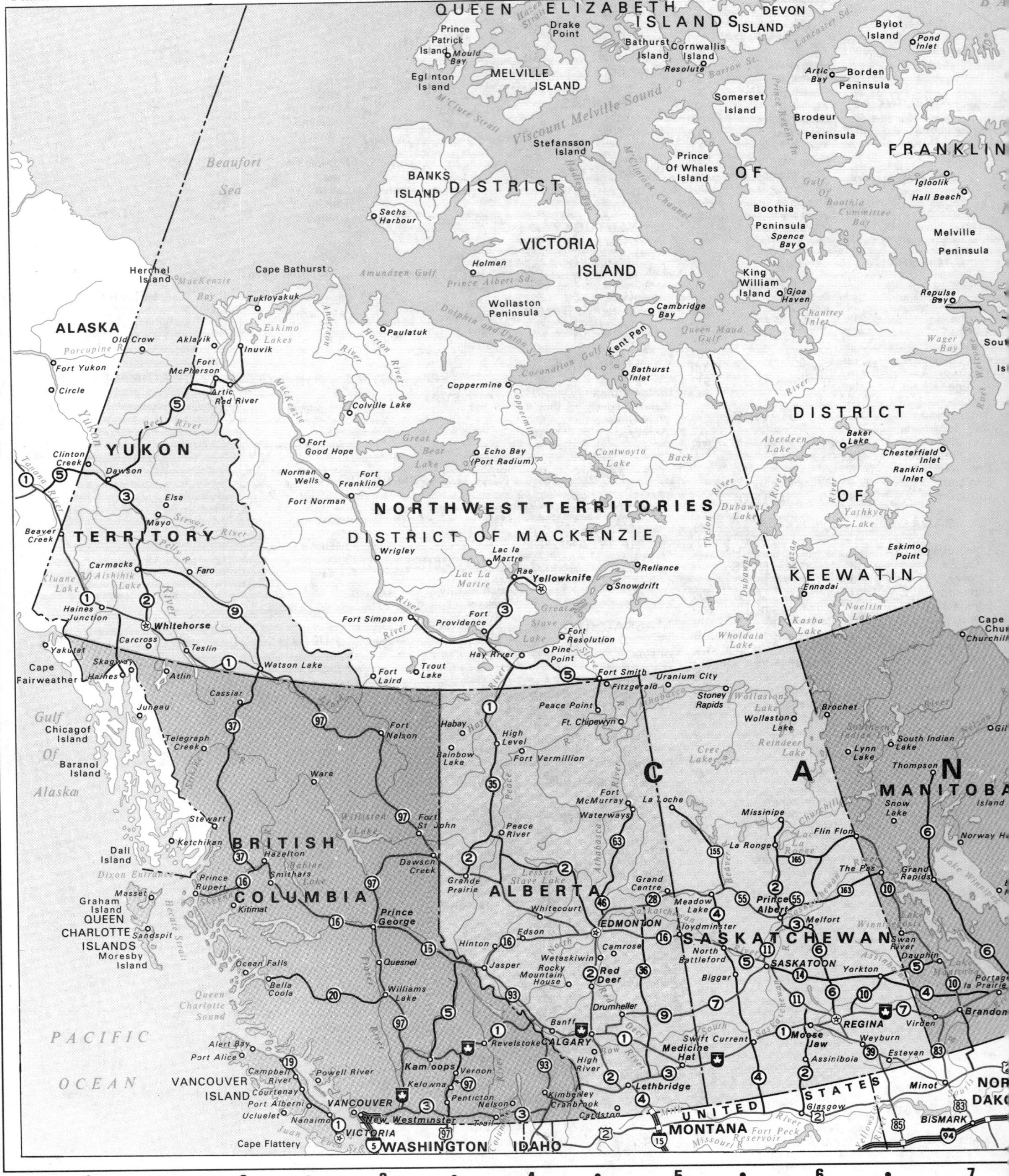

8 • 9 • 10 • 11 • 12 • 13 • 14

Goose Bay C-12
Grand Falls C-14
Hebron C-11
Hopedale C-11
Labrador City D-11
Makkovik C-12
Marystown D-14
Northwest River . . C-12
Nutak C-11
Placentia C-14
St. Anthony C-13
St. John's C-14
St. Pierre (France) . D-14
Stephenville D-13
Wabana C-14

N.W. TERRITORY

Aklavik C-2
Artic Bay A-6
Artic Red River D-2
Baker Lake D-6
Bathurst Inlet C-5
Cambridge Bay C-5
Cape Dorset C-8
Cape Dyer A-9
Chesterfield Inlet . . D-7
Clyde A-8
Colville Lake D-3
Coppermine D-4
Echo Bay (Port Radium) D-4
Ennadai E-6
Eskimo Point E-7
Ft. Franklin D-3
Ft. Good Hope D-3
Ft. Laird F-3
Ft. McPherson C-2
Ft. Norman D-3
Ft. Providence E-4
Ft. Resolution F-4
Ft. Simpson E-3
Ft. Smith F-4
Frobisher Bay B-9
Gjoa Haven C-6
Hall Beach B-7
Hay River F-4
Holman C-4
Igloolik B-7
Inuvik C-2
Lac la Martre E-4
Lake Harbour B-9
Mould Bay A-4
Norman Wells D-3
Panguirtung A-9
Paulatuk C-3
Pine Point F-4
Pond Inlet A-7
Rae E-4
Rankin Inlet D-7
Reliance E-5
Repulse Bay C-7
Resolute A-5
Resolution Island . . B-10
Sachs Harbour B-3
Snowdrift E-5
Spence Bay B-6
Trout Lake F-3
Tukloyakuk C-2
Wrigley E-3
Yellowknife E-4

NOVA SCOTIA

Amherst E-13
Bridgewater F-14
Canso E-14
Glace Bay E-14
Halifax F-14
Kentville F-13
New Glasgow E-14
Shelburne F-14
Sydney E-14
Truro E-13
Yarmouth F-13

ONTARIO

Armstrong G-9
Atikokan H-8
Barrie H-11
Belleville H-12
Blind River H-10
Brantford J-11
Brockville G-12
Chatham J-11
Cochrane G-10
Cornwall G-12
Deep River G-11
Favourable Lake . . G-8
Ft. Albany F-9
Ft. Frances H-8
Ft. Severn F-8
Geraldton H-9
Goderich J-11
Guelph H-11
Hamiton H-12
Hearst G-10
Kapuskasing G-10
Kenora H-8
Kingston H-12
Kirkland Lake G-10
Kitchener H-11
Lec Seul H-8
London J-11
Marathon H-9
Moosonee F-10
Nakina G-9
Niagra Falls H-12
Nipigon H-9
North Bay H-11
Oshawa H-11
Ottawa G-12
Owen Sound H-11
Parry Sound H-11
Pembroke G-11
Peterborough H-12
Pickle Lake G-9
Red Lake H-8
Renfrew G-11
St. Catharines H-12
St. Thomas J-11
Sault Ste. Marie . . . H-10
Sioux Lookout H-8
Smith's Falls G-12
Sudbury H-10
Thunder Bay H-9
Timmins G-10
Toronto H-11
Trenton H-12
Wawa H-10
Windsor J-11
Winisk F-9

PRINCE EDWARD ISLAND

Charlottetown E-13
Summerside E-13

QUEBEC

Alma F-12
Amos G-11
Arvida F-12
Baie Comeau E-12
Belin (Payne) C-10
Cape Smith D-9
Chandler E-12
Chicoutimi F-12
Deception C-9
Desmaraisville F-11
Drummondville . . . G-12
Eastmain F-10
Ft. Chimo C-10
Ft. George F-10
Ft. Rupert F-10
Gagnon E-11
Gaspe E-12
Granby G-12
Harve St. Pierre . . . D-12
Hull G-12
Inoucdjouac (Port Harrison) D-9
Ivujivik C-9
Koartac C-9
La Tugue F-12
Lac-Allard D-12
Levis F-12
Manicourgan E-12
Maniwaki G-11
Maricourt (Wakeham) C-9
Matagami F-10
Matane E-12
Mont-Laurier G-12
Montreal G-12
Nitchequon E-11
Noranda G-10
Nouveau-Quebec (George River) . . C-10
Port Alfred F-12
Port Cartier E-12
Poste-de-la-Baleine E-10
Povungnitak D-9
Quebec F-12
Rimouski E-12
Riviere-du-Loup . . . F-12
Rouyn G-11
St. Hyacinthe G-12
St. Jean G-12
St. Jerome G-12
Ste. Anne-des-Monts E-12
Schefferville D-11
Senneterre G-11
Sept. Iles E-12
Shawinigan G-12
Sherbrooke G-12
Shibougamau F-11
Sorel G-12
Thetford Mines . . . F-12
Trois-Rivieres G-12
Val-d'Or G-11

SASKATCHEWAN

Assiniboia J-6
Biggar H-5
Estevan J-7
La Loche G-5
La Rouge G-6
Lloydminister H-5
Meadow lake H-5
Melfort H-6
Missinipe G-6
Moose Jaw J-6
North Battleford . . H-5
Prince Albert H-6
Regina J-6
Saskatoon H-6
Stoney Rapids F-5
Swift Current J-5
Uramium City F-5
Weyburn J-6
Wollaston Lake . . . F-6
Yorkton H-6

YUKON

Beaver Creek E-1
Carcross E-1
Carmacks E-1
Clinton Creek D-1
Dawson D-1
Elsa D-2
Faro E-2
Haines Jct. E-1
Mayo E-1
Old Crow C-1
Teslin F-2
Watson Lake F-2
Whitehorse E-2

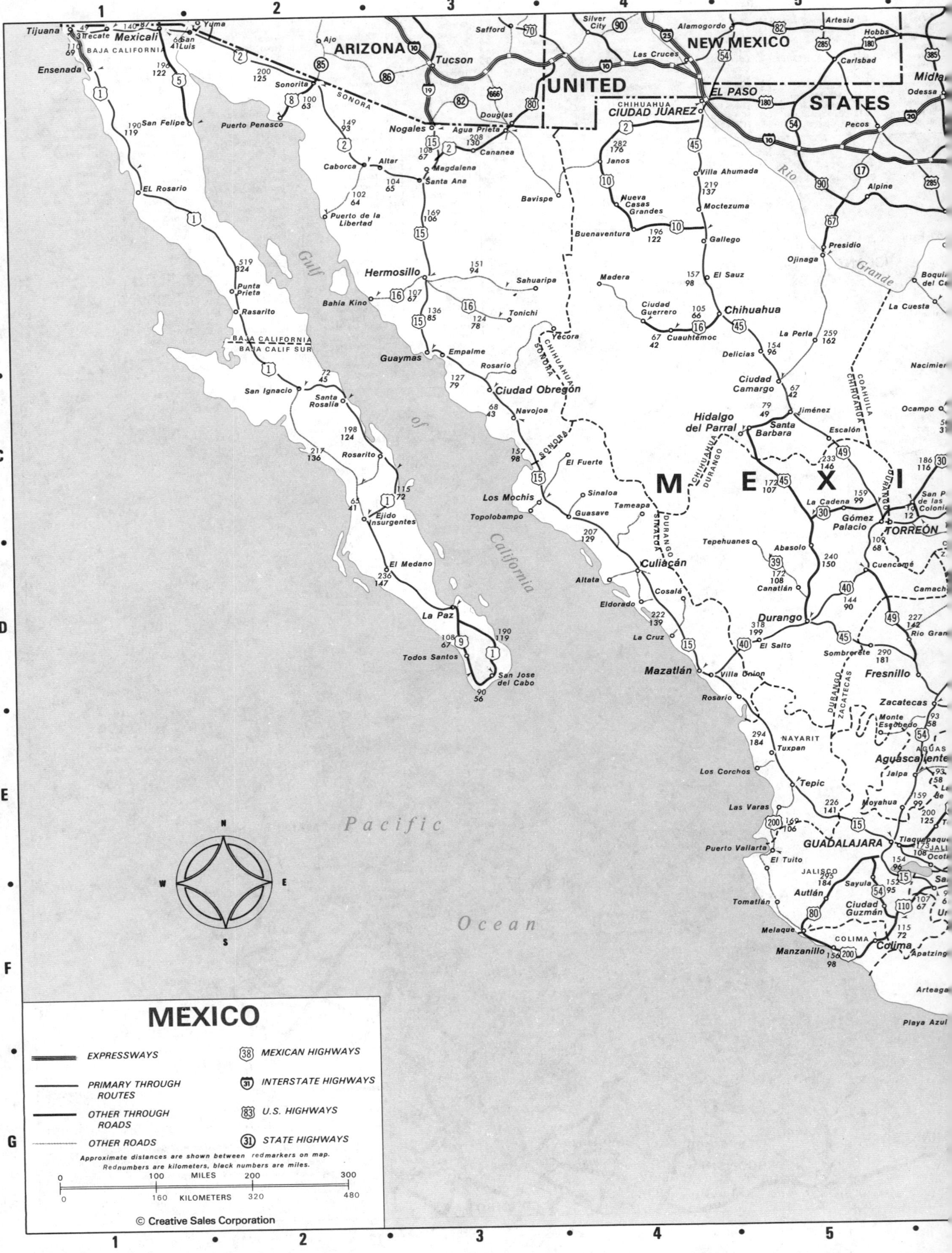
MEXICO
EXPRESSWAYS
PRIMARY THROUGH ROUTES
OTHER THROUGH ROADS
OTHER ROADS
MEXICAN HIGHWAYS
INTERSTATE HIGHWAYS
U.S. HIGHWAYS
STATE HIGHWAYS
Approximate distances are shown between redmarkers on map.
Rednumbers are kilometers, black numbers are miles.
0 100 MILES 200 300
0 160 KILOMETERS 320 480
© Creative Sales Corporation
N
S
E
W
Pacific
Ocean
Gulf
of
California
M E X I
UNITED
STATES
ARIZONA
NEW MEXICO
BAJA CALIFORNIA
BAJA CALIF SUR
SONORA
CHIHUAHUA
DURANGO
SINALOA
COAHUILA
NAYARIT
ZACATECAS
JALISCO
COLIMA
Rio Grande
Tijuana
Tecate
Mexicali
San Luis
Yuma
Ensenada
San Felipe
EL Rosario
Punta Prieta
Rasarito
San Ignacio
Santa Rosalia
Rosarito
Ejido Insurgentes
El Medano
La Paz
Todos Santos
San Jose del Cabo
Ajo
Tucson
Safford
Silver City
Las Cruces
Alamogordo
Artesia
Hobbs
Carlsbad
Midla
Odessa
Pecos
Alpine
EL PASO
CIUDAD JUAREZ
Douglas
Nogales
Agua Prieta
Cananea
Sonorita
Puerto Penasco
Caborca
Altar
Magdalena
Santa Ana
Puerto de la Libertad
Hermosillo
Bahia Kino
Sahuaripa
Tonichi
Guaymas
Empalme
Rosario
Ciudad Obregón
Navojoa
Yecora
Bavispe
Janos
Nueva Casas Grandes
Buenaventura
Villa Ahumada
Moctezuma
Gallego
El Sauz
Madera
Ciudad Guerrero
Cuauhtémoc
Chihuahua
Presidio
Ojinaga
La Cuesta
La Perla
Delicias
Ciudad Camargo
Jiménez
Hidalgo del Parral
Santa Barbara
Escalón
El Fuerte
Los Mochis
Topolobampo
Sinaloa
Guasave
Tameapa
Culiacán
Altata
Eldorado
Cosalá
La Cruz
Mazatlán
Villa Union
Rosario
Tepehuanes
Abasolo
Canatlán
Durango
El Salto
La Cadena
Gómez Palacio
TORREÓN
Cuencamé
Sombrerete
Fresnillo
Zacatecas
Monte Escobedo
Tuxpan
Los Corchos
Tepic
Las Varas
Puerto Vallarta
El Tuito
GUADALAJARA
Jalpa
Moyahua
Autlán
Sayula
Ciudad Guzmán
Tomatlán
Melaque
Manzanillo
Colima
Nacimier
Ocampo
Camach
Rio Gran
Arteaga
Playa Azul

MEXICO

Cities and Towns

Place	Grid
Abasolo	D-5
Acambaro	F-6
Acapulco	G-6
Acatlan	F-7
Acayucan	F-8
Agua Prieta	A-3
Aguascalientes	E-6
Altar	A-3
Altata	D-4
Alvarado	F-8
Apatzingan	F-6
Arcelia	F-6
Arriga	G-9
Arteaga	F-6
Arlixco	F-7
Autlan	F-5
Bahia Kino	B-2
Bavispe	B-4
Becal	E-10
Boquillas de Carmen	B-6
Buenaventura	B-4
Caborca	A-2
Camacho	D-6
Campeche	E-10
Cananea	A-3
Canatlan	D-5
Cardenas	F-9
Celaya	E-6
Celestun	E-10
Champoton	F-10
Chetumal	F-11
Chihuahua	B-5
Chilpancingo	F-7
China	C-7
Ciudad Acuna	B-6
Ciudad Camargo	C-5
Ciudad Guerrero	B-4
Ciudad Guzman	F-5
Ciudad Juarez	A-4
Ciudad Madero	E-7
Ciudad Mante	E-7
Ciudad Victoria	D-7
Ciudad de Carmen	F-9
Ciudad de Valles	E-7
Ciudad del Maiz	E-7
Coatzacoalcos	F-9
Colima	F-5
Comitan	G-9
Conception de Oro	D-6
Cordoba	F-8
Cosala	D-4
Cuauhtemoc	B-4
Cuencame	D-5
Cuernavaca	F-7
Culiacan	D-4
Delicias	B-5
Durango	D-5
Dzilam de Bravo	E-10
Ejido Insurgentes	C-3
Eldorado	D-4
El Fuerte	C-4
El Medana	D-3
El Rosario	A-1
El Sauz	B-4
El Tuito	E-5
Empalme	B-3
Ensanada	A-1
Escalon	C-5
Escarcega	F-10
Fresnillo	D-5
Gallego	B-4
Gomez Palacio	C-5
Guadalajara	E-5
Guasave	C-4
Guaymas	B-3
Hermosillo	B-3
Hidalgo del Parral	C-5
Hopelchen	E-10
Huajuapan de Leon	F-7
Iguala	F-7
Irapuato	E-6
Iturbide	F-10
Jalapa	F-8
Jalpa	E-5
Janos	A-4
Jimenez	C-5
Juchitan	G-8
La Cruz	D-4
La Cadena	C-5
La Cuesta	B-6
Lagos de Morena	E-6
La Paz	D-3
La Perla	B-5
La Pesca	D-7
La Piedad	E-6
Las Varas	E-5
Leon	E-6
Linares	D-7
Los Corchos	E-5
Los Mochis	C-3
Madera	B-4
Magdalena	A-3
Malpaso	G-9
Manuel	E-7
Manzanillo	F-5
Matamoros	C-7
Matehuala	D-6
Matias Romero	G-8
Mazatlan	D-4
Melaque	F-5
Merida	E-10
Mexicali	A-1
Mexico City	F-7
Miahuatlan	G-8
Mier	C-7
Minatitlan	F-8
Moctezuma	B-4
Molango	E-7
Moncloya	C-6
Monte Escobedo	E-5
Montemorelos	D-7
Monterrey	C-6
Morelia	F-6
Morelos	B-6
Moyahua	E-5
Nacimiento	C-6
Nautla	E-8
Navojoa	C-3
Nogales	A-3
Nueva Casas Grandes	B-4
Nueva Rosita	C-6
Nuevo Laredo	C-7
Oaxaca	G-8
Ocampo	C-6
Ocotlan	E-6
Ojinaga	B-5
Ometepec	G-7
Orizaba	F-8
Pachuca	E-7
Palenque	F-9
Papantla	E-7
Paraiso	F-9
Parras	C-6
Peto	E-10
Piedras Negras	B-6
Pijijiapan	G-9
Pinotepa Nacional	G-7
Piste	E-11
Playa Azul	F-6
Pochutla	G-8
Poza Pica	E-7
Progreso	E-10
Puebla	F-7
Puerto de la Libertad	B-2
Puerto Escondido	G-8
Puerto Juarez	E-11
Puerto Madero	G-9
Puerto Penasco	A-2
Punta Prieta	B-2
Queretaro	E-6
Rasarito	B-2
Reynosa	C-7
Rio Grande	D-6
Rio Lagartos	E-11
Rosario	C-3
Rosario	D-4
Sabinas	C-6
Sabinas Hidagalo	C-6
Sahuaripa	B-3
Salamanca	E-6
Salinas	C-6
Salina Cruz	G-8
Saltillo	C-6
San Andres Tuxtla	F-8
San Cristobal	G-9
San Felipe	A-2
San Fernando	D-7
San Ignacio	C-2
San Jose del Cabo	D-3
San Luis	A-2
San Luis Potosi	E-6
San Pedro de las Colonias	C-6
Santa Ana	A-3
Santa Barbara	C-5
Santa Rosalia	C-2
Sayula	F-5
Sinaloa	C-4
Sombrerete	D-5
Sonorita	A-2
Soto La Marina	D-7
Tameapa	C-4
Tampico	E-7
Tapachula	G-9
Tapanatepec	G-9
Taxco	F-7
Teapa	F-9
Tecate	A-1
Tehuacan	F-7
Tehuantepec	G-8
Temporal	E-7
Tepatitlan	E-6
Tepehuanes	D-5
Tepic	E-5
Ticul	E-10
Tijuana	A-1
Tiquicheo	F-6
Tlaciaco	G-7
Tlaxcala	F-7
Tlaxiaco	G-7
Todos Santos	D-3
Toluca	F-7
Tomatian	F-5
Tonichi	B-3
Topolobampo	C-3
Torreon	C-5
Totolapan	G-8
Tulancingo	F-7
Tulum	E-11
Tuxpan	E-5
Tuxpan	E-7
Tuxtepec	F-8
Tuxtla Gutierrez	G-9
Uruapan	F-6
Valladolid	E-11
Veracruz	F-8
Villa Ahumada	A-4
Villagran	D-7
Villahermosa	F-9
Villa Union	D-4
Xcan	E-11
Yecora	B-4
Zacatal	F-9
Zacatecas	E-6
Zamora	F-6
Zihuatanejo	F-6
Zimapan	E-7
Zitacuaro	F-6

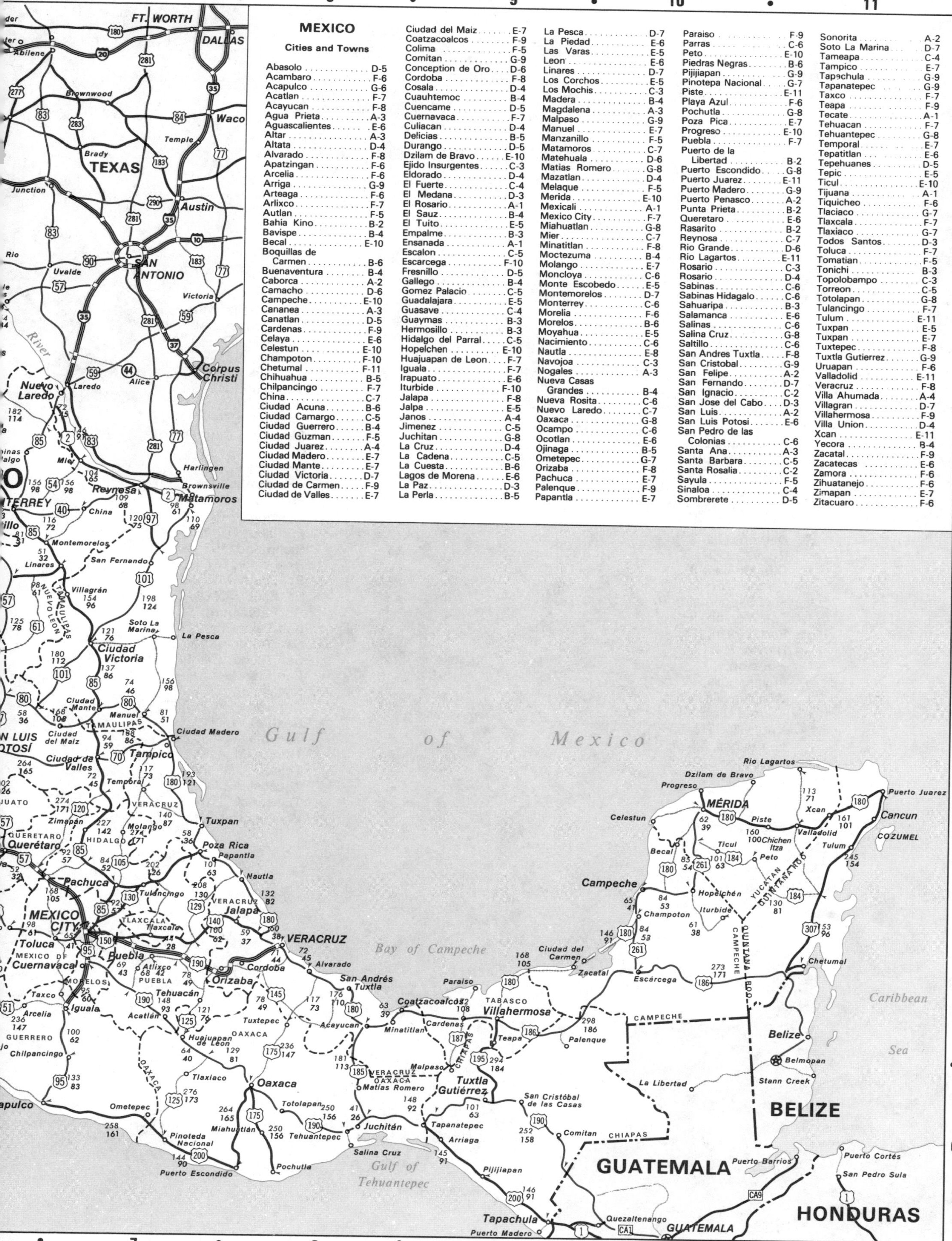

Detailed City Center Map Section

The maps in this section are intended to show in detail the central areas of each of the above 68 cities. The scale of each map was determined by the area of coverage, therefore they are not drawn to a common scale.

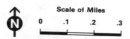

Scale of Miles
0 .1 .2 .3

ALBUQUERQUE

Ada Ct....F-8
Ada Pl....F-7
Alcade Pl....J-1
Alexander Blvd....A-8
Alexander Rd....B-1
Alhambra Ave....H-1
Altamonte Ave....C-3
Altamonte Pl....C-4
Apache Ave....E-3,F-8
Apache Ct....F-8
Arcadian Tr....B-2,B-3
Arias Ave....G-2
Arno St....D-5,G-5,J-4
Arvada Ave....F-4
Arvilla Ave....C-2
Ash St....J-7,K-6
Aspen Ave....F-1
....F-2,G-3,G-5
Atlantic Ave....K-3
Avenida Charada....D-1
Avenida Cristo....B-2
Avenida Curvatura....D-1
Avenida Entrada....C-2
Avenida Los Campanas....A-1
Avon St....C-4
Aztec Rd....C-3,D-8
Bayita Ln....A-2
Bellamah Ave....G-1-3
Bell Rose Ave....B-3,B-5
Berry Rd....A-4
Beryl Ct....E-1
Bezemek Ave....F-3
Broadview Pl....C-2
Broadway Blvd....G-5,J-4
Broadway Ext....E-5
Cacy Ave....D-5
Calle Los Vecinos....B-1
Camino....C-2
Camino Aplauso....C-2
Camino Ecuestre....D-2
Camino Gallo....D-2
Camino Raso....D-1
Camino Rosario....D-2
Campbell Ct....D-1
Campus....I-8
Candelaria Rd....C-2,D-6
Canna Dr....F-6
Carlton St....B-5,E-5
Carmony Rd....B-6
Carson Rd....G-1
Casaus Ave....K-3
Cedar St....K-6
Central Ave....I-3,J-7
Chacoma Pl....H-1
Chacon....H-2
Charlvoix St....G-1
Cherokee Rd....B-1,C-2
Church St....G-1
Claire Ct....H-2
Claremont Ave....D-4,E-7
Clyde St....C-4
Coal Ave....J-3,K-7
Coal Pl....K-6
Columbia Dr....D-7
....G-8,H-8,K-8
Commercial Ave.
....G-4,I-4
Commercial St....D-5
Conder Ln....D-4
Constitution Ave.
....G-4,H-8
Copper Ave....I-3,J-5
Cordero Rd....G-5
Cordova Ave....E-4
Cordova Pl....D-3
Cornell Dr....G-8,K-8
Coronado Ave....I-8
Coronaod Frwy....F-1,F-5
Covina Pl....D-1
Crespin Ave....G-5
Cromwell Ave....K-3,K-4
Cutler Ave....F-3,F-5,F-7
Cutler Ct....F-8
Cutter....D-7
Delmar Ave....A-3
Delmar Rd....A-3
Dietz Ct....A-1
Dietz Pl....A-1
Don Cipriano....I-5
Don Juan Ct....C-1
Douglas McArthur Rd....A-4
Dudley Rd....G-1
Edith Blvd....G-5,I-5
El Bordo Dr....K-3
El Ensueno Rd....A-7
Elfego Rd....A-1
Elm Dr....F-6,J-5
El Paseo Ave....A-4
El Paseo Dr....A-4
Engle Dr....F-8
Ensenada Pl....A-4
Escalante Ave....J-1
Eton Ave....K-7
Euclid....F-8
Fairfields Ave....D-4
Fairfields Ct....D-4
Fitzgerald Rd....D-3
Floral Dr....F-6
Foraker Pl....E-4
Forest Park....I-1
Forrester Ave....H-3
Franciscan St.
....D-5,F-5,H-5
Franz Hunning....I-1
Fredrick Pl....E-1
Freeman Ave....B-3,B-4
Fruit Ave....H-3,I-5
Garden Cir....D-2
Garfield Ave....K-8
Gold Ave....J-3,J-5,J-6
Gomez Ave....G-5
Grand Ave....I-4
Grande Ct....B-3
Grande Dr....B-3
Granite Ave....H-2,H-4,H-5
Griegos Commanche Ext....A-1,B-6
Guadalupe....A-2
Gusto....D-2
Haines....G-8
Haines Ave....F-3
Hannett Ave....G-3,G-5
Hannett Dr....G-8
Harold Pl....F-8
Harvard Ct....G-8
Harvard Dr....G-8,K-8
Hazeldine Ave.
....K-3,K-4,K-6
Headingly....B-1
Headingly Ave....C-3
Hendrix Rd....A-5
High St....D-6,G-5
....I-5,J-5
High Stone St....H-5
Hilton Ave....A-5
Hudson Ave....D-4
Indian School Rd.
....E-2,F-5,G-6
Industrial Ave....C-6
Iron Ave....J-2,K-5
John St....I-4
Juanita Ln....A-3
Jupiter St....B-5
Keleher Ave....I-3
Kinley Ave....G-3,H-5
Kit Carson Ave....I-1,J-1
La Cienega St....B-4
Laguna....I-1
La Luz....C-3
La Plaza Dr....C-1
La Poblana Rd.
....E-2,E-3,E-4
Larga Ave....G-8
La Rueda....A-4
Las Lomas Ave....I-6
Lead Ave....J-3,J-6
Leon Ct....B-1
Llano Ct....D-1
Lobo Ct....G-8
Lobo Pl....H-8
Locust St....D-6
Lomas Blvd....H-3,I-7
Lombardy Dr....F-6
Los Alamos Ave....I-1
Los Arboles Ave.
....D-2,D-3,E-8
Los Hermanos St....B-5
Los Tomases Dr....C-4,E-4
Luecking....B-8
Luke Cir....B-1
Luna Blvd....I-3
Lynch Ct....G-3
Lynch Pl....G-3
Maggies Ave....H-5
Main St....G-1
Major Ave....D-3
Manchester Dr....C-1
Manzano Ct....H-3
Maple St....I-7,J-6
Marble Ave....H-1
....H-3,H-5,H-8
Marie Pl....E-1
Marquette Ave....I-2,I-6
Martinez Ave....G-5
Mateo....C-2
Matthew Ave....D-5
McDonald Rd....D-1
Mcearl Ave....K-8
McKnight Ave....F-3,F-5
McMulden....D-3
Meadow View Dr....E-1
Medical Art Ave....I-6
Menaul Blvd....E-7
Menaul Ext....E-2
Menual Rd....F-7
Merritt Ave....H-1
Mesa St....K-7
Mesa Vista Rd....I-7
Mescalero Rd....C-5
Michelle Pl....A-2
Mildred Ave....D-3,D-4
Mill Pond Rd....F-1
Miller Cir....A-1
Milton Rd....D-1
Monk Ct....E-4
Montano Rd....A-6
Morrow Rd....F-8
Mountain Rd....H-3,H-8
Mulberry St....J-6
Natalie Ave....A-5
Newton Pl....F-8
Odelia Rd....G-5
Old Town Rd....H-1
Orchard Pl....H-2
Oxford Ave....K-7
Pacific Ave....K-3,K-4
Page Ave....H-5
Palo Duro Ave....A-3,A-4
Pan American Frwy.
....C-7,I-6
Park Ave....I-2
Park Rd....D-3
Pastura Pl....A-4
Patrick Ave....A-2
Pedrocelli Ct....B-2
Pedroncelli Rd....A-1
Phoenix Ave....D-2,E-4,E-8
Pine St....K-7
Pleasant Ave....B-5
Ponderosa Ave....A-3,A-4
Princeton Dr....E-8,F-8
....G-8,H-8,K-8
Prospect Ave....E-1,E-3,F-8
Pueblo Bonito Ct....G-1
Rankin Ln....C-7
Rankin Rd....C-6
Raynolds Ave....J-1
Rice Ave....E-1
Ridge Pl....I-6
Roma Ave....I-2,I-5,I-6
Romero St....H-1
Rosalee Rd....A-3
Rose Ave....F-1
Rosemont Ave....G-2
....H-3,H-5
Rutherford Ln....A-6
St. Cyr Ave....K-7
Saiz Rd....F-1
San Andres Ave.
....A-3,A-4,A-5
San Carlos Dr....I-1
Sanchez Rd....A-5
San Clemente Ave.
....B-2,B-4
San Cristobal Rd....I-1
San Felipe St....H-1
San Francisco....F-1
San Isidro St....B-2,E-1
San Lorenzo Ave.
....A-1,B-2,B-3
San Luis Pl....A-3
San Patricio Ave....I-1
San Pisquale Ave....H-1
Santa Fe Ave....K-3,K-4
San Venito Pl....E-1,F-1
Sawmill Rd....G-2
Saxton Ct....E-1
Schell Ct....F-8
Schell Pl....F-8
Shangri La....B-5
Shannon Pl....A-5
Shropshire Pl....D-4
Sierra Vista St....E-2
Sigma Chi Rd....I-6
Silver Ave....J-3,J-5,J-6
Slate Ave....H-1,H-3,I-5
Speronelli Rd....D-1
Spruce St....I-6,J-6
Sprunk Rd....G-5
Stanford Dr....C-8,D-8
....E-8,F-8,H-8
Stover Ave....J-2,K-3
Summer Ave....G-2,G-3
Sunland....C-3
Sycamore St....J-6
Tahoe Pl....A-7
Teodocio Rd....A-3
Terrace Dr....J-7
Tijeras Ave....I-2,I-4,J-6
Tiovio Cir....A-1
Toedoro Rd....A-1
Tokay St....A-7
Towner Ave....E-2,E-3
Tranquilino Ct....I-5
Trinity....B-3
Tucker St....H-8
Tulip Dr....F-6
Tyrone Ave....B-5
University Blvd....G-7,K-7
Valley Alto....C-2
Valley Haven Ct....B-1
Valley Heaven Park....C-1
Van Cleave Rd....B-2
Varsoviana....B-1
Vassar Dr....E-8
Veranda Rd....C-4
Vista Columbia Ave....G-8
Walter St....H-5,J-5
Willis Pl....H-1
Wilma Rd....D-1
Woodland Ave....E-8
Woodland Rd....E-3,E-5
Yale Blvd....K-8
1st St....G-4,J-4
2nd St....C-5,G-4,J-4
3rd St....B-5,C-4
....E-4,G-4,J-4
4th St....C-4,G-4,J-3
5th Ct....A-4
5th St....A-4,C-4
....D-4,E-4,G-4,J-3
6th Ct....A-4
6th St....A-4,C-4
....E-4,G-3,J-3
7th Ct....A-4
7th St....C-4,D-4,H-3,J-3
8th Ct....A-4
8th St....B-4,C-4
E-3, H-3, J-3
9th St....A-4,B-4,C-3
....E-3,F-3,J-3,K-2
10th Ct....A-4
10th St....B-4,C-3
....E-3,J-2,K-2
11th St....C-3,E-3
....I-2,J-2,K-2
12th St....A-3,D-3,I-1,J-2
13th St....C-3,I-2,J-2
14th Ct....B-3
14th St....I-2
15th Ct....B-3
15th St....C-2,I-2
16th Ct....B-2
16th St....H-2,I-1
17th Ct....B-2
17th St....E-2,H-2
18th St....E-1,H-2
19th St....E-1,G-1,H-1
20th St....E-1,G-1
21st St....G-1
22nd St....G-1
23rd St....G-1

POINTS OF INTEREST

C. L. Graves Park....F-3
Columbus Park....A-3
Coronado Park....F-4
Goodrich Park....A-5
Highland Park....J-5
McClelland Square Park....H-4
Netherwood Park....F-8
Rio Grande Park....K-2
Robinson Park....I-3
Roosevelt Park....K-6
Soldiers & Sailors Park....I-2
Spruce Park....I-6

ATLANTA

Abbott....E-1
Adair Ave....A-7,K-4
Adrian....B-7
Aiken....K-3
Alabama....E-4
Alamo....A-1
Alaska....D-7
Albion Av....C-8
Alice....F-3
Allen Ave....I-1
Allene Ave....J-1
Alexander St....C-3
Alloway....H-8
Alta Ave....D-8
Amal Dr....K-3
Angier Ave....C-5,C-6
Angier Pl....C-6
Anne....J-5
Argonne Ave....B-5
Arlington Pl....A-8
Arnold....C-6
Ashby....B-1,D-1,G-1
Ashby Cir....D-1
Ashby Pl....E-1
Ashland, W....D-7
Ashland Dr....D-7
Ashley....B-7
Athas....K-8
Athens Ave....J-2
Atlanta Ave....H-4,H-6
Atlantic....A-3
Atlantis....C-7
Auburn Ave....D-4,D-6
Augusta....G-5
Austin Ave....C-8,D-8
Avon Ave....I-1
Ashwood Ave....K-2
Avondale Ave....I-7
Bailey....E-2
Baker....D-4
Bankhead Ave....B-1
Barker Pl....D-6
Barnett Pl....C-7
Barnett St....B-7
Bass....G-5
Bass St....G-3,G-4,G-5
Battery Pl....D-8
Battle....E-1
Battle Ct....F-8
Beatie Ave....J-1
Beauregard....I-7
Beckwith St....E-1
Bedford St....B-1
Beechwood Ave....I-1
Belfast....J-1
Belgrade....C-7
Bell....E-5
Belmont Ave....J-2
Bender....G-2
Benjamin....G-2
Benteen....I-6,J-6
Benteen Way....J-6
Berean Ave....F-6
Berne St....G-6,G-7
Bernina....C-7
Beryl....H-2
Biglin St....I-1
Bird St....K-5
Bisbee Ave....J-4
Bishop....C-5
Bishop Al....C-5
Blashfield....J-5
Blossom....J-1
Blue Ridge Ave....B-8
Blue Ridge Ct....B-7
Bluff....G-2
Boley....C-1
Bonar....E-1
Bonaventure....B-7
Bonn....K-4
Bonnie Brae....H-1
Booker....I-3,J-3
Booker Wash. Dr....D-1
Boulevard....C-6,D-6
....G-6,I-6
Bouldvard Dr....E-8
Boulevard Pl....C-6
Bowen....K-5
Bowen Cir....J-3
Box Al....C-5
Boynton....I-4
Bradberry....E-3
Bradley....D-5,D-6,E-6
Brady Ave....A-1
Brantley....D-8
Briarcliff Pl....A-8
Brewer....K-1
Broad St....E-3
Brookline St....H-1
Brotherton St....E-3
Brown Ave....J-4
Bruce Cir....J-7
Bryan St....F-6
Buckeye....K-1
Buena Vista....H-3
Bulloch St....J-4
Burchill....J-1
Burns....J-1
Burns Dr....H-8
Burroughs St....J-6
Burton....K-5
Butler St....C-5,E-4,E-5
Byron....J-1
Caldwell....K-3
Cahoon St....K-1
Calhoun St....A-2
Capitol Ave....H-4
Carmel....C-8
Carnigie....D-4
Carroll....E-6
Carter St....D-1
Cassanova St....J-6
Casplan....K-2
Casplan Ct....K-1
Casplan St....K-1
Castleberry St....E-3
Catherine St....H-1
Central Ave....F-3,G-3
Chamberlain....E-6
Chapel....E-2
Chapel St....E-2
Charles Allen Dr....B-6
Charleston....K-5
Charlton Pl....J-2
Chastain....F-7
Cherokee Ave....G-6,H-6
Chester Ave....F-7
Chestnut Pl....D-1
Chestnut St....C-2,D-1
Christman....G-2
Circle....K-3
Claire Dr....K-1,K-4
Clemont Dr....A-7
Cleveland St....E-8
Clifton....C-5
Climax....I-5
Clinton....J-2
Clover Al....C-5
Cogins Dr....H-7
Cohen....H-2
Coleman St....I-2
Colquitt Ave....C-8
Columbia....A-4
Cone....D-4
Confederate....H-8
Confederate Ct....H-7
Connally St....G-5,H-5
Cooledge Ave....A-6
Cooper St....G-3
Copenhill....C-7
Corley....D-6
Cornelia....E-6
Courtland St....C-4,E-4
Crew St....H-4
Crogman....K-2
Crumley St....G-3
Curran....A-2
Currier St....C-4
Custer Ave....J-7
Cummings....E-8
Cypress....B-4
Dale Dr....J-7
Dallas St....C-6
Dalney St....A-3
Dalton St....I-5
D'Alvigney....B-1
Daniel....E-6
Danner....I-8
David....C-2
David Ct....C-7
Davage....J-4
Davis St....C-2
De Kalb Ave....E-6
De Leon St....A-7
Deckner....J-2
Deckner Ave....J-1
Degress....D-8
Delaware Av....H-8
Delbridge St....D-2
Delevan St....H-2
Delmar Ave....H-7
Desoto....D-1
Desoto Ave....J-1
Dewey....H-2
Dill Ave....J-1
Division....C-1
Dixie....D-7
Doane St....H-3
Dodd....G-3
Dora....F-2
Drewry St....A-7,A-8
Drud Cir....D-7
Drummond....E-1
Dunbar....I-2
Dupont Pl....J-7
Durant Pl....B-5
Dunlap....D-5
Earle....D-3
East Ave....C-6
Eastwood....H-8
Echo St....B-1
Echo St., W....B-1
Edgewood Ave....E-4,E-6
Edie Ave....I-7
Edith....C-7
Eden Ave....H-8
Elbert St....H-1
Electric....D-2
Elijah....D-1
Elizabeth St....C-7
Elleby Rd....J-7
Elliot St....D-3
Elm St....D-2,E-2
Eloise....G-7
Eloise Ct....G-7
Elvira St....J-5
Emerson Av....G-8
Emmett....C-2
Englewood Ave....I-5
English Ave....C-1
Erin....I-2
Erin Ave....I-1
Essie....H-8
Esten....E-8
Estoria St....F-7
Euclid....C-8
Euclid Ave....C-8,D-7
Eugenia....F-3
Euhrlee....E-1
Evans St....G-1
Everhart St....J-1
Fair St....E-2,E-3
Fairbanks St....J-1
Faith Ave....F-8
Farrington....H-5
Federal....J-7
Federal Ter....J-6
Fedler Dr....I-2
Felton Dr....C-5
Fern St....H-4
Field....E-7
Fisher Rd....J-7
Fitzgerald....E-6
Flat Shoals Ave....E-8
Fletcher St....I-2,I-3
Florence....D-7
Florida....F-8
Ford Pl....B-7
Forest Ave....C-5,C-6
Formwalt St....G-3
Fort St....D-5,E-5
Fortress Ave....I-3
Fortune....C-6
Forsyth St....E-3
Foundry St....D-1,D-2
Fowler....B-3
Fowler St....A-3
Fox St....B-1
Francis Ave....I-6
Frank....F-1
Franklin St....H-8
Fraser St....F-4,H-4
Fuller....D-3
Fulton....F-3
Fulton St....F-4
Fulton Terr....E-7
Funton....J-7
Gammon....I-4
Gardner....H-2
Garibaldi St....G-3,I-3
Garland St....J-4
Garnett St....E-3
Gartrell....E-5
Gault....J-6,I-6
Genesee Ave....J-1
Geneva Dr....J-8
Georgia Ave....G-3
Gerard....A-2
Giben Rd....K-3
Gibson St....F-8
Gift....F-8
Gilbert....H-8,I-8
Gillette....H-1
Glen Pl....C-6,G-4
Glendale Pl....A-1
Glendale Ter....B-5
Glenn St....G-1,G-3
Glenwood Ave.
....F-5,F-7,F-8
Glenwood Pl....G-8
Gordon....G-1
Gould....K-5
Graham St....J-1
Grant Cir....H-5
Grant Pl....C-4
Grant St....F-5,G-5,J-5
Grant Park Pl....H-5
Grape....D-6,I-4
Gray....C-3
Gray St....C-3
Green Field....A-3
Greens Ferry Ave....F-1
Greenwood....B-6,B-7
Gress....H-7
Griffin....C-1,D-1
Hale St....D-7
Hall Ave....G-8
Hamilton Ave....H-6
Hammond....F-1
Hampton St....A-2
Hannah....J-5
Hanover....E-8
Hansell....G-6
Hardee....D-8
Hardee St....D-8
Hardwick....K-4
Harold....E-7
Harriet St....J-5
Harris St....D-4
Harte Dr....K-1
Hartford Ave....J-1
Hartford Pl....I-1
Hatcher....H-4
Hayden....D-3
Haynes St....D-3
Hawthorne....E-8
Hazelrig Dr....K-8
Hemlock Cir....G-8
Hemphill....A-2
Hendrix....H-3
Highland Ave....B-8,D-6
Highland View....A-7
Hill....I-5
Hill St....F-5
Hillard St....D-5,E-5
Hills....F-2
Hillside Dr....J-2
Hilltop Cir....D-1
Hobart Ave....I-6
Hogue St....D-6
Holiday....D-8
Holtzclaw....F-8
Home Ave....H-6
Hobson....H-2
Hopkins....K-5
Houston....D-6
Houston St....D-4
Howell....E-6
Howell Pl....C-3
Howell St....D-6
Hubbard St....I-2
Hudson Dr....A-8
Hugh....G-2
Hulsey St....D-3
Humphries St....G-2
Hunnicutt....C-3
Hunter St....E-2,E-3,F-5
Hurt St....D-8
Inman....B-5
Ira St....G-3,I-3
Iris Dr....C-6
Irwin St....D-5
Iswald....F-7
Ivy St....D-4,E-4
Jackson....E-6
Jackson Pkwy....D-6
Jefferson St....B-1
Jenkins....K-4
Jett St....C-1
John St....C-3
Johnson....C-3
Jones Ave....C-2
Joyce....E-1
Joyland....J-3
Joyland St....K-3
Julian St....B-2
Juniper St....B-5
Kelly St....F-5
Kendrick Ave....H-5
Kennedy St....C-1
Kenneth....G-4
Kent....G-5
Kenyon....E-7
King....E-5
Killian....G-7
Kirkwood....E-7
Knott....I-8
Lake Ave....D-7
Lakewood Ave....I-5
Lampkin....D-6
Lansing St....J-4
Larkin St....F-2
Latimer....D-3
Lawshe....E-1
Lee St....I-1
Lethea St....K-5
Lester....H-7
Lexington Ave....I-1
Lillian....H-1
Linam....H-4
Lincoln Pl....K-3
Linden Ave....B-4
Lindsay St....C-1
Linwood Ave....C-8
Little St....G-4,G-5
Livermore....K-5
Logan....F-5
Loneta....I-6
Longview....C-5
Loring St....G-8
Love St....G-3,G-4,G-5
Lovejoy....C-3
Lowndes....H-1
Luckie St....D-3,D-4
Lucy....E-6
Lynch....A-2
Lyndale....H-8
Lynnhaven....J-2
Lynwood St....G-7
Lytle....F-8
Maderira....C-7
Magnolia St....D-2
Maiden Ln....B-7
Main St....A-1
Manford Rd....I-2,I-3
Mangum St....D-3
Manigault Ave....E-8
Maple St....D-2
Marcus....E-7
Margaret....J-5
Marietta....D-4
Marietta St....A-1,B-3
Marion....G-7,J-7
Markham....E-1
Martin....I-4,I-5,J-4
Martin St....F-4,H-4,I-5
Mary....H-2
Maryland....A-8,I-2
Mayes....D-3
Maygood Ave....H-4
Mayland....I-2
McCreary....I-4
McCullough....D-1
McDaniels St....F-2,I-2
McDonald....F-7
McDonald Dr....I-5
McDonough Blvd....I-5,I-7
McMillan....B-2
Mead St....H-6
Means St....B-2
Meldon Ave....J-4
Meldrum St....C-1
Mellview....J-2
Memorial Dr....F-4
Mercer Pl....G-7
Mercer St....G-7,G-8
Merritts....C-3
Merritts Ave....C-4
Michigan....D-1
Middleton....J-4
Mildred....E-1
Milledge Ave....G-5
Miller....J-5
Milton Ave....I-4
Milton St....E-1
Milton Ter....I-5
Mitchell St....E-1,E-2,E-4
Monroe....B-6
Monroe Cir....B-6
Moore....E-5
Moreland Ave....C-8,H-8
Moreland Dr....K-7
Morely....I-7
Moton....I-3
Moury Ave....J-4
Murphy Ave....G-1
Murray....J-4
Myrtle....B-5
Neal St....C-1
Nelson St....E-3
New Cir....K-7
Newcastle....E-1
Newport St....C-1
Newton....D-3
Napier....I-8
Narrow St....F-7
Nolan St....I-5
North Ave....B-1,B-3
....B-6,B-8
Northern....E-8
Northside Dr....A-2
Nuting....C-5
Oak Knoll Cir....K-5
Oakhill Ave....H-2
Oakland....F-5
Oakland Ave....G-6
Ogden....E-1
Old Flat....F-7
Old Wheat....D-5,D-6
Olive....K-4
Oliver St....C-1
Orlean....G-5
Ormewood Ave....G-6,G-8
Ormewood Ter....H-7
Ormond St....H-3,H-5
Ozone....E-1
Park Ave....G-6
....H-6,J-4,J-6
Park Rd....J-7
Park St....F-1
Parsons....K-5
Parsons St....E-1
Pavillion....G-5
Paynes....C-1
Peachtree Pl....A-4
Peachtree St....C-4,E-3
Peachtree St., W....C-4
Pear St....I-4
Pearce St....H-1
Pearl St....F-7
Pelham St....B-1
Penn Ave....B-5
Pickett....E-7
Piedmont....E-4
Piedmont Rd....B-5,D-5
Pine....C-6
Pine St....C-4
Play Lane....D-1
Plum....A-3
Ponce De Leon Ave.
....B-4,B-7
Ponce De Leon Ct.
....B-6
Ponce De Leon Ter.
....A-7
Pontiac....K-8
Pontiac Pl....J-8
Poole Pl....G-1
Poplar....D-4
Poplar Cir....D-8
Portland....G-8
Porter Pl....C-4
Pratt St....E-5
Prescott....C-4
Primrose Cir....I-5
Primrose St....H-5
Proctor....C-1
Prospect....H-8
Pryor Circle....K-3
Pryor Rd....I-3,K-3
Pryor St....E-4,G-3
Pullman St....H-4
Pylant....A-7
Rankin Pl....C-6
Rankin St....C-6
Rawlins....I-5
Rawlins St....H-5
Rawson....F-2
Raymond St....E-1
Reed....G-4
Reed Ave....J-5
Reinhard....E-6
Renfroe....E-8
Rhodes Ave....K-4
Rhodes St....D-2
Ridge Ave....H-4
Richardson St....F-3
Richmond....G-4,K-6
Richmond Cir....K-6
Roach....D-2
Roberts Dr....I-6
Robins....G-2
Robinson Ave....H-6
Rock....A-1-3
Rockwell St....H-2
Rosalie St....G-6
Rose Circle....H-1
Rosedale....G-6
Rosedale Dr....A-8
Roy St....I-2
St. Charles....B-6,B-8
St. Charles Ave....B-7
St. Louis Pl....B-8
St. Paul....F-5
Sampson St....D-7
Sanders....F-8
Savannah....E-6
Sawtell Ave....K-5
Schuyler....I-6
Sciple Ter....D-1
Scott....C-4
Seaboard Ave....D-8
Seal Pl....A-6
Selman....E-7
Seminole Ave....C-8
Shannon....J-2
Shaw St....J-4
Shelby Pl....I-8
Shelton....G-1
Shoals Rd....F-7
Short....E-7
Siloam Ave....G-8
Simpson St....C-2,C-3
Sims St....I-2
Sinclair Ave....C-8
Sloan Cir....I-7
Smith St....I-3
Somerset Ter....B-7
Soloman....F-4
South Ave....H-5
Spelman....I-5
Spencer St....D-1,D-2
Spring St....C-4,E-3
Stephens....G-2,G-3
Stonewall St....E-2
Stovall St....F-8
Strong....C-2
Sunset Ave....C-2
Sydney....F-5,F-6
Sylvan Pl....K-1
Sylvan Rd....I-1
Taft....A-6,K-3
Taliaferro St....D-1
Tech Pkwy....B-2
Techwood Dr.
....B-4,C-4,E-3
Tenelle St....E-6
Terry....G-4
Terry St....F-4
Thayer....J-4
Thirkeld Ave....J-4
Thomas Dr....K-8
Thomasville Blvd....K-7
Thorton....J-3
Thurmond St....D-1,D-2
Tift....G-1,H-2
Todd....A-8
Trammel St....C-1
Travis....B-2
Trenholm....F-2
Trinity Ave....E-3
Troup St....K-4
Trusco....G-2
Tudor....H-3
Turner....D-1
Turpin Ave....I-7
Tuskegee....H-5
Twiggs....J-4
Tyler....C-2,C-3
Underwood Ave....H-7
University Ave....I-2,I-4
Vanra Ave....H-4
Vaud....C-8
Vedado Way....B-6
Venable St....C-3
Vernon....C-5,G-7
Vickers St....I-8
Victoria....C-3
Victory Dr....K-1
Vine St....D-2,E-2
Violet....H-4
Virgil....D-7
Virginia....A-8
Virginia Ave....A-7
Virginia Cir....A-7
Wade....D-8
Waddel....D-7
Wall St....D-3
Walker Ave....H-7
Walker St....F-2
Walnut....C-2
Walnut St....E-2
Walthan St....E-8
Walton St....D-3
Warner St....I-1
Warren....B-2
Warwick....G-8
Washita Av....C-8
Washington St.
....F-4,G-4,H-4
Waverly Way....D-8
Wayne....J-2
Welch St....H-2,K-7
Wells St....G-2
Wellswood Dr....J-7
West Ave....I-3
West End Ave....F-1
Western Ave....C-2
Weyman....I-4
Whatley....K-5
Wheeler St....B-1
White St....H-1
Whitehall St....F-2
Whittaker St....B-1
Wilbur....F-8
Wilcox....J-4
Williams St....B-4,C-4
Williams Mill Rd....C-7
Willow St....B-5
Wilson....A-1
Windsor St....G-3,I-3
Winton Ter....C-6
Wood....F-6
Woodall St....G-6
Woodbourne Dr....K-1
Woodland Ave....G-8,I-8
Woodlawn Ave....J-8
Woodlawn Cr....J-8
Woodward Ave....F-5
Woodrow Pl....C-5
Woodrow St....I-1
Wylie St....E-7,E-8
Yonge....E-6
York Ave....G-1
3rd St....A-2,B-3,B-4
4th St....B-2,B-3,B-5
5th St....B-2,B-3,B-4,B-5
6th St....A-4
7th St....A-4,A-5
8th St....A-3,A-4,A-5
9th St....A-1,A-2,A-5
10th St....A-1,A-2,A-3,A-6
11th St....A-3,A-4

POINTS OF INTEREST

Adair Park....I-1
Atlanta Tech....J-2
Benteen Park....J-7
Chosewood Park....I-6
Clark College....E-1
Couch Park....A-2
Emman Milligan Park....J-2
Grant Park....H-6
Home Park....A-3
Joyland Park....J-3
Key Park....G-7
Morehouse College....E-1
Oaklane Cemetery....E-6
Parkerson Park....J-1
Piedmont Park Golf Course....A-5
Pittman Park....H-3
Roosevelt H.S....G-7
Smith H.S....G-5
U.S. Penitentiary....J-6

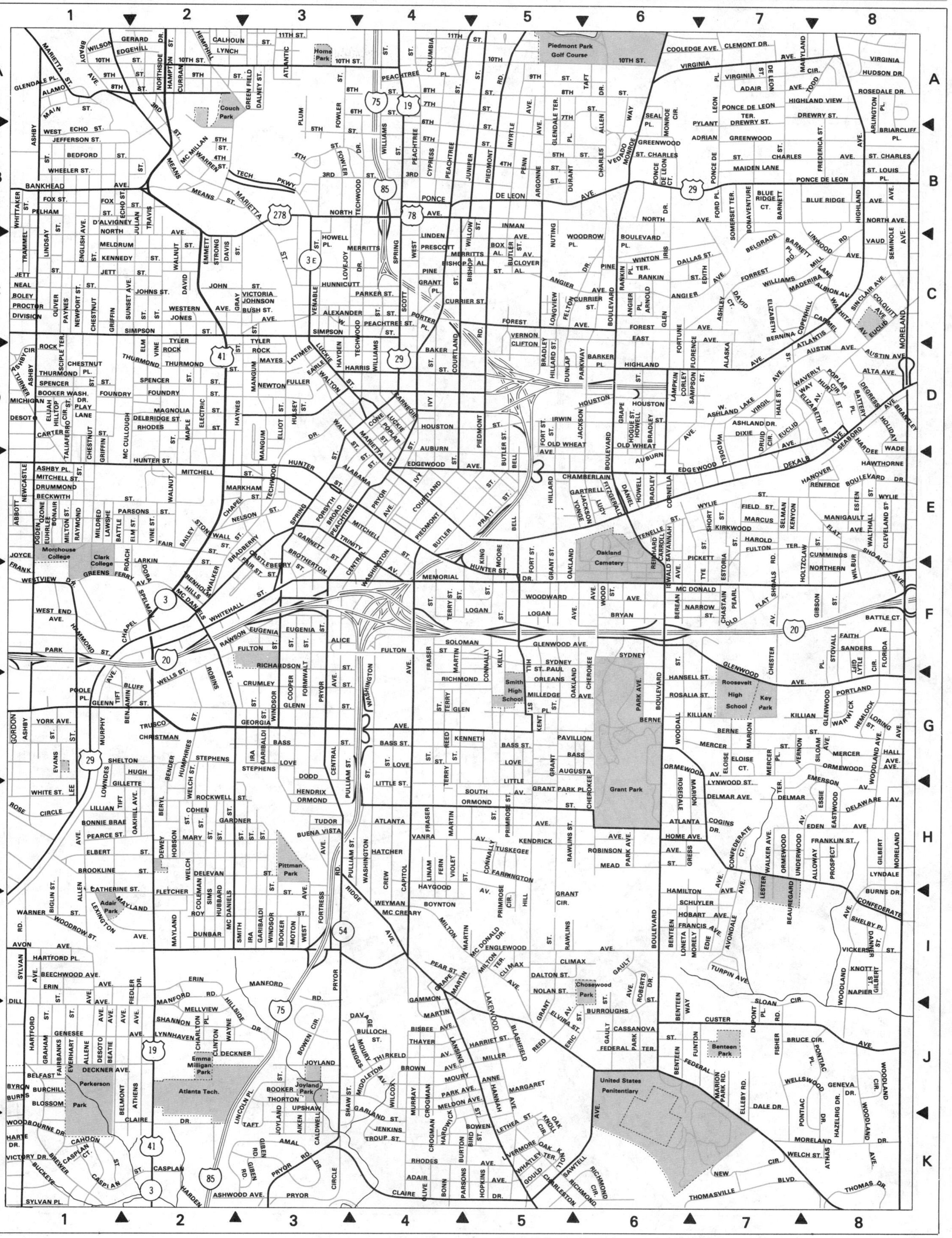
Scale of Miles
0 .2 .4 .6
N
1 2 3 4 5 6 7 8
A B C D E F G H I J K
Piedmont Park Golf Course
Couch Park
Home Park
Morehouse College
Clark College
Oakland Cemetery
Smith High School
Roosevelt High School
Key Park
Grant Park
Pittman Park
Adair Park
Chosewood Park
Benteen Park
Emma Milligan Park
Atlanta Tech.
Perkerson Park
Joyland Park
United States Penitentiary
PEACHTREE ST.
PONCE DE LEON AVE.
NORTH AVE.
MARIETTA ST.
BANKHEAD AVE.
MEMORIAL DR.
GLENWOOD AVE.
BOULEVARD
MORELAND AVE.
DEKALB AVE.
EDGEWOOD AVE.
HIGHLAND AVE.
PIEDMONT AVE.
JUNIPER ST.
SPRING ST.
WEST PEACHTREE ST.
CAPITOL AVE.
PRYOR ST.
CENTRAL AVE.
McDANIEL ST.
LAKEWOOD AVE.
McDONOUGH BLVD.
ASHBY ST.
WHITEHALL ST.
HUNTER ST.
MITCHELL ST.
DECATUR ST.
ALABAMA ST.
AUBURN AVE.
HOUSTON ST.
VIRGINIA AVE.
10TH ST.
TECH PKWY
FULTON ST.
GEORGIA AVE.
ORMOND ST.
ATLANTA AVE.
McDONALD DR.
BOULEVARD
CUSTER AVE.
WELCH ST.
THOMASVILLE BLVD.
SYLVAN RD.
CLAIRE DR.
75 85 19 29 278 78 3E 41 3 20 54

Scale of Miles 0 .2 .4 .6 N

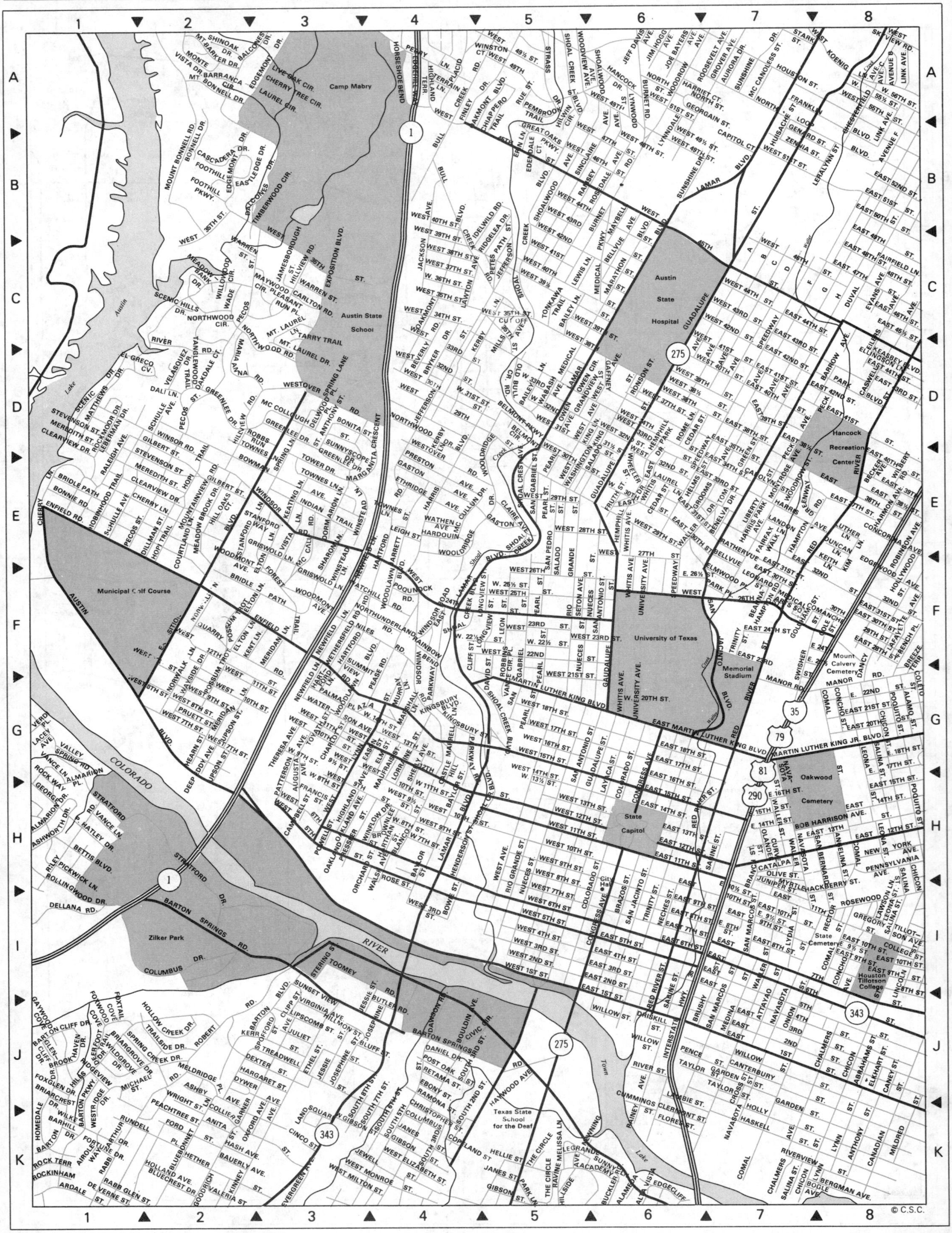

AUSTIN

Abrahams St....J-8
Academy Ln....K-5,K-6
Airole Way....K-1
Alameda....K-6
Alamo St....G-8
Almarion Dr....H-1
Almarion Pl....G-1
Alta Vista....K-6
Angelina St....H-8
Anita St....K-2
Anthony St....K-8
Ardale St....K-1
Arthur Rd....K-1
Ashby Ave....J-2
Ashworth Dr....H-1
Attayao St....J-7
Augusta Ave....G-3,H-3
Aurora Dr....A-7
Austin Blvd....F-1,G-2
Ave. A....C-7,D-6
Ave. B....A-8,C-7,D-7
Ave. C....A-8,C-7,D-7
Ave. D....C-7,D-7
Ave. F....B-8,C-7,D-7
Ave. G....C-8,D-7
Ave. H....C-8,D-7
Bailey Ln....C-5,D-5
Balcones Dr....A-2,A-3
Barhill Dr....K-1
Barranca Cir....A-2
Barrow Ave....D-8
Barton Blvd....I-3,J-3
Barton Cliff Dr....J-1
Barton Dr....J-1,K-1
Barton Pkwy....J-1,K-1
Barton Springs Rd. I-2,J-4
Baverly Ave....K-2
Baylor St....H-4
Beanna....F-7
Becker Ave....E-8
Bellvue Ave....B-6,C-6 ....E-7,F-7
Belmont Cir....D-5
Belmont Pkwy....D-5
Benelva Dr....E-7
Bergman Ave....K-8
Bettis Blvd....H-1
Beverly Rd....C-4,D-4
Blanco St....H-4
Bluebonnet Ln....K-2
Bluecrest Dr....K-2
Bluff St....J-3,J-4
Bob Harrison Ave. H-7,H-8
Bogle Ave....K-7,K-8
Bonita St....D-3
Bonnell Dr....B-2
Bonnie Rd....E-1
Bouldin Ave....J-4
Bowie St....I-4
Bowman Ave....E-2,E-3
Branch St....H-7
Brazos St....I-6
Breeze Terr....F-8,G-8
Briarcrest Dr....J-1
Briargrove Dr....J-1
Bridle Path....E-1,F-2,F-3
Brookhaven Dr....J-1
Brownlee St....H-4
Brushy St....J-6
Bryker Dr....C-4,D-4
Buckler Rd....K-6
Bull Creek Rd....A-4 ....B-4,C-4,C-5
Burnet Rd....A-6,B-6
Butler Rd....J-4
Campbell St....H-3
Canadian St....K-8
Caney St....J-8
Canterbury St....J-7
Capitol Ct....B-7
Carlton Rd....C-3
Carolyn St....E-7
Cascadera Dr....B-2
Castle Hill....G-4
Caswell Ave....C-8,D-8
Catalpa....H-7
Cedar St....D-6,E-6
Chalmers Ave....I-8 ....J-8,K-7
Charlot St....G-3
Cherry Ln....E-1,E-2
Cherry Tree Cir....A-3
Chesterfield Ave. A-8,B-8
Chiappero Trail....A-5
Chicon St....G-8,H-8 ....I-8,J-8,K-7
Christopher St....K-4
Cinco St....K-3
Circle, The....K-5
Civic Cir....J-4
Claire Ave....E-5
Clearview Dr....D-1,E-2
Clermont St....K-6
Cliff St....F-4
Clipp St....J-3
College St....I-8
Cole St....F-8
Coleto St....G-8
Collier St....K-2,K-3
Colorado St....G-6,H-6,I-5
Columbus Dr....I-2
Columbus St....K-4
Comal St....G-8,H-8 ....I-8,J-7,K-7
Comanche....F-7,F-8
Concho St....G-8
Concordia Ave....E-8
Congress Ave....G-6,H-6,I-6
Copeland St....K-4
Courtland Ln....E-2
Cross St....J-7
Cullun Dr....E-4,E-5
Cummings St....J-6
Curve Orlander St....H-7
Dalcones Dr....B-2,B-3
Dali Ln....D-2
Daniel Dr....J-4
Dancy....F-8,G-8
David St....G-5
Dawson Rd....J-4
Deep Eddy Ave....G-2,H-2
Deerfoot Trail....J-1
Dellana Rd....I-1
Delwood Pl....D-3
DeVerne St....K-1
Dexter St....J-2,J-3
Dillman St....E-2
Dorm Arion Ln....E-3
Dressier St....H-3
Driskill St....J-6
Duncan Ln....E-8
Duval St....B-8,C-8
Dywer Ave....J-2
Eason St....G-3,G-4
East Dr....E-6
Ebony St....J-4
Edendale Ct....B-5
Edgecliff....K-6
Edgehill Way....A-4
Edgemont Dr....A-3,B-2
Edgewood Ave....F-8
Eilers Ave....C-8,D-8
Elizabeth St., West....K-4
El Greco Cv....D-1,D-2
Elkhart St....J-8
Ellingson Ln....D-8
Elm St....G-4
Elmwood Pl....F-7
Elton Ln....E-3,F-2,F-3
Enfield Rd....E-1,F-3,G-3
Erin Ln....B-5
Ethel St....J-3
Ethridge Ave....E-4
Evans Ave....C-8
Evergreen Ave....K-3
Exposition St....B-3 ....C-3,E-2,F-2
Fairfaild Ln....C-8
Fairfax Walk....F-7
Finley Dr....A-4,A-5
Flores St....K-6
Foothill Eastledge Dr. B-2,B-3
Foothill Pkwy....B-2
Ford St....K-2
Forest Trail....F-3
Fortune Dr....K-1
Foxglen Dr....J-1
Foxtail Cove....J-1
Foxwood Cove....J-1
Francis St....H-3
Franklin Blvd....A-7,B-8
French Pl....F-8
Fruth St....E-6
Gaffney St....D-6
Garden St....J-7,K-7
Garner Ave....J-2,J-3,K-2
Gaston Ave....E-4,E-5
Gaywood Cove....J-1
Genard St....B-7
Georgain St....A-6,A-7,B-7
George P. Hatley Dr....H-1
Gibson St....K-4,K-5
Gibson St., W....K-3
Gilbert St....D-2,E-2
Glencliff Dr....J-1
Goldham St....F-7
Goodrich St....K-2
Grande St....E-5,F-5
Grandview....D-5,D-6
Great Oaks Pkwy....B-5
Greenlee Dr....D-2 ....D-3,E-3
Green St....D-7,E-7
Greenway....E-7
Gregory St....I-8
Griswold Ln....E-3,F-3
Grooms Ave....E-6,E-7
Grover Ave....A-7
Guadalupe St....B-7,C-6 ....E-6,F-6,G-6
Hampton Rd....E-7,E-8,F-7
Hancock Dr....A-6
Hardouin....E-4
Hargaret St....J-2,J-3
Harmon Ave....E-8
Harriet Ct....A-6,A-7
Harris Ave....E-7,E-8
Harris Blvd....D-4,E-4
Harris Park Ave....E-7
Hartford Ln....G-3
Hartford Rd....E-4 ....F-3,F-4
Harthan St....H-4
Hash Ave....K-2
Haskell St....K-7
Haywood Ave....J-5
Hearn St....G-2
Hellie St....K-5
Helms St....E-6
Hemphill Dr....E-6
Hemphill Park....D-6
Henderson St....H-4
Hether St....K-2
Highland Ave....H-3
Highland Terr....A-4
Hillmon St....J-3
Hill Oaks Ct....E-2
Hills Dr....J-1
Hillside Ave....K-5
Hillview Rd....C-3,D-2
Hilwin Cir....A-5
Holland Ave....K-2
Hollow Creek Dr....J-2
Holly St....K-7
Hollywood St....F-8
Homedale....J-1,K-1
Hopi Trail....D-2,E-2
Horseshoe Bend....A-4
Houston St....A-7
Huisache St....A-7,B-7
Indelwild Rd....B-5,C-4
Indian Trail....E-3
Interstate Hwy. 35 ....I-6,J-6
Inwood Pl....F-2
Jackson Ave....B-4,C-4
Jamesborough St. B-3,C-3
Janes St....K-4,K-5
Jarrett St....E-4
Jeff Davis Ave....A-6
Jefferson St....B-5 ....C-4,C-5,D-4
Jessie St....I-4,J-3
Jewell....K-3,K-4
Jim Hogg Ave....A-6
Joe Bayers Ave....A-6
Josephine St....J-3,J-4
Juliet St....J-3
Juniper St....I-7
Keasbey Blvd....D-8
Keating Ln....E-3
Keith Ln....E-8,F-8
Kent Ln....F-2
Kerby Ln....C-5,D-4
Kerr St....J-2
Kim Ln....E-8,F-8
Kingsbury Blvd....G-4
Kingsbury St....G-4
King St....D-6
King Ln.,West....D-5 ....D-6,E-5
Kinney Ave....K-2,K-3
Koenig Ln.,West....A-8
Lacey Ave....G-1
Lafayette Ave....F-8
Lamar Blvd....B-6,B-7 ....C-6,D-5,E-5,F-4,H-4
Lambie St....J-6
Land Square....K-3
Laurel Cir....A-3
Laurel Ln....E-6
Lawson Ave....I-8
Lawton Ave....C-4
Layaca St....G-6,H-6
Leberman Dr....D-1
Legrande....K-5,K-6
Leigh St....E-4
Leonard St....F-7
Leona St....G-8,H-8,I-8
Leon St....F-5
Leralynn St....B-8
Lewis Ln....C-5
Liberty St....E-7
Lincoln St....I-8
Link Ave....A-8,B-8
Lipscomb St....J-3
Live Oak Cir....A-3
London Ln....E-7
Longview St....F-5
Loop Blvd.,North A-7,B-7,B-8
Lorraine St....G-4
Luther Ln....E-8
Lydia St....I-7
Lynndale....A-6,B-6
Lynn St....K-8
Lynn St., West....G-3,H-3
Lynwood St....A-6
Manor Rd....G-7,G-8
Marathon Blvd....B-6,C-6
Marganita Crescent D-4,E-3,E-4
Maria Anna Rd....D-2,D-3
Marrell Ln....G-4
Marshall Ln....G-4
Martin Luther King Blvd....G-5
Martin Luther King Blvd. East....G-6
Martin Luther King, Jr. Blvd....G-7,G-8
Mattews Dr....D-1
Maufraisi St....G-4,H-4
Maybelle....B-6
Maywood Cir....C-3
McCall Rd....E-3,F-3
McCanoless St....A-7
McCollough St....D-3
Meadowbank Dr....C-2
Meadowbrook Dr....E-2
Medical Arts Sq. St....F-7
Medical Pkwy....C-6
Medina St....J-7
Meldridge Pl....J-2
Meredith St....D-1,E-2
Meridan Ln....F-3,G-2
Michael St....J-1
Mildred St....K-8
Mills Ave....C-5,D-5
Milton St., West....K-3
Monroe St., West....K-3,K-4
Monte Vista Dr....A-2
Montrose Ave....E-7
Mountainview Rd....E-2
M.. Barker Dr....A-2
Mt. Bonnell Dr....A-2
Mount Bonnell Rd. B-1;B-2
Mt. Laurel Dr....C-3
Mt. Laurel Ln....C-3
Murray Ln....G-4
Myrtle Hackberry St. I-7,I-8
Navasota St....G-7 ....H-7,J-7,K-7
Neches St....I-6
Newfield Ln....E-4 ....F-3,G-3
Newning....K-5,K-6
New York Ave....H-8
Niles Rd....F-3,F-4
North St....A-6,A-7
Northunderland Rd. F-3,F-4
Northwood Cir....C-2
Northwood Dr....D-4
Northwood Rd....C-2,D-3
Norwalk Ln....F-2,G-2
Nueces St....F-5,F-6,H-5
Oakdale Ct....D-2
Oakland Ave....H-3
Oakmont Blvd....A-5 ....B-4,C-4
Old Bull Cr. Rd....D-5
Olive St....H-7
Onion St....J-7
Orchard St....H-3
Owen Ave....D-5
Owen Cir....D-5,D-6
Oxford Ave....K-2
Palma Plaza....G-3
Park Blvd....D-8
Park Ln....K-5
Park Pl....F-7
Parkway Rd....G-4
Patterson Ave....G-3,H-3
Peachtree St....J-2,K-2
Pearl Ave....D-5,E-5
Pearl St....E-5,F-5,G-5
Pease Rd....G-4
Peck Ave....D-7,D-8,E-7
Pecos St....C-2,D-2,E-1
Pembrook Trail....A-5
Pence St....J-6
Pennsylvania Ave....H-8
Perry Ln....A-4
Petes Path....C-5
Pickwick Ln....H-1
Placid....A-4
Pleasant Run Pl....C-3
Poquito St....G-8,H-8
Poqunock Rd....F-4
Possum Trot....F-2,G-2
Post Oak St....J-4
Powell St....H-3
Preston Ave....E-4
Pruett St....G-2
Quarry Rd....F-2
Rabb Glen St....K-1
Rabb Rd....K-1
Rainbow Bend....F-4
Rainey Ave....J-6,K-6
Raleigh Ave....D-1,E-1
Ramona St....J-4
Ramsey Ave....A-6,B-5,B-6
Rathervue....E-7,F-7
Ravine Melissa Ln....K-5
Rector St....I-8
Red River St....D-8 ....E-8,E-7,F-7,G-7 ....I-6,J-6,H-6
Retama St....J-4
Ridgelea Dr....B-5,C-5
Ridgeview....J-1
Ridge Dr., West....J-1,K-1
Riley Rd....H-1
Rio Grande St....H-5
River Rd....C-2,D-2
River St....J-6
Riverview St....K-7
Robbins Pl....F-5
Robbs Run....D-3
Robert Rd....J-2
Robinhood Trail....E-1
Robinson Ave....E-8,F-8
Rockinham....K-1
Rockmoor Dr....D-1
Rock Terr....K-1
Rockway....G-1,H-1
Rollingwood Dr. H-1,I-1
Rome Ln....D-6
Ronson St....D-6
Roosevelt Ave....A-6,A-7
Rose St....H-4
Rosewood....I-8
Rosindale Ave....B-6
Rue St....A-5
Rundell Pl....K-1,K-2
Sabine St....H-7,I-6,J-6
St. Anthony St....D-3
Salado St....D-6,E-5 ....E-6,F-5
Salina St....G-8,H-8 ....I-8,K-7
San Antonio St....F-6,G-5
San Bernard St....H-8
San Gabrial St....E-5 ....F-5,G-5
San Jacinto St....I-6
San Lacinto Blvd. F-7,G-7
San Marcos St....I-7,J-7
San Pedro St....E-5,F-5
Scenic Dr....D-1
Scenic Hills Dr....C-2
Schulle Ave....D-2,E-1
Seton Ave....F-5
Sharon Ln....E-3,F-3
Shelly Ave....G-4
Shinoak Dr....A-2
Shoal Creek Blvd....A-5 ....B-5,C-5,E-5,F-4 ....G-5,H-4,H-5
Shoal Crest Ave....D-5,E-5
Shoalwood Ave....A-6,B-5
Sinclaire Ave....A-6 ....B-5,B-6
Skyview Rd., West....A-8
Speedway....C-7,D-7 ....E-6,F-6
Spring Creek Dr....J-1,J-2
Spring Ln....D-3,E-3
Spufford St....J-3
Stanford Ln....E-2,E-3
Stanford Way....E-3
Stark St....A-7
Stering St....I-3
Stevenson St....D-1,E-2
Strass Dr....
Stratford Dr....H-1,H-2
Summit View....F-3
Sunny Ln....K-6
Sunnyscope Dr. D-4,E-4
Sunsetview....I-3
Sunshine Dr....A-7,B-6
Swisher St....F-7,G-7
Tanglewood Trail....D-2
Tarry Trail....C-3
Taylor St....J-6,J-7
Terrian Ln....A-4
Theresa Ave....G-3
Tillotson Ave....I-8
Timberwood Cir....B-3
Tonkawa Trail....C-5
Toomey Rd....I-3
Tower Dr....E-3
Townes Ln....D-2,E-3,E-4
Toyath St....G-3
Trailside Dr....J-2
Treadwell St....J-3
Trinity St....F-7,I-6
University Ave....F-6,G-6
Upson St....G-2
Valasquez Dr....D-2
Valeria St....K-2
Valley Springs Rd....G-1
Vance Cir....F-5,G-5
Vance Ln....G-1,H-1
Verdi Pl....G-1
Virginia Ave....J-3
Vista Ln....E-3
Wabash Medical Ave....D-5
Wade Cir....C-2
Waller Dr....E-6,E-7
Waller St....H-7,J-7
Walsh Ave....H-4
Warren St....C-2,C-3
Washington....E-5
Watchill....F-3,F-4
Water-Son Ave....G-3
Wathen Ave....E-4
Wayside Dr....F-2,G-2
West Ave....D-5,D-6,H-5
Westover Rd....D-3 ....D-4,E-4
Wethersfield Rd....F-3
Wheeler St....E-6
Whitis Ave....E-6,F-6,G-6
Whitis, East....E-6
Wilbert Rd....E-8
Wildgrove Dr....J-1
Willowood Cir....C-2
Winsor Rd....F-4,G-4
Windsor Rd. East....F-4
Winflow Dr....H-3,H-4
Winsor Rd....D-2
Winstead Ln....E-3,F-3
Winston Ct....A-5
Wilke Dr....K-1
Willow St....J-6,J-7
Windsor Rd....E-3
Woodlawn Blvd....F-4,G-3
Woodmont Ave....E-2,F-3
Woodrow Ave....A-6
Woodrow St....E-7
Woodview Ave....A-5
Woolridge....D-5,E-4
Wright St....J-2
Zennia St....B-7
1st St. East....I-6J-7
1st St. West....I-5
2nd St. East....I-6,J-7
2nd St. South....J-4,K-4
2nd St. West....I-5
3rd St. East....I-6,J-7
3rd St. South....J-4,K-4
3rd St. West....I-4,I-5
4th St. East....I-6,I-7,J-7
4th St. West....I-5
5th St. East....I-6,I-7,J-7
5th St. South....J-4,K-4
5th St. West....H-3,I-5
6th St. East....I-6,I-7
6th St. South....J-4,K-3
6th West....H-3,I-5
7th St. East....I-6,I-7
7th St. South....J-4,K-3
7th St. West....G-2,H-4,I-5
8th St. East....I-6,I-7
8th St. South....J-3,K-3
8th St. West....G-1,G-2 ....G-3,H-3,H-4,H-5
9th St. East....I-6,I-7,I-8
9th St. West....G-2,G-3 ....H-3,H-4,H-5
9½ St. E....I-7,I-8
9½ St. West....G-3,H-4
10th St. East....I-6,I-7,I-8
10th St. West....F-1,F-2 ....G-2,G-3,G-4,H-4,H-5
10½ St. East....I-7
11th St. East....H-6,I-7
11th St. West....F-2,G-3 ....H-4,H-5
12th St. East....H-6,H-8
12th St. West....F-2,G-3 ....G-4,H-5,H-6
13th St. East....H-6,H-8
13th St. West....G-4,H-5
13½ St. W....H-5
14th St. East....H-6,H-7,H-8
14th St. W....G-4,G-5
15th St. East....H-6 ....H-7,H-8
15th St. West....G-5
16th St. East....H-6,H-7
16th St. West....G-5
17th St. East....G-6,G-8
17th St. West....G-5
18th St. East....G-6,G-8
18th St. West....G-5
20th St. East....G-8
20th St. W....G-6
21st St. East....G-8
21st St. West....G-5
22nd St. E....G-8
22nd St. West....F-5
22½ St. W....F-4,F-5
23rd St. East....F-7
23rd St. West....F-5,F-6
24th St. East....F-7,F-8
24th St. West....F-4,F-5
25½ St. W....F-5
26th St. West....F-5,F-6,F-7
26½ St. E....F-6
27th St. West....E-6
28th St. E....F-6
28th St. West....E-5,E-6
29th St....F-8
29th West....D-4,D-5,E-5,E-6
30th St. East....E-6,E-7 ....F-7,F-8
30th St. West....D-4,E-5,E-6
31st St. East....E-7 ....E-6,F-7,F-8
31st St. W....D-4,D-5,E-6
31½ St....D-6,E-6
32nd St....F-8
32nd St. East....F-7,F-8
32nd St. West....D-4 ....D-5,D-6,E-6
33rd St. East....E-6,E-7
33rd St. West....C-4 ....D-4,D-5,D-6
34th St. East....E-7
34th St. West....C-4,D-6
35th St....C-5,D-5
35th St. East....D-7,E-7
35th St. West....B-2 ....B-3,C-2,C-3,C-4,C-5
36th St. W....C-4
37th St. East....E-8
37th West....C-4,D-6
38th St. East....D-7,E-8
38th St. West....C-4,C-5,D-6
38½ St. East....D-7,E-7,E-8
38½ St. West....D-6,D-7
39th St. East....D-7,E-8
39th St. West....B-4 ....C-4,C-5,C-6,D-6,D-7
39½ St. West....C-5,C-6
40th St. East....D-7,E-8
40th St. West....B-4 ....C-5,C-6,D-6,D-7
41st St. East....D-7,D-8
41st St. West....C-5,C-6,D-7
42nd St. East....D-7,D-8
42nd St. West....B-5 ....C-6,C-7
43rd St. East....C-7 ....D-7,D-8

BALTIMORE

Abell....A-5
Abbotson St....A-8
Abbott St....E-8
Aiken St....D-7
Aisquity St....B-7 ....C-7,E-7,G-7
Albemarle....H-7
Aliceanna....I-7
Alluvion St....J-3
Amity St....H-2
Annapolis Rd....K-3
Ann St....I-8
Arclay St....D-6
Argeant St....I-2
Argyle Ave....E-2
Arlington Ave....H-2
Art Museum Dr....A-4
Ashland Ave....F-7
Atkinson St....B-4
Baker St....D-1
Baltimore St....G-7,H-4
Bank St....H-7
Barclay St....B-5,D-6
Barnes St....E-8
Barney St....K-5,K-6
Barre St....I-3,I-4,I-5
Bartlett Ave....B-6
Battery Ave....I-6,K-6
Bayard Rd....J-3
Bayard St....J-2
Beason St....K-8
Belt St....K-6
Belvidere St....D-6
Bethel St....D-8,I-8
Bevan....J-5
Biddle St....E-6,F-3
Block St....I-7
Bloom St....D-2
Bolton Pl....E-4
Bolton St....C-3
Bonaparte Ave....B-7
Bond St....F-8,G-7
Boone St....B-6,C-6
Booth St....H-1,H-2
Boyle St....K-7
Bradley....F-3
Brantley....F-2
Brentwood Ave....B-5,E-5
Broadway St....D-8,H-8
Brookfield Ave....C-2
Brooks Lane....C-2
Brunt St....E-2
Bush St....J-2
Byrd St....K-6
Calender St....H-2
Calhoun St....H-1
Callow Ave....C-2
Calvert St....B-5,H-5
Camden St....H-4
Carey St....D-1,I-2
Carlton St....G-2,H-2
Caroline St....I-7
Carroll St....I-3,J-2
Carrolton St....G-2,H-2
Carswell St....A-8
Cathedral St....E-4
Cecil Ave....B-7,C-6
Center St....F-4
Central St....F-7
Chapel St....D-8,F-8
Charles St....H-5,J-5
Chase St....E-4
Chauncey Ave....C-2
Chestnut Ave....A-3
Clarkson St....K-5
Clay St....G-4
Clement St....J-5,J-6,K-7
Clendenin Ave....D-2
Cleveland St....J-2
Cliftview Ave....B-7
Cloverdale Rd....C-1
Cokesbury Ave....C-6
Colvin St....F-6
Commerce St....H-6
Constitution St....F-6
Conway St....I-3,I-5,J-3
Cooksie St....K-8
Covington St....J-6
Cresmont....A-4
Cresmont Ave....A-4
Cross St....I-2,J-4
Cuba....K-8
Cumberland....D-1
Curtain Ave....C-6
Dallas St....F-8,G-8
Darley Ave....B-7,C-8
Davis St....G-5
Decatur....K-8
Dexter St....I-3
Division St....D-1
Dock St....I-7
Dolphin St....E-3
Dorn St....F-3
Druid....C-1
Druid Hill Ave....C-1,E-3
Ducatel St....C-2
Durham St....D-8,I-8
Eager St....E-5
East St....F-6
Eastern Ave....H-7
Eden St....E-7
Edmonson Ave....F-1
Edyth St....F-7
Eislen St....I-3
Ellerslie Ave....A-6
Ellsworth St....D-8
Etting St....D-1,E-3
Eutah Pl....C-1,E-4
Eutaw St....H-4,J-4,K-3
Exeter St....F-6,H-7
Exeter Hall Ave....A-6
Fairmont Ave....G-4 ....G-7,H-1
Faith La....E-8
Falls Rd....B-3
Fallscliff Rd....A-2
Fawcett....C-4
Fawn St....H-7
Fayette St....G-1,G-7
Federal St....D-5,D-7
Fenwick Ave....A-8
Fillmore St....A-7
Fleet St....H-7
Fort Ave....K-5,K-7
Francis St....C-1
Franklin St....G-4
Frederick St....H-6
Fremont Ave....E-2,G-3
Friendship....B-7
Frisby St....A-6
Front St....F-6,G-6
Garrett Ave....B-7
Gay St....F-7,H-6
George St....F-3
Germania Ave....C-7
Gilbert St....F-2
Gittings St....J-5,J-6
Glyndon St....I-2
Gold St....D-1
Gorsuch Ave....A-7
Gough St....H-7
Granby St....H-6
Graves St....F-6
Greene St....H-4
Greenmount Ave....E-6
Guilford Ave....B-5,F-5
Gutman Ave....B-6
Haines St....K-3
Hamburg St....I-3,J-5
Hamilton St....F-4
Hampden....C-4
Hampden Ave....B-4
Hanover St....H-5,K-5
Harford Ave....E-7,F-6
Harford Rd....B-8
Harlem Ave....F-1
Harvey St....K-7
Haubert St....K-8
Heath St....K-5,K-6
Henneman Ave....E-7
Henrietta....I-5
Herkimer St....I-1
High St....F-6,H-7
Hill St....I-5
Hillen St....F-6
Hillman St....E-6
Hoffman St....D-6 ....E-4,F-3
Holbrook St....E-6
Holiday....G-6
Hollins St....A-1
Holly Cross La....C-8
Homestead St....A-7
Homewood Ave....A-7 ....C-6,E-6
Hope St....D-7
Hopkins Pl....H-4
Howard St....B-4,H-4,J-4
Hughs St....I-5
Hull St....K-8
Hunter Ave....F-5
Hunter St....E-5
Huntingdon....C-4
Huntingdon Ave....A-4
Ilchester Ave....A-5
Independence St....A-6
Irvine Pl....G-8
Jackson St....K-6
James St....I-2
Jasper St....F-4
Jefferson St....F-8
John St....D-4
Johnson St....K-6
Jones Fall Expwy....A-2
Josephine St....G-3
Kennedy....B-7
Kennedy Ave....C-6
Kensett....C-1
Keswick Rd....A-4
Key Hwy....I-5,J-6,K-7
Kirk Ave....B-7,C-6
Lafayette Ave....D-4 ....D-8,E-3,F-1
Lakeview Ave....C-2
Lamont Ave....E-8
Lamont St....D-7
Lancaster....I-7
Lanvale St....D-5,E-3,F-1
Latrobe St....D-5
Laurens St....E-1,E-2
Lawrence St....K-7
Leadenhall St....J-4
Lee St....I-5
Lemmon ST....H-1
Lennox St....C-3
Lexington St....G-4,G-6
Liberty St....G-5
Light St....H-5,K-5
Linden Ave....C-2,E-3,F-4
Llewelyn Ave....D-8
Lloyd St....G-7
Loch Raven Rd....B-6
Lombard St....H-1,H-4
Lorraine Ave....B-4,B-5
Lovegrove St....A-5,C-5
Low St....G-6
Lowman....K-8
Ludlow St....K-7
McAllister St....D-5
McColluh St....C-1,E-3
McDonough St....F-8
McElderry St....F-8
McHenry St....H-2
McKim St....F-6
McMechan St....E-2
Madison Ave....C-1,E-3
Madison St....E-3,F-4
Market Pl....H-6
Market St....J-5
Marriott....K-8
Mary St....F-3
Maryland Ave....B-4,E-4
May St....G-7
Miles Ave....B-4
Miller St....F-8
Mill Rd....A-3
Milliman St....F-8
Monroe St....J-1
Montgomery St....I-4,I-6
Montpelier St....A-6,B-7
Monument St....F-4
Mosher St....D-3,F-1
Mount St....I-1
Mt. Clare St....H-2
Mt. Royal Ave....D-4
Mt. Royal Terr....C-3
Mt. Vernon Pl....F-5
Mulberry St....G-4
Mullikin St....G-8
Mura St....E-6
Myrtle Ave....F-2,G-3
Nanticoke St....J-2
Newington Ave....C-2
Normal Ave....C-8
Norris St....I-1
Oler St....K-3
Oliver St....D-4,D-7
Olive St....J-5,J-6
Orchard St....F-3
Orleans St....G-7
Ostend St....I-2,J-3,J-5
Oxford....F-3
Paca St....I-3,J-3
Pacific St....A-3
Park Ave....E-4
Parkin St....H-3
Park St....F-4
Park Lake Dr....C-2
Parrish St....F-1,I-1
Patapsco St....J-5,K-5
Pearl St....G-3
Penn St....H-3
Pennsylvania Ave. C-1,F-3
Perry St....H-5
Philpot St....I-7
Pierce St....G-3
Pine St....G-3
Pitcher....E-1
Pleasant....G-4
Polk St....B-8
Poppleton St....G-2,H-2
Portland St....H-3
Poultney St....J-5
Pratt St....H-4,H-7,H-8
President St....I-7
Presstman St....D-2
Preston St....E-6,F-3
Proctor St....E-6
Race St....J-5
Ramsay St....I-3
Randall St....K-5
Read St....E-4,F-5
Redwood St....H-3,H-5
Reese St....A-6,B-6
Regester St....D-8,I-8
Remington Ave....A-3
Reservoir St....C-3
Retreat....D-1
Richardson St....K-8
Ridgely....I-3,K-3
Riggs Ave....E-1
River St....J-6
Riverside Ave....K-6
Robert St....E-2
Russell St....K-3
Rutland Ave....D-8,F-8
Ryan St....I-2
St. Ann's....B-6
St. James St....F-7
St. Lo Dr....C-8
St. Paul Pl....G-5
St. Paul St....E-5
Sarah Ann St....G-2,G-3
Saratoga St....G-4
School St....E-1
Schroeder St....H-2
Scott St....J-3
Severn St....J-2
Shakespeare St....I-8
Sharp St....H-4,J-4
Shields Pl....E-2
Sinclair La....C-8
Sisson St....B-3,C-4
Smithson....E-2
Somerset St....E-7
South St....H-5
Spring St....D-7,I-7
Stanford Pl....D-1
Sterrett St....I-3
Stevenson St....K-7
Stiles St....H-6
Stirling St....F-7
Stockton St....E-1,H-2
Stricker St....F-1,I-1
Suther St....F-8
Thames St....I-8
The Alameda....A-8
The Fallsway....G-6
Tilden Dr....A-3
Tivoly Ave....A-8
Towson St....K-8
Truck....H-3
Tyler....B-7
Tyson St....F-4,G-4
Upton St....F-2
Valley St....E-6
Vincent St....F-1,I-1
Vine St....G-1,G-3
Vineyard Lane....A-5
Wards St....J-2
Warner St....K-3
Warren Ave....I-5
Washington Blvd. I-3,K-1
Washington St....D-8
Water St....H-6
Watson St....G-7
Webb St....E-7
Webster St....K-6
Welcome....I-5
West....J-4
What Coat St....F-1
Wheeling....J-5
Whitelock St....C-2
Whitridge....B-5
Wicomico St....J-2
William St....K-6
Wills St....I-7
Wilmer Ct....E-2
Wilson....E-2
Winchester St....E-1
Wirton St....E-6
Wolffe St....D-8,I-8
Woodall....K-7
Woodbrook Ave....C-1
Woodyear St....E-1,I-1
Worchester St....J-3
Wyeth....H-3,I-3
Wyman Park Dr....A-3
Wyman Pl....A-4
York St....I-5
20th St....C-4,C-8
21st....C-4
22nd St....C-4
23rd St....C-4
24th St....C-4
25th St....B-4,C-8
26th St....B-4,B-6
27th St....B-4
28th St....A-4,B-3,B-6
29th St....A-5,A-8,B-3
30th St....A-4,A-5,A-8
31st St....A-3,A-5,A-8
32nd....A-3

POINTS OF INTEREST

Carroll Mansion Park....J-1
Clifton Park....B-8
Druid Hill Park....A-1
Federal Hill....I-6
Riverside Park....K-6
Wyman Park....B-3

Scale of Miles
0 .1 .2 .3 .4

N

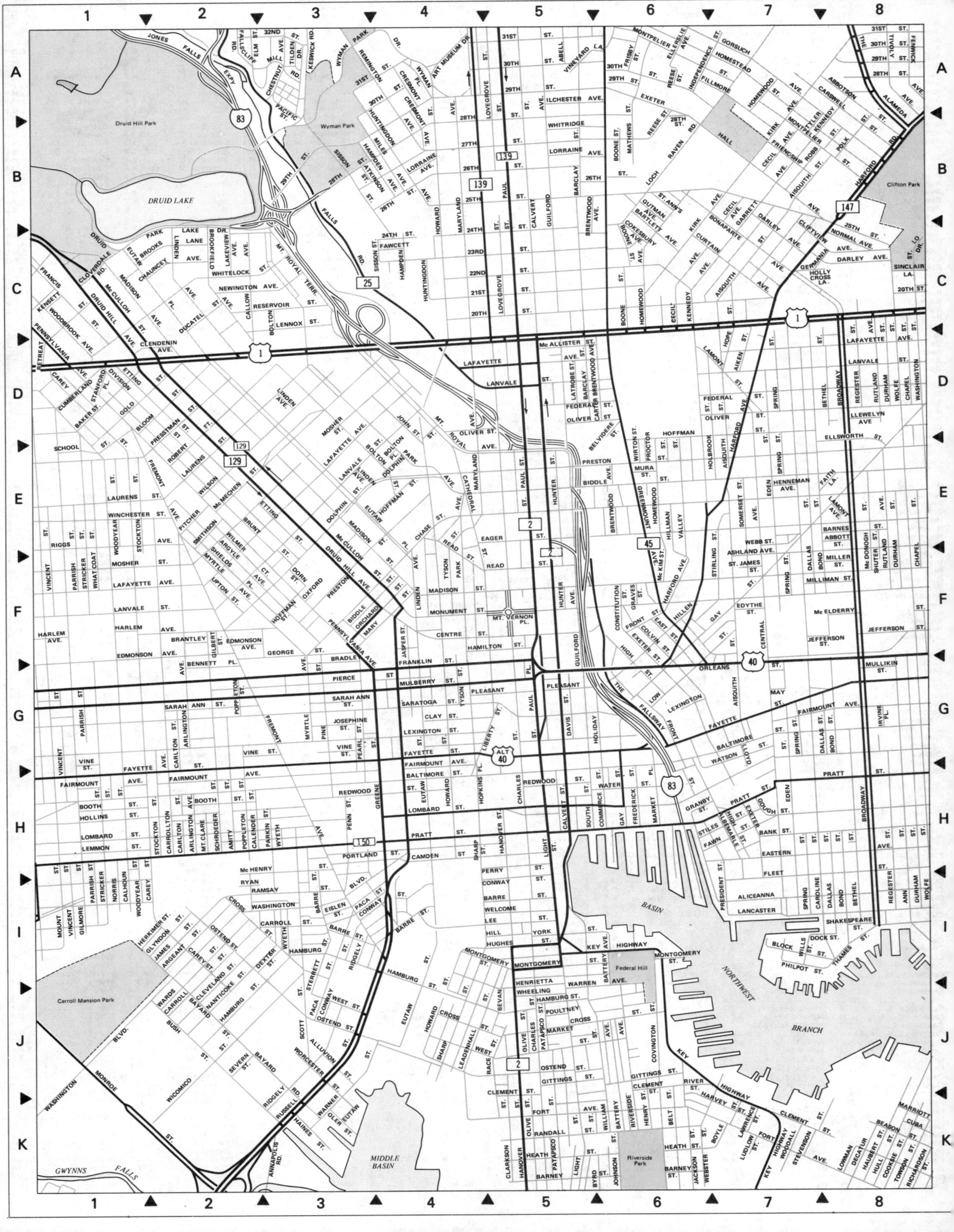

Scale of Miles
0 .1 .2 .3 .4 .5

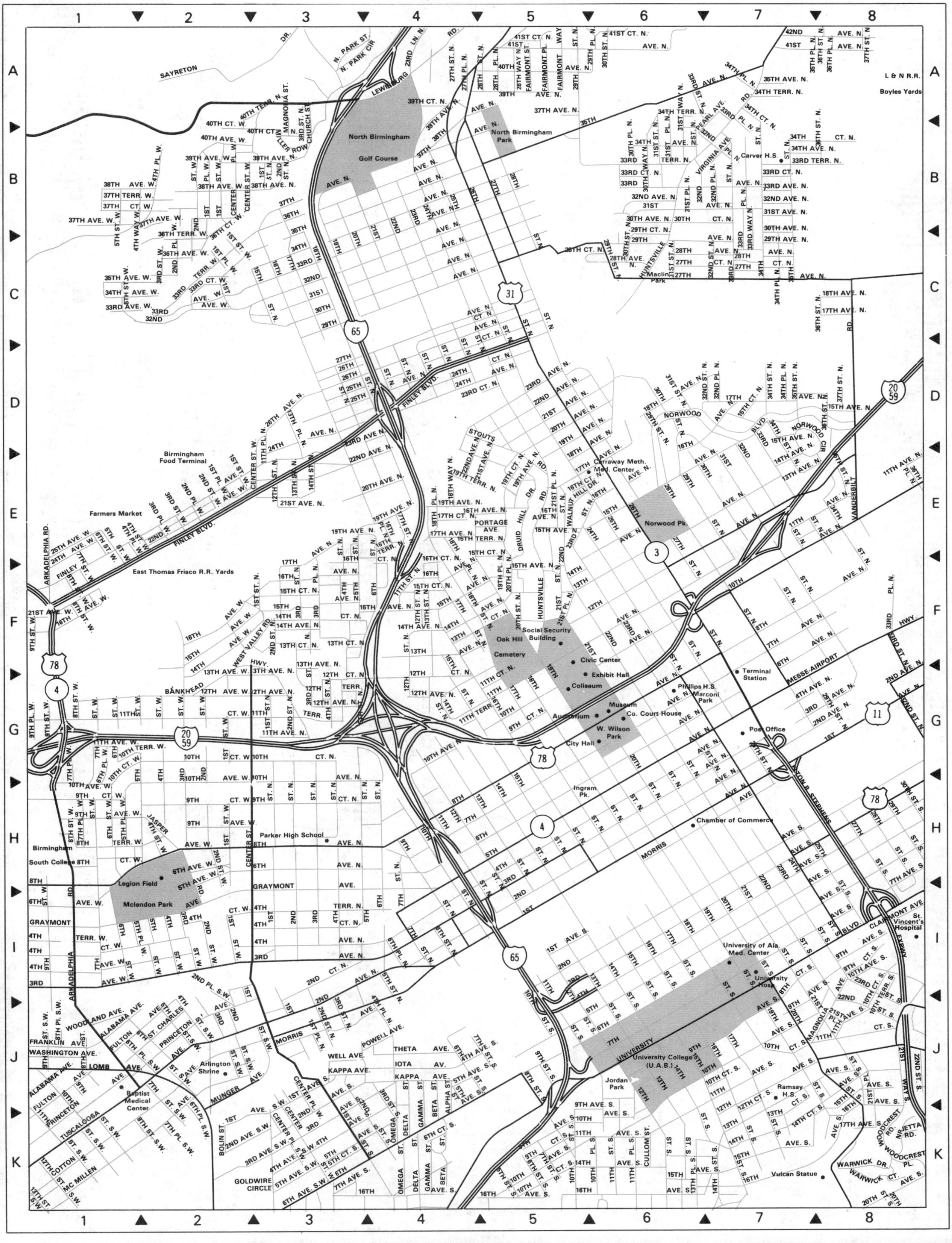

BIRMINGHAM

Alabama Ave. ... J-1
Alpha St. ... J-4
Arkadelphia Rd. ... E-1,I-1
Bankhead Hwy. ... G-2
Beta St. ... K-4
Bolin St. ... K-2
Center Pl. S.W. ... K-3
Center Pl. W. ... B-2,J-3
Center St. ... H-2
Center St. W. ... B-2,E-3,K-3
Church St. ... B-3
Claremont Ave. ... I-8
Cotton Ave. ... K-1
Cullom St. ... K-8
Delta St. ... K-4
Druid Hill Dr. ... E-5
Elton B. Stephens
Expwy. ... H-7
Fairmont Pl. ... A-5
Fairmont St. ... A-5
Fairmont Way ... A-5
Finley Ave. ... F-1
Finley Blvd. ... D-4,E-2
Franklin Ave. ... J-1
Fulton Ave. ... J-1
Gamma St. ... K-4
Goldwire Circle ... K-3
Graymont Ave. ... H-3,I-1
Henrietta Rd. ... K-8
Huntsville Rd. ... C-6,F-5
Iota Ave. ... J-4
Jasper Rd. ... H-2
Kappa Ave. ... J-3,J-4
Lewisburg Rd. ... A-4
Lomb Ave. ... J-1
Magnolia Ave. ... J-8
Magnolia St. ... A-3
McMillen Ave. ... K-1
Messe Airport Hwy. ... G-7
Miller Row ... B-3
Morris Ave. ... H-6,J-3
Munger Ave. ... J-2
N. Park Cir. ... A-3
N. Park St. ... A-3
Norwood ... D-6
Norwood Cir. ... D-7
Omega St. ... K-4
Pearl Ave. ... A-7
Portage Ave. ... E-5
Powell Ave. ... J-4
Princeton Ave. ... J-1,J-2
Sayreton Dr. ... A-2
St. Charles ... J-2
Stouts Rd. ... D-5
Theta Ave. ... J-4
Tuscaloosa Ave. ... K-1
University Blvd. ... J-6
Vanderbilt Rd. ... E-8
Virginia Ave. ... B-7
Walnut Hill Dr. ... E-5
Warwick Ct. ... K-8
Warwick Dr. ... K-8
Washington Ave. ... J-1
Well Ave. ... J-3
West Valley Rd. ... F-2
Woodcrest Pl. ... K-8
Woodcrest Rd. ... K-8
Woodland Ave. ... J-1
1st Ave. N. ... G-8,I-5
1st Ave. S. ... I-5,J-3
1st Ave. S.W. ... K-2
1st Pl. N. ... J-3
1st Pl. W. ... B-2,C-2,E-2
1st St. N. ... B-3,F-3,G-3,I-3
1st St. S. ... K-3
1st St. S.W. ... I-2
1st St. W. ... B-2,C-2,-2,G-2
... H-2,I-2
2nd Ave. N. ... G-8,I-3,I-5
2nd Ave. S. ... I-5,K-3
2nd Ave. S.W. ... K-2
2nd Ct. N. ... I-3
2nd Pl. S.W. ... I-2
2nd Pl. W. ... C-2,E-2
2nd St. N. ... B-3,F-3,G-3
... I-3,J-3
2nd St. S. ... J-3
2nd St. S.W. ... J-2
2nd St. W. ... B-2,E-2,G-2
... H-1,I-2
3rd Ave. N. ... G-7,H-5,I-3
3rd Ave. S. ... I-5,K-3
3rd Ave. S.W. ... K-3
3rd Ave. W. ... I-1
3rd Pl. N. ... F-3
3rd Pl. W. ... E-2
3rd St. N. ... B-2,F-3,G-3
... I-3,J-3
3rd St. S. ... J-4
3rd St. S.W. ... J-2
3rd St. W. ... C-2,E-2,G-2,I-2
4th Ave. N. ... G-7,H-5,I-3
4th Ave. S. ... I-5,J-4,K-3
4th Ave. S.W. ... K-3
4th Ave. W. ... I-1
4th Ct. N. ... I-3
4th Ct. W. ... I-1,I-2
4th Pl. N. ... J-4
4th Pl. W. ... B-2,E-1
4th St. N. ... F-3,G-3,I-3
4th St. S.W. ... J-2
4th St. W. ... E-1,G-2
... H-2,I-2
4th Terr. N. ... I-3
4th Terr. W. ... I-1
4th Way W. ... C-1
5th Ave. N. ... H-5
5th Ave. S. ... J-6,K-3
5th Ave. S.W. ... K-3
5th Ave. W. ... H-2
5th Ct. S. ... K-3
5th Pl. W. ... H-1,I-2
5th St. N. ... F-3,G-3,I-3,I-4
5th St. S. ... J-4,K-5
5th St. S.W. ... J-2
5th St. W. ... B-1,C-1,E-1
... G-1,I-2
6th Ave. N. ... F-7,H-3,H-5
6th Ave. S. ... J-6,K-3
6th Ave. S.W. ... K-3
6th Ave. W. ... H-2,I-1
6th Ct. S. ... K-4
6th Pl. N. ... I-4
6th Pl. S.W. ... J-1,J-2
6th Pl. W. ... G-1
6th St. N. ... F-4,I-4
6th St. S. ... J-4,K-5
6th St. S.W. ... J-2
6th St. W. ... E-1,G-1,H-1,I-1
7th Ave. N. ... F-7,H-4
7th Ave. S. ... H-8,J-6,K-3
7th Pl. S.W. ... K-2
7th Pl. W. ... G-1,H-1
7th St. N. ... I-4
7th St. S. ... J-5,K-5
7th St. S.W. ... J-2
7th St. W. ... F-1,G-1,I-1
8th Ave. N. ... F-7,H-3,H-4
8th Ave. W. ... H-1
8th Ct. S. ... I-7
8th Ct. W. ... H-1
8th Pl. S.W. ... J-1
8th St. N. ... I-4
8th St. S. ... J-5
8th St. S.W. ... K-2
8th St. W. ... F-1,G-1,H-1
8th Terr. W. ... H-1
9th Ave. S. ... I-8,J-5,J-6
... J-7,K-5
9th Ave. W. ... H-1,H-2
9th Ct. N. ... G-5,H-3
9th Ct. S. ... I-8,K-5
9th Ct. W. ... H-1,H-2
9th Pl. W. ... G-1
9th St. N. ... H-4
9th St. S. ... J-5
9th St. S.W. ... J-1
9th St. W. ... F-1,G-1,I-1
10th Ave. N. ... FG-7,G-3
... G-4,G-5
10th Ave. S. ... I-8,J-7,K-5
10th Ave. W. ... G-2,H-1
10th Ct. N. ... G-3
10th Ct. S. ... J-7,J-8,K-5
10th Ct. W. ... G-1,G-2
10th St. N. ... H-4
10th St. S. ... J-5,K-5
10th St. S.W. ... J-1
10th Terr. S. ... J-8
10th Terr. W. ... G-1
11th Ave. N. ... E-7,E-8
... G-3,G-5
11th Ave. W. ... G-1
11th Terr. N. ... G-3
11th Ct. W. ... G-1
11th Ct. N. ... G-5
11th Terr. N. ... G-4
11th Ave. S. ... J-7,J-8,K-5
11th Ct. S. ... J-8
11th St. N. ... F-4,H-4
11th St. S. ... I-5,K-6
11th Pl. S. ... K-6
11th St. S.W. ... K-1
12th Ave. N. ... F-6,G-3,G-4
12th Ave. S. ... J-7
12th Ave. W. ... G-2
12th Ct. N. ... G-3,G-4
12th Ct. S. ... J-7
12th St. N. ... E-3,F-4
... G-4,H-4
12th St. S. ... I-5,J-6
12th St. S.W. ... K-1
12th Terr. N. ... G-3
13th Ave. N. ... E-7,F-3
... F-4,F-5
13th Ave. S. ... K-7
13th Ave. W. ... G-2
13th Ct. N. ... F-3,F-4
13th Ct. S. ... K-7
13th Pl. N. ... D-3
13th Pl. S. ... K-6
13th St. N. ... E-3,F-4,H-5
13th St. S. ... I-6,J-6
13th St. S.W. ... K-1
14th Ave. N. ... E-7,F-3
... F-4,F-5
14th Ave. S. ... K-5,K-7
14th Ave. W. ... F-2
14th Ct. N. ... F-3
14th Ct. S. ... K-7
14th St. N. ... E-3,G-4,H-5
14th St. S. ... I-6,J-6,K-7
15th Ave. N. ... D-7,D-8,E-6
... E-5,F-3,F-4,F-5
15th Ave. S. ... J-8,K-6,K-7
15th Ave. W. ... F-2
15th Ct. N. ... D-7,E-5
... F-3,F-4
15th St. N. ... C-3,F-4,H-5
15th St. S. ... I-6,J-6
15th Terr. N. ... E-4
16th Ave. N. ... D-6,E-4,E-5
... E-6,F-3,F-4
16th Ave. S. ... K-4,K-5
... K-7,K-8
16th Ave. W. ... F-1,F-2
16th Ct. N. ... E-3,E-4,E-5
16th Pl. N. ... E-4
16th St. N. ... C-3,G-5
16th St. S. ... I-6,J-7
16th Terr. N. ... E-4
17th Ave. N. ... C-8,D-7
... E-4,E-5,F-3
17th Ave. S. ... K-8
17th Ct. N. ... E-4
17th St. N. ... C-3,E-4
... F-4,G-5
17th St. S. ... I-6,J-7
18th Ave. N. ... C-8,D-6,E-5
18th Pl. N. ... E-4
18th St. N. ... C-3,F-4,G-5
18th St. S. ... I-6
18th Way N. ... E-4
19th Ave. N. ... D-5,E-3
... E-4,E-5
19th Ct. N. ... E-5
19th Pl. N. ... F-5
19th St. N. ... C-3,G-5
19th St. S. ... I-7,J-7
19th Terr. N. ... E-4
20th Ave. N. ... D-5,E-4
20th Ave. S. ... K-8
20th Pl. N. ... F-5
20th St. N. ... C-3,F-5,G-6
20th St. S. ... I-7,J-7,K-8
21st Ave. N. ... D-5,E-3,E-5
21st Ave. W. ... F-1
21st Pl. N. ... E-5,F-5
21st Pl. S. ... J-8
21st St. N. ... C-4,F-5,F-6
21st St. S. ... I-7,J-7
21st Way S. ... J-8
22nd Ave. N. ... D-5,E-3,E-4
22nd Ave. W. ... E-2
22nd St. N. ... B-4,E-5,F-6
22nd St. S. ... H-7,J-8
23rd Ave. N. ... D-3,D-5
23rd Ct. N. ... D-4
23rd Ln. N. ... A-4
23rd St. N. ... B-4,E-5,F-6
23rd St. S. ... H-7,I-8
24th Ave. N. ... D-3,D-4
24th Ave. W. ... E-1
24th Ct. N. ... D-4
24th St. N. ... B-4,E-6
24th St. S. ... H-7
25th Ave. N. ... D-3
25th Ave. W. ... E-1
25th Ct. N. ... D-3
25th St. N. ... B-4,E-6,G-7
25th St. S. ... H-8
26th Ave. N. ... D-3
26th Ct. N. ... D-3
26th St. N. ... B-4,E-6
27th Ave. N. ... C-6,D-3
27th Ct. N. ... C-6,C-7
27th Pl. N. ... A-5
27th St. N. ... A-4,B-5,E-6
27th St. S. ... H-8
28th Ave. N. ... C-6,C-7
28th Ct. N. ... C-5
28th Pl. N. ... A-5
28th St. N. ... A-5,B-5,E-6
28th St. S. ... H-8
28th Way N. ... A-5
29th Ave. N. ... C-3,C-6,C-7
29th Ct. N. ... C-6
29th Pl. N. ... A-5
29th St. N. ... A-5,C-6
... D-6,E-6,G-8
29th St. S. ... H-8
30th Ave. N. ... B-6,B-7,C-3
30th Ct. N. ... B-6
30th Pl. N. ... B-6
30th St. N. ... A-6,C-6
... D-6,E-7
30th St. S. ... H-8
30th Way N. ... B-6
31st Ave. N. ... B-6,B-7,C-3
31st Pl. N. ... B-6
31st St. N. ... B-6,C-6
... D-6,E-7
31st Way N. ... A-6
32nd Ave. N. ... B-6,B-7,C-3
32nd Ave. W. ... C-2
32nd Pl. N. ... B-7,D-7
32nd St. N. ... B-6,C-7
... D-6,E-7,G-8
33rd Ave. N. ... B-6,B-7,C-3
33rd Ave. W. ... C-1,C-2
33rd Ct. N. ... B-6,B-7
33rd Ct. W. ... C-2
33rd Pl. N. ... B-7,C-7,F-8
33rd St. N. ... A-6,C-7
... D-7,F-8
33rd Terr. N. ... B-6,B-7
33rd Terr. W. ... C-2
33rd Way N. ... B-7
34th Ave. N. ... B-6,B-7,C-3
34th Ave. W. ... C-1
34th Ct. N. ... A-7,B-7
34th Pl. N. ... A-7,C-7,D-7
34th St. N. ... C-7,D-7,E-8
34th Terr. N. ... A-6,A-7
35th Ave. N. ... A-7,B-3,B-5
35th Ave. W. ... C-1
35th Pl. N. ... A-7
35th St. N. ... C-7,D-7,E-8
36th Ave. N. ... B-3
36th Ave. W. ... C-2
36th Ct. W. ... B-2
36th Pl. N. ... A-8,E-8
36th St. N. ... A-8,B-8
... C-8,D-8
36th Terr. W. ... C-2
37th Ave. N. ... A-5,B-3,B-4
37th Ave. W. ... B-1,B-2
37th Ct. W. ... B-1
37th St. N. ... A-8,D-8
37th Terr. W. ... B-1
38th Ave. N. ... B-3,B-4
38th Ave. W. ... B-1,B-2
39th Ave. N. ... A-5,B-3,B-4
39th Ave. W. ... B-2
39th Ct. N. ... A-4
40th Ave. N. ... A-5
40th Ave. W. ... B-2
40th Ct. N. ... B-3
40th Ct. W. ... B-2
40th Terr. N. ... A-3
41st Ave. N. ... A-5,A-7
41st Ct. N. ... A-5,A-6
42nd Ave. N. ... A-7

POINTS OF INTEREST

Arlington Shrine ... J-2
Auditorium ... G-5
Baptist Medical
Center ... J-1
Birmingham Food
Terminal ... E-2
Birmingham South
College ... H-1
Carraway Meth. Med.
Center ... E-6
Carver H.S. ... B-7
Chamber of
Commerce ... H-7
City Hall ... G-5
Civic Center ... F-6
Coliseum ... G-5
Co. Court House ... G-6
East Thomas Frisco
R.R. Yards ... F-2
Exhibit Hall ... G-6
Farmers Market ... E-1
Ingram Pk. ... H-5
Jordan Park ... J-6
Legion Field ... H-2
L. & N. R.R. Boyles
Yards ... A-8
Maclin Park ... C-6
Marcorn Park ... G-7
Mclendon Park ... I-2
Museum ... G-6
North Birmingham
Golf Course ... B-4
North Birmingham
Park ... B-5
Norwood Pk. ... E-6
Oak Hill Cemetery
... F-5
Parker H.S. ... H-3
Phillips H.S. ... G-6
Post Office ... G-7
Ramsay H.S. ... J-7
St. Vincent's
Hospital ... I-8
Social Security
Building ... F-5
Terminal Station ... G-7
University College
(U.A.B.) ... J-6
University
Hospital ... I-7
University of Ala.
Med. Center ... I-7
Vulcan Statue ... K-7
W. Wilson Park ... G-6

BOSTON

A St. ... B-6
Abbotsford Rd. ... K-7
Aberdeen St. ... I-7
Acorn St. ... J-5
Adams St. ... K-7
Adams St. ... D-1
Adrian St. ... I-1
Albany St. ... C-6,D-8
Albany St. ... I-4
Alger St. ... B-8
Allen St. ... I-1
Allston St. ... J-5
Ames St. ... G-4
Amherst St. ... G-4
Amory St. ... J-7
Amory St. ... I-3
Anderson St. ... E-3
Andrews St. ... K-5
Antrim St. ... J-3
Appleton St. ... E-6
Arch St. ... C-4
Arundel St. ... I-7
Ashburton Pl. ... D-3
Asylum St. ... D-6
Athens St. ... K-3
Atkinson St. ... D-8
Atlantic Av. ... B-2,C-5
Atlantic St. ... A-7
Auburn St. ... J-4
Audrey St. ... I-5
Austin St. ... E-1
Austin St. ... J-3,I-3
Autumn St. ... I-8
Avery St. ... D-5
Avon St. ... C-4
B St. ... A-5,B-7
Babbitt St. ... I-6
Babcock St. ... K-7
Back St. ... I-6
Baldwin St. ... B-6
Ball ... E-8
Banks St. ... K-3
Battery St. ... C-2,C-3
Bay St. ... K-3
Bay State Rd. ... I-6
Beach St. ... C-5
Beacon St. ... K-8
Beacon St. ... D-4,F-5
Bedford St. ... C-4
Beech Rd. ... J-8
Belvidere St. ... G-6
Bent St. ... G-3
Benton St. ... F-8
Berkeley St. ... E-5
Berkeley St., E. ... D-6
Berkshire St. ... H-3
Bigelow St. ... J-3
Billerical St. ... D-2
Binney St. ... G-3,H-3
Blackstone St. ... K-4
Blagden St. ... E-6
Blanche St. ... I-4
Blandford St. ... I-6
Blossom St. ... E-3
Boardman St. ... I-3
Boden St. ... J-4
Bolton St. ... I-2
Bolyston St. ... F-6
... G-7,H-7
Bonner Av. ... I-1
Border St. ... B-1
Borland St. ... J-7
Boston Univ. Bridge
... J-6
Bowdoin ... J-1
Bowdoin St. ... D-3
Braddock Pl. ... E-7
Bradford St. ... D-7
Branch St. ... E-4
Bremen St. ... A-1
Brimmer St. ... E-4
Bristol St. ... C-6
Bristol St. ... H-3
Broad St. ... C-3
Broadway ... D-5,H-3
Bromfield St. ... D-4
Brookline Ave. ... I-8
Brookline St. ... J-5
Brookline St., E. ... D-7
Brookline St., W. ... E-7
Brownie St. ... K-7
Bryant St. ... K-1
Buckingham St. ... E-6,J-2
Buick St. ... K-6
Bullock St. ... A-6
Burbank St. ... G-7
Burke St. ... F-8
Burlington St. ... H-7
Buswell St. ... I-7
Byron St. ... E-4
C St. ... B-7
Cabot St. ... F-8
Calahan Tunnel ... B-2
Calender St. ... K-4
Calvin St. ... J-1
Cambridge St. ... D-3,H-2
Camden St. ... E-8
Canal St. ... D-2
Canton St. ... E-6
Canton St., E. ... D-7
Canton St., W. ... E-7
Carleton St. ... G-4
Carlisle St. ... I-2
Carlton St. ... F-7,J-1,J-7
Carver St. ... D-5,K-1
Causeway St. ... D-2
Cedar St. ... E-4
Central St. ... C-3
Centre St. ... J-3
Chalk St. ... J-4
Chandler St. ... E-6
Chapel St. ... J-8
Chaplin St. ... A-6
Charles St. ... E-3,E-4
... G-2,K-8
Charlesgate East ... G-6
Charlesgate West ... G-6
Charles River Dam ... E-2
Charlestown Ave. ... F-2
Charlestown St. ... H-1
Charlestown Bridge ... D-2
Charter St. ... C-2
Chatham St. ... C-3,J-3,J-8
Chelsea St. ... A-1,D-1
Cherry St. ... I-3
Chestnut St. ... E-4,J-5
Chilton St. ... J-7
Church ... J-1
Church St. ... D-5
Churchill St. ... J-7
Clarendon St. ... E-5
Claremont Pk. ... F-7
Clark St. ... C-2,H-3,I-1
Clearway St. ... F-7
Cleveland St. ... K-3
Clinton St. ... C-3,J-3
Colchester St. ... J-8
Columbia St. ... I-2-4
Columbus Av. ... I-1
Commercial Av. ... F-3
Commercial St. ... C-2,C-3
Common St. ... D-5
Commonwealth Av. ... F-6
Concord Av. ... I-1
Concord St., E. ... D-8
Concord St., W. ... E-7
Concord Sq. ... E-7
Congress St. ... B-5,C-3
Copley St. ... K-7
Cordis St. ... D-1
Corning St. ... D-6
Cortes St. ... E-6
Cottage St. ... A-2,J-4
Cottage Farm Rd. ... J-7
Court St. ... C-3
Cross St. ... C-3
Cumberland St. ... F-7
Cummings St. ... C-8
Cummington St. ... I-7
Cunard St. ... F-8
Cypher St. ... B-6
D St. ... B-7
Dalton St. ... G-6
Dana St. ... K-3
Dane Av. ... J-1
Dane St. ... J-1
Darnell St. ... B-8
Dartmouth Pl. ... E-6
Dartmouth St. ... F-6
Davenport St. ... F-8
Decatur St. ... J-4
Dedham St., E. ... D-7
Dedham St., W. ... E-7
Deerfield St. ... H-6
Devonshire St. ... C-4
Dewolee St. ... K-3
Dilworth St. ... F-8
Dimick St. ... J-2
Dorchester Ave.
... B-5,B-7,B-8
Douglass Ct. ... I-4
Drapers Ln. ... E-7
Dummer St. ... K-7
Durham St. ... F-7,J-1
Dwight St. ... D-6,K-8
E St. ... B-7
Earle St. ... H-1
Edgerly Rd. ... G-7
Egmont St. ... K-7
Eighth St. ... G-2
Elba St. ... K-7
Eliot St. ... K-1
Eliot Kneeland St. ... D-5
Ellery St. ... K-3
Ellisworth Ave. ... J-2
Elm St. ... I-3
Embankment Rd. ... E-4
Emily St. ... I-5
Emmons St. ... A-1
Endicott St. ... C-2
Erie St. ... J-5
Essex St. ... D-5,I-3,J-7
Euston St. ... J-7
Evans Way ... H-8
Everett St. ... I-1
Exeter St. ... F-5
F St. ... A-8
Fairfield ... F-5
Fairmont St. ... J-4
Fargo St. ... A-5
Farnsworth St. ... B-4
Farrar St. ... K-1
Fay St. ... D-6
Fayette St. ... D-5,J-3
Federal St. ... C-4
Fellows St. ... E-8
Felton St. ... K-2
Fenway ... H-8
Fiarmont Av. ... K-5
Field St. ... G-8
Fifth St. ... G-3
First St. ... F-3
Fisk Pl. ... I-3
Fitchburg St. ... G-1
Flagg St. ... K-3
Fleet St. ... C-2
Florence St. ... K-5
Follen St. ... F-6
Forsyth St. ... G-8
Forsyth Way ... G-8
Foundry St. ... C-6
Francis Av. ... K-1
Frankfort St. ... A-1
Franklin St. ... C-4,J-3
Freeman St. ... K-7
Friend St. ... D-2
Front ... I-4
Fruit St. ... E-3
Fulkerson St. ... H-3
Fullerton St. ... H-7
Fulton St. ... C-2
Gaffney St. ... K-6
Gainsborough St. ... G-7
Garden St. ... D-3
Gardner St. ... I-2
Garrison St. ... F-6
Gates St. ... A-8
Glenwood Av. ... J-5
Gloucester St. ... G-5
Gore St. ... A-1,G-2
Granby St. ... I-6
Granite St. ... B-6,J-5
Green St. ... I-4,K-3,K-8
Greenleaf St. ... G-8
Greenough Av. ... J-2
Greenwich St. ... F-8
Grove St. ... E-3
Hamilton St. ... J-5
Hammond St. ... F-8,J-2
Hampshire St. ... H-3
Hancock St. ... D-3,J-3
Hanover ... C-3
Hanson St. ... D-6,J-1
Harcourt St. ... F-6
Harding St. ... H-2
Hardwick St. ... H-2
Harrison Av. ... D-7
Harrison St. ... K-1
Harvard Bridge ... G-5
Harvard St. ... D-5,H-3,J-3
Haviland St. ... G-6
Havre St. ... A-1
Hawes Pl. ... J-8
Hawes St. ... J-8
Hawkins St. ... I-1
Hawley St. ... C-4
Hayes St. ... K-3
Hayward St. ... G-4
Hemenway St. ... G-7
Henley St. ... D-1
Henry St. ... J-5
Herald St. ... D-6
Hereford St. ... G-6
High St. ... C-4
Highland Ave. ... J-2
Hingham St. ... K-4
Hinsdale St. ... I-6
Holden St. ... K-1
Hollis St. ... C-5
Holyoke St. ... E-6
Horrace St. ... H-1
Houghton St. ... I-2
Hovey Ave. ... J-2
Howard St. ... D-1,J-4
Hudson St. ... C-5
Hull St. ... C-2
Huntington Ave. ... F-7
Hurley St. ... G-2
Ilavado St. ... K-1
India St. ... C-3
Inman St. ... J-3
Ipswich St. ... H-7
Irving St. ... D-3,K-1,K-2
Irving Terr. ... K-2
Isabella ... E-6
Ivy St. ... J-7
James St. ... E-8,K-8
James Storrow ... H-6
Jay St. ... J-4
Jefferson St. ... H-2
Jersey St. ... H-7
John St. ... K-8
John Fitzgerald
Expwy. ... C-7
Joseph St. ... I-1
Joy St. ... D-3,H-1
Kelly Rd. ... J-4
Kendall St. ... F-8
Kenmore St. ... H-6
Kent St. ... J-8
Keswick St. ... I-7
Kilmarnock St. ... H-7
Kingman Rd. ... I-2
Kinnaird St. ... K-3
Kirkland Pl. ... K-2
La Grange St. ... D-5
Lake St. ... J-1
Lansdowne St. ... H-7,I-4
Lattmore Ct. ... E-8
Lawrence St. ... E-6,J-4
Lee St. ... J-3
Lenox St. ... F-8,J-7
Leon St. ... G-8,J-2
Leonard Av. ... J-2
Lime St. ... E-4
Lincoln Pkwy. ... J-1
Lincoln St. ... C-5,I-1,I-2
Line St. ... J-1
Liverpool ... B-1
Linwood St. ... H-1
London St. ... B-1
Longfellow Bridge ... F-3
Longwood Av. ... J-8
Lopez Av. ... F-2
Lopez St. ... J-4
Louis St. ... B-6
Louis Pasteur Av. ... H-8
Lowell St. ... D-2
Magee St. ... K-4
Magnolia Ave. ... K-2
Magazine St. ... J-5
Magnus ... J-1
Main St. ... H-4,I-4
Maitland St. ... I-7
Malden St. ... D-7
Manchester Rd. ... K-7
Mansfield St. ... H-1
Maple Ave. ... J-2
Marcella St. ... H-2
March Oliver St. ... C-4
Marginal ... A-1
Marie Av. ... J-2
Marion St. ... H-2,J-2
Market St. ... C-3,H-3
Marlborough St. ... F-5
Marney St. ... H-2
Marshall St. ... J-8
Martha Way ... E-2
Marys St. ... I-7
Mason St. ... D-4,J-7
Massachusetts Ave.
... F-7,G-6,H-4
Matthews St. ... C-4
Maverick St. ... A-1
Melcher St. ... B-5
Melrose St. ... D-5
Memorial Dr. ... G-5,H-5
Mercer St. ... A-8
Merchants Row ... C-3
Medford St. ... D-2
Merriam St. ... H-1,I-5
Midway st. ... B-6
Milford St. ... D-6
Milk St. ... C-4
Mill St. ... A-1
Miner St. ... I-7
Monmouth Ct. ... I-7
Monmouth St. ... I-7
Montgomery St. ... E-7
Monument Ave. ... D-1
Mountfort St. ... I-7
Mt. Vernon St. ... E-3
Mt. Washington St. ... B-5
Moore St. ... C-8
Morgan St. ... K-1
Munroe St. ... G-3
Munson St. ... I-7
Museum Rd. ... G-8
Museum St. ... K-1
Myrtle St. ... E-4
Mystic St. ... D-7
Nashua St. ... E-2
Necco St. ... B-5
New St. ... B-1
Newbury St. ... F-6,H-6
Newton ... J-5
Newton St. ... I-1
Newton St., E. ... D-8
Newton St., W. ... F-7
Norfolk St. ... I-2,I-3
North St. ... C-3
Northampton St. ... E-8
Northern Av. ... B-4
Northfield St. ... F-8
Norway St. ... G-7
Oak St. ... D-5,I-2
O'Brien Hwy. ... F-2
Old Colony Av. ... B-7
Old Harbor St. ... A-8
Opera Pl. ... G-7
Orleans St. ... A-1
Osborn St. ... H-4,K-7
Otis St. ... C-4,G-2
Otter St. ... E-4
Overland St. ... H-7
Pacific St. ... I-4
Palermo St. ... H-2
Paris St. ... A-1
Park Dr. ... H-8
Park St. ... D-1,D-4,J-3,K-1
Parkdale ... J-1
Parkman St. ... K-8
Parker ... J-1
Parker St. ... G-8
Parkman St. ... E-3
Paul St. ... K-7
Pearl St. ... C-4,J-5
Pelham St. ... G-4
Pembroke St. ... E-7
Perry St. ... J-1,J-4
Peterborough St. ... H-7
Peters ... J-5
Phillips St. ... E-3
Pilgrim Rd. ... I-8
Pinckney St. ... E-4
Pine St. ... I-4
Pittsburgh St. ... B-5
Pleasant St. ... J-5,K-8
Plymouth ... H-3
Plymouth St. ... I-8
Plymton St. ... D-7
Poplar St. ... H-1
Portland St. ... D-2,H-3
Portsmouth ... H-3
Potter St. ... G-3
Powell St. ... J-7
Prescott St. ... J-7,K-3
Prince St. ... C-2
Prospect St. ... I-3
Providence St. ... E-5
Province St. ... C-4
Puchase St. ... C-4
Purrington ... I-4
Putnam Av. ... J-5,K-3,K-4
Queensbury St. ... H-7
Quincy St. ... J-1,K-3
Raleigh St. ... H-6
Randolph St. ... D-7
Reed St. ... E-8
Revere St. ... E-4
Richmond St. ... C-2
River St. ... E-4
Riverway ... I-8
Roberts Rd. ... K-2
Rockwell St. ... J-4
Rodgers St. ... G-3
Rose ... J-1
Rossmore ... H-1
Ruggles St. ... G-8
Russell St. ... D-3
Rutherford ... E-1
Rutherford Av. ... E-1
Rutland St. ... E-7
Rutland St., W. ... F-7
St. Botolph ... F-7
St. George St. ... D-7
St. Germain St. ... F-6
St. James Av. ... E-5
St. Mary St. ... I-2
St. Stephens St. ... G-7
Salem ... C-2
Sanborn ... I-1
School St. ... C-4
... E-1,I-4,J-1
Sciarappa St. ... G-2
Scotia St. ... G-6
Scott St. ... K-1
Seckel ... H-3
Second St. ... F-3
Seventh St. ... G-2
Sewall Av. ... K-8
Shawmut Av. ... D-6
Sheafe St. ... C-2
Sherborn St. ... I-6
Short St. ... I-8
Sidney St. ... I-5
Sixth St. ... G-3,G-4
Skehan St. ... J-1
Sleeper St. ... B-4
Smart St. ... H-4
Snowhill St. ... C-2
Somerset St. ... D-3
Somerville Av. ... J-1
South St. ... C-5,H-2
South Bay Av. ... D-8
Spring St. ... G-2
Springfield St.
... F-7,I-2
Spruce St. ... D-4
Stanhope St. ... E-6
State St. ... C-3,I-4
Stearns Rd. ... J-8
Sterling St. ... F-8
Stetson St. ... K-7
Still St. ... J-7
Stillings St. ... A-5
Stillman St. ... C-2
Stone St. ... I-1
Stuart St. ... E-6
Sudbury St. ... D-3
Suffolk St. ... I-3
Summer Rd. ... K-2
Summer St. ... B-5,C-4
Sumner St. ... A-1
Sumner Tunnel ... B-2
Surrey St. ... K-3
Symphony Rd. ... G-7
Tavern Rd. ... G-8
Telegraph St. ... A-8
Temple Pl. ... D-4
Temple St. ... D-3,J-3
Tetlow St. ... H-8
Thatcher St. ... K-7
Thayer St. ... C-6
Third St. ... G-2,G-3
Thorndike St. ... G-2
Tileston ... C-2
Topeka St. ... D-8
Traveler St. ... D-6
Traverse St. ... D-3
Tremont St. ... E-7,F-8,I-3
Tremont St. ... I-3
Trinity Pl. ... E-6
Trotter Ct. ... E-8
Trowbridge ... K-3
Tudor St. ... I-4
Tufts St. ... C-5,J-5
Tyler St. ... C-5,J-1
Union St. ... E-1,I-3
Union Park St. ... D-7
Unity St. ... C-2
Upton St. ... J-4
Utica St. ... C-5
Valentine St. ... J-4
Vancouver St. ... G-8
Van Ness St. ... H-7
Vassar St. ... I-5
Viaduct St. ... A-5
Village St. ... J-1
Vine St. ... K-1
Wadsworth St. ... G-4
Waldo St. ... J-2
Walnut St. ... D-4
Waltham St. ... D-6
Wapole St. ... F-8
Ward St. ... H-1
Ware St. ... K-3
Wareham St. ... D-7
Warren Av. ... E-6
Warren St. ... E-1,H-2,I-1
Washington St. ... D-2
... D-6,E-1,E-8,H-3,I-3,J-1
Water St. ... C-3
Watson St. ... F-7,J-4
Waverly St. ... I-5
Webster Av. ... H-3
Webster St. ... A-1,K-8
Well Rd. ... J-8
Wellington St. ... F-7
West St. ... B-6,D-4,J-3
Westland Av. ... G-7
Willow St. ... H-2
William St. ... J-4
William Cardinal
O'Connell Way ... D-3
Windsor St. ... F-8,H-2,I-3
Winter St. ... D-4,G-2
Winthrop St. ... D-1
Winton St. ... B-8
Worcester St. ... E-8,I-3
Worcester Sq. ... E-8
Wormwood St. ... B-5
Worthington St. ... H-8
Wyatt ... J-1
Yarmouth St. ... E-6
York St. ... H-2
1st St. W. ... B-6
2nd St. W. ... B-7
3rd St. W. ... B-7
4th St. W. ... B-7,C-6
5th St. W. ... B-7
6th St. W. ... B-7
7th St. W. ... B-7
8th St. W. ... B-7
9th St. W. ... B-8

POINTS OF INTEREST

Ahern Field ... G-2
Boston Common ... D-4
Black Bay Fens
Park ... H-8
Blackstone Sq. ... E-7
Central Sq. ... J-4
Donnelly Field ... H-2
Fenway Park ... H-7
Franklin Sq. ... D-7
Hoyt Field ... K-4
Knyvet Sq. ... J-7
Lincoln Park ... J-1
Longwood Sq. ... J-8
Madison Park ... F-8
Mason Sq. ... J-7
Nickerson Field ... K-6
Public Garden ... E-5
Sennott Park ... I-3
Telegraph Hill
Park ... A-8
Winthrop Sq. ... K-7

Scale of Miles
0 .1 .2 .3 .4

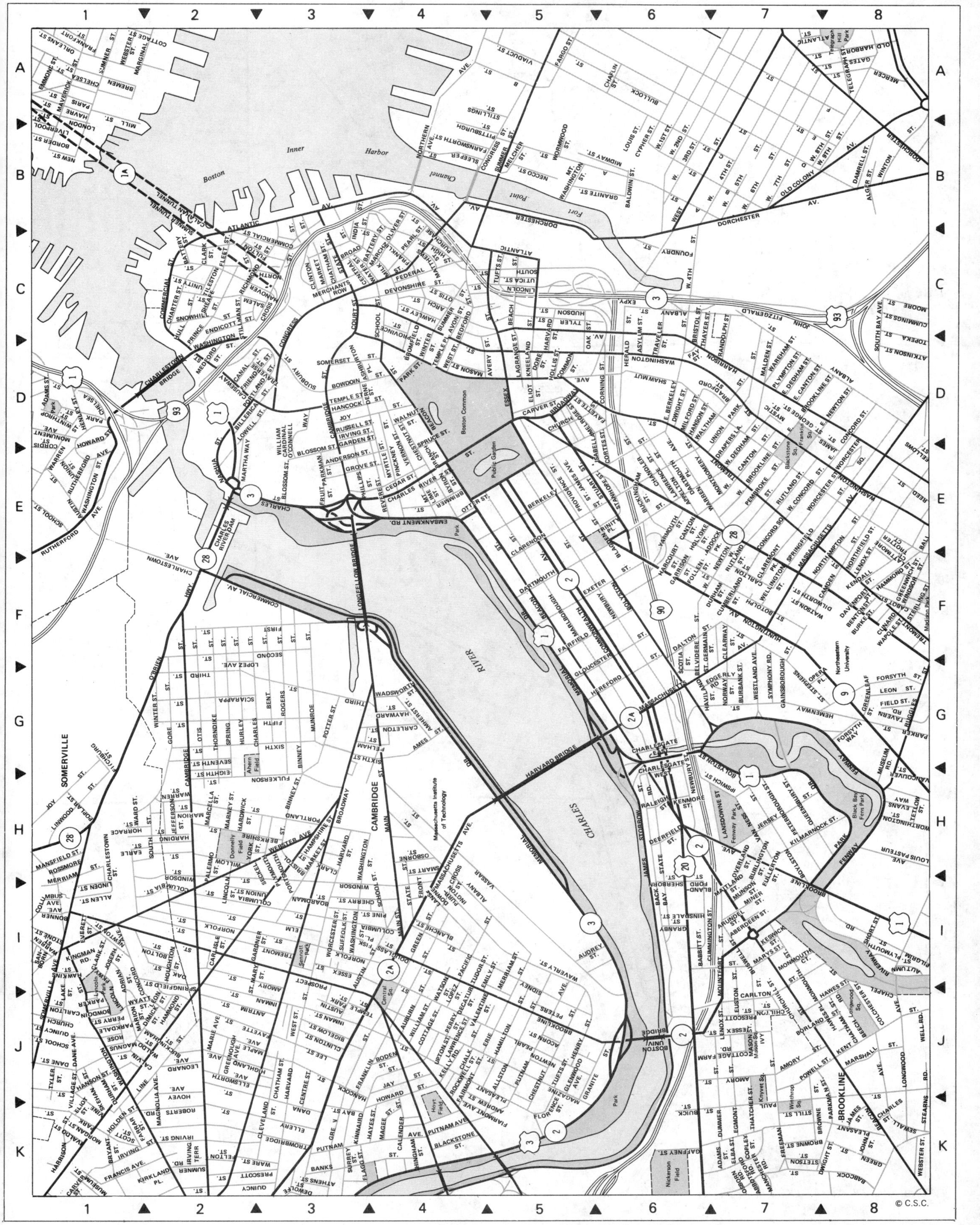

© C.S.C.

Scale of Miles
0 .1 .2 .3 .4 .5

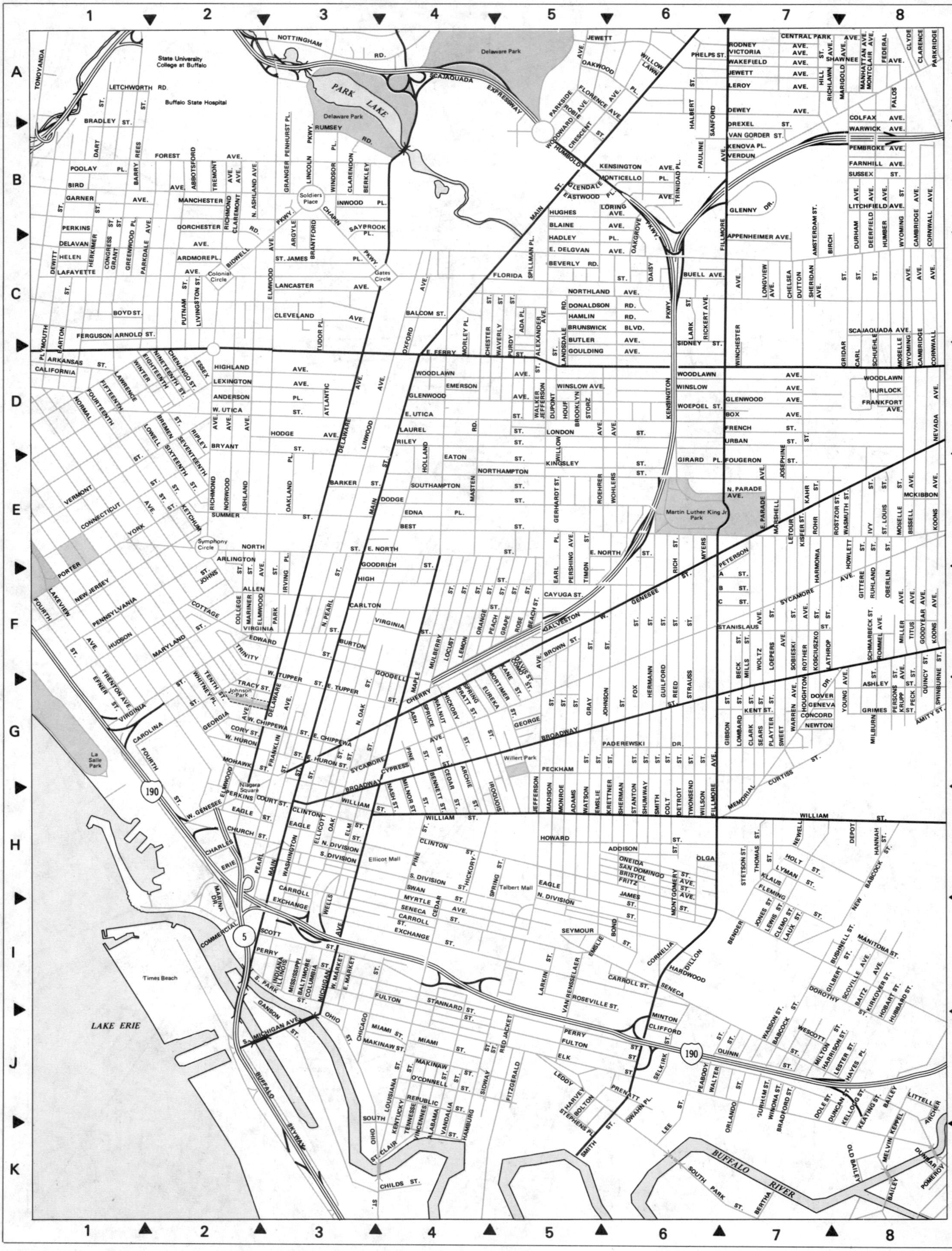

BUFFALO

A St. ... F-7
Abbotsford ... B-2
Adams St. ... H-5
Ada Pl. ... C-5
Addison ... H-6
Alabama St. ... K-4
Alexander Ave. ... C-5
Amity St. ... G-8
Amsterdam St. ... C-7
Anderson Pl. ... D-2
Appenheimer Ave. ... C-7
Archer ... J-8
Archie St. ... G-4
Ardmore Pl. ... C-2
Argyle ... C-3
Arkansas St. ... D-1
Arlington ... E-2
Ashland Ave. ... E-2
Ashland Ave., N. . B-2,E-2
Ashley St. ... G-8
Ash St. ... G-4
Atlantic ... D-3
B St. ... F-7
Babcock St. ... J-7
Bailey ... J-8,K-8
Baitz Ave. ... I-8
Balcom St. ... C-4
Baltimore ... I-3
Barker St. ... E-3
Barryrees St. ... B-1
Barton St. ... C-1
Beach St. ... F-5
Beck St. ... F-7
Bender ... I-7
Bennett St. ... G-4
Berkley ... B-3
Bertha ... K-7
Best St. ... E-4
Beverly Rd. ... C-5
Bidwell Pkwy. ... C-2
Birch ... C-7
Bird Ave. ... B-1
Bissell Ave. ... E-8
Blaine Ave. ... B-5
Bolton ... J-5
Bond ... I-6
Box Ave. ... D-7
Boyd St. ... C-1
Bradford St. ... J-7
Bradley St. ... A-1
Brantford ... C-3
Bremen ... D-2
Bristol St. ... H-6
Broadway St. ... G-5,H-3
Brooklyn ... D-5
Brown St. ... F-5
Brunswick Blvd. ... C-5
Bryant St. ... D-2
Buell Ave. ... C-6
Buffalo Skyway. . J-2,K-3
Burton ... F-3
Bushnell St. ... I-8
Butler Ave. ... C-5
C St. ... F-7
California ... D-1
Cambridge Ave. . B-8,D-8
Carl St. ... D-8
Carlton St. ... F-3
Carolina St. ... G-1
Carroll St. ... H-3,I-4,I-6
Cayuga St. ... F-5
Cedar ... I-4
Cedar St. ... G-4
Central Park Ave. ... A-7
Chapin Pkwy. ... B-3
Charles ... H-2
Chelsea ... C-7
Chenango St. ... D-2
Cherry ... G-4
Chester St. ... C-4,D-4
Chicago St. ... J-3
Childs St. ... K-4
Chippewa St., E. ... G-3
Chippewa St., W. ... G-2
Church St. ... H-2
Claremont Ave. ... B-2
Clarence ... A-8
Clarendon ... B-3
Clark St. ... G-7
Clemo St. ... I-7
Cleveland Ave. ... C-3
Clifford ... J-6
Clinton St. ... H-3,H-4
Clyde ... A-8
Colfax Ave. ... B-8
College St. ... F-2
Colt St. ... H-6
Columbia ... I-3
Commercial ... I-2
Como St. ... F-5
Concord ... G-7
Congress St. ... C-1
Connecticut St. ... E-1
Cornelia ... I-6
Cornwall Ave. ... B-8,D-8
Cory St. ... G-2
Cottage ... F-2
Court St. ... H-3
Crescent Ave. ... B-5
Curtiss St. ... G-7
Cypress ... G-4
Daisy ... C-6
Dart St. ... B-1
Davis St. ... F-5
Deerfield Ave. ... B-8
Delaware Ave. ... D-3,G-3
Delgvan Ave. ... C-1
Delgvan Ave., E. ... C-5
Depot ... H-8
Detroit St. ... H-6
Dewey Ave. ... A-7
Dillon ... I-6
Division St., N. . . H-3,H-5
Division St., S. . . H-3,H-4
Dodge St. ... E-4
Dole St. ... J-7
Donaldson Rd. ... C-5
Dorchester Rd. ... B-2
Dorothy St. ... I-7
Dover ... G-7
Drexel St. ... B-7
Dunbar ... K-8
Duncan St. ... J-8
Dupont St. ... D-5
Durham Ave. ... B-8,C-8
Dutton ... C-7
Eagle St. ... H-2,H-5
Earl Pl. ... F-5
Eastwood Pl. ... B-5
Eaton St. ... E-4
Edna Pl. ... E-4
Edward St. ... F-2
Efner St. ... G-1
Eighteenth St. ... D-2
Elk St. ... J-5
Ellicott ... H-3
Elm St. ... H-3
Elmwood Ave. ... C-3
... F-2,G-2
Emerson ... D-4
Emslie St. ... H-5,I-5
Erie ... H-2
Essex ... D-2
Eureka ... G-4
Exchange St. ... I-3,I-4
Farnhill Ave. ... B-8
Federal ... A-8
Ferguson Arnold
St. ... C-1
Ferry St., E. ... D-4
Fifteenth St. ... D-1
Fillmore Ave. B-7,C-7,H-6
Fitzgerald ... J-5
Fleming St. ... H-7
Florence Ave. ... A-5
Florida St. ... C-5
Forrest Ave. ... B-2
Fougeron St. ... E-7
Fourteenth St. ... D-1
Fourth St. ... F-1,G-2
Fox St. ... G-6
Frankfort Ave. ... D-8
Franklin Ave. ... G-3
French St. ... D-7
Fritz Ave. ... H-6
Fulton St. ... I-4,J-5
Galveston ... F-5
Ganson St. ... J-3
Garner Ave. ... B-1
Genesee St., W. . . F-6,H-2
Geneva ... G-7
George ... G-5
Georgia ... G-2
Gerhardt St. ... E-5
Gibson St. ... G-7
Gilbert St. ... I-8
Girard Pl. ... E-6
Gittere St. ... E-8
Glendale ... B-5
Glenny Dr. ... B-7
Glenwood Ave. . . D-4,D-7
Goodell ... F-4
Goodrich St. ... E-3
Goodyear Ave. ... F-8
Goulding Ave. ... D-5
Granger Penhurst
Pl. ... B-3
Grant St. ... C-1
Grape St. ... F-5
Gray St. ... G-5
Grimes St. ... G-8
Greenwood Pl. ... C-1
Gridar St. ... D-8
Guilford St. ... G-6
Gurham St. ... J-7
Hadley Pl. ... C-5
Halbert St. ... A-6
Hamburg ... K-4
Hamlin Rd. ... C-5
r _nnah St. ... H-8
Hardwood ... I-6
Harmonia St. ... F-7
Harrison St. ... J-7
Harvey ... J-5
Hayes Pl. ... J-8
Helen ... C-1
Herkimer St. ... C-1
Hermann St. ... G-6
Hickory St. ... G-4,H-4
Highland Ave. ... D-2
High St. ... F-3
Hill St. ... A-7
Hobart St. ... I-8
Hodge Ave. ... D-3
Holland ... E-4
Holt St. ... H-7
Houf ... D-5
Houghton ... G-7
Howard St. ... H-5
Howlett ... E-8
Hubbard St. ... J-8
Hudson ... F-1
Hughes Ave. ... B-5
Humber Ave. ... B-8,C-8
Humboldt Pkwy. ... B-5
Hurlock ... D-8
Huron St., E. ... G-3
Huron St., W. ... G-2
Illinois ... I-3
Indiana ... I-3
Inwood Pl. ... B-3
Iroquois ... H-5
Irving Pl. ... F-3
Ivy St. ... E-8
James St. ... H-6
Jefferson Ave. . . D-5,H-5
Jewett Ave. ... A-5,A-7
Johnson St. ... G-6
Jones St. ... I-7
Josephine ... E-7
Kahr St. ... E-7
Kane St. ... F-5
Keating St. ... J-8
Kellogg St. ... J-8
Kenova Pl. ... B-7
Kensington Ave. ... B-6
Kensington Pkwy. ... D-6
Kent St. ... G-7
Kentucky St. ... J-4
Ketchum ... E-2
Kingsley St. ... E-5
Kirkover St. ... I-8
Kisfer St. ... E-7
Klaus ... H-7
Koons Ave. ... E-8,F-8
Kosciuszko St. ... F-7
Krettner St. ... H-6
Krupp Ave. ... G-8
Lafayette Ave. ... C-1
Lakeview Ave. ... F-1
Lancaster Ave. ... C-3
Landsdale Rd. ... D-5
Larkin St. ... I-5
Lark St. ... C-6
Latchworth St. ... A-1
Lathrop St. ... F-7
Laurel St. ... D-4
Laux St. ... I-7
Lowell ... D-2
Lawrence ... D-1
Lee St. ... K-6
Leddy ... J-5
Lemon St. ... F-4
Leroy Ave. ... A-7
Lester St. ... J-8
Letour ... E-7
Lewis St. ... I-7
Lexington Ave. ... D-2
Lincoln Pkwy. ... B-3
Linwood Ave. ... D-3
Litchfield Ave. ... B-8
Littell ... J-8
Livingston St. ... C-2
Locust St. ... F-4
Loepers St. ... F-7
Lombard St. ... G-7
London St. ... D-5
Longview Ave. ... C-7
Loring Ave. ... B-6
Louisiana St. ... J-4
Lyman St. ... H-7
Madison St. ... H-5
Main St. ... B-5,E-3,H-3
Makinaw St. ... J-3,J-4
Manchester ... B-2
Manhattan Ave. ... A-8
Manitoba St. ... I-8
Maple ... G-4
Marigold Ave. ... A-8
Marina Dr. ... H-2
Mariner St. ... F-2
Market, E. ... I-3
Market, W. ... I-3
Marshell ... E-7
Maryland St. ... F-2
Masten Rd. ... E-4
McKibbon ... E-8
Melvin Keppel ... K-8
Memorial Dr. ... H-7
Miami St. ... J-4
Michigan Ave., S. . I-3,J-2
Milburn St. ... G-8
Miller Ave. ... F-8
Mills St. ... F-7
Milnor St. ... G-4
Milton St. ... J-7
Minton ... J-6
Mississippi ... I-3
Mohawk St. ... G-2
Monroe St. ... H-5
Montclair Ave. ... A-8
Montgomery St. . . H-6,I-6
Monticello Pl. ... B-6
Morley Pl. ... C-4
Mortimer St. ... G-5
Moselle St. ... D-8,E-8
Mulberry St. ... F-4
Myers ... E-6
Myrtle Ave. ... I-4
Nash St. ... H-4
New Babcock St. . H-8,I-8
Newell ... H-7
New Jersey ... F-1
Newton ... G-7
Nevada Ave. ... D-8
Nineteenth St. ... D-2
Normal Ave. ... D-1
North St., E. ... E-4,E-6
Northampton St. ... E-4
Northland Ave. ... C-5
North St. ... E-2
Nottingham Rd. ... A-3
Norwood Ave. ... E-2
Oak ... H-3
Oak St., N. ... G-3
Oak Grove ... C-6
Oakland Pl. ... E-3
Oakwood Pl. ... A-5
Oberlin St. ... F-8
O'Connell St. ... J-4
Ohio St. ... J-3,K-3
Old Bailey ... K-8
Olga ... H-6
Oneida St. ... H-6
Orange St. ... F-4
Orlando St. ... J-7
Owahn Pl. ... J-6
Oxford Ave. ... C-4
Paderewski Dr. ... G-6
Palos ... A-8
Parade Ave., E. ... E-7
Parade Ave., N. ... E-7
Park St. ... F-3
Parkdale Ave. ... C-1
Parkridge ... A-8
Parkside Ave. ... A-5
Pauline ... B-6
Peabody St. ... J-6
Peach St. ... F-5
Pearl St. ... H-2
Pearl St., N. ... F-3
Peck St. ... G-8
Peckham ... G-5
Pembroke Ave. ... B-8
Pennsylvania ... F-1
Perkins ... B-1
Perry St. ... I-2,J-5
Pershing Ave. ... F-5
Persons St. ... G-8
Peterson ... E-7
Phelps St. ... A-6
Pine St. ... G-4,H-4
Playter St. ... G-7
Plymouth Dewitt
St. ... C-1
Pomeroy ... K-8
Poolay Pl. ... B-1
Porter ... E-1,F-1
Pratt St. ... G-4
Prenatt ... J-6
Purdy St. ... C-5
Putnam St. ... C-2
Quincy St. ... G-8
Quinn St. ... J-7
Red Jacket ... J-5
Reed St. ... G-6
Republic St. ... J-4
Richlawn Ave. ... A-7
Rich St. ... E-6
Richmond Ave. . . B-2,E-2
Rickert Ave. ... C-6
Riley St. ... D-4
Ripley ... D-2
Robie St. ... A-5
Rodney Ave. ... A-7
Roehrer Ave. ... E-5
Rohr St. ... E-7
Rommel Ave. ... F-8
Rose St. ... F-5
Roseville St. ... I-5
Rostzor St. ... E-8
Rother Ave. ... F-7
Ruhland St. ... F-8
Rumsey Rd. ... B-3
St. Clair ... K-4
St. James Pl. ... C-3
St. Johns ... F-2
St. Louis St. ... E-8
San Domingo Ave. . . H-6
Sanford ... B-6
Saybrook Pl. ... B-3
Scajaquada Ave. ... C-8
Scajaquada Expwy. . . A-4
Schmarbeck St. ... F-8
Schuehle St. ... D-8
Scott St. ... I-3
Scoville Ave. ... I-8
Sears St. ... G-7
Selkirk St. ... J-6
Seneca St. ... I-4,I-6
Seventeenth St. ... D-2
Seymour St. ... I-5
Shawnee Ave. ... A-8
Sheridan Ave. ... C-7
Sherman ... H-6
Shumway St. ... H-6
Sidney St. ... C-6
Sidway St. ... J-4
Sixteenth St. ... D-2
Smith St. ... H-6,K-5
Sobieski St. ... F-7
Southampton St. ... E-4
South St. ... J-3
South Park St. ... I-3,K-6
Spillman Pl. ... C-5
Spring St. ... G-4,H-5
Spruce St. ... G-4
Stanislaus St. ... F-7
Stannard St. ... I-4
Stanton St. ... H-6
Stephens Pl. ... J-5
Stetson St. ... H-7
Storz ... D-5
Strauss St. ... G-6
Summer St. ... E-2
Sussex St. ... B-8
Swan St. ... H-4
Sweet Ave. ... G-7
Swinburne St. ... G-8
Sycamore Ave. . . F-7,G-3
Tennessee ... J-4
Tenth St. ... F-2
Thomas St. ... H-7
Timon St. ... F-5
Titus Ave. ... F-8
Tonoyanda ... A-1
Tracy St. ... G-2
Tremont ... B-2
Trenton Ave. ... G-1
Trinidad Pl. ... B-6
Trinity ... F-2
Tudor Pl. ... C-3
Tupper St., E. ... G-3
Tupper St., W. ... F-3
Townsend St. ... H-6
Utical St., E. ... D-4
Utica St., W. ... D-2
Urban St. ... D-7
Vandalia St. ... K-4
Vangarder St. ... B-7
Van Rensselaer ... I-5
Verdun ... B-7
Vermont St. ... E-1
Victoria Ave. ... A-7
Vincennes ... K-4
Virginia St. ... F-2
... F-4,G-1
Wakefield Ave. ... A-7
Walker St. ... D-5
Walnut ... G-4
Walter St. ... J-6
Warren Ave. ... G-7
Warwick Ave. ... B-8
Washington St. ... H-3
Wasmuth St. ... E-8
Wasson St. ... J-7
Watson St. ... H-5
Waverly St. ... C-5
Wells ... I-3
Wescott ... J-7
Whitney Pl. ... F-2
William St. . . H-3,H-4,H-7
Willow ... D-5,E-5
Willow Lawn ... A-6
Wilson St. ... H-6
Winchester Ave. ... D-7
Windsor Pl. ... B-3
Winona St. ... J-7
Winslow Ave. ... D-5,D-6
Winter St. ... D-1
Woepoel St. ... D-6
Wohlers Ave. ... E-6
Woltz Ave. ... F-7
Woodlawn Ave. ... D-4
... D-6,D-8
Woodward AVe. ... B-5
Wyoming St. ... B-8,D-8
York St. ... E-1
Young Ave. ... G-8

POINTS OF INTEREST

Colonial Circle ... C-2
Delaware Park . . A-3,A-5
Ellicot Mall ... H-3
Gates Circle ... C-4
Johnson Park ... G-2
La Salle Park ... G-1
Martin Luther King,
Jr. Park ... E-6
Niagra Square ... H-2
Soldiers Place ... B-3
Symphony Circle ... E-2
Talbert Mall ... H-5
Times Beach ... I-2
Willert Park ... G-5

CHARLOTTE

A Ave. ... A-3
Abbey Pl. ... K-3
Ablewood ... B-2
Academy ... D-7
Academy St. ... D-7
Addison Dr. ... K-8
Admiral ... D-8
Alabama ... B-1
Alberto ... H-5
Alexander, N. ... D-6,F-4
Alexander, S. ... F-4
Alice Ave. ... D-1
Alma Ct. ... B-4
Altondale Ave. ... H-5
Ambassador ... D-1
Amber Dr. ... D-1
Ameron Dr. ... B-6
Amble Dr. ... A-6
Amherst ... G-5
Anderson ... D-7
Anderson St. ... D-8
Andover Rd. ... J-6
Andrill ... D-3
Anthony Cir. ... J-7
Ansley ... J-6
Anson St. ... I-1
Applegate ... J-1
Arcadia ... K-4
Arden St. ... C-4
Ardmore ... H-2
Ardsley ... H-4
Argyle ... B-7
Arlington ... F-3
Armour ... D-4
Armoury Dr. ... F-5
Arnold Dr. ... F-8
Arosa Ave. ... G-3
Arty Ave. ... F-1
Asbury Ave. ... B-5
Ashby ... D-5
Ashcraft Ln. ... J-2
Ashland Ave. ... F-7
Ashworth Rd. ... I-7
Atando Ave. ... B-5,C-6
Atmore St. ... D-8
Attaberry ... E-7
Auburn Ave. ... I-2
Audubon Rd. ... K-6
Augusta ... B-3
Auten Rd. ... A-4,D-2
Avant St. ... G-4
Aylesfora ... J-6
Azalea ... B-5
B Ave. ... A-3
Bacon ... D-2
Badger ... C-4
Baldwin ... G-5
Baltimore ... H-1
Bancroft St. ... C-5
... D-4,D-5
Bank St. ... H-1
Barkley Rd. ... K-2
Barnette ... G-5
Barnhill Dr. ... G-7
Barringer Dr. ... G-1
Barry St. ... E-6
Bartow ... G-5
Barwick ... J-7
Bascom St. ... G-6
Basin ... G-1
Baxter St. ... G-4
Bay St. ... G-6
Baylor Dr. ... K-1
Beal St. ... I-7
Bearwood Ave. ... C-8
Bellaire ... B-2
Belleterre ... E-6
Belmont Ave. ... E-5
Belor Ave. ... G-3
Belot ... A-5
Belrose Ln. ... J-2
Belton St. ... H-1
Belvedere Ave. ... E-6,F-7
Benard ... C-6
Bennett ... B-8
Benson ... C-4
Berkeley Ave. ... G-3
Berkshire ... H-2
Berryhill ... E-1
Bertonley Ave. ... J-7
Bethel Rd. ... F-1
Beverly Dr. ... I-5
Billingsley Rd. ... I-6
Bingham ... C-8
Black ... B-1
Blackthorne Rd. ... I-1
Blackwood ... D-8
Blairmore ... K-8
Bland, W. ... F-2
Blanton ... G-1
Blazer ... C-3
Blythe Blvd. ... H-4
Bobby Ln. ... I-7
Booker ... C-2
Bolling Rd. ... I-5
Bonwood Dr. ... J-6
Boone St. ... C-3
Botany St. ... B-2
Boyd ... C-1
Bradbury ... K-2
Brandon Cir. ... J-5
Brandon Rd. ... I-4
Brandywine Ave. ... K-3
Brantham Rd. ... J-8
Brentwood Dr. ... F-1
Brevard St., N. ... F-4
Brevard St., S. ... F-3
Briabend ... J-1
Briarcliff Pl. ... J-4
Briar Creek Rd. ... G-7
Brice St. ... D-1
Bridlepath Ln. ... J-8
Brighton Pl. ... H-8
Bromley Rd. ... H-4
Brook Hill Rd. ... G-1
Brookhurst ... H-8
Brookhurst Dr. ... I-7
Brookridge ... K-6
Brookshire Frwy. C-2,D-3
Brookwood ... K-5
Browning Sprague ... F-6
Brownstone ... B-3
Bruns Ave. ... D-2
Brunswick Ave. ... H-4
Bryant ... E-2
Buchanan St. ... H-3
Bucknell ... I-4,J-4
Bulford Ave. ... H-7
Bungalow ... C-1
Burbank Rd. ... B-2
Burch Dr. ... A-4
Burklane ... I-7
Burleigh ... K-7
Burrough ... B-8
Burton ... D-3
Butterfield ... C-7
C Ave. ... A-3
Caldwell St., N. ... F-4
Caldwell St., S. ... F-4
Callahan ... D-4
Calvert ... E-2
Cameron ... G-6
Campus ... C-2,D-2
Cambridge Rd. ... I-2
Camden ... G-2
Candy Stick ... B-8
Canterbury, N. ... J-7
Canterbury S. ... J-6
Card ... D-7
Carmine St. ... B-4
Carol ... D-1
Carolyn Dr. ... G-8
Carowil ... J-3
Carter St. ... H-8
Cartier Way ... F-1
Cassamia Pl. ... J-5
Castleton Rd. ... J-8
Castlewood ... J-2
Caswell Rd. ... G-5
Catalina Ave. ... C-5
Catawba ... E-6
Cedar, N. ... E-3
Cedar St. S. ... E-3
Celia ... B-2,C-2
Cemetery ... C-2
Central Ave. ... F-6
Centre ... B-1
Chamberland ... D-2
Chandler Pl. ... K-7
Charles Ave. ... D-6
Charmapeg Ave. ... K-8
Chase St. ... G-5
Chatman Ave. ... F-7
Cheddington Dr. ... J-8
Cherokee Pl. ... H-5
Cherokee Rd. ... I-5
Cherry ... G-4
Chesterfield Ave. ... G-6
Chestnut Ave. ... F-6
Cheswick Rd. ... J-7
Chicago AVe. ... G-1
Chillingworth ... K-7
Chilton Pl. ... J-4
Chipley Ave. ... H-7
Chippendale Rd. ... I-8
Chlemsford Rd. ... J-6
Church St., N. ... D-5,E-4
Church, S. ... F-3
Churchill Rd. ... I-6
Cinderella ... B-8
Clarice Ave. ... G-6
Clark ... E-8
Clarkson, N. ... E-3
Clay ... D-1
Clayton Dr. ... I-3
Clement Ave. ... F-6,G-5
Clemson ... D-7
Cleveland ... G-2
Clifford ... F-2
Cloudman ... A-1
Clover ... K-6
Club Rd. ... F-7
Clyde Dr. ... C-1
Clydesdale Rd. ... D-1
Coates ... B-8
Cochran ... E-6
Coddington Pl. ... J-6
Coker ... D-1
Colfax ... B-2
Collanade Dr. ... H-7
College St., N. ... E-4
College St., S. ... F-3
Collingwood ... J-1
Colliseum Dr. ... H-7
Colonial Ave. ... G-5
Colony Rd. ... K-4
Columbus Pl. ... E-1
Colville Rd. ... H-5,I-5
Colwick ... J-7
Commerce ... F-2
Commercial ... D-8
Commodore ... I-8
Commonwealth Ave.
... G-6,H-8
Concordia ... C-5
Concordia Ave. ... C-5
Condon St. ... C-3
Coniston Pl. ... H-4
Connecticut ... E-8
Connecting Rd. ... J-1
Conway Ave. ... I-1
Cooper Dr. ... K-1
Cornelius ... C-6
Cornell Ave. ... J-6
Coronet Way ... C-1
Corporation Circle ... A-1
Cosby Pl. ... F-8
Cotes St. ... E-3
Cottage Pl. ... H-5
Cottonwood ... A-6
Country Club ... E-7
Country Club Rd. ... E-7
Coventry Rd. ... J-6
Coxe Ave. ... D-2
Craghead Rd., W. ... B-6
Craig Ave. ... I-8
Cranbrook Ln. ... H-6
Creek ... D-3
Creger St. ... B-1
Creighton ... G-8
Crest Dr., E. ... G-7
Crestdale ... A-3
Crestview ... C-2
Crestway ... C-2
Cricketeer Dr. ... A-2
Crosby ... K-6
Croydon Rd. ... J-4
Crystal ... G-8
Cullman Ave. ... C-6
Cumberland Ave. ... I-3
Cummings Ave. ... B-3
Cunningham ... D-1
Currituck Dr. ... K-1
Curtiswood ... C-8
Cushman St. ... B-7
Custer ... B-3
Cyrus Dr. ... G-8
Dakota ... A-1
De Lane Ave. ... J-8
Dalehurst Dr. ... D-8
Dalton Ave. ... D-4
Darby Ave. ... B-1
Dare Dr. ... B-7
Darsey ... D-3
Dartmouth ... H-5
Davidson St., N.
... C-7,D-6,F-4
Davidson St., S. ... F-4
Dawson ... C-2
Dean St. ... C-3
Dearborn ... C-4
De Armon Dr. ... F-7
Dellwood ... K-3
De Paul ... B-2
Devon ... J-3
Diana Dr. ... H-2
Dickinson ... I-4
Dilworth Rd. ... H-3
Dilworth, E. ... G-3
Dinglewood Ave. ... C-8
Distribution St. ... G-2
Dixon ... D-2
Doggett ... G-2
Dogwood Ave. ... C-5
Domino Ct. ... H-7
Donna ... D-8
Doris Ave. ... I-8
Dorothy ... H-2
Dotger Ave., N. ... H-6
Dotger, S. ... H-6
Double St. ... C-4
Dover ... I-1
Downs Ave. ... D-7
Dresden Dr., W. ... H-8
Drexel Pl. ... K-3
Drexmore Ave. ... K-3
Druid Cir. ... C-4
Drum ... E-1
Drummond Ave. ... E-6
Drury Dr. ... B-7
Duckworth ... D-2
Dunavant St. ... H-2
Dunbar St. ... E-2
Dundeen St. ... C-2
Dunkirk ... F-2
Dunlavin Way ... F-8
Dunn St. ... H-7
Dupree ... B-1
Durham ... G-5
Durwood Dr. ... G-4
Dwelle ... B-1
Earle ... D-4
East Boulevard ... H-3
Eastover Rd. ... H-5
Eaastview ... I-8
Eastwood ... E-8
Echo Glen Rd. ... A-8
Edgehill Rd. N. ... H-4
Edgehill Rd. S. ... H-4
Edgerton ... B-8
Edison St. ... C-4
Edwin ... C-4
Effingham ... D-1
Elder Ave. ... I-8
Eldridge ... F-3
Ellington ... I-7
Ellison ... G-4
Ellsworth ... I-7
Elmhurst Rd. ... H-2
Elizabeth Ave. ... F-4
Elkwood ... D-8
Ella St. ... A-6
Ellen Ave. ... E-8
Elm ... E-4
Elon St. ... D-1
Emerson ... H-6
Emory Ln. ... J-8
Englehardt St. ... B-2
English Dr. ... B-2
Ennis Ave. ... C-5
Enterprise St. ... C-6
Erie St. ... B-3
Erskine Dr. ... E-8
Eastway Dr. ... D-8
Essex ... D-8
Estelle St. ... C-2
Euclid ... G-3,H-2
Eureka ... C-4
Everett ... E-6
Evergreen ... E-1
Ewing Ave. ... H-3
Exeter ... J-6
Fairmont ... C-3
Falson ... D-6
Fannie Cir. ... H-6
Farmcrest ... A-7
Farmington Ln. ... F-8
Faulkner ... I-7
Fenton Pl. ... H-5
Fenwick ... K-2
Ferguson ... F-8
Ferncliff ... K-6
Ferncliff Rd. ... K-5
Fieldbrook ... K-3
Fireside ... B-8
Firth ... F-7
Firwood Ln. ... J-1
Flamingo ... E-8
Fleetwood Rd. ... E-1
Flint ... D-2
Floral Ave. ... H-3
Florida Ave. ... E-7
Flynwood ... F-8
Fontana Ave. ... D-4
Ford Rd. ... B-3
Ford Rd., E. ... E-7
Fordham Rd. ... F-1
Forest Dr. ... K-5
Fort St. ... E-7
Fortune ... H-7
Foster ... H-1
Fox ... G-4
Franklin ... C-5
Frazier ... D-3
Freeland ... I-1
French ... D-3
Frew Rd. ... C-6
Friendly ... A-8
Fugate Ave. ... H-7
Fulton ... F-7
Furman Pl. ... K-1
Galax ... C-8
Gardenter ... H-4
Gardner Ave. ... D-2
Garnette ... B-3
Gay St. ... F-1
Gaynor Rd. ... K-7
Gene Ave. ... H-6
Geneva Ct. ... I-3
Gentry Pl. ... K-2
Georgia Ave. ... E-7
Gibbs St. ... C-3
Gilbert St. ... B-3
Glendale ... K-4
Glenn St. ... G-8
Glory St. ... B-7
Gondola ... B-7
Goodwin Ave. ... H-8
Gordon St. ... F-6
Goshen ... J-8
Grace ... E-6
Graham St., N. . . A-6,D-4
Graham, S. ... F-2
Graham St., S. ... E-3
Grandin Rd. ... E-2
Grant ... C-1
Granville Rd. ... H-4
Graybark Ave. ... F-8
Greenleaf ... E-2
Green Oaks ... G-7
Greensboro St. ... C-7
Greenway Ave. ... G-5
Greenwich Rd. ... J-7
Greenwood Cliff ... G-4
Gregg Ave. ... D-2
Greystone Rd. ... I-1
Grier St. ... C-3
Griffith St. ... H-1
Grimes St. ... C-5,D-5
Guilford ... I-2
Gunn ... C-3
Habersham ... I-2
Haines ... B-3
Haleworth ... J-8
Hall St. ... F-6
Halsey ... C-1
Halstead ... K-2
Hamilton St. ... D-4
Hammet St. ... I-8
Hampshire ... D-8
Hampton Ave. ... I-5
Hanover ... G-6
Hanson Dr. ... J-5
Hardianway ... K-7
Harding Pl. ... G-4
Hardwick Rd. ... K-7
Harris Rd. ... J-5
Harrison St. ... C-1
Hartford ... I-4
Hartford Ave. ... I-1,J-1
Hartley St. ... B-5
Harvard ... H-5
Harvey ... A-6
Hassell Pl. ... K-3
Hasting ... J-4
Hatteras Ave. ... B-3
Haven Dr. ... J-3
Havilon Ct. ... K-8
Hawkins ... G-2
Hawkins St. ... G-2
Hawthorne Lane ... F-6
Heathcliff ... E-2
Heather Ln. ... J-2
Heathwood Rd. ... J-7
Hedgemore ... K-3
Heflin ... H-6
Heil ... C-3
Hempstead Pl. ... H-5,I-5
Henley Pl. ... H-4
Hermitage ... H-5
Hermitage Rd. ... H-5
Herrin ... D-7,E-8
Hershey St. ... B-8
Hickory ... A-4
Hickorynut St. ... H-8
Hidden Brook Dr. ... H-8
Hidden Valley Rd. ... B-8
Hildebrand ... B-2
Hill St., E. ... F-3
Hill St., W. ... E-2,F-3
Hillard ... E-8
Hillcrest St. ... B-7
Hillsdale ... J-4
Hillside Ave. ... J-3
Hilo Dr. ... C-7
Hobbs ... D-5
Hodgson ... K-7
Holland ... B-4
Hollis Rd. ... I-1
Holly St. ... B-3
Hollyday Ct. ... K-2
Holroyd ... J-6
Holt Ct. ... D-7
Homorton Pl. ... F-6
Honeywood Ave. ... B-1
Hope Dale ... H-4
Horne Dr. ... C-4
Hoskins Rd. ... A-1
Hough Rd. ... J-2
Howie Cir. ... C-8
Hudson ... D-7
Hughes ... A-8
Hungerford Pl. ... I-6
Hunter Ln. ... K-7
Huntley Pl. ... H-5
Hyde Dr. ... B-7
Ideal Way ... H-2
Idlewood Cir. ... I-3
Independence Blvd.
... F-1,G-6
Industry Rd. ... I-1
'nwood Dr. ... K-1
rby ... J-3
Iris Dr. ... F-7
Irma ... B-3
Ironwood St. ... B-7
Irwin ... E-3
Isenhour ... B-4
Ison ... F-1
Iverson Way ... H-2
Ivey Dr. ... G-7
Jackson ... F-5
Jameston Dr. ... I-3
Jasper ... F-3
Jay St. ... E-1
Jeff St. ... E-8
Jefferson ... F-2
Jefferson Davis ... C-4
Jenkins ... D-2
Jennings ... B-3
Jersey ... J-2
Jessie Ct. ... B-4
Jewel St. ... H-6
Joe St. ... A-6
Johnson ... D-4
Johnston Rd. ... B-6
Jones St. ... C-1
Jonquil St. ... I-7
Jordan Pl. ... D-6
Judith ... J-7
Judson ... C-1
Julia Ave. ... B-4
Julien St. ... G-6
June ... H-8
Justice Ave. ... B-4
Kasaw ... A-5
Kay ... C-3
Keller Ave. ... B-3
Kendall ... A-2
Kenilworth ... H-3
Kenmore ... G-5
Kennesaw Dr. ... B-3
Kenney St. ... C-3
Kennon St. ... E-6
Kensington Dr. ... F-6
Kentbrook ... B-8
Kentucky ... B-1
Kenwood ... F-6
Keswick ... D-5
Kings Dr., S. ... G-4,H-4
Kingsbury Dr. ... G-6
Kingston Ave., E. ... G-3
Kingston Ave., W. ... F-2
Kirkland ... D-1
Kirkwood ... H-3
Knollwood ... K-6
Kohler ... C-4
Kotonah ... D-2
Laburnum Ave. ... G-6
Lake ... D-1
Lakeview ... C-1
Lakewood ... C-1
Lamar Ave. ... G-5
Lambeth Dr. ... B-8
Lander St. ... C-1
La Salle ... C-1
La Salle St. ... B-2
Laurel Ave. ... G-6,H-5
Leafmore ... C-8
Leigh Ave. ... D-6
Lenox Ave. ... G-3
Leota Dr. ... B-6
Leroy St. ... I-6
Lexington ... G-3
Liberty ... F-3
Libeth St. ... E-8
Liddell St., W. ... E-4
Lilac Rd. ... I-3
Lilington Ave. ... G-4
Lincoln ... F-2
Lincrest ... K-8
Linda Ln. ... J-7
Linden Ln. ... E-5
Linganore ... G-3
Linwood Ave. ... B-1
Lima ... D-2
Litchfield ... I-8
Little Hope ... J-2
Lloyd ... D-4
Lockhart Dr. ... H-3
Lockley Dr. ... I-5
Lockridge Rd. ... J-1
Log Cabin Rd. ... A-8
Logie Ave. ... F-7
Lola Ave. ... E-6
Loma Ln. ... E-8
Lomax Ave. ... J-8
Lombardy Cir. ... H-4
Long ... F-4
Long Branch ... F-5
Longfellow ... G-8
Longwood Dr. ... K-2
Lorene Ave. ... J-4
Louise Ave. ... F-5
Lucena St. ... C-5
Ludlow ... B-2
Lunsford Pl. ... D-6
Lyndhurst Ave. ... G-2
Lynnwood ... J-3
Lyon ... F-7
Lyttleton ... K-8
Macathur Ave. ... B-4
Madison ... D-3
Madrid Rd. ... B-3
Magnolia Ave. ... G-2
Malvern Rd. ... I-5
Manhasset ... J-1
Maple Grove ... A-2
Marguerite ... E-7
Maribe Ave. ... B-2
Marlwood Ter. ... I-3
Marsh Rd. ... H-2
Marshall ... H-2
Martin St. ... D-3
Marvin Rd. ... I-7
Mavista ... J-3
Maryland Ave. ... I-4
Masonic ... F-7
Matheson Ave. . . D-6,E-7
Mathis ... D-1
Mattoon ... C-2
May St. ... H-1
Mayfield ... I-2
May View Dr. ... H-7
Maywood ... E-8
McAlway ... I-7,J-7
Mc Call St. ... D-4
Mc Cauley St. ... I-8
Mc Clintock Rd. ... G-6
Mc Donald ... B-2,H-2
Mc Dowell St. ... E-5
Mc Dowell St., N.
... D-7F-4
Mc Dowell St., S. ... F-4
Mc Millan St. ... D-8
Mc Quay ... D-1
Meacham St. ... H-2
Meadow Brook ... I-6
Meadow Ln. ... D-8
Melboure Ct. ... H-2
Melchor Ave. ... I-7
Melita ... C-2
Mellow Dr. ... B-8
Mercury St. ... C-7
Merlane Dr. ... A-7
Merriman Ave. ... F-2
Merry Oaks ... G-8
Merwick Cir. ... J-7
Metals Dr. ... A-6
Meyer, N. ... D-6
Middleton Dr. ... H-5
Midfield ... B-7
Miles Ct. ... C-3
Millbrook Rd. ... I-7
Millerton Ave. ... E-1
Mimosa Ave. ... E-6
Mint St. ... F-3
Mitchell St. ... B-3
Mockingbird Ln. ... K-3
Mohigan ... H-7
Mona ... K-3
Montclair ... K-7
Monterey ... B-2
Montford Dr. ... K-2
Montgomery ... D-2
Montrose Ct. ... H-6
Mooney ... D-7
Moorehead St., E. ... F-3
Moorehead St., W. ... E-2
Moravian Ln. ... H-5
Moretz Ave. ... C-4
Morningside Dr. ... G-7
Morrow ... F-4
Morson ... D-1
Moss St. ... C-4
Moultrie St. ... I-1
Mt. Kisco Dr. ... A-8
Mt. Vernon ... G-3
Mulberry ... C-3
Murdoch Rd. ... D-7
Murray Hill Rd. . . J-1,K-1
Museum Dr. ... I-6
Museum Pl. ... H-6
Myers St. ... F-4
Myrica ... A-8
Myrtle ... G-3
Nandina St. ... F-6
Nancy Dr. ... I-8
Nassau Blvd. ... F-6
Nelson Ave. ... B-1
New Castle ... C-3
New Hope ... H-3
Newland ... C-4
Newland Rd. ... B-3
Norcross ... E-7
Norfolk ... H-1
Norris Ave. ... C-4
Northaven Dr. ... B-7
Northcliffe ... A-2
Northcrest ... B-7
Northerly Rd. ... B-4
North Gate ... J-1
Northmore ... C-7
Norton Rd. ... I-4
Norwell ... D-7
Norwood Dr. ... C-1
Nottingham ... K-8
Oaklawn Ave. ... D-4
Oakmont Ave. ... G-8
Oaks Rd. ... C-4
Oakwood Ave. ... D-7
October ... C-1
Olando Ave. ... C-5
Onyz ... C-2
Opal St. ... D-1
Orange St. ... H-6
Ordermore ... H-3
Oregon St. ... C-1
Orvis St. ... C-3
Osborne ... G-5
Osmond ... F-1
Otts St. ... F-5
Overhill Rd. ... K-5
Oxford Pl. ... I-5
Paddock ... J-2
Palm ... E-8
Palmer ... F-2,F-3
Pamlico St. ... F-6
Park Ave. ... G-3
Park Ave., E. ... G-3
Park Ave., W. ... F-2
Park Dr. ... F-5
Park Rd. ... J-3,H-3
Parkside Dr. ... D-1
Parkway Dr. ... D-1
Parkwood Ave. ... E-6
Patch ... B-4
Patterson ... C-7
Patton Ave. ... C-3
Paxton ... B-8
Pearson St. ... E-6
Pebble St. ... A-6
Pecan Ave. ... F-6,G-5
Pelton St. ... H-1
Pembroke ... I-4
Pender ... J-4
Penman ... F-2
Pennsylvania ... B-1
Perrin Pl. ... H-5
Phifer ... E-4
Philemon ... C-7
Phoenix Pl. ... K-6
Picaroy ... J-4
Pickens ... F-8
Pierce St. ... H-3
Pine St. ... E-3
Pine St., N. ... D-5
Pinecrest Ave. ... G-8
Pine Grove Ave. ... B-6
Pinehurst ... K-3
Fineville Rd. ... K-1
Pinewood Cir. ... J-5
Pinkney Ave. ... D-6
Pitts Dr. ... C-2
Placid ... I-6
Plainwood ... A-1
Plantation ... J-3
Planters ... C-1
Plum Hearty ... K-7
Plymouth Ave. ... D-4
Poindexter Dr. ... H-2
Polk St. ... D-4
Pompano St. ... A-1
Pondella Dr. ... A-8
Poplar St., N. ... D-5,E-3
Poplar, S. ... E-3
Portland ... I-5
Post St. ... F-2
Prospect ... F-5
Prince St. ... B-1
Princeton Ave. ... I-3
Providence ... J-5
Providence Rd. ... H-5,I-5
Pryor St. ... D-1
Purnell Ct. ... J-5
Queens ... I-4
Queens Rd. ... H-4
Queens Rd., E. ... J-4
Queens Rd., W. ... I-4
Quentin Pl. ... B-2
Quincy ... F-2
Rachel St. ... C-5
Radcliffe Ave. ... I-4
Radio ... E-2
Rainbow ... B-6
Raleigh St. ... C-7,C-8
Ramona ... C-1
Rampart ... G-2
Randall ... F-6
Randolph Rd. ... I-6
Ravencroft Dr. ... D-1
Rayon St. ... B-1
Redbud ... C-2
Redwood Ave. ... C-8
Reece ... J-3
Renner ... C-3
Rennsselar ... G-3
Rensford Ave. ... I-5
Remington ... B-2
Remus ... G-1
Reynolds Dr. ... J-2
Richland Dr. ... I-8
Ridgecrest ... I-7
Ridgedale ... A-7
Ridgeway Ave. ... G-5
Ridgewood ... J-3
Ringwood ... D-1
Ritch Ave. ... C-6
Roanoke Ave. ... H-8
Robin Rd. ... K-7
Robinhood Rd. ... K-8
Robinson Ave. ... C-6
Rockbrook Dr. ... K-4
Rockford ... J-1
Rocklyn ... J-3
Rockway Dr. ... G-7
Rodman ... I-6
Roland ... F-7
Rolling Hill Dr. ... B-8
Rollins Ave. ... H-8
Romany Rd. ... G-3
Rose ... D-1
Rosetta ... C-2
Rosewood ... J-8
Roslyn Ave. ... C-2,D-2
Roswell Ave. ... J-4
Rothwood Dr. ... K-6
Royal Ct. ... F-3
Rozzelles Ferry
Rd. ... D-2
Runnymede ... K-4
Rush ... D-1
Russell Ave. ... C-3
Rutgers Ave. ... B-7
Rutledge ... K-7
St. Andrews Ln. ... F-7
St. Bernard ... C-6
St. George St. ... G-7
St. John ... B-3
St. Luke ... B-3
St. Mark ... B-3
St. Paul ... B-3
Samuel ... B-4
Sandalwood Rd. ... H-6
Sanders ... C-2
Sandridge ... K-1
Salem Dr. ... I-3
Scaleybark ... I-1
School St. ... F-6
Scotland Ave. ... I-5
Scott Ave. ... H-3
Sedgefield ... I-2
Sedgewood ... J-6
Seldon Dr. ... C-2
Selwyn Ave. ... K-3,I-4
Senior ... B-2
September Ln. ... D-1
Service St. ... B-5
Shamrock ... E-8
Sharon Ave. ... K-5
Sharon Lane ... K-6
Shawee Dr. ... I-2
Shenandoah Ave. ... G-6
Sherwood ... I-4
Shoreham Dr. ... K-6
Silabert Ave. ... I-8
Simplicity ... B-5
Simpson Dr. ... E-7
Skyland Ave. ... H-6
Skyview Rd. ... F-1
Sloan St. ... I-1
Smallwood ... C-2
Smith St. ... E-4
Snow White Ln. ... B-8
Sofley Rd. ... B-7
Solomon ... D-2
Somerset Dr. ... I-3
South Blvd. ... G-2,H-2
Southwest Blvd. ... B-2
Southwood ... F-2
Sparrow Mill Rd. ... D-3
Spencer ... D-7
Spratt St. ... D-4
Spring St. ... D-4
Springdale ... H-2
Springview Rd. ... B-8
Spruce St. ... F-1
Squirrel Hill Rd. ... A-8
Stafford ... K-8
Stancill Pl. ... I-6
Stanley Ave. ... H-7
Stanford Pl. ... I-4
Starita Rd. ... A-6
State St. ... D-2
Statesville Ave. . . B-4,D-4
Sterling Rd. ... J-3
Stevens Seigle ... F-5
Stoneybrook Rd. ... E-7
Stonewall, E. ... F-3
Stonewall, W. ... F-3
Stratford ... E-7
Suffolk Pl. ... J-6
Sugar Creek ... C-7
Sugar Creek Rd. ... C-8
Summitt Ave. ... D-3,E-2
Summit Ave., W. ... F-2
Sumter ... D-2
Sunderland ... J-5
Sunnyside Ave. ... F-5
Sunset Dr. ... I-2
Suttle Ave. ... F-1
Sutton ... B-2
Sycamore ... E-3
Sylvania ... D-5
Syracuse Dr. ... B-2
Tangle Dr. ... J-8
Tanglewood Ln. ... J-5
Tappan Pl. ... D-7
Tate ... C-2
Taylor Ave. ... B-3
Television Ln. ... H-7
Templeton ... G-3
Tennessee ... B-1
Terrybrook Ln. ... D-8
Thackery ... G-8
The Plaza ... D-7
Thera Dr. ... B-7
Thomas ... F-6
Thornwood Dr. ... A-8
Thrift Rd. ... E-1
Thrush Ln. ... A-6
Tippan Ave. ... F-6
Toal St. ... B-5
Tom Hunter Rd. ... A-8
Toomey Ave. ... G-1
Topaz St. ... B-6
Topsfield Rd. ... I-8
Torrence St. ... G-4
Townes Rd. ... J-3
Trade St. ... D-2,F-4
Trade St., E. ... F-4
Trade St., W. ... E-3
Tranquil ... J-3
Tremont ... G-2,G-3
Trentwood ... A-3
Trinity Pl. ... K-7
Truman Rd. ... F-7
Tryclan ... I-1
Tryon St., N. ... C-7,E-4
Tryon St., S. ... F-3,H-1
Tuckoseegee Rd. ... E-2
Turner Ave. ... D-2
Twiford Pl. ... I-5
Twinfield ... A-2
Tyngway ... J-6
Tyson St. ... I-1
University ... J-1
Unstead St. ... E-6
Van Buren ... D-3
Van Every St. ... F-5
Van Ness ... H-5
Vance, E. ... F-3
Vance, W. ... F-3
Vancouver ... A-8
Vanderbuilt ... C-4,F-5
Vane Ct. ... B-5
Vanizer ... D-1
Vernon Dr. ... J-6
Victoria ... E-3
Vine ... D-2
Vinewood ... H-7
Vinton ... C-3
Virginia Ave. ... E-7
Waco St. ... G-4
Waddell St. ... C-3
Wadsworth ... E-5
Wainwright ... B-4
Wakefield ... K-3
Wales ... J-3
Walnut Ave. ... E-2
Walter Oak Rd. ... J-7
Ware St. ... B-5
Warp St. ... C-7
Washburn Ave. ... H-7
Washington St. ... C-3
Washington, W. ... G-2
Waterbury ... J-2
Webster Pl. ... I-1
Weddington ... G-6
Wedgewood Dr. ... K-2
Weldon ... D-8
Welker ... G-4
Wellesley Ave. ... I-4
Wellingford St. ... B-8
Wells St. ... C-5
Wembley Dr. ... G-7
Wendover Rd. ... J-5
Wendwood Ln. ... I-6
Wenworth Pl. ... K-2
Wesley ... D-7
Westbrook ... E-3
Westbury Rd. ... K-6
Westfield Rd. ... J-3
Westminster ... J-4
Westmoreland St. ... G-7
Westover St. ... G-6
Wheatley Ave. ... I-6
Whisnant ... D-3
Whitby Ln. ... J-7
Whitehaven ... D-2
White Oak ... K-1
White Plains Rd. ... A-8
Whiting ... D-7
Wickford ... G-2
Willow Oak Rd. ... J-3
Wilmore Dr. ... F-2
Wilson Ave. ... A-3
Wilson Ln. ... A-7
Windemere Ln. ... J-8
Windingwood ... K-4
Windsor Ave. ... I-3
Windsor Dr. ... K-4
Winnifred ... F-2
Winston ... C-5
Winston Dr. ... D-7
Winter St. ... F-7
Wintergreen Pl. ... K-6
Winthrop ... H-2
Wolfberry ... D-5
Wolfe ... F-7
Wonderwood Dr. ... K-7
Woodcrest ... G-2
Woodhaven Ln. ... K-5
Woodland ... G-8
Woodlawn Rd. ... K-1,K-3
Woodlark Ln. ... J-7
Woodruff Pl. ... E-2
Woodside Ave. ... D-6
Woodvale ... D-2
Wood Valley ... A-2
Woodward Ave. ... C-4
Worthington Ave. ... G-3
Woyt St. ... C-4
Wren ... F-1
Wrenwood ... J-6
Wright Ave. ... J-8
Wriston ... I-2
Wyanoke ... G-6
Yale Pl. ... I-3
Yellowstone ... D-1
Yonkers ... B-6
Yorkshire ... I-1
Youngblood ... H-1
Yuma St. ... A-8,B-8
1st ... G-4
1st, E. ... F-3
1st St., W. ... E-2,F-3
2nd St., E. ... F-3
2nd St., W. ... E-2,F-3
3rd St., E. ... F-3
3rd, W. ... E-3
4th St., E. ... F-4
4tth St., W. ... E-2,E-3
4th St. Ext. ... E-2
5th St., E. ... F-4,G-5
5th, W. ... E-3
6th St., E. ... F-4
6th, W. ... E-3
7th St ... G-5
7th St., E. ... E-4
7th, W. ... E-3
8th St., E. ... E-4,G-5
8th St., W. ... E-4
9th St., E. ... E-4,G-6
9th St., W. ... E-4
10th St. ... F-5
10th St., E. ... E-4
10th St., W. ... E-4
11th St., E. ... E-4
11th St., W. ... D-3,E-4
12th St. ... E-4
12th St., W. ... D-3
13th St., E. ... E-5
15th St. ... E-4
15th St., E. ... E-5
16th St., E. ... E-5
17th St., E. ... E-5
18th St., E. ... E-6
19th, E. ... E-5
19th St., E. ... E-6
20th, E. ... E-5
20th St., E. ... E-6
21st, E. ... E-5
22nd, E. ... E-5
23rd, E. ... D-5
24th, E. ... E-6
24th St., W. ... D-5
25th, E. ... D-6
26th, E. ... D-6
26th, W. ... D-5
27th, E. ... D-6
27th, W. ... D-5
28th St., E. ... D-6
28th, W. ... D-6
29th, W. ... C-6
30th St., W. ... C-6
31st, W. ... C-6
32nd St. ... D-6
32nd St., W. ... C-6
33rd St., E. ... D-6
34th St., E. ... D-6
35th St., E. ... D-7
36th St., E. ... D-7
37th St., E. ... D-7

POINTS OF INTEREST

Independence Park . . G-5
Revolution Park ... G-1

Charlotte, NC

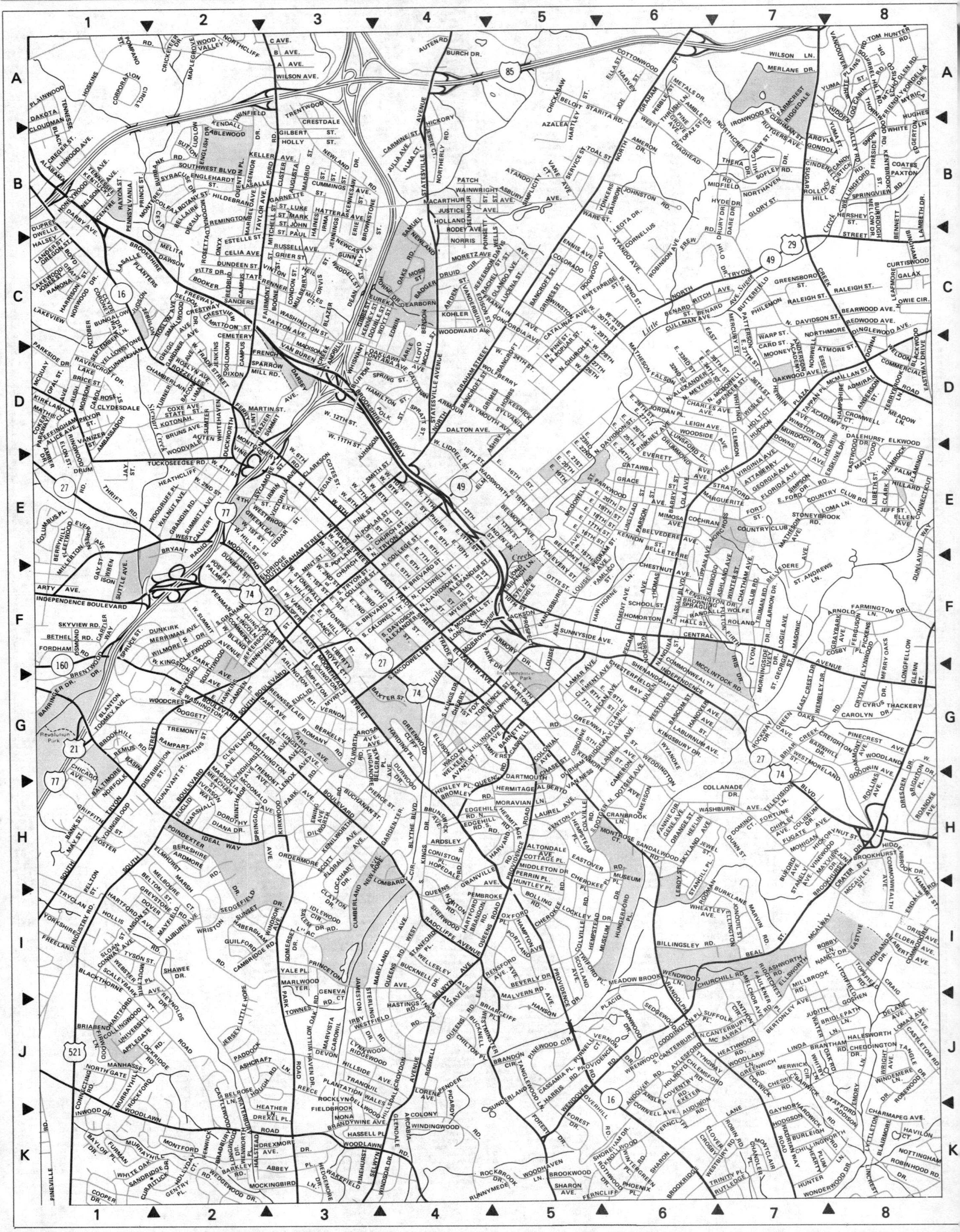

Scale of Miles 0 .2 .4 .6 .8

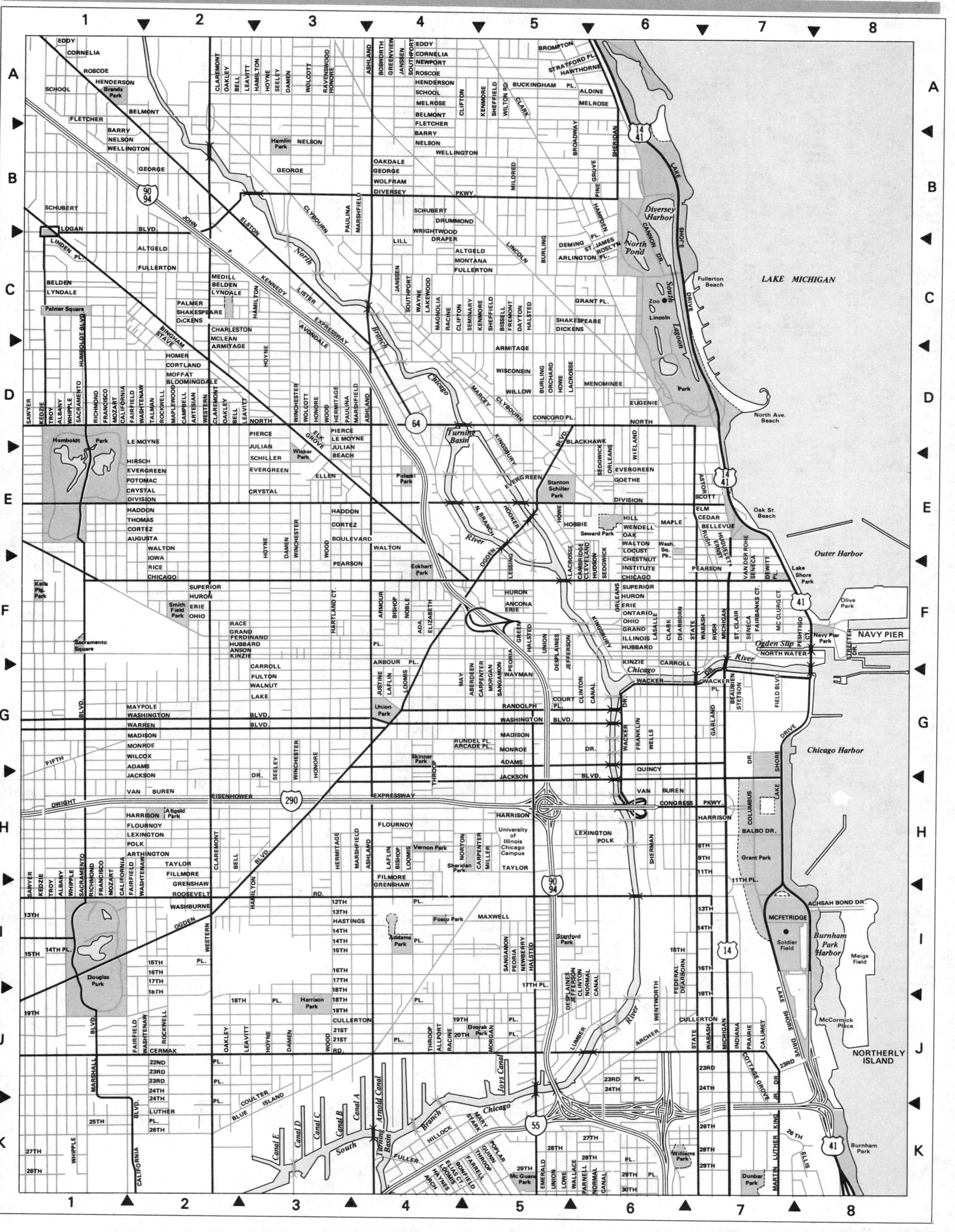

Chicago, IL

CHICAGO

Aberdeen G-5
Achsah Bond Dr. I-8
Ada F-4
Adams G-2,G-5
Albany D-1,H-1
Aldine A-6
Allport J-4
Altgeld C-2,C-4
Ancona F-5
Anson F-2
Arbour Pl. F-4
Arcade Pl. G-4
Arch K-4
Archer J-6
Arlington Pl. C-5
Armitage D-2,D-5
Armour F-4
Artesian D-2
Arthington H-2
Ashland A-4,D-4,H-4
Astor E-7
Augusta Blvd. E-2
Avondale C-3
Balbo Dr. H-7
Barry A-1,B-4
Beach E-3
Beaubien Ct. G-7
Belden C-1,C-2
Bell A-2,D-2,H-2
Bellevue E-7
Belmont A-1,A-4
Bingham C-2
Bishop F-4,H-4
Bissell A-5,C-5
Blackhawk D-5
Bloomingdale D-2
Blue Island K-2
Bonfield K-4
Bosworth A-4
Branch, N. E-5
Broadway B-5
Brompton A-5
Buckingham Pl. A-5
Burling C-5,D-5
California D-1,H-1
California Blvd. K-2
Calumet J-7
Campbell D-2
Canal G-6,I-6,K-6
Cannon Dr. B-6
Carpenter G-5,H-5
Carroll F-3,F-6
Cedar E-7
Cermack Rd. J-2
Charleston C-2
Chestnut E-6
Chicago F-2,F-6
Claremont A-2,D-2,H-2
Clark A-5,F-6
Clifton A-4,C-4
Clinton G-6,I-6
Clybourn B-3,D-5
Columbus Dr. H-7
Concord Pl. D-5
Congress Pkwy. H-6
Cornelia A-1,A-4
Cortez E-2,E-3
Cortland D-2
Cottage Grove J-7
Coulter J-3
Court Pl. G-5
Crystal E-2,E-3
Cullerton J-3,J-7
Damen A-3,E-3,J-3
Dayton C-5
Dearborn F-6,I-6
Deming Pl. C-5
Deming St. C-5
Des Plaines F-5,J-5
Dewitt Pl. F-7
Dickens C-2,C-5
Diversey Pkwy. B-4
Division E-2,E-6
Draper C-4
Drummond B-4
Dwight Eisenhower Expwy. H-1-5
Eddy A-1,A-4
Elias Ct. K-4
Elizabeth F-4
Elk Grove D-3
Ellen E-3
Ellis K-8
Elm E-7
Elston B-2
Emerald K-5
Erie F-2,F-5,F-6
Ernst E-7
Eugene D-6
Evergreen E-2,E-3,E-5,E-6
Fairbanks Ct. F-7
Fairfield D-1,H-1,J-2
Farrell K-5
Federal I-6
Ferdinand F-2
Fifth G-1
Fillmore H-2,H-4
Fletcher A-1,A-4
Flournoy H-2,H-4
Francisco D-1,H-1
Franklin G-6
Fremont C-5
Fuller K-4
Fullerton C-2,C-4
Fulton G-3
Garland G-7
George B-2,B-3,B-4
Goethe E-6
Grand F-2,F-6
Grant Pl. C-6
Green F-5
Greenview A-4
Grenshaw H-1,I-4
Haddon E-2,E-3
Halsted C-5,F-5,I-5
Hamilton A-3,C-3,I-3
Hampden B-6
Harrison H-2,H-5,H-7
Hartland Ct. F-3
Hastings I-3
Hawthorne A-5
Haynes K-4
Henderson A-1,A-4
Hermitage D-3,H-3
Hill E-6
Hillock K-4
Hirsch E-2
Hobbie E-5
Homer D-2
Honore A-3,D-3,G-3
Hooker E-5
Howe D-5,E-5
Hoyne A-3,D-3,E-3,J-3
Hubbard Pl. F-2,F-6
Huguelet E-7
Humboldt Blvd. D-1
Huron F-2,F-5,F-6
Illinois F-6
Indiana J-7
Institute F-6
Iowa E-2
Jackson Blvd. H-5
Jackson Dr. H-2
James C-6
Janssen A-4,C-4
Jefferson F-5,I-5
John F. Kennedy Expwy. B-2,C-3
Julian D-3
Justine G-4
Kedzie D-1,H-1
Kenmore A-5,C-5
Kingsbury D-5,F-6
Kinzie F-2,F-6
La Crosse D-5,F-5
Laflin G-4,H-4
Lake G-3
Lake Shore Dr. B-6,G-7
Lakewood C-4
La Salle F-6
Leavitt A-2,D-2,J-3
Le Moyne D-2,D-3
Lessing F-5
Lexington H-2,H-6
Lill C-4
Lincoln C-5
Linden Pl. C-1
Lister C-3
Locust E-6
Logan Blvd. B-1
Loomis G-4,H-4,K-4
Lowe K-5
Lumber J-6
Luther C-2
Lyndale C-1,C-2
Madison G-2,G-5
Magnolia C-4
Maple E-6
Maplewood D-2
Marcey D-5
Marshall Blvd. J-1
Marshfield B-3,D-3,H-4
Martin Luther King, Jr. Dr. K-7
Mary K-5
Maxwell I-5
May G-4
Maypole G-2
McClurg F-7
McLean C-2
Medill C-2
Melrose A-4,A-6
Menominee D-6
Michigan F-7,J-7
Mildred B-5
Miller H-5
Moffat D-2
Monroe G-2,G-5
Montana C-4
Morgan G-5,J-5
Mozart D-1,H-1
Nelson B-1,B-3,B-4
Newberry I-5
Newport A-4
Noble F-4
Normal I-6,K-6
North D-3,D-6
North Water F-7
Norton H-4
Oak E-6
Oakdale B-4
Oakley A-2,D-2,J-2
Ogden Blvd. I-2,E-5
Ohio F-2,F-6
Ontario F-6
Orchard D-5
Orleans E-6,F-6
Palmer C-2
Parnell K-6
Paulina B-3,D-3
Pearson F-3,F-7
Peoria F-5,I-5
Peshtigo Ct. F-8
Pierce D-3
Pine Grove B-6
Polk H-2,H-6
Poplar K-5
Potomac E-2
Prairie J-7
Quincy G-6
Quinn K-5
Race F-2
Racine C-4,J-4
Randolph G-5
Ravenswood A-3
Rice F-2
Richmond D-1,H-1
Rockwell D-2,J-2
Roosevelt Rd. I-2
Roscoe A-1,A-4
Roslyn C-6
Rundel Pl. G-4
Rush F-7
Sacramento Blvd. D-1,H-1
Sangamon G-5,I-5
Sawyer D-1,H-1
Schiller E-3
School A-1,A-4
Schubert B-1,B-4
Scott E-7
Sedgwick E-6,F-6
Seeley A-3,G-3
Seminary C-4
Seneca F-7
Shakespeare C-2,C-5
Sheffield A-5,C-5
Sheridan B-6
Sherman H-6
Southport A-4,C-4
St. Clair F-7
Stark K-5
Stave C-2
Stratford Pl. A-5
Streeter Dr. F-8
State F-7,J-7
Superior F-2,F-6
Talman D-2
Taylor H-2,H-5
Thomas E-2
Throop H-4,J-4,K-5
Troy D-1,H-1
Union F-5,K-5
Van Buren H-2,H-6
Wabash F-7,J-7
Wacker Dr. G-6
Wallace K-5
Walnut G-3
Walton E-2,E-4,E-6
Warren Blvd. G-2
Washburne I-2
Washington Blvd. G-2,G-5
Washtenaw D-2,H-2,J-2
Wayman G-5
Wayne C-4
Wellington B-1,B-4
Wells G-6
Wendell E-6
Wentworth J-6
Western D-2,I-2
W. Lake Shore Dr. I-7,J-7
Whipple D-1,H-1,K-1
Wieland D-6
Wilcox G-2
Willow D-5
Winchester D-3,E-3,G-3
Wisconsin D-5
Wolcott A-3,D-3
Wolfram B-4
Wood D-3,E-3,J-3
Wrightwood B-4
8th H-7
9th H-7
11th H-7
11th Pl. H-7
12th Pl. I-3
13th I-1,I-3,I-7
14th I-3,I-7
14th Pl. I-1
15th I-1,I-3,I-6
15th Pl. I-2
16th I-2,I-3,I-7
17th I-2,I-3
17th Pl. I-5
18th J-2,J-7,I-3
18th Pl. J-2,J-3
19th J-1,J-3
19th Pl. J-4
20th Pl. J-4
21st J-3
21st Pl. J-3
22nd Pl. J-2
23rd J-2,J-7
23rd Pl. J-2,J-6
24th J-2,J-6,J-7
24th Pl. J-2
25th Pl. K-1
26th K-2,K-7
27th K-1,K-6
28th K-1,K-5,K-7
28th Pl. K-6
29th K-5,K-7
29th Pl. K-6
30th K-6

POINTS OF INTEREST

Adams Park I-4
Altgeld Park H-2
Brands Park A-1
Douglas Park I-1
Dunbar Park K-7
Dvorak Park J-5
Eckhart Park F-4
Fosco Park I-4
Grant Park H-7
Hamlin Park B-3
Harrison Park J-3
Humboldt Park D-1
Kells Plg. Park F-1
Lake Shore Park F-7
Lincoln Park C-6
McGuane Park K-5
Navy Pier Park F-8
Pulaski Park E-4
Seward Park E-6
Sheridan Park H-4
Skinner Park G-4
Smith Field Park F-2
Stanford Park I-5
Stanton Schiller Park E-5
Union Park G-4
Vernon Park H-4
Washington Sq. Park E-6
Wicker Park E-3
Williams Park K-6

CINCINNATI

Adela K-1
Adler E-1
Agnes A-1
Alabama C-2
Alaska Ave. B-7
Alaska Ct. A-7
Albion F-6
Alfred E-2
Alpine F-8
Altamont J-3
Alter A-8
Altoonia D-8
Alvin F-6
Amor F-1
Ann H-4,K-8
Armory G-4
Ash J-2
Atkinson E-5
Auburn F-6
Auburncrest E-6
Audrey F-6
Augusta St. J-5
Avon D-2
Back G-5
Bader D-3
Bains G-8
Baltimore D-1
Bank F-3
Barker A-7
Barnard F-3
Bates C-2
Bathgate D-7
Bauer G-4
Baumer H-7
Baymiller F-3
Beech I-8
Beecher D-8
Beekman E-1
Beekman St. C-1
Beldare B-5
Bella Vista F-7
Bellevue E-6,J-3
Belsaw Pl. A-4
Bethesda C-6
Betts H-4
Biddle B-5
Bigelow F-6
Bishop C-5
Blackwell K-5
Blaine E-1
Blair C-8
Blair Conn. C-8
Bleeker D-1
Boal G-6
Bodmann C-4
Bogart B-8
Bond J-3
Boone E-7
Borden A-1
Borrman D-7
Bosley E-5
Boston H-1
Bowdle B-3
Bowman D-7,G-1
Branch E-1
Braxton C-8
Brent Spence Bridge J-4
Broadway I-6
Brookline B-5
Bryant B-4
Buck E-3
Budd I-3
Buenavista D-8
Burbank E-7
Burgoyne E-1
Burlington D-2
Burnett D-7,F-6
Burns I-1
Burton A-8
Butler I-7,J-1
Byron F-4
Calhoun E-5
Calumet F-5
Camden A-7
Canyon A-1
Carll D-1
Carmalt F-6
Carneal J-2
Carney H-7
Carplin C-7
Catherine C-7
Celestial H-7
Central E-3,F-4,K-7
Central Bridge J-7
Central Pkwy. B-2,H-5
Chalfonte B-6
Channing G-6
Chappel D-8
Charles H-5
Charlotte G-3
Charlton E-6
Chestnut H-5,K-7
Chickasaw E-4
Church K-1
Clark H-4,K-3
Claypole G-1
Clearwater F-3
Cleveland C-8
Cleveland Ave. C-8
Cliff E-5,G-8
Clinton G-4
Clifton B-4
Clifton Crest B-3
Clifton Hills B-3
Clifton Hills Terr. B-3
Clifton View C-3
Cloister C-5
Clybourn E-3
C & O Bridge J-5
Colfrain D-3,F-3
Columbia K-8
Concord E-2
Concordia D-7
Conroy F-3
Convention Way I-5
Cook E-3
Coon E-4
Copelin E-8
Cornell B-4
Cormany C-3
Corry E-6
Cortlandt G-3
Court H-4,H-5,J-6
Craig K-5
Crescent K-4
Crescent, N. A-8
Crescent, S. A-8
Crestmont B-5
Crooked Stone B-3
Cross E-8
Crown E-7
Culvert H-6
Cumber G-6
Cumberland E-6
Cummins D-2
Curtis E-8
Cutter H-4
Cypress Garden A-4
Dalton H-3,I-3
Dandridge G-6
Daniels D-6
Daves J-1
David G-4
Dawson A-1
Dayton F-4,J-8
Deerfield F-7
Delleva A-5
Dellway C-8
Dempsey D-1
Denman G-3
Dennis E-5
Depot H-1
Detzel E-5
Deverhill K-1
Devotie D-3,D-4
Dick B-6
Digby D-4
Dirr A-1
Division K-3
Dixmyth C-3
Donahue D-6
Dorsey G-6
Dover E-7
Draper E-2
Dreman A-1
Drexel C-8
Duke D-3
Duluth B-5
Dunkirk A-6
Dunlap F-4
Dunore B-3
Dury C-6
Earnshaw F-4
Eden B-6,E-6
Edgehill A-8
Edinburg F-6
Edmunds D-7
Eggleston H-6
Ehrman B-6
Eighth K-7
Eighth St. H-5
Eighth St. Viaduct H-2
Elam C-2,D-2
Eleanor F-5
Eleventh K-8
Elgin G-7
Eliza E-3
Elizabeth H-4
Elland C-6
Elland Cir. C-6
Elliot D-4
Elm J-1,K-1,K-5,K-7
Elmore Ct. A-2
Elmore St. A-1
Elsinore G-7
Elysian D-5
Emma B-1
Emming F-4
English St. F-5
Erkenbrecker C-6
Ernst A-6
Esmond F-3
Essex E-7
Estelle F-6
Ethan C-2
Euclid C-6,D-6,J-1
Eupeka F-5
Eutaw A-6
Evans H-1
Evanswood B-4
Evening Star C-3
Eyre A-4
Fairmont E-1
Fairview A-6
Fairview Pl. F-3
Faulkner G-3
Fifth J-7,K-5
Fifth St. H-7,I-3,I-5
Filson H-7
Findlay G-3,G-5
Fitzpatrick E-4
Flora E-8
Florence F-8
Flint G-3
Follett A-1
Forest J-1,K-3
Forest Park B-7
Foretaker D-8
Fortune E-4
Fort View H-7
Fosdick D-6
Foulke F-3
Fourth J-7,K-5,K-6
Fourth St. I-5
Forest Ave. B-6
Fourteenth H-5
Fort Washington Way I-6
Fox B-1
Francisco F-8
Frank G-6
Fredonia D-8
Freeman F-3,J-3
Freeman Ave. I-1
Fricke B-1
Front St. I-7
Fuller H-7
Fulton F-8
Gage F-5
Gano C-4
Garrard D-2,K-6
George I-5
Genessee H-5
Gerard D-6
Gest H-1,I-5
Gholson B-7
Gilbert C-8,H-6
Glencoe F-6
Glendora C-5,D-6
Gleneste A-6
Glenmary B-5
Glenridge A-6
Glenwood J-1
Glenwood Ave. A-6,B-7
Gilbert D-8
Goeth G-6
Goodman D-6
Graham F-5
Grand St. I-5
Greendale A-5
Greenhill A-5
Greenup E-6
Greenwood A-8
Gregory G-7
Guido G-7
Hale C-6
Hallwood C-7
Halmar D-3
Halstead E-3
Hamer G-5
Hammond H-6
Harriet I-3
Harrison F-3
Hartford C-8
Hartshorn E-5
Hastings F-3
Hatch H-8
Hathaway J-3
Hatmaker I-1
Haven B-6
Hazen K-2
Hearne C-6
Hebron A-1
Hedgegrow B-4
Helen E-6,K-1
Hemlock E-7
Henry F-5
Henshaw C-2,D-3
Herman E-4
Heywood D-3
Hickman C-7
Hickory B-7
High K-3
Highland E-6,G-6
Hill H-7,K-3
Hillcrest J-3
Hilton E-6
Hollister E-5
Hooper J-1
Hopkins H-1,H-3
Hopple Ct. D-1
Hopple St. Viaduct D-1
Hosea C-5
Howard K-1
Howard Taft E-6
Howell C-3
Hughes G-5
Hulbert C-3
Hull D-4
Huntington F-6
Hutchins B-8
Highway Ave. K-3
Ida G-7
Iowa E-7
Imperial D-5
Intervine B-5
Interwood Ave. B-5
Inwood E-6
Iroquois E-1
Irving B-6
Isabella K-7
Jackson H-5
James E-8
Jay C-7
Jean F-1
Jefferson C-5,D-5
Jerome H-7
Jessamine D-2
John G-4,K-3,K-8
John St. I-5
Johnson K-5
Joselin D-4
Josephine G-6
Juergens A-5
Juliaann C-3
June E-7
Justis F-5
Kasota F-8
Kemper E-8,F-8
Kenner G-3,J-1
Kenton E-7
Kerper D-8
Keturah K-7
Kilgour H-7
Kindel F-3
Kinsey E-6
Klotter F-3,F-4
Koebel F-3
Kottman E-3
Knob C-1
Knott C-7
Knox E-2
Lafayette A-3,A-4
Lafayette Cir. A-5
Lafayette Ln. A-5
Lake K-1
Lakewood D-5
Lakes F-8
Landon C-7
Lane F-1
Lange G-5
Laredo E-8
Larona B-6
Latta J-1
Lauk A-5
Laurel K-1
Lawson Ct. I-6
Leblie C-2
Lee B-8
Lehman G-1
Leroy F-6
Lexington B-8,I-8,J-3
Liberty G-3,G-4,K-7
Liberty Hill G-6
Library H-5
Lidell E-1
Lillie B-1
Lincoln D-8
Lincoln Park Dr. H-4
Lincoln Pl. D-8
Linden D-1,J-1,K-1
Lindsey K-7
Linton D-7
Lionel F-1
Livingston G-3,J-3
Llewellyn A-1
Lloyd E-3
Lock St. H-7
Lockhurst G-3
Locust J-2
Logan G-4
Lorraine B-5
Lossing B-8
Loude G-7
Louis C-6
Lowell C-3,K-7
L & N Bridge I-7
Ludford K-1
Ludlow J-2
Ludlow Ave. B-3
Luna E-4
Luray F-8
Lyleburn B-4
Lyon E-5
MacAuley E-6
Madison K-6
Malvern F-6
Main G-5,K-5
Maiseldeckebach D-3
Manchester F-4
Mantiou F-7
Mann B-8
Manor Hill B-3
Mansfield G-8
Maple C-7
Maplewood F-6
Marmet C-5
Marquis F-7
Marshall D-3
Martin G-8
Maryland I-1
Mason F-5,K-2
Massachusetts D-3
Mathers D-8
May St. E-7
McAlpin B-3
McAlpin Pl. B-3
McCormick E-6
McFarland I-5
McGregor F-7
McGregory F-7
McLean F-3
McMicken E-3,F-3
McMillan E-4
Meadow A-5
Meeker D-2
Mehring J-5
Mehring Way I-3
Melbourne C-8
Melish D-6
Melrose E-8
Memorial I-1
Mentor D-8
Mercer G-5
Mill H-4
Mill Creek Expwy. C-3
Millvale Ct. B-1
Milton C-8,G-6
Minnesota E-7
Mistletoe G-1
Moerlein E-5
Mohawk Pl. F-4
Mohawk St. F-4
Montclair J-2
Monfort D-8
Monmouth C-2,J-8
Monroe F-7,J-8
Montrose J-2
Moore G-5
Moosewood C-1
Morgan C-6
Morrison B-3
Mound St. H-4
Mulberry F-5
Muriel E-4
Myrtle E-8
Nassau F-8
Neave I-8
Nelson I-8
Nevada H-1
New St. H-6
Neyer B-1
Ninth K-7
Ninth St. H-5
Nixon C-5
Northeast Expwy. I-5
Northern B-6
Northern Blvd. C-1
Norway A-7
Norwich Ln. A-6
Oak D-6,E-8,E-7,K-1,J-1
Odeon G-5
Old Ludlow B-3
Oliver G-4
Omaha D-7
Orchard K-8
Oregon St. H-7
Ormond C-4
Osterfield F-1
Overton J-8
Oxford C-5
Paradome G-7
Parchman A-6
Paris E-6
Park E-8,J-8,K-1
Parker F-4
Parkside G-7
Parson H-8
Patchen I-7
Patterson F-3
Pavillion H-7
Peete F-5
Peggie I-1
Pendleton H-6
Perkins C-8
Perr I-5
Philadelphia K-5
Piedmont D-6
Pike K-6
Pike St. I-7
Pinetree E-1
Pleasant G-5
Plum H-5
Polk E-5
Poplar G-3,J-1
Post J-2
Postal I-6
Powers Ave. A-1
Powers Pl. A-1
Powers St. A-2
Probasco D-4
Produce St. J-5
Prospect C-7
Providence G-4
Prior H-5
Pulte D-1
Purdue B-6
Putnam K-8
Queen E-1
Race G-5
Rachel D-3
Ralston B-1
Randolph B-5
Rankin E-1
Ravine F-4
Rawson Woods Cir. A-4
Rawson Woods Ln. B-4
Reading E-7,H-6
Reedy H-6
Renner F-4
Renner St. F-4
Renshaw E-5
Republic G-5
Resor Pl. B-4
Revel A-7
Rice F-5
Richmond St. H-4
Riddle D-3
Riddle Crest C-4
Riddleview D-4
Ridge K-3
Ridgeway C-7
Ringgold G-6,J-1
River Rd. J-2
Riverside I-8,J-6
Robert J-8
Rochelle D-6
Rockdale B-6
Rogers E-8
Rohs E-4
Roll A-1
Rose St. J-4
Rural A-5
Russell K-5
Ruther C-5
Ryan F-7
St. Clair D-5
St. Clair Ext. C-4
St. James F-8
St. Paul St. H-7
Sanford K-6
Saratoga G-1,J-8
Sassafras C-2
Sauer E-5
School D-7
Scioto D-5,E-5
Scott K-6
Second I-8,J-6,J-7
Second St. J-5
Seegar D-1
Seitz F-5
Selim F-1
Seminole D-6
Senator B-5
Sentinel H-6
Seventh K-6,K-7
Seventh St. I-4
Severn A-5
Shadewell Clara F-1
Shields C-6
Shelby G-1
Sherlock C-4
Sherman G-3
Shiloh B-4
Sidney C-3,D-3
Sinton F-8
Sixth K-6,K-7
Sixth St. Expwy. I-3
Slack G-6
Sloo I-1
Sohn F-4
Somerset J-1
South H-1
Southern F-6
South Gate J-7
Southview J-7
Spring G-6,K-3
Springs A-7
Springhouse A-7
Stokesay H-1
Stadium Dr. J-6
Stanton E-8
Storrs I-1
Staedler I-1
Stark F-4
State F-1
Sterrett G-1
Stetson D-6
Stewart C-7
Stonewall F-4
Stratford D-4,E-4
Straight E-3
Summer H-1
Sunset K-3
Suspension Bridge J-6
Sutter D-1
Swain J-4
Sycamore H-6
Sylvan A-1
Symmes E-7
Syracuse D-8
Tafel E-3
Tallant B-6
Taylor C-3
Telford B-4
Tennis D-7
Tenth K-8
Terrace C-3
Thill F-5
Third I-8,J-7,K-5,K-6
Third St. I-6
Thirteenth G-6
Thrall B-4
Tillotson E-4
Tower B-5
Townsend St. A-1
Townsend Pl. A-1
Township D-3
Tremont E-1
Trevor D-1
Twelfth St. H-6
Union D-7
University D-4,D-5
Uphill K-2
Valencia F-5
Valeroy F-6
Valley D-2,E-2
Valley View E-4
Vanantwerp Pl. B-7
Van Buren D-7
Van Lear E-5
Van Meter H-7
Vaughn D-6
Vernon D-7
Vestry E-4
Victor E-4
Victoria J-1
View J-3
View Ct. J-3
Vine A-6,E-6,G-5
Vinecrest B-5
Vinton E-1
Volker E-4
Wade G-3,G-4
Wagner D-4
Walker G-6
Wall A-6
Wallace G-1
Walnut G-5
Walter D-8
Wareham Dr. H-7
Warner E-4
Warren A-4
Washington B-7,J-8
Waverly E-1
Wayne E-7
Weber A-1
Webman B-1
Wehrman D-8
Wellington E-6
Wentworth C-5
Wesley St. H-4
West E-4
Western F-3,K-4
Western Hills Viaduct E-2
Westwood E-1
Whatley H-1
Wheeler E-4
Whitefield B-4,C-4
Whiteman F-4
Whittaker H-8
Whittier C-7
Wilder H-1
Wilkinson F-7
Wm. Howard Taft E-8
Willow D-2
Wilstach G-3
Winchell F-3,G-3
Windham C-8
Windsor F-8
Winkler F-5
Wirham C-3
Wood Ave. B-4
Woodrow H-1
Woodside D-5
Woodward G-6
Woolper B-5
Wright K-4
Yale E-8
York F-3,G-3,K-8
Young G-6

POINTS OF INTEREST

Burnet Woods C-5
Coy Field & Playground D-4
Devon Park K-2
Dury Ave. Play Area B-6
Eden Park G-7
Fleischmann Gardens B-7
Goeber Park K-5
Haven Tot Lot B-6
Millvale Play Area B-1
Mt. Storm Park A-3
Rawson Woods B-4
Shirley Bonne Camp A-6
St. Clair Heights Park E-1
University of Cincinnati D-5
Windham Park C-8
Zoological Gardens B-6

Scale of Miles 0 .1 .2 .3 .4 .5

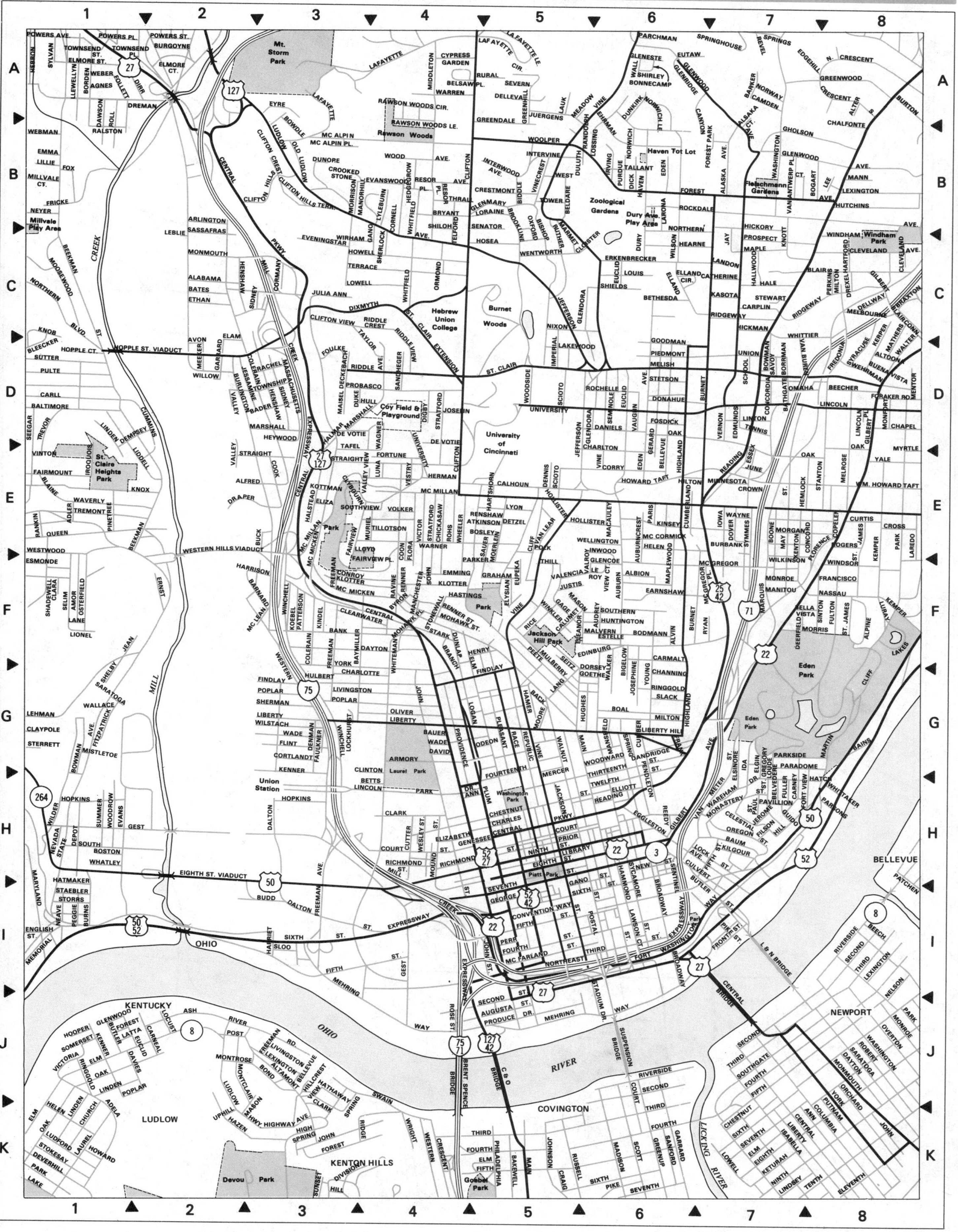

Scale of Miles
0 .1 .2 .3 .4
N

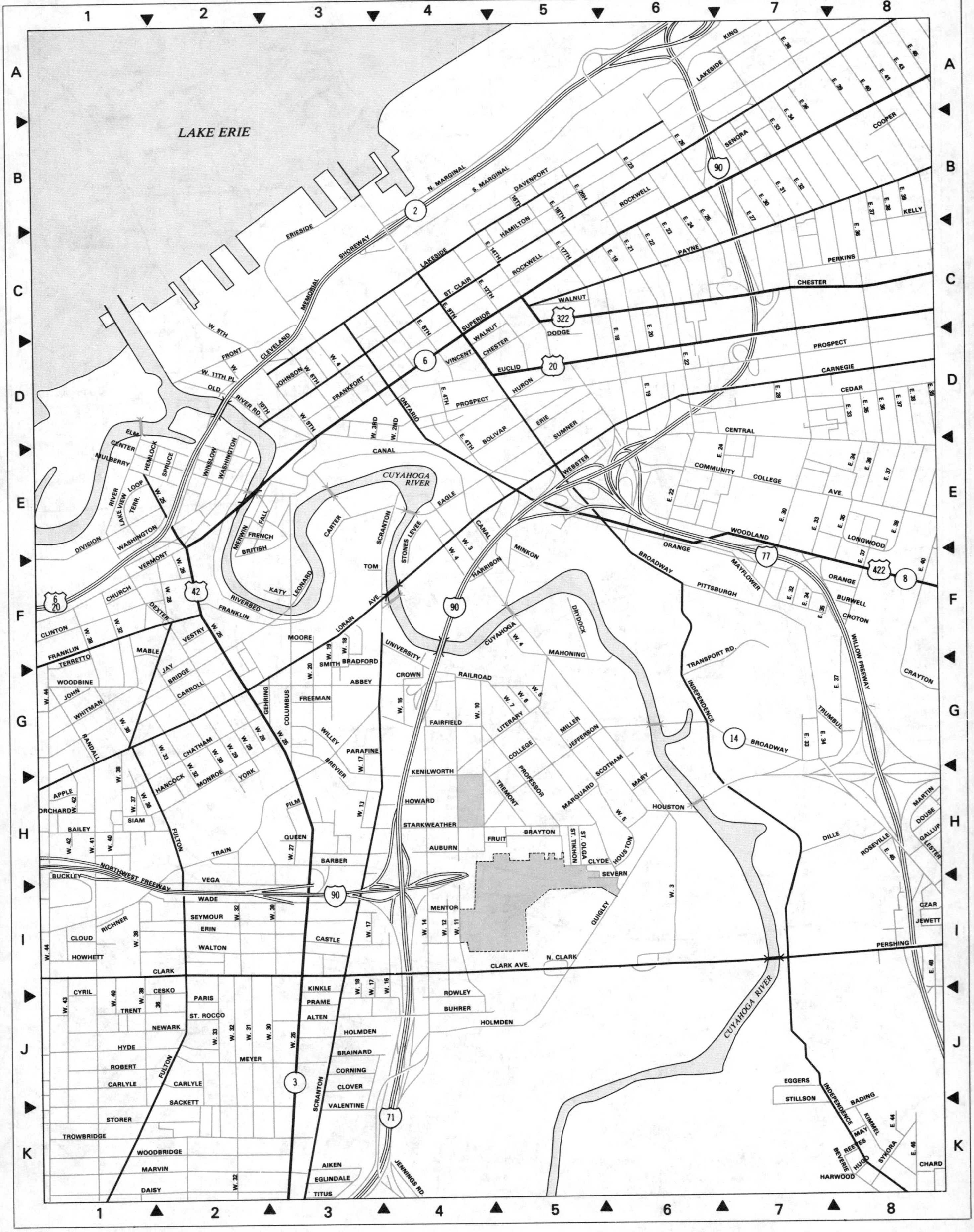

CLEVELAND

Abbey G-3
Aiken K-3
Alten J-3
Apple H-1
Auburn H-4
Bading K-8
Bailey H-1
Barber H-3
Beverie K-8
Bolivar D-5
Bradford F-3
Brainard J-3
Brayton H-5
Brevier G-3
Bridge G-2
British E-2
Broadway F-6,G-7
Buckley H-1
Buhrer J-4
Burwell F-8
Canal E-4
Carlyle J-1,J-2
Carnegie D-8
Carroll G-2
Carter E-3
Castle I-3
Cedar D-8
Center E-1
Central D-7
Cesko I-2
Chard K-8
Chatham G-2
Chester C-7,D-5
Church F-1
Clark I-2
Clark, N. I-5
Clark Ave. I-5
Cleveland Memorial
Shoreway C-3,D-3
Clinton F-1
Cloud I-1
Clover J-3
Clyde H-5
College G-5
Columbus G-3
Community College
Ave. E-7,E-8
Cooper B-8
Corning J-3
Crayton G-8
Croton F-8
Crown G-4
Cuyahoga F-5
Cyril I-1
Czar I-8
Daisy K-1
Davenport B-5
Dexter F-2
Dille H-7,H-8
Division E-1
Dodge C-5
Douse H-8
Drylock F-5
Eagle E-4
Eggers J-7
Eglindale K-3
Elm D-1
Erie D-5
Erieside B-3,C-3
Erin I-2
Euclid D-5
Fairfield G-4
Fall E-3
Film H-3
Frankfort D-3
Franklin F-1,F-2
Freeman G-3
French E-2
Front D-2
Fruit H-5
Fulton H-2,J-1
Gallup H-8
Gehring G-3
Hamilton B-5
Hancock H-2
Harrison F-5
Harwood K-8
Hemlock E-2
Holmden J-3
Houston H-6
Howard H-4
Howhett I-1
Hugo K-8
Huron D-5
Hyde J-1
Independence G-6,K-8
Jefferson G-5
Jennings Rd. K-4
Jewett I-8
John G-1
Johnson D-3
Katy F-3
Kelly B-8
Kenilworth H-4
Kimmel K-8
King A-7
Kinkle I-3
Lakeside A-6,A-7,C-4
Lakeview Loop
Terr. E-1
Leonard F-3
Literary G-5
Longwood E-8
Mable F-2
Mahoning F-5
Marginal, N. B-4
Marginal, S. B-5
Marquard H-5
Martin H-8
Marvin K-1
Mary H-6
May K-8
Mayflower F-7
Mentor I-4
Merwin E-2
Meyer J-2
Miller G-5
Minkon E-5
Monroe H-2
Moore F-3
Mulberry E-1
Newark J-2
Northwest Frwy. H-1
Old River Rd. D-2
Ontario D-4
Orange E-6,F-8
Orchard H-1
Parafine G-3
Paris J-2
Payne C-6
Perkins C-8
Pershing I-8
Pittsburgh F-6
Prame J-3
Professor H-5
Prospect D-4,D-8
Quigley I-5
Railroad G-4
Randall G-1
Reeves K-8
Robert J-1
Rockwell B-6,C-5
Roseville H-8
Rowley J-4
Richner I-1
River E-1
Riverbed F-2
Sackett J-2
St. Clair C-4
St. Olga H-5
St. Rocco J-2
St. Tikhon H-5
Scotham H-6
Scranton E-4,K-3
Senora B-7
Severn H-6
Seymour I-2
Siam H-1
Smith F-3
Spruce E-2
Starkweather H-4
Stillson K-7
Stones Levee E-4
Storer K-1
Summer D-5
Superior C-4
Sykora K-8
Terretto F-1
Titus K-3
Tom F-3
Train H-2
Transport Rd. F-6,F-7
Tremont H-5
Trent J-1
Trowbridge K-1
Trumbul G-7,G-8
University F-4
Valentine K-3
Vega H-2
Vermont F-1
Vestry F-2
Vincent D-4
York H-2
Wade I-2
Walnut C-4,C-5
Walton I-2
Washington E-1,E-2
Webster E-5
Whitman G-1
Willey G-3
Willow Freeway G-8
Winslow E-2
Woodbine G-1
Woodland E-7
Woodbridge K-1
2nd West D-4
3 West E-4,I-6
3rd West D-4
4th East D-4,E-5
4 West E-4
4th West D-4
5 West G-5,H-6
6th East C-4
6th West D-3,G-5
7 West G-5
9th East C-4
9th West C-2,D-3
10th West D-2,G-4
11 West I-4
11th Pl. West D-2
12th East C-5
12 West I-4
14th East C-5
14 West I-4
15 West G-4
16th B-5
16 West I-4
17th East C-5
17 West G-3,I-3
18th East B-5,C-6
18 West F-3,H-3,I-3
19 East C-6,D-6
19 West F-3
20 East C-6
20th East B-5
20 West G-3
21 East C-6
22 East C-6,D-6,E-6
23 East B-6,C-6
24 East E-7
24th East C-6
25 East B-7
25 West E-2,F-2,G-3,J-3
26 East B-6
26 West G-2
27 East B-7
27 West H-3
28 East D-7
28 West F-2,G-2
29 West G-2
30 East B-7,E-8
30 West G-2,I-3,J-3
31 East B-7
31 West J-2
32 East B-7,F-7
32 West F-1,G-2
I-2,J-2,K-2
33 East B-7,D-8,E-7,G-7
33 West G-2,J-2
35 East D-8,E-8,F-7
36 East A-7,C-8,D-8,E-8
36 West H-1,J-2
37 East B-8,D-8
E-8,F-8,G-7
37 West H-1
38 East A-7,B-8,D-8,E-8
38 West F-1,H-1,I-1
G-1,J-1
39 East A-8,B-8,D-7
40 East A-8,F-8
40 West H-1,J-1
41 East A-8
41 West H-1
42 West H-1
43 East A-8
43 West J-1
44 East K-8
44 West G-1,I-1
45 East A-8,H-8
46 East K-8
48 East I-8

COLUMBUS

Aberdeen Ave. B-5,B-6
Abner B-5
Ackerman Rd. C-2
Action Rd. A-3
Adams Ave. C-3
Advance J-7
Afton B-1
Agawam Cir. A-7
Agler B-8
Agler Rd. B-6
Akola Ave. B-4
Alamo Ave. B-4
Albert Ave. A-6
Alcott K-5
Alden C-4
Allegheny E-8
Allen G-5
Alum H-8
Alum Creek Dr. I-8
Alvason C-6
Amazon A-2
Amberly A-1
Amherst Ave. I-1
Arcadia C-3
Arden Rd. A-3
Ardmore Rd. F-8
Argyle D-7
Arlington B-4
Arlington Ave. B-5
Armstrong F-4
Ashbourne F-8
Ashdowne Rd. D-1
Ashland Ave. E-1
Astor G-8
Atcheson St. F-5
Atwood A-5,C-5
Atwood Ter. B-5
Auburn F-6
Audrey A-6
Audubon Rd. B-4
Avalon E-7,E-8
Avondale F-1,G-3
Avon Lea A-8
Azelda Ave. B-4
Baitz J-5
Bancroft St. C-6
Bar Harbor C-7
Bartha A-8
Barthman Ave. J-5
Bassett E-6
Baughman Ave. B-7
Beaumont Rd. D-1
Beautyview Ct. A-1
Beck St. H-5
Becker J-5
Bedford G-6
Belle St. G-6
Bellevue J-8
Bellevue Ave. J-8
Bellows Ave. H-2
Bellwood E-8
Belmont Ave. D-3
Belvidere I-1
Benfield Ave. K-5
Bernard B-1
Berrel C-6
Berrel Ave. B-6
Bethesda C-7
Beulah Rd. A-4
Bevis Rd. B-2
Bexford F-8
Bexley Park Rd. G-8
Birchmont A-1
Blake Ave. C-3,C-6
Blenkner H-4
Bluff Ave. F-1
Bonham D-4,D-5
Boston F-8
Boyleston A-7
Bradford B-1
Brehl Ave. H-2
Bremen A-5
Bremen St. A-5
Brentnell C-7
Brentnell Ave. C-7
Brentnell Blvd. B-7
Brentford Dr. D-1
Brentwood Rd. G-8
Bretton D-6
Brevoort A-3
Briarwood Ave. B-5
Brickel F-4
Bricker B-1
Bridgeview Dr. A-7
Bridgewalk A-7
Brighton B-2,B-4
Broad St. G-5
Broadbelt F-3
Brockton C-7
Brookcliff D-7
Brooksgerald D-5
Brown Rd. I-2
Brown Leaf Rd. J-2
Bruck H-5,J-5
Brunson F-7
Bryden Rd. G-5,G-8
Buckeye Park Rd. J-6
Buckingham F-4
Bulen Ave. K-7
Burley Dr. J-7
Burnbrae C-2
Burr F-2
Burrell F-2
Butler I-1
Buttles Ave. F-3
Cable G-2
Caldwell Ct. F-5
California Ave. B-3
Cambro I-8
Camden Ave. E-5
Campbell Ave. H-2
Caniff B-1
Capital St. G-5
Caralee Dr. B-8
Cardiff Rd. D-1
Carlisle Ave. A-4
Caroline A-5,E-8
Cassady A-8,F-8
Cassady Ave. K-8
Cassady Pl. B-8
Cassingham Rd. E-8,G-8
Castle K-5
Catherine H-2
Central H-2
Century Dr. B-7
Chambers Ave. E-1
Champion Ave. H-6
Charles G-8
Chauncy D-6
Chelford Dr. A-8
Chesapeake Ave. E-1
Chester E-7
Chestnut St. F-4
Cherry St. G-6
Chicago G-2
Chilcote C-4
Chittenden D-5
Chittenden Ave. D-4
Civic Center Dr. G-4
Claredon I-1
Clarendon Ave. H-1
Clark E-3,I-1
Clearview B-1
Cleveland A-6
Cleveland Ave. D-5,F-5
Clifton Ave. F-6,F-7
Clinton C-4,C-5
Clinton Heights Ave.
B-3
Cochrane J-5
Cole St. G-6
Colerain Ave. A-3
College Ave. G-8
College Hill Dr. C-1
Collins Ave. F-3
Columbia Ave. E-8
Columbian I-1
Columbus E-8,H-4
Columbus St. H-7
Commonwealth Park
N. F-7
Commonwealth Park S.
F-7
Como Ave. B-4
Como St. B-2
Coolidge H-3
Copeland F-2
Cordell C-6
Corr Rd. K-6
Corrugated E-4
Corvair I-8
Corwin E-6
Courtland E-4
Crestview Rd. B-3
Criswell Dr. A-1
Cullman K-5
Cumberland E-7
Curtis Ave. F-5
Cypress G-2
Dakota G-2
Dale F-8
Dale Ave. F-8
Dana Ave. H-2
Dartmouth E-7
Daugherty E-4
Davis Ave. G-3
Dawnlight Ave. B-7
Dawson E-8,F-8
Dayton C-3
Deckebach Rd. I-4
Delamere B-1
Deibert C-6,D-6
Delhi Ave. B-2
Delmar E-8
Delno B-5
Delray Rd. K-5
Delta, N. A-2
Deming Ave. C-4
Dennison F-4
Denune Ave. B-7
Denver F-8
Deporres D-7
Deshler Ave. I-5,I-7
Devonsh C-7
Dewberry Rd. K-7
Dewey D-6
Dick Ave. E-5
Dillward A-8
Dodridge St. C-2
Doone Dr. D-1
Doren H-1
Doris Ave. B-2
Doten E-2
Douglas G-6
Dover E-2
Dow E-4
Drake C-8
Dresden A-5
Dresden St. A-5
Drexel E-8
Drexel Ave. E-8
Drummond Island A-1
Dublin Ave. G-3
Dublin Rd. F-2
Dunbar Rd. A-6
Duncan C-3
Dunedin A-4,A-6
Dunedin Rd. A-3
Dunham I-1
Dunning C-7
DuPont Ave. E-5
Durham Dr. H-1
Duxberry Ave. C-4
Eagle Ave. K-6
Eakin Rd. I-1
Earl Ave. B-6
Earncliff A-8
East Ave. B-3,C-3
Eastfield Dr. N. J-1
Eastview E-2
Eastwood F-6
Eaton I-4
Eddyston A-4
Eddystone Ave. A-6
Edenburch C-7
Edgar B-4
Edgefield C-1
Edgehill Rd. E-2
Edsel K-7
Edwards St. F-5
Eisenhower Rd. A-4
Elda St. F-6
Eldorn I-7
Elm F-8
Elm St. G-4
Elmwood Ave. E-1
Elsmere H-5
Elwood J-6
Emerald F-7
Emerson H-1
Enderly C-6
Engadine Ave. K-2
Engler St. G-5
Erie D-5
Essex E-5
Essex Rd. D-1
Euclaire Ave. G-8
Euclid D-3
Eulalia A-5
Eureka J-1
Evergreen Rd. K-7
Faber Ave. K-7
Faculty B-1
Fair G-6
Fair Ave. G-8
Fairbank Rd. K-7
Fairfield E-6
Fairmont Ave. H-1
Fairview Ave. F-1
Fairwood G-7
Fairwood Ave. H-7
Fairwood Rd. K-7
Fallis Rd. A-3
Feddern K-2
Fern Ave. B-6
Ferndale H-8
Fields E-4
Filmore I-4
Findley Ave. C-3
Finland Ave. K-2
Floral Ave. H-1
Forest J-6
Forest St. H-5,H-7
Fornoff Rd. K-5
Fradena Ave. C-4
Frambes D-3
Framingtion Dr. A-7
Francis Ave. G-8
Frank Rd. K-3
Frankfort St. H-7
Franklin J-1
Franklin Ave. G-6
Franklin Rd. I-8
Franklin Park S. G-7
Franklin Park W. F-7
Franllin G-5
Frebis Ave. I-5
Frey Rd. A-8
Friar B-1
Front St. G-4
Fulton St. G-6,H-5
Gantz Rd. K-1
Gardendale D-7
Garfield Ave. F-5
Garling Ave. I-2
Garrett A-1
Gate Rd. B-1
Gates St. I-5
Gault St. H-7
Gay G-3
Gay St. F-6,G-4
Geers H-7
Genessee Ave. B-5,B-6
Geneva I-1
Gerbert A-5,C-5
Gerbert Rd. A-5
Gerrard E-2
Gibbard E-5
Gibbard Ave. E-6
Gift St. G-3
Gilbert St. H-6
Gladden F-2
Glencoe Rd. A-3
Glendower K-6
Glendower Ave. K-6
Glen Echo C-4
Glenmawr B-4
Glenn Ave. E-1
Glenwood H-2
Goodale Blvd. F-1,F-2
Governor F-6
Grafton B-1
Graham F-6
Granden A-3
Grant E-5
Grant Ave. G-5
Granville F-6
Grasmere C-5
Gray E-5
Greenlawn Ave. I-3
Greenleaf Rd. J-2
Greenway F-7
Greenwich A-6
Greenwich St. B-6
Greenwood E-3
Grenoble Rd. D-1
Griggs Ave. H-3
Grogan E-2
Grove F-5
Groveport Rd. K-6
Grovewood K-7
Grubb St. G-3
Guilford Rd. D-1
Halstead C-1
Hamilton F-5
Hamlet St. E-4
Hanford St. I-5,I-7
Hanna Dr. B-7
Hanover E-3
Hardy Pkwy. K-2
Harley Dr. B-2
Harmon Ave. J-4
Harrison F-3
Hart Rd. J-2
Hartford G-3
Harvard F-6
Haskell A-8
Havendale B-1
Hawkes G-3
Hawthorne F-6
Hayden G-2
Heiman K-6
Helen H-2
Helena Ave. D-6
Hendrix Dr. K-2
Hennepin A-3
Hess E-2
Heyl Ave. H-6
Hiawatha A-4,C-4
Hickory St. G-4
Higgs F-2
High St. B-3,G-4
Highland A-1,E-3,H-1
Hildreth Ave. F-6
Hilltonia I-1
Hingham Ln. A-7
Hinkle J-5
Hinman Ave. J-5
Holburn I-7
Holloway I-1
Hollywood E-1
Holt Ave. D-7
Holton Ave. H-2
Holtzman G-7
Homecroft A-4
Homestead A-5
Homewood I-1
Hope F-2
Hopkins J-3
Hopkins Ave. J-2
Hosack I-4
Hoster H-4
Hosack J-5
Howard St. E-5
Howey C-5
Hubbard F-3
Hudson C-3,C-5
Humphrey Ave. I-1
Hunt Ave. I-1
Hunter D-3
Hunter Ave. E-3
Huntington Rd. K-8
Ida Ave. E-1
Independence E-1
Indianola E-4
Indianola Ave. D-4
Ingleside F-3
Innis Ave. J-7
Innis Pl. J-5
Innis Rd. A-6
Integrity Dr. N. I-8
Integrity Dr. S. I-8
Ipswick Cir. A-7
Isabell D-5
Iuka D-4
Jackson Rd. I-2
Jade I-2
Jaeger St. H-5
Jane D-7
Jefferson C-5,F-5
Jefferson Pl. F-5
Jenkins Ave. I-5
Jeri C-7
Jermain B-7
John Ave. G-2
Jonathan J-7
Joyce Ave. B-6,D-6
Kail K-5
Karon D-7
Kelenard A-8
Kelso Rd. B-3
Kelton H-7,I-7
Kemper D-6
Kendall G-6
Kenlawn A-6
Kenley A-1
Kenmore Rd. C-6
Kennedy H-5
Kenny E-2
Kenny Rd. C-1
Kenraydor A-8
Kent St. H-5
Kenton G-8
Kenwood A-4
Kenworth Rd. A-4
Kermit I-7
Kessler E-5
Kettering Rd. B-2
Keywest D-6
Kian Ave. J-5
Kilbourne F-4
Kimball H-6
Kimberley Dr. A-4
King Ave. E-1
Kingston J-5
Kinnear C-3
Kinnear Rd. D-1
Kitchner J-7
Koebel Ave. K-6,K-8
Koebel Rd. K-7
Kohr Pl. C-6
Korbel D-8
Kossuth H-4
Kossuth St. H-5,H-7
Kramer F-2
Kutchins Pl. G-6
Lafayette St. G-4
Lakeview Ave. B-2
Lambeth B-1
Lancashire C-7
lansing St. H-5
Lansmere E-1
Larcomb H-1
Latham Ct. A-1
Laurel I-2
Lawn J-5
Lawndale J-8
Lawndale Ave. J-8
Lawrence Dr. J-6
Lazelle St. G-4
Lear St. H-5
Lechner H-1
Lee D-6
Lenore A-5
Leon B-8
Leona Ave. E-5
Leonard Ave. E-6,F-5
Lexington D-5
Lilley I-7
Lincoln St. F-4
Linden C-6
Linnet I-2
Linview B-6
Linwood J-6
Linwood Ave. H-6
Liscomb I-7
Liston Ave. J-8
Little Ave. J-2
Livingston Ave. H-5,H-7
Lockbourne Rd. H-6
Locust St. G-4
Loew E-5
Long St. G-4
Longview B-3,B-4
Longwood Ave. K-2
Loretta C-6
Loretta Ave. C-5
Louis D-6
Loxley Dr. K-5
Lucas St. G-3
Lynn St. G-4
Mabel C-3
Madison Ave. G-6
Main St. G-5,G-7
Maize A-4
Manchester Ave. B-5
Manning G-7
Maple St. F-3
Marburn Dr. A-1
Marcia Dr. B-7
Marconi G-4
Margaret E-7,E-8
Margaret Pl. E-7
Marina-Toni C-7
Marion Rd. J-6
Markison Ave. I-6,J-5
Marsdale J-1,K-2
Marston C-7
Martin G-3
Martha H-2
Maryland St. E-8
May G-3
Mayfield H-8
Maynard C-3,C-5
McAllister
McClain F-2
McClelland D-5
McCoy F-5
McDowell G-3
McGuffy C-5
McKinley G-2
McKinley Ave. G-1
McMillen E-2,E-3
Meade I-1
Meadow E-2
Meadowdale D-7
Mecca Rd. A-6
Medary Ave. C-3
Medbrook A-2
Medhurst A-1
Medina A-5
Medinah Ave. A-5
Melrose B-4,B-5
Melrose Ave. B-7
Memory Ln. H-8
Menlo Pl. F-6
Mennesota Ave. B-5,B-6
Meredith D-7
Merrimac G-2
Merryhill F-7
Miami F-6
Michigan F-3
Middlehurst C-7
Midgard B-4
Midland I-1,J-1
Midland Ave. H-1
Midway K-7
Milford Ave. B-4,B-5,B-7
Millcreek A-1
Miller Ave. G-7
Milton Ave. B-2
Miner I-3
Mithoff St. I-5
Mohawk H-5
Moler St. I-5,I-7
Monroe Ave. F-5,G-6
Montrose A-2
Montrose Ave. G-8
Mooberry G-7
Moon Rd. A-4
Morning I-1
Morrill Ave. J-5
Morrison G-7
Mound H-3
Mound St. G-5,G-6
Mt. Pleasant E-4
Mt. Vernon Ave. F-5
Mura B-4
Murray Ave. B-2
Myrtle Ave. B-5,B-6
Nace Ave. H-2
Naghten F-5
Nashoba I-1
Nason I-7
Neff Ave. K-5
Neil C-3
Neil Ave. B-3
Neilston F-4
Nelson Rd. G-7
Newton Ave. H-6
Niantic Dr. A-7
North St. C-3
North Broadway A-3
Northglen A-7
Northmoor A-3
North Star Ave. C-1
Northview D-8
Northwest Blvd. E-2
Northwood Ave. C-3,C-4
Norton Ave. E-2
Norway B-1
Norwich C-3,C-4
Norwood A-5
Norwood St. A-5
Nuway K-7
Oak St. G-5,G-6
Oakland Ave. C-3,F-1
Oakland Park Ave.
A-3,A-5
Oaklawn A-6
Oaklawn St. A-5
Oakwood Ave. H-6
Ohio Ave. H-5
Ohlen D-4
Olentangy A-2
Olentangy St. B-3
Oletangy River Rd.
B-2
Olmstead Ave. C-3
Olpp J-5
Omar Dr. J-7
Ontario A-5
Ontario St. A-5
Orchard Ln. A-3
Oregon Ave. E-3
Oriole D-7
Osborn Dr. D-1
Osceola A-4
Osceola Ave. B-4
Overlook Dr. A-1
Oxford D-5
Oxley E-2,F-2
Pacemount Rd. B-2
Palmer Ave. F-2
Pamella K-7
Pannell I-7
Park Dr. F-7
Park Leigh A-1
Parkview Ave. E-8
Parkway N. E-2
Parkwood C-6,D-6
Patterson Ave. C-3
Pauline A-5
Pauline Ave. A-5
Payne G-8
Peabody J-1
Pearl E-4
Pearl St. G-4
Peasley D-3
Pegg B-1
Pembrooke F-7
Pennsylvania Ave. E-3
Penny E-4
Perry Ave. E-3
Peters E-5
Pickwick C-1
Piedmont A-4,A-6
Piedmont Rd. A-3
Pierce Dr. H-3
Pleasant Ridge G-8
Pontiac C-4
Pontiac Ave. B-4
Poplar F-4
Powell F-8
Presidential E-1
Preston Rd. F-8
Price E-4
Princeton G-2
Princeton Ave. H-2
Progress I-8
Purdue Ave. B-7
Puritan D-6
Quay F-2
Rainbow Park H-7
Rankin C-7
Ransburg Ave. I-2
Raynor A-8
Rea Ave. I-1
Red Rock Blvd. K-1
Reeb A-8
Reeb Ave. J-5,J-6
Refugee Rd. J-7
Reinhard Ave. H-5
Remington F-8
Renick St. H-3
Republic C-6
Republic Ave. C-5
Reynolds E-5
Rhoads Ave. H-7,K-7
Rhoda E-2
Rich H-2
Rich St. G-5-7, H-3
Richards Rd. A-3
Richmond F-7
Richmond Rd. J-2
Richter Rd. J-2
Ridge C-8
Ridge St. F-1
Rightmire Blvd. B-1
Riverside Dr. B-2
Riverview Dr. B-2
Robert B-6
Roberts I-7
Rodgers G-2
Rose E-7
Rosedale Ave. J-1
Rosemont I-1
Rosewood D-7
Ross E-7
Rudwick A-8
Ruhl E-8
Ruhl Ave. E-8
Russell F-4
Ryan H-2
Ryder F-2
Safford Ave. I-1
Sagamore C-7
St. Clair D-5,F-5
St. Clair Ave. F-5
Sampson D-6
Sandlin B-5
Saugus Cir. A-7
Say Ave. E-4
Schenley C-7
Schultz G-2
Scioto I-4
Scott Rd. I-2
Scott St. G-3
Sells E-2
Seneca Park Pl. F-8
Seymour Ave. H-7
Shady Ln. J-2
Shady Hill C-1
Shadywood C-1
Sharon A-3
Shattuck A-1
Shattuck Ave. B-1
Sheldon I-6
Sheldon Ave. I-5
Sherbourne F-7
Sheridan Ave. G-8
Sherwood Rd. G-8
Shoemaker Ave. E-5
Short St. H-4
Sidney E-5
Siebert St. H-5
Sigsbee D-6
Silver Dr. A-4
Skidmore St. G-3
Smith E-3
Smith Rd. I-6,I-7
Somersworth D-7
Souder Ave. G-3
South Ave. E-2
South Ln. H-5
Southard K-5
Southwood Ave. J-5
Spring St. F-5,G-3
Springmont I-1
Spruce St. F-3
Stambaugh J-6
Stanbery F-8
Stanhope B-1
Stanley Ave. H-5
Starling G-4
Starr E-4,E-5
State St. G-5
Steelwood E-1
Stevens G-2
Stewart Ave. I-5
Stimmel Rd. I-3
Stinchcomb Dr. B-2
Stoddart G-7
Stonington Ave. K-1
Stratford F-7
Studer Ave. H-6
Sullivant Ave. H-3
Summit D-4,E-4
Sunbury B-8
Sunbury Dr. D-7
Suncrest I-1
Sunny Hill C-1
Swan St. F-5
Sycamore H-4,H-5
Sycamore St. H-7
Talmadge St. F-5
Taylor D-6,E-6
Thelma I-2
Thomas F-2,H-2
Thomas Ave. H-3
Thomas Ln. B-1
Thorn F-6
Thornwood F-6
Thurber F-3
Thurman Ave. I-5
Tibet E-4
Tibet Rd. B-3
Tilbur Ave. A-1
Tompkins C-3
Toronto F-6
Torrence Rd. A-3
Town St. G-5
Townsend H-2
Trentwood B-1
Tulane B-3,B-4
Tulane Rd. B-3
Tuller St. C-3
Tuttle Park Pl. D-3
Twin Rivers G-3
Union H-2,I-1
Universal Rd. J-7
Urana A-4
Valcon I-7
Valley B-8
Varsity B-1
Vassar Dr. C-1
Vaughn I-1
Velma Ave. C-5
Vendome C-7
Vernon F-6
Vine St. F-4
Virginia E-2
Waldeck C-3
Walhalla Rd. B-3
Wall St. G-4
Walmar Dr. A-5
Walnut St. G-5
Walsh H-2
Walters E-5
Wareham C-1
Warren St. F-4
Washington E-5,J-5
Washington Ave.
G-5
Watkins K-8
Watkins Rd. K-7
Weber Rd. B-3,B-5
Webster Park A-2
Wedge B-7
Weiler I-7
Welch Ave. J-5
Weldon Ave. B-4,B-5
Wellesley Dr. C-1
Wendell G-2
Wentworth D-6
Westfield Dr. N. J-1
Westland Ave. F-8
Westminster Dr. C-1
Weston A-2
Westwood Ave. E-1
Wheatland H-1
Whitehead I-1
Whitehorn J-1
Whitehorne I-1
Whitethorne Ave. H-1
Whittier St. H-5,H-7
Wildwood E-7
Willamont E-7
Willard F-2
Williams F-2
Willow H-5
Wilnis Ave. C-4
Wilson Ave. H-6,K-6
Windsor Ave. D-6
Winslow Dr. J-8
Winthrop A-2
Wisconsin G-2
Withers Ave. I-2
Wood Rd. C-2
Woodbury H-1
Woodcroft Rd. J-1
Woodford Ave. D-6
Woodland F-7
Woodland Ave. B-7,D-7
Woodmere A-1
Woodnell D-7
Woodrow Ave. J-5,J-6
Woodruff Ave. D-3
Woodward D-7
Worthington E-3
Wrexham I-1
Wyandotte C-4
Wyandotte Ave. E-1
Yale Ave. H-2
Yolanda J-7
Yorkcliff A-8
Zebulon Ave. A-5
Zimpfer St. I-5
1st Ave. E-4,F-1,F-3
2nd E-2
2nd Ave. E-3,E-4
3rd E-4
3rd Ave. E-1,E-3,E-5
3rd St. G-4,I-5
4th E-6,E-8
4th Ave. E-3,E-4,E-5
4th St. E-4,G-4,I-5
5th Ave. E-1,E-3,E-5,E-7
5th St. E-4,G-5
6th E-3,E-4,E-8,F-4
6th Ave. E-1
6th St. E-4,G-5
7th E-3,E-4,E-8
7th Ave. E-1
8th D-8,E-5
8th Ave. E-3
9th D-2,D-8
9th Ave. E-3
9th St. G-5
10th D-2,D-8
10th Ave. D-3
11th D-2,D-8
11th Ave. D-3,D-4
12th D-4,D-6,D-8
12th Ave. D-5
13th D-4,D-8
13th Ave. D-5
14th D-4,D-5
14th Ave. D-8
15th D-4
15th Ave. D-5
16th D-4,D-6
16th Ave. D-5
17th D-3,H-6,I-6
17th Ave. D-4,D-5
17th St. F-5,G-6
18th D-3,D-4,H-6,I-6
18th Ave. D-5
18th St. F-6,G-6
19th D-4,E-6,I-6
19th Ave. D-5
20th D-4,E-6,G-6
20th Ave. D-5
20th St. F-6,I-6
21st Ave. C-5
21st St. E-6,F-6,G-6
22nd E-6,G-6
22nd Ave. C-5
22nd St. F-6,H-6
23rd C-6,E-6
23rd Ave. C-5
24th C-6
24th Ave. C-5
25th Ave. C-5
26th Ave. C-5

POINTS OF INTEREST

Fort Hays F-5
Franklin Park F-7
Goodale Park F-4
Lincoln Park I-6
Schiller Park H-5
Southview Park I-4
Sunshine Park H-3

Scale of Miles
0 .2 .4 .6 .8 1
N

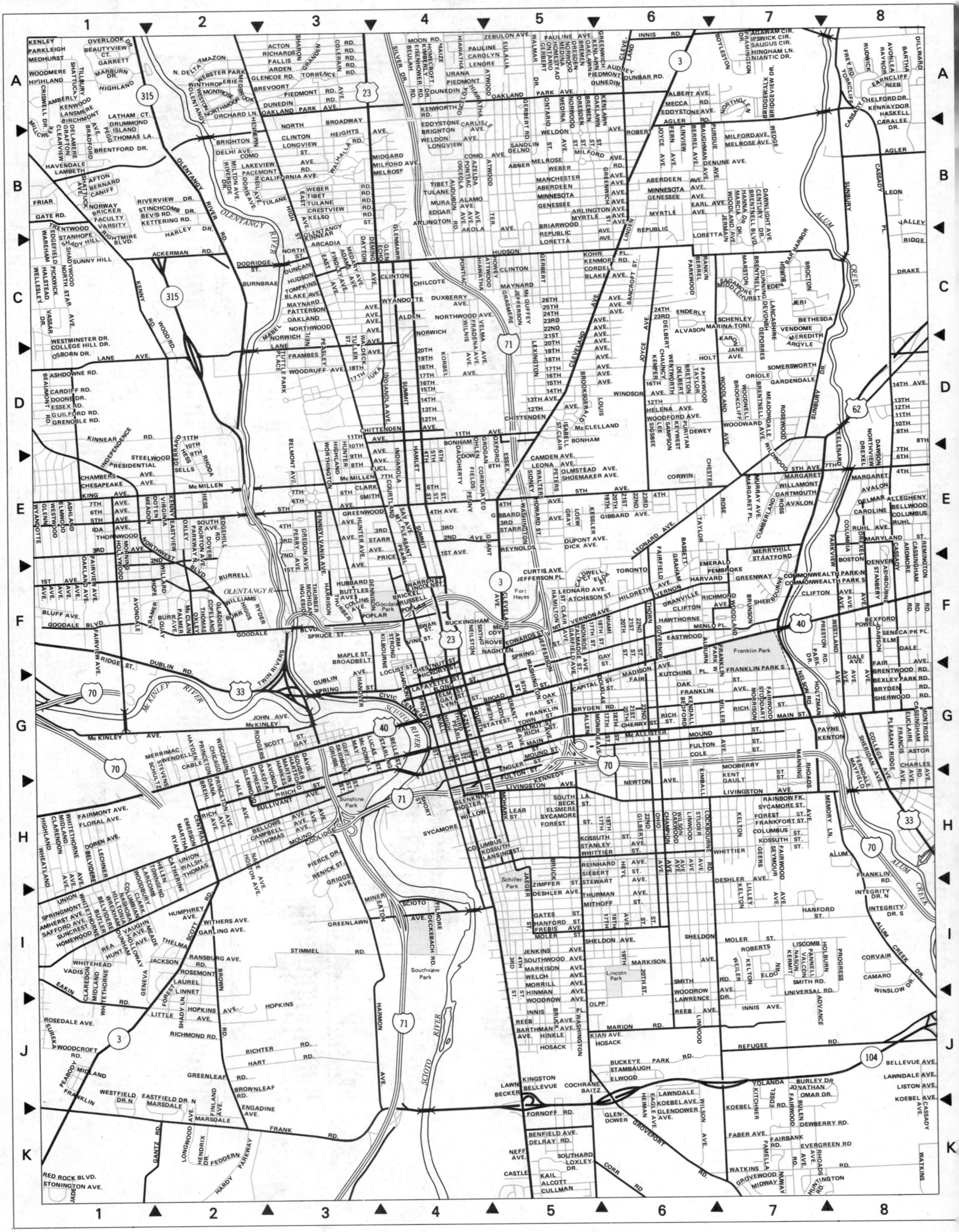

Scale of Miles

0 .1 .2 .3 .4

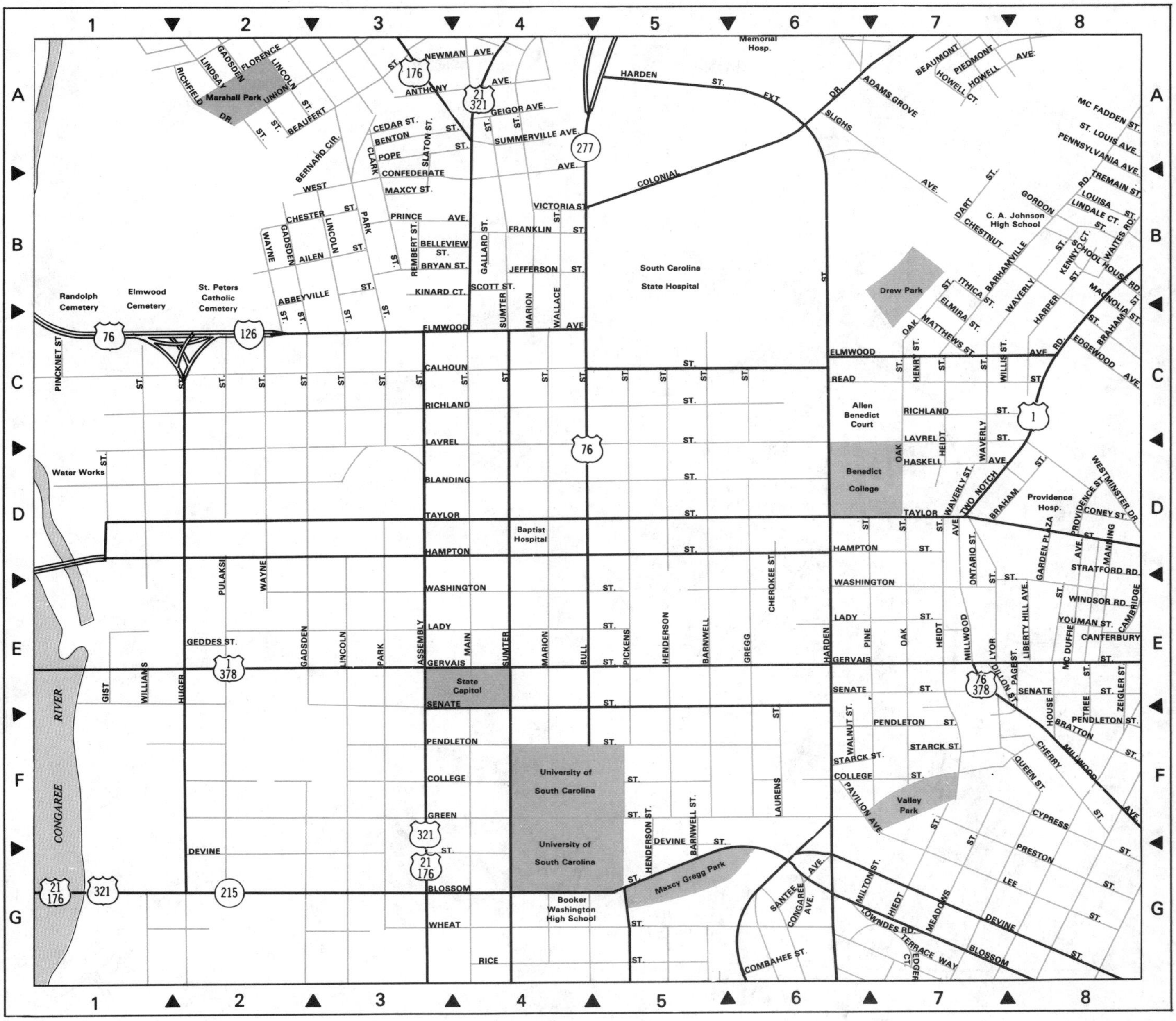

COLUMBIA

Abbeyville St.........B-2
Adams Grove........A-7
Allen St..............B-3
Anthony Ave.........A-3
Assembly St..........E-3
Barhamville Rd.......B-8
Barnwell St...........E-5
.................F-5,G-5
Beaufert St...........A-2
Beaumont Ave.......A-7
Belleview St..........B-3
Benton St.............A-3
Bernard Cir...........A-3
Blanding St...........D-3
Blossom St......G-3,G-7
Braham St........C-8,D-7
Bratton St............F-8
Bryan St..............B-3
Bull St...............E-4
Calhoun St...........C-3
Cambridge E-8
Canterbury E-8
Carver St.............A-7
Cedar St..............A-3
Cherokee St..........E-6
Cherry St.............F-8
Chester St............B-2
Chestnut St..........B-7
Clark St..............A-3
College St.........F-3,F-6
Colonial Dr...........B-5
Columbia St..........A-3
Combahee St.........G-6
Coney St.............D-8
Confederate Ave.....B-3
Congaree Ave.......G-6
Cypress St............F-8
Dart St...............B-7
Devine St.............F-5
................G-2,G-7
Dillon St.............E-7
Edgerton Ct..........G-7
Edgewood Ave.......C-8
Elmira St.............C-7
Elmwood Ave....C-3,C-6
Florence St...........A-2
Franklin St...........B-4
Gadsden St...........A-2
..................B-2,E-2
Gallard St............B-4
Garden Plaza.........D-8
Geddes St............E-2
Gervais St........E-3,E-6
Geigor Ave...........A-4
Gist St...............E-1
Gordon St............B-8
Green St.............F-3
Gregg St.............E-6
Grove St.............A-6
Hampton St.....D-3,D-6
Harden St............E-6
Harden St. Ext.......A-5
Harper St............B-8
Haskell Ave..........D-7
Heidt St.....D-7,E-7,G-7
Henderson St....E-5,G-5
Henry St.............C-7
House St.............F-8
Howell Ave...........A-7
Howell Ct............A-7
Huger St.............E-2
Ithica St.............B-7
Jefferson St.........B-4
Kenney Ct............B-8
Kinard Ct............B-3
Lady St..........E-3,E-6
Laurel St.........C-3,C-7
Laurens St...........F-6
Lee St...............G-7
Liberty Hill Ave......E-8
Lincoln St....A-2,B-3,E-3
Lindale Ct............B-8
Lindsay St...........A-2
Louisa St............B-8
Lowndes Rd..........G-7
Lyor St..............E-7
Magnolia St..........B-8
Main St..............E-4
Manning.............D-8
Mapion St............C-4
Marion St............E-4
Matthews St.........C-7
Maxcy St.............B-3
McDuffie Ave.........E-8
McFadden St.........A-8
Meadows St..........G-7
Millwood Ave....E-7,F-8
Milton St.............G-6
Newman Ave.........A-3
Oak St.......C-7,D-7,E-7
Ontario St...........D-7
Page St..............E-8
Park St......A-2,B-3,E-3
Pavilion Ave.........F-6
Pendicton St.........F-3
.................F-7,F-8
Pennsylvania Ave....A-8
Pickens St...........E-5
Piedmont Ave........A-7
Pincknet St..........C-1
Pine St..............E-6
Pope St..............A-3
Preston St...........G-8
Prince Ave...........B-3
Providence St.......D-8
Pulaksi St...........D-2
Queen St.............F-8
Read St..............C-6
Rembert St..........B-3
Rice St..............G-4
Richfield Dr.........A-2
Richland St......C-3,C-7
St. Louis Ave........A-8
Santee Ave..........G-6
School House Rd....B-8
Scott St.............B-4
Senate St............E-3
...............E-6,E-8
Slaton St.............A-3
Slighs Ave............A-6
Starck St.........F-6,F-7
Stratford Rd.........D-8
Summerville Ave....A-4
Sumter St........C-4,E-4
Taylor St........D-3,D-7
Terrace Way.........G-7
Tree St...............E-8
Tremain St...........B-8
Two Notch Rd.......D-7
Union St.............A-2
Victoria St...........B-4
Waites Rd............B-8
Wallace St...........C-4
Walnut St............F-6
Washington St...E-3,E-6
Waverly St.......B-8,D-7
Wayne St.........B-2,D-2
West.................B-3
Westminster Dr......D-8
Wheat St.............G-3
Williams St......E-1,G-1
Willis St.............C-7
Windsor Rd..........E-8
Youman St...........E-8
Zeigler St............E-8

POINTS OF INTEREST

Allen Benedict Court...............C-6
Baptist Hospital.....D-4
Benedict College....D-6
Booker Washington H.S.................G-4
C. A. Johnson H.S...B-7
Drew Park...........B-7
Elmwood Cemetery..B-1
Marshall Park........A-2
Maxcy Gregg Park...G-5
Providence Hosp....D-8
Randolph Cemetery.B-1
Richland Memorial Hosp................A-6
St. Peters Catholic Cemetery...........B-2
South Carolina State Hospital B-5
State Capitol........E-4
University of South Carolina..F-4,G-4
Valley Park..........F-7

Corpus Christi, TX

Scale of Miles
0 .2 .4 .6

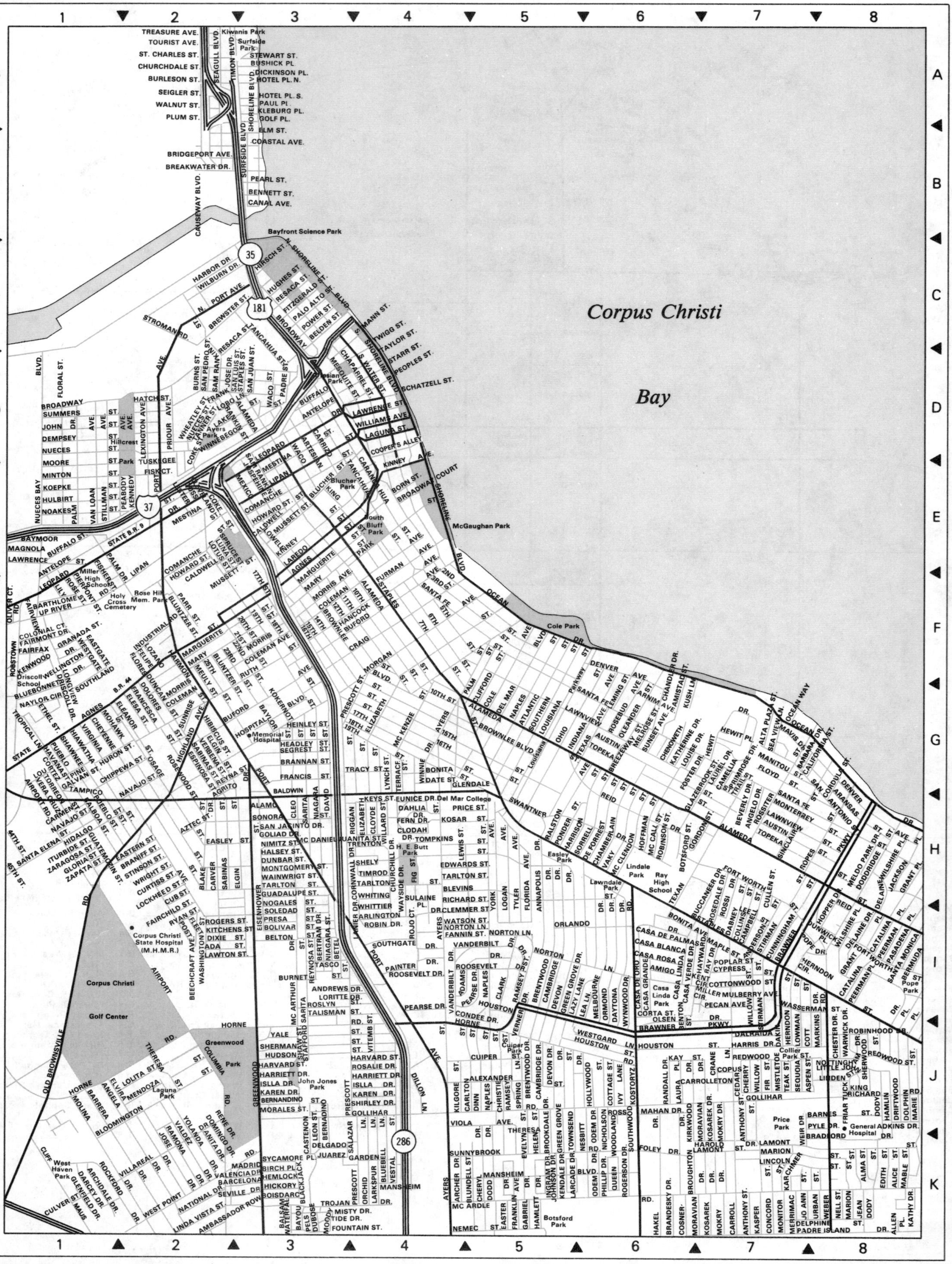

CORPUS CHRISTI

Ada St. I-2
Adams I-4
Adkins Dr. J-8
Agnes St. E-3,G-1
Agrito G-2
Airport Rd. . . . G-1,H-1,I-2
Alameda D-3,F-4
Alamo H-3
Alexander St. J-5
Alice St. K-8
Allen Pl. K-8
Alma St. K-8
Alameda St. . . . G-5,H-7
Alta Plaza St. G-7
Ambassador Row . . . K-2
Amigo I-6
Amistad St. G-6
Andrews Dr. I-3
Angela Dr. J-1
Angelo Dr. H-7
Anita Dr. K-2
Annapolis Dr. H-5
Antelope St. . . . D-3,E-1
Anthony St. J-7K-7
Aransas St. H-8
Archdale Dr. K-1
Archer Dr. K-4
Arlington Dr. I-4
Arnim Ave. G-6
Artesian D-3
Aspen St. J-7
Atlantic St. G-5
Austin G-6
Austin St. H-7
Ayers G-4,I-4,K-4
Aztec St. H-2
Balsam K-3
Barcelona K-3
Barnes St. J-8
Barrera Dr. . . . G-7,J-1
Barthlome Rd. F-1
Baylor G-3
Baymoor E-1
Bayou K-3
Beechcraft Ave. I-2
Belden St. C-3
Belton St. I-3
Bennett St. B-3
Benton St. I-6
Bermuda I-8
Bernanding St. J-3
Bernadino J-3
Betel St. J-3
Bertram Dr. I-3
Beverly Dr. H-7
Birch Pl. K-3
Blackjack K-3
Blake St. H-2
Blevins St. H-4
Bloomington St. J-2
Blucher St. E-3
Bluebell Ln. K-4
Bluebonnet Dr. G-1
Blundell St. K-5
Bluntzer St. F-2
Boisdarc K-3
Bolivar St. I-3
Bonita Ave. I-6
Bonita St. G-4
Born St. E-4
Botsford St. H-6
Bradford Dr. J-8
Brandesky Dr. K-6
Braniff St. H-2
Brannan St. G-3
Brawner Pkwy. . . . I-7,J-6
Breakwater Dr. B-2
Breezeway St. G-6
Brentwood Dr. . . . I-5,J-5
Brewster St. C-2
Bridgeport Ave. I-2
Broadway C-3,D-1
Broadway Court E-4
Brookdale Dr. J-5
Broughton K-6
Brownlee F-3
Brownlee Blvd. G-5
Buccaneer Dr. H-7
Buffalo St. . . . D-3,E-1
Buford St. . . . F-4,G-2
Burleson St. A-2
Burnet St. I-3
Burns St. D-2
Bushick Pl. A-3
Caldwell St. . . . E-2,E-3
California St. G-7
Cambridge Dr. . . . I-5,J-5
Camellia G-7
Campbell St. I-7
Canal Ave. B-3
Caranca Hua E-4
Carlton St. J-5
Carmen H-1
Carrizo D-3
Carroll Dr. K-7
Carrolleton J-7
Carver Dr. H-2
Casa Blanca I-6
Casa De Oro Rd. I-6
Casa De Palmas I-6
Casa Grande I-6
Casa Linda I-6
Casa Rosa I-6
Casa Verde Dr. I-6
Castenon J-3
Catalina Pl. I-8
Causeway Blvd. B-2
Cedar J-7
Chamberlain St. H-6
Chandler Dr. G-6
Chaparral St. D-4
Chennoweth G-6
Cherry J-7
Cheryl Dr. K-5
Chester Dr. J-8
Cheyenne St. G-1
Chippewa St. G-1
Christie St. J-5
Churchdale St. A-2
Churchhill Dr. H-4
Clark Dr. I-5
Clemmer St. I-4
Cleo H-3
Cleveland E-2
Clifford St. G-5
Clodah Dr. H-4
Cloyde St. H-4
Coastal Ave. B-3
Coke St. . . . D-2,E-2
Cole Ave. G-5
Coleman Ave. . . F-3,G-2
Collins St. I-7
Colonial Ct. F-1
Comanche St. . . . E-2,E-3
Concord St. K-7
Condee Dr. I-5
Cooper's Al. D-4
Copus J-7
Cordula St. G-8
Cornwall Dr. H-4
Corta St. I-6
Cortez G-1
Cosner Dr. K-6
Cott St. J-7
Cottage St. J-6
Cottonwood St. I-7
Craig F-4
Crane J-7
Cub St. H-2
Cuiper St. J-5
Cullen St. H-7
Culver St. K-1
Cunningham St. I-7
Curtiss St. H-2
Cypress St. I-7
Dabney St. I-7
Dahlia Dr. H-4
Dakin J-7
Dalraida J-7
Darcey Dr. K-1
Date St. G-4
David St. H-3
Daytona Dr. I-6
De Forest St. H-6
DeLaine Dr. I-8
Delaine Wilshire Pl. . . H-8
Delgado K-3
Del Mar Blvd. G-5
Delphine St. K-8
Dempsey St. D-1
Denver Ave. . . . F-6,G-8
Derson St. I-7
Devon Dr. I-5,J-5
Dickinson Pl. A-3
Dillon Ln. J-4
Dinn St. J-5
Dixie St. I-2
Dodd Dr. K-5
Doddridge St. H-7
Dody St. J-8,K-8
Dolphin Pl. J-8
Dolores St. G-2
Domingo Dr. J-2
Doss E-2
Driftwood Pl. J-8
Driscoll Dr. G-1
Dubose K-3
Dunbar St. H-3
Duncan St. G-2
Dunwick Pl. I-8
Easley St. H-2
Easter Dr. K-5
Eastern St. H-2
Eastgate F-1
Edith St. K-8
Edwards St. H-4
Eisenhower St. I-3
Eleanor St. G-2
Elesa St. G-2
Elgin St. G-2,H-2
Elizabeth St. . . . G-4,H-4
Elm St. B-3
Elvira Dr. J-2
Espinosa St. G-2
Ethel St. G-1
Eunice Dr. H-4
Evelyn St. K-5
Fairchild St. I-2
Fairfax F-1
Fairmont Dr. F-1
Fairview F-1
Fannin St. I-4
Felipe F-2
Fern Dr. H-4
Fig St. H-4
Fir St. J-7
Fisher St. I-1
Fisk Ct. E-2
Fitzgerald St. C-3
Fleet I-2
Floral St. D-1
Flores F-2
Florida Ave. H-5
Floyd St. G-7
Foley Dr. K-6
Fort Worth St. . . . H-7,I-8
Foster Dr. G-6
Fountain St. K-4
Francesca St. G-2
Francis St. G-3
Frank D-2
Franklin Ave. K-5
Friar Tuck J-8
Furman Ave. F-4
Gabriel Dr. K-5
Galvan St. G-1
Garden K-4
Glazebrook St. G-7
Glendale G-4
Glenfield Dr. H-1
Gloria St. H-1
Golf Pl. A-3
Goliad Dr. H-3
Gollihar J-4,J-7
Gordon St. C-2
Granada St. F-1
Grant Pl. H-8,I-8
Green Grove Dr. . . . I-5,J-5
Greenwood Dr. J-3
Guadalupe St. H-3
Guatemozin St. H-1
Hakel Dr. H-6
Halsey St. H-3
Hamlett Dr. K-5
Hamlin Dr. J-8
Hancock Ave. F-4
Harbor Dr. C-2
Harmon St. F-2
Harold Dr. K-7
Harriett Dr. J-3,J-4
Harris Dr. J-7
Harrison St. H-3
Harvard St. J-3,J-4
Hatch St. D-2
Hudson St. J-3
Hughes St. C-3
Hulbirt St. E-1
Huron St. G-1
Havana St. G-1
Hayward I-7
Headley St. G-3
Heinley St. G-3
Helen St. K-5
Hemlock K-3
Herndon St. J-7
Hewit Pl. G-7
Hiawatha G-1
Hibiscus St. G-2
Hickory K-3
Hidalgo St. H-1
Highland Ave. G-2
Hirsch St. C-3
Hoffman St. H-6
Hollywood J-6
Horne J-5
Hopper Dr. I-8
Horne Rd. J-1,J-3
Hospital Blvd. G-3
Hotel Pl. N. A-3
Hotel Pl. S. A-3
Houston St. H-5
Howard St. E-2,E-3
Indiana G-5
Industrial Rd. F-2
Ingram Dr. K-5
Islla Dr. J-3,J-4
Iturbide St. H-1
Ivy Lane K-4
Jackson Pl. H-8
Jean St. K-8
Jo Ann St. K-7
John St. D-1
Johnson Dr. K-5
Jose Dr. D-2,K-2
Josephine K-3
Juarez K-3
Karchmer K-7
Karen Dr. J-3,J-4
Kasper St. K-7
Katherine Dr. G-6
Kathy Dr. K-8
Kay St. J-6
Kendale Dr. K-5
Kennedy Ave. . . . E-2,E-4
Kent Cir. I-7
Kenwood F-1
Keys St. H-4
Kilgore St. K-5
King Richard Rd. J-8
Kinney St. E-3
Kirkwood Dr. J-6
Kitchens St. I-2
Kleburg Pl. A-3
Koepke St. E-1
Kokernot G-3
Kosar St. H-4
Kosarek Dr. J-7,K-7
Kostoryz J-6
Kush Ln. G-6
Laguna St. D-4
Lake St. D-2
Lamont St. K-7
Lanier Dr. I-4
Laredo St. E-2
Larkspur La. K-4
Larcade Dr. K-5
Laura Pl. J-6
Laurel Dr. G-7
Lawnview St. . . . G-5,H-7
Lawrence St. . . . D-4,E-1
Lawton St. I-2
Lazy Lane I-5
Lily F-1
Lincoln St. K-7
Linda Vista St. K-2
Linden St. J-8
Lipan E-2,E-3
Little John J-8
Lobo Ln. D-2
Lockhead St. H-2
Logan Ave. H-5
Lolita St. J-2
Loritte Dr. I-3
Lotus St. E-2
Lou St. G-1
Louise Dr. G-6
Louisiana St. G-5
Lowell E-3
Lowman St. J-7
Lozano F-2
Lea Ln. I-6
Lee St. I-7
Leming St. G-6
Leon St. J-3
Leopard Dr. . . . D-3,F-1
Lester E-2
Lewis St. H-4
Lexington Ave. D-2
Luna St. E-2
Lynch St. G-4
Mable St. K-8
Madrid K-3
Magnola E-1
Mahan Dr. J-6
Manitou St. G-7
Mann St. C-4
Manshum Blvd. . . . K-4,K-5
Maple St. I-7
Marguerite St. . . . E-3,F-2
Marie St. I-1
Marion St. . . . K-7, K-8
Markins Dr. J-8
Mavis Dr. G-7
Mary F-2,F-3
McArdle Rd. K-5
McArthur Dr. I-3
McCall St. H-6
McClendon St. H-6
McDaniel Juanita St. . . H-3
McGaughan Park E-5
McKenzie St. G-4
Melbourne I-6
Meldo Park Dr. H-8
Melrose St. G-6
Mendoza St. J-2
Merrimac K-7
Mestina St. E-2,E-3
Mesquite St. D-3
Meuly St. F-2
Mexico E-3
Miller Cir. I-7
Minton St. E-1
Mistletoe J-7
Misty Dr. K-3
Mohawk St. G-1
Mokry Dr. J-7,K-7
Molina Dr. J-1
Monitor St. K-7
Monterey St. H-7
Montgomery St. H-3
Moody K-3
Moore St. E-1
Morales St. J-3
Moravian Dr. . . . J-7,K-6
Morgan St. F-4
Morris Ave. F-3,G-2
Mulberry Ave. I-7
Mussett St. E-3,F-2
Naples St. . . . G-5,I-5,J-5
Naterfal K-3
National Dr. K-2
Navajo St. G-2,H-1
Naylor Circle G-1
Nell St. K-8
Nemec St. K-5
Nesbitt Dr. J-6
Niagara St. H-3,I-3
Nicholson St. J-6
Nimitz St. H-3
Noakes St. E-1
Nogales St. H-3
Norton Ln. I-4,I-5
Nottingham J-8
Nueces St. D-1,D-2
Nueces Bay Blvd. E-1
Ocean Dr. F-5,G-7
Ocean Way G-7
Odem Dr. J-6,K-6
Ohio St. G-5
Old Brownsville Rd. F-1,J-1
Oleander St. G-6
Oliver Ct. F-1
Olsen Dr. I-6
Orchid Ln. K-4
Orlando I-5
Ormond Dr. I-6
Osage G-2
Padre St. D-3
Padre Island Dr. K-8
Painter Dr. I-4
Palboa St. H-1
Palermo St. F-5
Palm Dr. E-1
Palo Alto St. C-3
Park St. E-4
Parr St. F-2
Pasadena I-8
Paul Pl. A-3
Peabody Ave. E-2
Pearl St. B-3
Pearse Dr. I-4,I-5
Pecan Ave. I-7
Peerman Pl. I-8
Pel's K-3
Peoples St. D-4
Phillip Dr. K-6
Pierpont St. F-1
Pine G-1
Plum St. A-2
Ponder St. H-5
Pope Dr. J-3
Poplar St. I-7
Port Ave. E-2,G-3,I-4
Port Avenue N. C-2
Post I-2
Power St. C-3
Pueblo St. G-1,G-2
Prasa St. I-3
Prescott St. . . G-3,J-3,K-4
Price St. H-4
Primrose Dr. G-7
Priour Ave. D-2
Pyle Dr. J-8
Queen K-6
Ralston Ave. H-5
Ramona Dr. K-2
Ramsey St. I-5,J-5
Randall Dr. J-6
Rankin St. D-2
Ray Dr. I-7
Redwood St. J-7,J-8
Reid Dr. H-6,H-8
Rene Dr. J-2
Resaca St. C-2,C-3
Reyna St. J-2
Reynosa St. I-3
Richard St. H-4
Riggan St. H-4
Robin Dr. I-4
Robinhood Dr. J-8
Robinson St. H-6
Rockford Dr. K-1
Rogers St. I-2
Rogerson Dr. K-6
Rojo Ct. I-4
Roosevelt Dr. I-4,I-5
Ropes St. H-7
Rosalie Dr. J-4
Rose St. F-1
Rosebud Ave. G-6
Rosedale Dr. H-7
Rosewood St. G-2
Roslyn St. I-3
Ross J-6
Rossi Dr. H-7
Rossiter St. H-7
Ruth F-3
Ryan St. I-2
St. Charles St. A-2
Sabinas St. G-2,H-2
Salazar K-4
Sam Rankin St. D-2
San Antonio St. H-8
Santa Elena St. H-1
Santa Fe St. G-6,H-6
San Jacinto Dr. H-3
San Juan St. D-3
San Luis St. D-2
Santa Monica I-8
San Pedro St. D-2
San Rankin F-3
Sarita St. H-3,I-3
Schatzell St. D-4
Sea Gull Blvd. A-2
Sea View Ln. G-7
Segrest St. E-3
Seigler St. A-2
Sequoia J-7
Seville Dr. K-3
Shaw St. J-3
Shawnee St. G-1
Shely St. H-4
Sherman St. J-3
Sherwood J-8
Shirley Dr. J-4
Shoreline Blvd. . . . A-3,E-4
S. Shoreline Blvd. . . . D-4
Sinclair St. I-7
Southgate Dr. I-4
Soledad St. I-3
Sonora H-3
Sorrell St. H-6
Southern St. G-5
Southland F-1
Southwood J-6
Spring Ln. J-5
Spruce St. E-2
Stafford J-3
Staples St. . . . D-3,F-4,I-7
Starr St. E-3
Stewart St. A-3
Stillman Ave. E-1
Stinson St. H-2
Stirman St. I-7
Stromanro C-2
Sulaine Pl. H-4
Summers St. D-1
Sunnybrook Rd. K-5
Sunrise G-2
Sunset Ave. G-6
Surfside Blvd. B-3
Swantner H-5
Sycamore Pl. K-3
Talisman St. I-3
Tampico G-1
Tancahua St. C-3,E-4
Tanner St. D-2
Tarlton St. H-3,H-4
Tasco I-3
Taylor St. C-4
Teak St. J-7
Terrace St. G-4
Texan H-6
Texas Ave. G-6
Theresa St. J-2,J-5
Tide Dr. K-3
Timon Blvd. A-2
Timrod J-6
Tompkins St. H-4
Topeka G-6,H-7
Torreon G-1
Tourist Ave. A-2
Townsend St. J-5
Tracy St. G-4
Trail G-7
Treasure Ave. A-2
Trenton St. H-4
Trojan Dr. K-3
Tropical Ln. K-3
Tuskegee E-2
Twigg St. C-4
Tyler Ave. H-5
Up River F-1
Urban St. K-8
Vaky St. H-6
Valdez Dr. J-2
Valencia Dr. K-3
Vanderbilt Dr. I-4,I-5
Van Loan Ave. E-1
Vera Cruz G-1
Verbena St. G-2
Verner Dr. J-5
Vestal St. K-4
Villareal Dr. K-2
Viola Ave. J-4
Virginia G-1
Vitemb St. J-4
Waco St. D-3
Wainwright St. H-3
Walnut St. A-2
Warwick Dr. J-8
Washington St. I-2
Wasserman St. I-7
Water St., S. D-4
Watson St. I-4
Wayside Dr. H-4
Weber Rd. K-8
Weir Dr. J-7
Wellington F-1
Westgard Ln. J-6
Westgate F-1
West Point Rd. K-2
Wheatley St. D-2
Whiting St. H-4
Whittier H-4
Wilburn Dr. C-2
Willard St. H-4
Williams Ave. D-4
Willow St. I-7,J-7
Wilshire Pl. I-8
Winnebago St. D-2
Winnie Dr. G-4
Woodland K-6
Wright St. H-2
Wynwood Dr. I-6
Yale St. J-3
Yolanda Dr. J-2
York Ave. H-5
Zapata St. H-1
Zaragosa St. H-1
2nd St. F-4
3rd St. F-4
5th St. F-4
6th St. F-4
7th St. F-4
10th St. G-4
11th St. F-3
12th St. F-3
14th St. F-3
15th St. F-3,G-4
16th St. F-3,G-4
17th St. F-3,G-4
18th St. F-3,G-4
19th St. F-3,G-4
20th St. F-3
21st St. F-3
22nd St. F-3
23rd St. F-2
25th St. F-2
44th St. H-1
45th St. H-1

POINTS OF INTEREST

Artesian Park D-3
Ayers Park D-2
Bayfront Science Park B-3
Blucher Park E-3
Botsford Park K-5
Casa Linda Park I-6
Cole Park F-5
Collier Park J-7
Corpus Christi Golf Center I-1
Corpus Christi State Hospital (M.H.M.R.) . I-2
Cuiper Park J-5
Del Mar College H-4
Driscoll School F-1
Easley Park H-5
General Hospital J-8
Greenwood Park J-2
H. E. Butt Park H-4
Hillcrest Park E-1
Holy Cross Cemetery . F-1
John Jones Park J-3
Kiwanis Park A-2
Laguna Park J-2
Lawndale Park H-6
Lindale Park H-6
Louisiana Parkway . . G-5
Memorial Hospital . . . G-3
Miller H.S. F-1
Pope Park I-8
Price Park J-7
Ray H.S. H-6
Rose Hill Memorial Park F-2
South Bluff Park E-4
Surfside Park A-3
West Haven Park K-1

DALLAS

Abbott B-6
Abbott Ave. D-6
Acorn D-1
Adair G-7
Addison J-4
Adolph G-4
Afton E-3
Airfreight B-1
Air Line Rd. A-7,B-7
Akard H-5
Akard St. I-6
Albright K-5
Alcott D-6,E-6
Alexander J-6
Algiers F-1
Alice Cir. C-5
Allen G-6
Allison J-2
Amelia E-2
Amesbury A-8
Amonette H-3
Andrews B-5
Angelina G-1
Anita B-7,B-8
Ann H-8
Annex F-7
Apple G-7
Arcady C-3,C-4
Armstrong D-6
Armstrong Pkwy. B-4
Arnold J-6
Arroyo E-3
Asbury B-6
Ash I-7
Ash Ln. H-8
Ashland G-4
Athens Ave. A-6
Atlanta I-7
Atoka E-6
Atwater C-6
Atwell C-2
Aubrey C-2
Auburndale B-6
Austin H-5,I-5
Bank E-8
Bataan H-2
Baylor H-7
Bayonne I-2
Bayside G-1
Beatrice I-3
Beaver J-2
Beckley Ave. K-3
Beeville I-2
Belclaire C-3,C-4
Belfort C-1
Bell E-8
Belleau J-1
Bellview I-6
Belmont Ave. E-7
Belmont Rd. D-7
Bengal E-2
Bennett Ave. E-7
Benson H-8
Beverly C-3,C-6
Bickers G-1,H-2
Binkley B-6
Birch A-8,G-8
Bird G-7
Birmingham Ave. J-8
Bishop K-3
Blakney I-6
Blaylock Dr. K-4
Bluebonnet D-7
Boaz A-3
Bobbie K-5
Boedecker A-7
Boll G-6
Bomar C-1
Bonita D-7
Bookhout F-8
Bordeaux B-3,C-4
Borger H-1
Bowen St. E-4
Bowser D-4
Bowser Ave. C-4
Bradford D-2
Bradley J-1
Brantley H-2
Bremen C-8
Bristol A-2
Brook A-6
Broom H-4
Browder I-6
Brown E-3,F-4
Bryan E-8,G-8
Bryan Pkwy. E-8
Buena Vista E-5
Buffalo J-6
Burgess F-1
Burlew F-7
Burr I-2
Butler E-2
Byron C-6
Cabell Dr. F-6
Caddo F-6
Cadis St. I-6
Cadiz H-6,I-5
Cadiz St. Viaduct J-4
Cagemi B-1
Caillet A-3
Calvary F-5
Cambrick E-5
Cambridge C-6
Camden Ave. B-8
Campbell F-6
Canada Dr. G-1
Cantegral G-6
Canterbury Ct. J-1
Canton H-6,H-7
Canty St. K-2
Carnation E-1
Carrol Ave. F-7
Capitol Ave. E-6
Carlisle F-5
Cass E-2
Cedar D-3,F-5
Cedar Crest Blvd. K-7
Cedar Hill Rd. . . . J-2,K-2
Cedar Plaza Ln. D-3
Cedar Springs Rd. C-2,E-4
Central H-6
Central Expwy. E-6
G-6,I-7
Chambers E-7
Chattanooga D-1
Chemical F-2
Cherrywood Ave. D-2
Chicago H-1
Chihuahua H-1
Clara E-3
Clark F-5
Cleburne A-7
Clyde F-5
Clarence J-7
Cleaves K-5
Clinton K-1
Cobb G-6
Cochran F-6
Cockrell I-6
Colby G-5
Cole F-5,G-3
Cole Ave. E-5
Coleman K-7
College B-7
Colonial K-8
Colorado Blvd. . . . J-1,J-3
Colson G-8
Comal K-3
Commerce St. . . . H-5,H-8
Commerce St. Viaduct I-3
Conant F-2
Concho D-8
Concord B-1
Congress E-4
Conklin H-2,I-2
Conner F-6
Connerly B-5
Conrad B-1
Conroe H-2
Continental Ave. H-4
Continental Viaduct H-3
Convent G-7
Converse F-2
Coombs I-7
Cooper J-8,K-7
Corbin H-5
Corinth St. J-6
Cornell C-6
Coronet H-2
Corsicana I-6
Cortland B-1
Cowan A-2
Cragmont D-5
Crampton F-2
Crescent D-6
Crest D-3
Cresthaven A-2
Crockett G-5
Crossman H-1
Crowdlis H-7
Crutcher G-8
Culcourt A-2
Cullen E-7
Curtis St. H-7
Dallas-Ft. Worth Tpk. I-2
Daniels A-6
Dartmouth C-6
Dathe J-8
Dawson H-7,I-7
Deere F-6
Delano F-6
Delmar Dr. E-8
Delta H-1
Denley K-5
Denton E-2
Denton Dr. C-1
Dickason E-4
Dorothy St. C-3
Douglas E-3,E-4
Douglas Ave. . . . A-4,C-4
Dragon G-4
Drane Dr. B-3
Drexel B-6
Driskell K-8
Druid Ln. B-5
Druid Ln. A-5
Dublin A-7
Duluth I-2
Dumas F-8
Dumont F-8
Durham A-7
Dyer B-7
Eads K-4
Eastern E-3
Eastside H-8
Eastus Dr. B-2
Edgefield I-1
Edgefield Dr. K-1
Edgewater D-5
Edgewood J-8
Edison G-4
Edmondson C-3
Edwards B-2
El Benito I-1
El Dorado K-3
Elihu H-8
Elizabeth E-6
Ellis F-5
Ellsworth C-7
Elm St. H-5,H-7
Elsbeth K-3
Emerson A-3,A-4
Englewood Rd. K-4
Enid F-4
Ervay St. H-5,I-6
Eton C-5
Euclid C-5,E-7
Eugene K-8
Evergreen H-8,J-2
Ewing Ave. K-4
Exposition H-8
Express G-2
Fairfax C-3
Fairfield C-5
Fairfield Ave. C-5
Fairley C-3
Fairmount F-4
Fairway D-4
Famous I-2
Farrington F-1,G-3
Federal H-5
Ferris I-7
Fielder Ct. C-1
Fitzhugh Ave. . . . D-6,E-6
Flanders I-1
Fleetwood D-2
Fletcher H-8
Flora G-5
Floride G-7
Floyd G-6
Folsom I-2
Fondren A-7
Fordyce G-3
Forest J-7,J-8
Ft. Worth Ave. J-1
Fox I-2
Fuqua E-7
Gallagher H-2
Gano I-6
Garrett E-7
Gaston Ave. G-7
Gilbert C-3,D-4
Gilmer I-2
Glass G-3
Glencoe D-7
Glenwick Ln. . . . A-3,A-4
Glenwood Ave. D-5
Golf B-5
Goliad D-8
Good Latimer G-6
Goodwin D-7,D-8
Gordon G-7
Granada B-6
Grand Ave. I-8,J-7
Grassmere A-4,A-5
Green K-2
Greenbriar J-2,J-3
Greenville Ave. D-8
Greenway B-4
Greenway, W. A-3
Greer K-8
Gregg D-2
Gretna F-1
Griffin H-5
Griffin, N. I-5
Griffin, S. I-6
Guest I-2
Guilden H-3
Guillot G-5
Gunter H-8
Guymon I-1
Haggar C-2
Haines J-3,K-2
Hall D-1,D-3,E-4
Hall St. G-6,H-7
Hamburg K-7
Handley J-3
Hardwick I-3
Harlem F-5
Harry Hines Blvd. E-2,G-4
Harston G-1,I-1
Hart K-5
Hartford E-4,F-4
Harvard C-6
Harwood G-4,G-5 H-6,I-6
Haskell Ave. F-7
Haskill E-5
Harvester G-3
Hawes C-3
Hawkins G-6,H-6
Hawthorne E-3
Hawthorne Ave. D-4
Haynie A-6
Hearne I-1
Hedgerow Dr. D-2
Henderson Ave. E-7
Henning J-6
Henson F-4
Herbert H-2
Herschel D-4
Hester D-6
Hickman K-8
Hickory I-8,I-7
Highland C-5
High School B-6
Hiline G-3
Hill G-7,K-1
Hillcrest Ave. B-6
Holland D-5
Holland Ave. C-3
Homeland G-1
Homer D-7,E-6
Hondo E-3
Hood F-4
Hope K-8
Hopkins Ave. A-2
Hord H-5
Horrace F-6
Hoskins E-8
Houston I-4
Houston St. Viaduct J-4
Howell F-6,H-3
Hubert E-8
Hudnall St. D-2
Hudson B-3
Hugo F-5
Hunt G-4
Hunters Glen Rd. A-5
Hursey A-6
Iberia F-1
Indiana H-7
Industrial Blvd. . . . F-3,J-5
Inspiration G-4
Inwood Rd. B-3,D-2
Irving D-5
Irving Blvd. F-1
Ivan G-4
Jackson H-5
Jefferson Blvd. Viaduct J-4
Jeffries H-7,I-8
Jewette F-6
Johnson F-6
Jordan J-8
Julian J-3
Junior J-2,J-3
Junius F-8,G-7
Kay G-2
Kaywood Dr. A-3
Kelly J-7
Kelton Dr. A-2
Kenwell D-4
Kenwood C-8
Kessler Ave. J-2
Kessler Pkwy. J-1,J-2
Key B-6
Kidd Springs K-2
Kimsey Dr. D-2
Kings Hwy. K-1
Kings Rd. E-3
Knight F-3
Knott Pl. J-2
Knox J-7
Kyle K-1
La Clede F-5
Ladd H-1
Lafayette F-6,F-7
Lafoy Blvd. C-3
Lagoon K-5
Lahoma D-3
Lake E-3
Lake Cliff Dr. K-3
Lakeside C-5
Lamar J-7
Lamar St. H-4
Lamesa J-6
Lancaster K-4
Lane I-7
Laneri D-7
Langford B-3
Lansing K-4
Larchmont B-4
Lark Dr. B-3
La Salle AVe. D-4
Latimer I-7
La Vista E-8
La Vista Ct. E-8
Lear I-6
Leath G-1
Leatrice J-2
Lee E-1
Lee Ave. E-6
Lee Pkwy. E-5
Lemmon C-3
Lemmon Ave. A-1,E-4
Lenway J-8,K-7
Levee St. G-3
Lewis F-6
Liberty G-6
Lincoln I-7
Lindell E-8
Lindenwood C-6
Linnet Ln. B-2
Live Oak St. F-7,G-6
Livingston B-3
Llano D-8
Lockheed B-2
Lofland E-2
Logan I-7
Lomo Alto A-4,C-4
Longview C-7
Loomis K-8
Lorraine Ln. C-3
Louise I-7
Lovers Ln. A-2,A-6
Lucas Ave. E-3
Lupo E-1
Mabel B-2
Mac Arthur D-3
Macatee E-2
Mack A-6
Madison K-3
Magnolia H-5
Mahanna Springs D-3
Main G-8
Main St. H-5
Malt H-8
Manett E-6
Manett Ave. D-7
Manor E-1
Manor Wy. C-1
Manufacturing G-2
Maple E-3
Maple Ave. C-1,F-4
Maplewood B-5
March A-2
Marilla I-5
Market H-5
Marquita C-8
Marsalis Ave. K-4
Martel C-7
Mary E-8
Mary Cliff K-1
Matalee C-7
Matilda D-8
Matilda St. A-8
Matton F-5
May I-3
Mayo F-6
McBroom H-1,H-2
McCommas Blvd. C-7
McCoy G-6
McDonald K-8
McFarlin Blvd. . . . A-4,B-7
McKee I-8,J-8
McKell F-7
McKinney G-5
McKinney Ave. E-6
McKinnon F-4
McMillan D-7
Meadow I-8
Medical Center E-1
Melrose E-7
Mercedes C-7
Merrimac C-7
Meyers I-8
Milam D-5
Miles C-3
Milton A-6,A-8
Mississippi F-1
Mobile I-2
Mockingbird C-1
Mockingbird Ln. B-4
Monarch E-7
Monitor F-2
Montclair K-1
Montclair Rd. J-1
Montgomery J-8
Monticello C-7,C-8
Montrose B-3
Moody G-3
Moore K-5
Moreland F-7
Morgan J-3
Morningside C-7
Morton A-3
Moser E-7
Motor E-2,F-1
Mt. Vernon B-6
Muncie I-1
Munger F-6-8,G-5,H-5
Murphey H-5
Myrtle I-8
Nakoma B-3
Nash F-5
Navarro H-1,I-1,J-1
Neal I-1,J-1
Neches K-2
Neola B-3
Newmore A-2
New Orleans D-1
Newton Ave. D-4
Nomas H-2
Nob Hill J-2
Noble E-5,F-5
Normandy B-4,B-5
Northway Dr. A-8
Nusbaume G-7
Oak G-6,H-8,I-7,J-2
Oakenwald J-3
Oak Grove F-5
Oakland K-7
Oakland Ave. H-7,I-8
Oak Lawn G-3
Oak Lawn Ave. E-4
Obenchain H-2
Olive G-5
Oliver C-6
Olympia J-1
Oram E-8
Oregon J-3
Orleans Ave. I-7
Ormsby H-2
Overhill D-5
Ownby B-5
Oxford B-7,C-6
Pacific Ave. H-5
Palo Pinto D-8
Park A-5,H-6,J-8,I-7
Park Rd. D-1
Paker J-6
Parkhouse I-5
Parkland D-2
Parkmont E-8
Parvia H-2
Pastor I-2
Patterson H-5
Payne G-4,H-3
Peabody J-7
Peabody Ave. J-8
Peak St. F-7
Pear H-8
Pearl F-4,G-5,H-6
Pearlstone H-7
Pecan K-5
Pecos G-6
Pennsylvania J-7,K-7
Penrose C-8
Pershing D-6
Pine K-8
Pittman J-2
Pittsburg H-3
Plowman J-3,K-3
Poe E-6
Poplar K-8
Potomac B-5
Potomac, W. B-4
Powhattan I-5
Poydras H-5
Prairie View E-1
Prentice B-7
Prescott D-4
Preston B-5
Preston Rd. C-5
Princeton C-6
Prospect E-8
Prosper B-2
Pueblo H-1
Quaker F-1
Rainbow J-2
Raleigh D-3
Ralston C-2
Rampart E-2
Randall E-8
Ranier K-1
Rankin A-5
Rawlins C-3,E-4
Reagan E-4,F-3
Record I-5
Redfield F-2
Revere C-8
Rheims Pl. D-4
Richard D-7
Richardson I-7
Richmond Ave. D-7
Ridgedale C-7
Rio Vista J-3
River H-4
Roberts Pkwy. B-6
Robin Rd. A-3
Rock Creek B-5
Rock Island Rd. J-5
Roe J-5
Roland Ave. D-4
Romine K-8
Roper B-2
Rosedale A-6
Rosewood E-3
Ross H-5
Ross Ave. E-8,F-6
Roswell E-4
Routh F-4,G-5
Rowena E-7
Rusk E-6
Rutz H-1
Sadler Cir. D-2
St. John D-5
St. Johns C-6
St. Joseph G-7
St. Louis H-7
St. Paul G-5
Sale E-5
Salmon K-2
Sam Dealy J-2
San Carlos B-4
Sandhurst Ln. B-8
Sanger J-6
San Juacinto G-6,H-5
Santa Fe H-8
Savage B-2
Savannah I-6
Scurry F-7
Seale I-2
Sears E-8
Seegar J-6
Sewanee C-5
Shannon B-5
Shaw H-1
Shelby F-4
Shenandoah B-4,B-5
Shreveport G-7
Simpson G-7
Singleton Blvd. H-1
Skiles G-6
Slocum G-3,G-4
Sneed F-5
Snider Plaza A-6
Somerville B-8
South J-7
Spann J-3
Sparks K-5
Spence K-8
Springbrook D-5
Springs Blvd. D-3
Stacey G-6
Stanhope B-4
Starling Cir. B-3
Starr K-3
State F-6,G-5
Stemmons J-3
Stemmons Frwy., N. . G-4
Stigall Dr. A-2
Stone Bridge D-5
Stoneman K-8
Stonelegh D-2
Stratford C-5
Stutz Dr. D-1
Sullivan I-6
Sulphur I-3
Summit E-7
Swiss G-7
Sycamore F-7
Sylvan Ave. H-2
Sylvester E-3,F-4
Sylvi K-2
Taft K-1
Taos A-2
Taylor H-7,I-6
Texas E-8
Tex Oak E-2
Thackeray B-6
Thedford B-2
Thomas F-6,G-5
Thornton Frwy. K-4
Throckmorton . . . D-5,E-4
Thrush B-3
Tilden J-3
Timbergrove K-1
Topeka H-2,I-2
Toronto H-1
Travis E-5
Treadway D-1
Tremont F-8
Tully E-2
Turner Ct. J-2,K-2
Turtle Creek G-3
Turtle Creek Ln. A-5
Tyler K-2
Tyree B-2
University B-7
University Blvd. A-2,A-5,A-7
Vagas E-3
Valdina F-2
Vanelia D-3
Vanderbilt D-7,D-8
Vandlia D-3
Vantage F-2
Vassar A-5
Velasco D-8
Versailles, N. C-4
Versailles, S. C-4
Viaduct K-5
Vickery Blvd. D-7
Vicksburg F-1
Victor G-7
Victoria B-2
View D-3
Vilbig Rd. H-1,J-1
Villars G-6
Virginia F-7
Wade G-6
Wake H-2
Wales I-3
Walkway I-2
Wall I-6
Walton H-7
Wanetka B-3
Warren J-7,J-8
Washington F-6,H-8
Wateka Rd. B-2,B-3
Watt F-6
Webb C-6
Webster B-2
Welborn E-4
Welbourn G-4
Weldon F-6
Wendelkin K-8
Wenoah B-3
Westchester A-4
West Main I-2
Westminster A-6
West Side C-4
Westward I-2
Westway D-4
Westwick Rd. B-5
Wheeler D-3
Wichita G-4,H-4
Wickford K-2
Willard A-7
Williams Dr. B-5
Williams Pkwy. B-5
Willis D-7
Willow G-8,H-8
Windomere J-1,K-1
Windsor B-4
Windsor Pkwy. B-5
Winnetak H-2,I-1,K-1
Winton B-8,C-7
Wolf F-4
Wood H-5
Woodall Rogers Frwy. G-5
Woodlawn K-2
Woodside K-5
Worcola B-8,D-7
Word G-6
Worth G-7,G-8
Worthington F-5
Wren B-3
Wycliff D-4
Wycliff Ave. D-4 E-3,F-2
Yeargan F-5
Young H-5,H-6
Yuma J-2
Zang J-4
Zangs Blv.d K-3
1st H-7,H-8
2nd H-7,H-8
3rd H-8
4th H-8
5th St. K-2
6th St. K-2

POINTS OF INTEREST

Buckner Park G-8
Cole Park E-6
Exall Park G-6
Greenbelt Park . . G-2,K-5
Greenway Park B-4
Grigge Park F-6
Highland Park C-6
Kidd Springs Park . . . K-2
Lake Cliff Park K-3
Lee Park E-5
Love Field Municipal Airport B-1
Reverchon Park F-4
University Park B-6

Dallas, TX

Scale of Miles
0 .2 .4 .6 .8
N

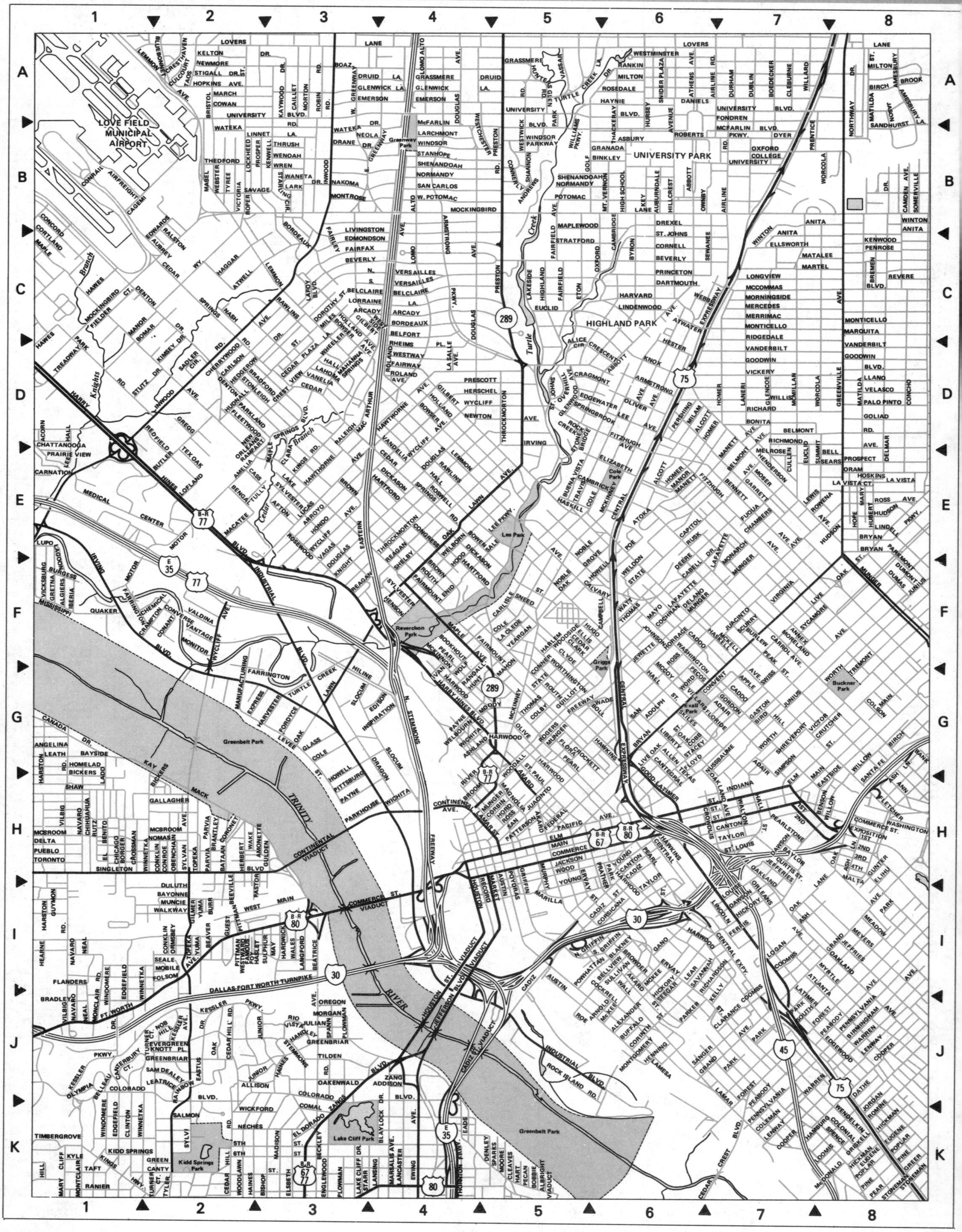

N

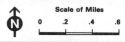

Scale of Miles

0 .2 .4 .6

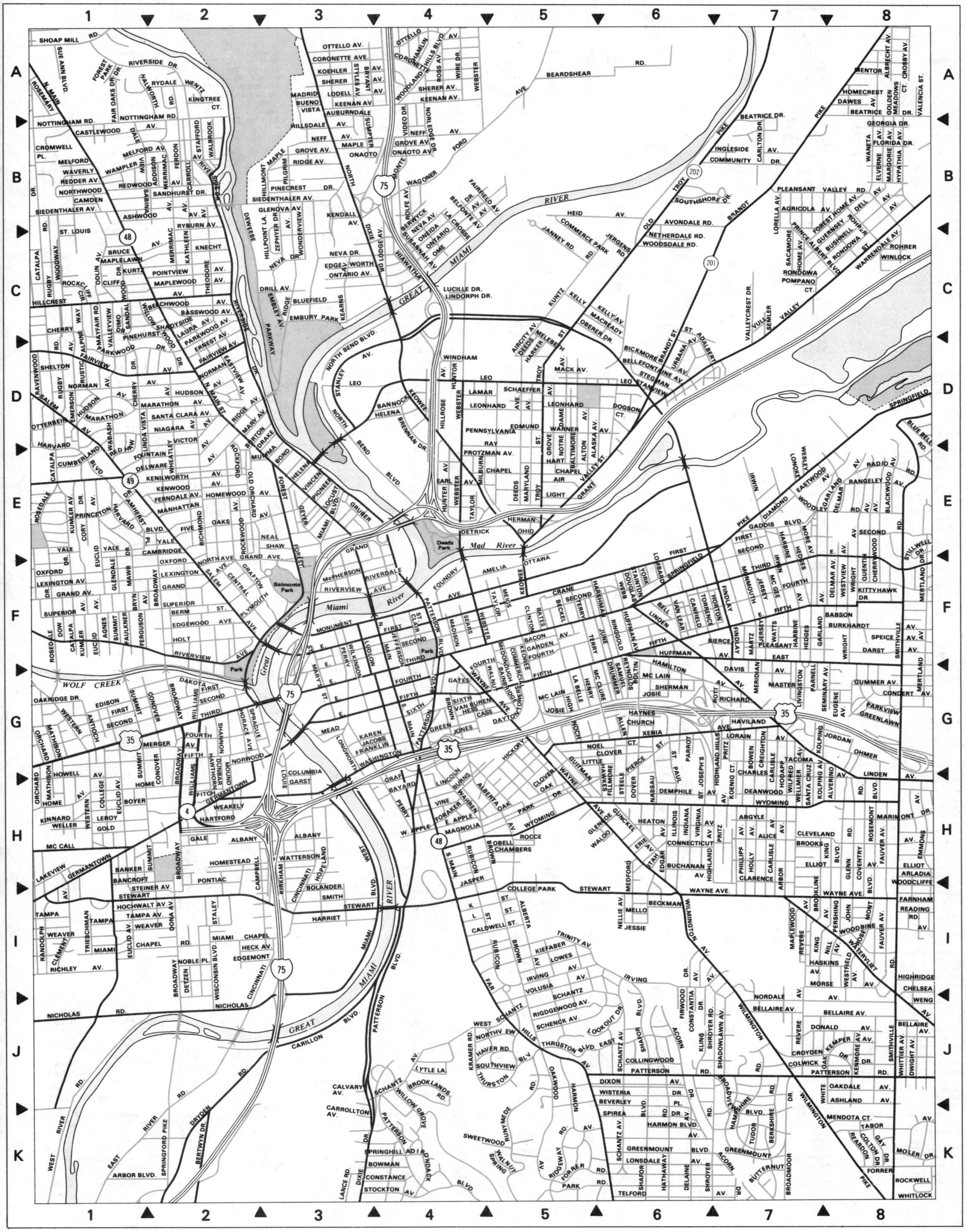

DAYTON

Acorn Dr. J-6,K-7
Addison B-2
Adirondack K-4
Agnes F-1
Agricola Av. B-7
Air E-5
Aircity Av. C-5
Alaska Av. D-5
Albany H-2,H-3
Alberta Ave. H-4,I-5
Albrecht Av. A-8
Alice H-7
Allen G-6
Alpine Way C-1
Alton v. D-5
Alverino H-8
Amelia F-5
Amherst Blvd. E-1
Antioch G-1
Apple,E. H-4
Apple,W. H-4
Arbor H-7
Arbor Blvd. K-1
Argyle H-7
Arladia H-8
Ashland Av. J-8
Ashwood Av. B-1
Auburndale A-3
Avondale Rd. B-6
Babson F-8
Bacon F-5
Bainbridge G-5
Baltimore D-5
Bancroft H-1
Banker H-1
Bannock D-4
Basswood Av. C-2
Bates F-5
Bayard H-4
Beardshear Rd. A-5
Beatrice Dr. A-7
Beckel F-5
Beckman I-6
Beechwood Av. C-2
Belfonte Av. B-4
Bell F-6
Bellaire Av. J-7,J-8
Bellefontaine Av. D-6
Berkshire Rd. K-7
Berm St. F-2
Bertwyn Dr. K-2
Berwick B-4
Beverley Pl. J-6
Bickmore Av. D-6
Bierce F-7
Blackwood E-8
Blue Bell Rd. D-8
Bluefield C-3
Bolander H-3
Boltin G-6
Bond E-3
Bowen G-7
Bowman K-4
Boyer H-1
Brandt St. D-6
Brandt Pike B-7
Brennan Dr. D-4
Broadmoor Dr. K-7
Broadvie Blvd. J-7
Broadway F-2,G-2
H-2,I-2
Brooklands Rd. J-4
Brookline H-7
Brooks H-7
Brown G-4,H-5
Bruce Av. C-1
Bryan Av. F-1
Bryant A-3
Buchanan Av. H-6
Burkhardt Av. F-8
Burns H-4
Burton D-2
Bushnell Av. C-8
Butternut K-7
Caldwell St. I-5
Calvary Av. J-3
Cambridge E-2
Camden B-1
Campbell H-2
Canfield F-6
Carillon Blvd. J-2
Carl Av. E-4
Carlisle Av. G-7,H-7
Carlton Dr. B-4
Carroll B-2
Carrollton Av. K-3
Cass G-4
Castlewood Av. B-1
Catalpa Dr. C-1,E-1,F-1
Central F-2
Chambers H-5
Chapel E-5
Charles G-7
Chelsea I-8
Cherrwood Av. F-8
Cherry Dr. C-1,D-1
Church G-6
Cincinnati H-3,I-2
Clarence H-7
Clement Av. I-1
Cleveland H-7
Cliff C-1
Clinton F-5
Clover G-6
College H-1
College Park I-5
Collingwood J-6
Colton Dr. K-8
Columbia G-3
Colwick Dr. J-7
Commerce Park B-5
Commercial F-5
Community Dr. B-7
Condert Av. G-8
Connecticut H-6
Conover G-2
Constance K-4
Constantia Av. J-6
Coronett Ave. A-3,A-4
Cory Dr. E-1
Coventry Rd. H-8
Crane F-5
Creighton G-7
Cromwell Pl. B-1
Crosby Av. A-8
Croyden Dr. J-7
Cumberland E-1
Dakota G-2
Dale View B-1
Darst Av. F-8
Davis Av. G-7
Dayton Towers G-5
Deanwood H-7
Deeds Ave. D-5,E-5
Delaine Ave. K-6
Delmar Av. E-8,F-8
Delware Av. E-2
Demphile H-6
Detrick E-4
Detzen I-2
Dewesse Pkwy. B-3
Diamond E-7
Dixie Dr. K-3
Dixon Av. J-6
Dogson Ct. D-6
Dona Av. I-2
Donald Av. J-8
Douglas F-6
Dover H-6
Dow F-1
Drake D-3
Drill Av. C-3
Drummer G-6
Dryden Rd. J-2,K-1
Dunbar G-2
Dwight Av. J-8
East River Rd.
J-2,K-1
East View Av. D-2
Eastwood Av. E-8
Edgar H-6
Edgemont I-2
Edgewood Ave. F-2
Edgeworth C-3
Edison G-1
Edmund D-5
Elliot H-7,H-8
Elverine Av. B-8
Embley Av. C-3
Embury Park C-3
Emerson Av. D-1
Emmons H-8
Erie H-6
Ernest Av. D-2
Euclid Av. E-1,F-1
H-1,I-1
Eugene Av. G-8
Fairfield Av. B-4
Fair Oaks Dr. A-1
Fairview Av. D-1,D-2
Faulkner F-1
Fauver Av. H-8,I-8
Far Hills Av. J-5
Farnham I-8
Ferdon Rd. B-2
Ferguson F-1
Ferndale Ave. E-2
Fifth F-6,G-2
Fifth, E. F-7,G-3
Filmore G-6
Findlay F-7
First E-6,E-7
F-4,G-1,G-2
Firwood Dr. J-6
Fitch G-1
Five Oaks Av. E-2
Florida Dr. B-8
Foraker H-4
Forest E-3
Forest Home Av. B-8
Forest Park Dr. A-1
Forrer Rd. K-5,K-8
Foundry F-4
Fountain Av. E-2
Fourth F-5,F-7,G-2,G-4
Fourth, E. G-3
Franklin G-3
Gaddis Blvd. E-7
Gale H-2
Garden Av. F-5
Garland Av. E-8,F-7
Garst H-3
Gates G-4
Gay Dr. K-8
Georgia Dr. B-8
Germantown H-1
Geyer E-3
Glencoe H-5
Glendale F-1
Glenn Rd. H-8
Glenoua Av. B-3
Gold H-1
Golden Meadows Ct. A-8
Graf H-4
Grafton F-2
Grand Ave. E-2,E-3
F-1,F-2
Grant E-5
Greenlawn G-8
Greenmount Blvd. K-6
Grove Av. D-5
Gruber E-3
Guernsey Dell Av. B-8
Gummer Av. G-8
Gunckel H-6
Halworth A-2
Hamilton G-6
Hamlin A-4
Hampshire Rd. J-7
Harbine Av. E-7,F-7
Harker D-5
Harmon Blvd. J-5,K-6
Harriet I-3
Harshman F-6
Hart E-5
Hartford H-2
Harvard Blvd. D-1,E-1
Haskins Av. I-7
Hathaway Rd. K-6
Haver Rd. J-5
Haviland G-7
Hawkes G-6
Hawthorn G-2
Haynes G-6
Heaton H-6
Heck Av. I-2
Hedges E-7,F-7
Heid Av. B-5
Helena D-4,E-3
Henry G-5
Herman E-5
Hess G-4
Hiawatha C-4
Hickory G-5
Hillcrest Av. C-1
Hilldale Av. B-3
Hillmont B-3
Hill Point Ln. B-3
Hill Rose Av. D-4
Highland H-6
Highland Hills G-7
High Noch G-5
High Ridge I-8
Hochwalt Av. I-1
Hodapp G-7
Holly Av. H-7
Holt F-2
Home Av. H-1
Homecreast A-8
Homestead H-2
Homewood Av. E-2
Hopeland H-3
Horace Ave. G-8
Horton F-7
Howe Av. C-7
Howell Av. G-1
Hudson Av. D-1,D-2
Hunter Av. E-4
Huntor D-4
Huffman Av. F-6
Huffman Av. East F-6
Hypathia Av. B-8
Illinois H-6
Imo C-1
Indiana H-6
Ingleside Av. B-7
Irving Av. I-5,I-6
Irwin E-7,F-7
Jacobs G-3
Janney Rd. C-5
Jasper H-4
Jefferson F-4
Jergens Rd. C-6
Jersey F-7
Jessie I-6
John Glen Rd. I-8
Jones G-4
Jordan G-8
Joseph's G-6
Josie G-5,G-6
June F-6
K St. I-5
Karen G-3
Kathleen Av. C-2
Kearns C-3
Keenan Av. A-3,A-4
Kelly Ave. C-5,C-6
Kendall Av. B-3
Kenilworth Av. E-2
Kenimore Av. J-8
Kenwood Av. E-1
Keowee D-4,G-5
Kiefaber I-5
King Av. H-8,I-7
King Tree Ct. A-2
Kinnard H-1
Kirkham H-3
Kitty Hawk Dr. F-8
Kling Av. J-6
Kling Dr. J-6
Knecht C-2
Koehler Av. A-3
Koeing Ct. H-7
Kolping Av. G-7,H-7
Kramer Rd. J-4
Kumler Av. E-1,G-1
Kuniz Rd. C-5
Kurtz C-1
L St. I-5
La Belle G-5
La Crosse B-4
Lakeview H-1
Lamar D-4
Lance Rd. K-3
Laura Av. C-2
Leo D-3,D-4,D-5
Leonhard D-4,D-5
Leroy H-1
Lexington Av.
F-1,F-2
Light E-5
Lincoln H-4
Linda Vista D-1
Linden Av. F-6,H-8
Lindorph Dr. C-4
Little G-5
Livingston G-7
Locust E-3
Lodell Av. A-3
Lodge Av. C-4
Lombard F-6
Longworth G-3
Lonoke E-7
Lonsdale Av. K-6
Lookout Dr. J-5
Lorain Av. G-7
Lorella Av. B-7
Louie G-3
Lowes I-5
Lucille Dr. C-4
Ludlow F-3
Lytle Ln. J-4
Mack Av. D-5
Macready C-6
Madrid Bueno
Vista A-3
Madson F-4
Magnolia H-4
Main St., N. A-1
D-2,F-4
Main, S. G-4,H-4
Manhattan E-2
Martz F-7
Maple Grove Av. B-3
Maple Lawn C-1
Maplewood Av. C-2,I-7
Marathon Av. D-1
Margoire Av. B-8
Marimont Dr. H-8
Mary Av. D-2
Maryland Av. E-5
Master G-7
Mathison G-1,H-1
Mawr Dr. F-1
Mayfair Rd. C-1
McCall H-1
McClure G-5
McDonough F-5
McGee F-7
McLain G-5,G-6
McPherson F-3
Mead G-3
Medford H-6
Meigs F-5
Melbeth C-5
Melford Av. B-1
Mello I-6
Mendota Ct. K-8
Mentor A-8
Merger Av. G-2
Meridian G-7
Merrimac Av. B-2,C-2
Mertland Dr. F-8
Miami Blvd. E-3
Miami Blvd.,W. I-3
Miami Chapel I-1
Milburn E-4
Moler Dr. K-8
Monmouth F-7
Monte Video Dr. B-4
Monument Ave. F-3
More Av. E-7
Morse I-7
Mound G-2
Mumma E-3
Nassau H-6
Neal E-3
Neff Av. B-3,B-4
Nellie Av. I-6
Netherdale Rd. C-6
Neva Av. B-4
Neva Dr. C-3
Niagara Av. D-2
Nicholas Rd. J-1,J-2
Nill Av. I-8
Noble Pl. I-2
Noel G-5
Nordale Av. J-7
Norledge Dr. B-4
Norman Av. D-1,D-2
North Ave. E-2
North Bend Blvd. D-3
North Dixie B-3
Northwood B-1
Northview J-5
Norwood G-2
Notre Dame Av. D-5
Nottingham Rd. A-1
Oak H-5
Oak Dale Av. J-8
Oak Kemper Av. J-8
Oakridge Dr. G-1
Oakwood Av. J-5
Obell H-5
Oberer Dr. C-5
Odlin Av. C-1
Ohio E-5
Ohmer G-8
Old Orchard E-2
Old Troy Pike B-6
Ome Av. C-4
Onaoto Av. B-3
Oneida Dr. B-4
Ontario Av. C-3,C-4
Orchard G-1,H-1
Ottawa F-5
Ottello Av. A-3
Otterbelli D-1
Oxford E-2,F-1
Park Dr. H-5
Park Rd. K-5
Parkview G-8
Parkway C-3
Parkwood Av. C-2
Parkwood Dr. C-1
Parnell G-7
Parrot G-6
Patterson Blvd.
F-4,G-4,I-4
J-6,J-8,K-4
Pennsylvania D-4
Perry F-3,H-4
Pershing Blvd. I-8
Phillips Av. H-7
Pierce St. G-6
Pilgrim B-3
Pioneer E-3
Pinecrest Dr. B-3
Pinehurst C-1
Pleasant F-7
Pleasant Valley Rd. B-7
Plymouth F-2
Pointview Av. C-2
Pompano Ct. C-7
Pontiac H-2
Prince Albert Blvd. C-7
Princeton Dr. E-1
Pritz G-7,H-7
Protzman Av. E-4
Quentin Av. F-8
Quitman G-5
Radio Rd. E-8
Randolph I-1
Rangelley Av. E-8
Ravenwood D-1
Ray D-4
Reading Rd. I-8
Reardon K-8
Reddar Av. B-1
Red Haw D-1
Redwood Av. B-1
Revere Av. I-7,J-7
Reynolds G-6
Richard G-7
Richley Av. I-1
Richmond E-2
Ridge Av. C-3,D-2
Ridgeway Rd. K-5
Ridgewood Ave. J-5
Ringgold F-6
Riverdale F-3
Riverside Dr. A-2
B-2,C-2
Riverview Ave. F-2,F-3
Rocce H-5
Rockcliff Cir. C-1
Rockford E-2
Rockwell K-8
Rockwood Av. E-2
Rohrer B-8,C-8
Rolfe Av. B-4
Rondowa C-7,C-8
Rosedale E-1,F-1
Rosemary A-1
Rosemont Blvd. H-8,I-8
Ross Av. A-4
Rott G-7
Rubicon H-4,I-5
Rugby Rd. C-1,D-1
Runymede Rd. K-5
Rustic Av. D-1
Ryburn Av. B-2
Rydale Wentz A-2
Sabina B-2
Sacamore C-7
St. Adalbert C-6
St. Brown I-5
St. Clair F-4
St. Louis B-1
St. Mary's St. F-3
St. Paul G-6
Salem Av. D-1,F-2
Samuel G-6
Sandal C-1
Sandhurst Dr. B-2
Santa Clara Av. D-2
Santa Cruz H-7
Schaefer D-5
Schantz J-4,J-5,J-6
Schenck Av. J-5
Sears F-4
Second E-1,E-8,F-1
F-5,G-1,G-2
Seminary Av. G-8
Semler C-7
Shaddy Side C-2
Shadowlawn Av. J-7
Shafor Blvd. J-6,K-6
Shannon G-2
Shaw E-3
Shelton D-1
Sherer Av. A-3,A-4
Sherman G-6
Shoapmill Rd. A-1
Shroyer Rd. J-6,K-6
Siedenthaler Av. B-1
Sixth G-4
Smith I-3
Smithville Rd. E-8,F-8
H-8,I-8,J-8
Southshore Dr. B-6
Southview J-5
Speice Av. F-8
Spirea Dr. K-6
Sprague G-2
Springfield Pike
D-8,E-7,F-6
Springford Pike K-2
Spring Hill K-4
Stafford B-2
Stainton F-6
Staley I-2
Stanley Av. D-3
Stanview D-6
Steele G-6
Stegman D-6
Stewart I-3,I-1
Stewart Wayne Ave.
I-5,I-6
Stillwell Dr. E-8
Stockton Av. K-4
Styles Av. A-3
Sue Ann Blvd. A-1
Summit F-1,G-1,H-2
Sumter A-
Superior F-1,G-2
Susannah Av. C-4
Sweetwood K-5
Tabor Av. K-8
Tacoma G-7
Tampa I-1
Taylor E-4,F-5
Telford Av. K-6
Terry F-5
Theodore Av. C-2
Third F-4,G-1,G-2
Third, E. F-7
Thruston Blvd., E. J-5
Thurston Blvd. J-5
Trieschman I-1
Trinity Av. I-5
Torrence F-6
Troy St. D-5,E-5
Tudor K-7
Utah Av. H-6
Urbana Av. D-6
Valencia St. A-8
Valley St. C-7,E-5
Valleycrest Dr. C-7
Valleyview C-1
Van Buren G-4
Van Lear F-6
Victor Av. D-2
Vincent E-3
Virginia H-6
Volusia Av. I-5
Vull C-7
Wabash Av. D-1
Wagner Ford Rd. B-4
Walbrook B-2
Waldo H-5
Walnut G-5
Walnut Spring K-5
Wampler Av. B-1
Waneta Av. B-8
Warner Av. D-5
Warren H-4
Warrendale Av. C-8
Washington G-3
Watervliet Av. I-8
Watterson H-3
Watts F-7
Wayne Ave. G-4,H-5,I-8
Waverly B-1
Weakely H-2
Weaver I-1
Webb F-6
Webster A-4,D-4,E-4
Weller H-1
Wellmier H-7
Wesley E-7
Western G-1,H-1
Westfield Av. I-8
West River Rd. J-1,K-1
West Schantz J-4
Westview Av. F-8
Wheatley Av. E-2
White J-8
Whitlock K-8
Whittier Av. J-8
Wilford G-7
Wilkinson F-3
Williams G-2
Willow Grove J-4
Wilmington Av. I-6
Wilmington Pike J-7,K-7
Willow Wood Dr. C-2
Windham D-4
Winlock C-8
Wire Dr. A-4
Wisconsin Blvd. I-2
Wisteria Dr. J-6
Wood Dr. C-1
Woodbine Av. I-8
Woodcliffe I-8
Woodland Hills Blvd.
A-4
Woodley Rd. E-7
Woodsdale Rd. C-6
Woodway C-1
Wonderview B-3
Wright Av. F-8
Wyoming H-5,H-7
Xenia Ave. G-6
Yale E-1
York F-6
Zephyer Dr. B-3

DENVER

Acoma St. A-4,H-4,K-4
Alcott St. B-1,F-1,K-1
Allcott Way H-1
Arapahoe St. F-3
Archer Pl. K-3
Argyle Pl. D-1
Arkins Ct. D-4
Baldwin Ct. A-6
Bannock St. H-4,J-4
Barberry I-1
Bassett St. E-2
Bayaud Ave. K-3
Beach St. A-1
Blake St. D-4,F-3
Boulder St. D-1
Bryant St. D-1,F-1,I-1
Bryant Way K-1
Brighton Blvd. A-7,C-5
Broadway A-4,G-4,J-4
Bryon Pl. E-1
Bunker Pl. E-1
Cahita B-4
California St. G-4
Cedar Ave. K-1,K-8
Chaffee B-2
Champa St. F-3
Cherokee St. B-4,H-4,K-4
Cherry Creek North
Dr. K-8
Cherry Creek South
Dr. K-8
Chestnut Pl. C-5
Circle Dr. J-7
Clarkson St. H-5,K-5
Claude B-7
Clayton St. B-8,H-8,J-8
Colfax Ave. G-1,G-6
Columbine St. B-8
H-8,J-8
Corona St. H-6,K-6
Court Pl. F-5,G-4
Crescent Dr. F-1
Curtis St. F-3,G-2
Delaware St. B-4,H-4,J-4
Delgany St. C-5,D-4,F-2
Denargo St. D-4
Detroit St. I-8
Dixie Pl. A-2
Downing St. H-6,K-6
Elati St. A-4
C-4,H-4,J-4
Elgin Pl. A-5
Elizabeth St. E-8,I-8
Elk Pl. A-1,A-3
Ellsworth Ave. K-3
Emerson St. H-5,K-5
Erie St. D-2
Explande G-8
Fairway Ave. H-1
Fife Ct. D-1
Fillmore St. A-8
D-8,I-8
Firth Ct. E-1
Fox St. A-3,C-3,E-3,K-3
Franklin St. A-6
H-6,J-6
Gaithness Pl. D-1
Galapago St. C-3
K-3,H-3
Gaylord St. A-7
H-7,J-7
Gilpin St. E-7,H-6,J-7
Glenarm Pl. E-5
F-5,G-4
Globeville Rd. C-4
Grant St. A-5,H-5,J-5
Grinell Ct. E-2
Hawthorne Pl. J-7
High St. A-7,H-7,J-7
Holden Pl. H-1
Humboldt St. A-6
D-6,H-6
Inca St. C-3,E-3,K-3
Irvington Pl. K-2
Jason St. C-3
Lawrence St. F-3,G-2
Leaf Ct. A-4
Lincoln St. A-4,H-4,J-4
Lipan St. D-3,H-3
Logan St. A-5,H-5,J-5
Lyle St. D-1
Josephine St. D-7
H-7,J-7
Kalamath St. A-3
C-3,H-3,K-3
Kensing Ct. E-2
Lafayette St. H-6
Larimer St. F-3
Maple Ave. K-2,K-4
Marion St. H-6
Mariposa St. D-2,H-2,J-2
Market St. F-3
Milwaukee St. B-8
D-1,I-8
Mulberry Pl. I-1
Navajo St. D-2,I-2
Ogden St. H-6,K-5
Osage St. D-2,H-2,J-2
Park Ave. F-5
Park Pl. F-7
Pearl St. A-5,H-5,J-5
Pecos St. D-2,H-2
Pennsylvania St.
A-5,H-5,J-5
Quieto Ct. B-2
Quivas St. A-2,B-2
D-2,J-2
Race St. A-7,H-7,J-7
Raritan A-2,B-2
Raritan Way J-2
Ringsby Ct. C-5
Rio Ct. H-2
River Dr. F-1
St. Paul St. B-8,D-8,I-8
Santa Fe St. H-3,K-3
Scott Pl. B-1
Sheer Blvd. H-4
Sherman St. A-4,H-4,J-4
Shoshone St. D-2,H-2
Steavenson Pl. A-7
Steele St. B-8,D-8,I-8
Stout St. G-3
Tejon St. B-1,I-1,K-1
Thompson Ct. B-8
Tremont Pl. F-5,G-4
Umatilla St. C-1,E-1,I-1
Vallejo St. B-1,D-1,J-1
Viaduct G-1
Vine St. A-7,H-7,J-7
Warner Pl. A-3
Washington St. H-5,K-5
Water St. F-1
Wazee St. C-5,F-2
Welton St. G-4
Westwood Dr. J-7
Wewatta St. F-2
Williams St. A-7
D-7,J-7
Wyandot St. B-1,D-1,J-1
Wynkoop St. C-5
Xinca St. H-1
York Ln. A-7
York St. B-7,D-7,H-7
Yuma St. K-1
Zuni St. B-1,H-1,K-1
1st Ave. K-6
2nd Ave. J-3,J-8
3rd Ave. J-3,J-6
4th Ave. J-3,J-6
5th Ave. J-3,J-6
5th St. G-2
6th Ave. I-2,I-6
6th St. G-2
7th Ave. I-2,I-7
7th St. G-2
8th Ave. I-2,I-6
8th St. G-2
9th Ave. I-2,I-6
9th St. G-2
10th Ave. H-2,H-8
11th Ave. H-2,H-7
12th Ave. H-2,H-6
12th Pl. H-1
12th St. F-2
13th Ave. H-1,H-3,H-6
13th St. F-3,G-3
14th Ave. H-3,H-6
14th St. G-3
15th St. E-2
16th Ave. G-6
16th St. E-2
17th Ave. G-6,G-8
17th St. D-2,F-3
18th Ave. G-6
18th St. D-2,E-3
19th Ave. F-6
19th St. E-3
20th Ave. F-6
20th St. E-3
21st Ave. F-6
21st St. E-4
22nd Ave. F-6
22nd St. E-4
23rd Ave. F-6
23rd St. E-4
24th Ave. F-6
24th St. E-4
25th Ave. E-6
25th St. E-4
26th Ave. E-6
26th St. E-5
27th Ave. E-6
27th St. E-5
28th Ave. E-6
29th Ave. E-3,E-6
29th St. D-5
30th Ave. D-3,E-6
30th St. D-5
31st Ave. D-3,D-6
31st St. D-5
32nd Ave. D-1,D-6
32nd St. D-5
33rd Ave. D-1,D-6
33rd St. D-5
34th Ave. D-1,D-6
34th St. C-5
35th Ave. D-1,D-6
35th St. C-6
36th Ave. C-1,C-6
36th St. C-6
37th Ave. C-1,C-6
38th Ave. C-1
38th St. B-5
39th Ave. C-1,C-3
39th St. B-5
40th Ave. C-1,C-3,C-6
40th St. C-6
41st Ave. B-1,B-3,B-8
42nd Ave. B-1,B-3,B-8
43rd Ave. B-1,B-4,B-8
44th Ave. B-1,B-4,B-8
45th Ave. B-1,B-4,B-8
46th Ave. A-1
47th Ave. A-1,A-5,A-7
48th Ave. A-4,A-7,A-8
49th Ave. A-4,A-7,A-8

POINTS OF INTEREST

Chessman Park H-6,H-7
City Park F-8
City Park Golf
Course F-8
Congress Park I-8
Denver Botanical
Gardens I-7
Lincoln Park H-2
Sunken Gardens H-3

Scale of Miles 0 .1 .2 .3 .4 .5

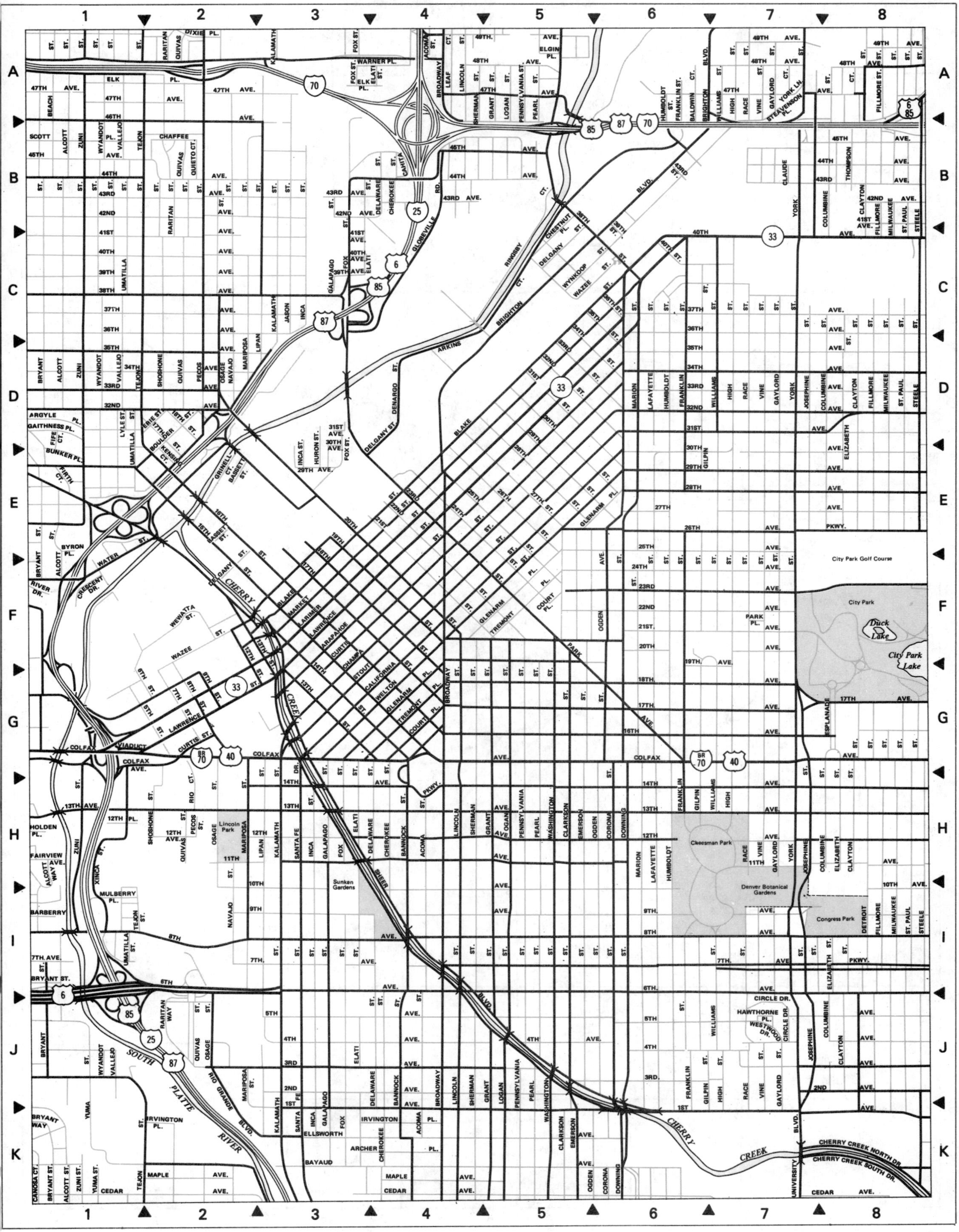

Des Moines, IA

Scale of Miles

0 .1 .2 .3 .4 .5

N

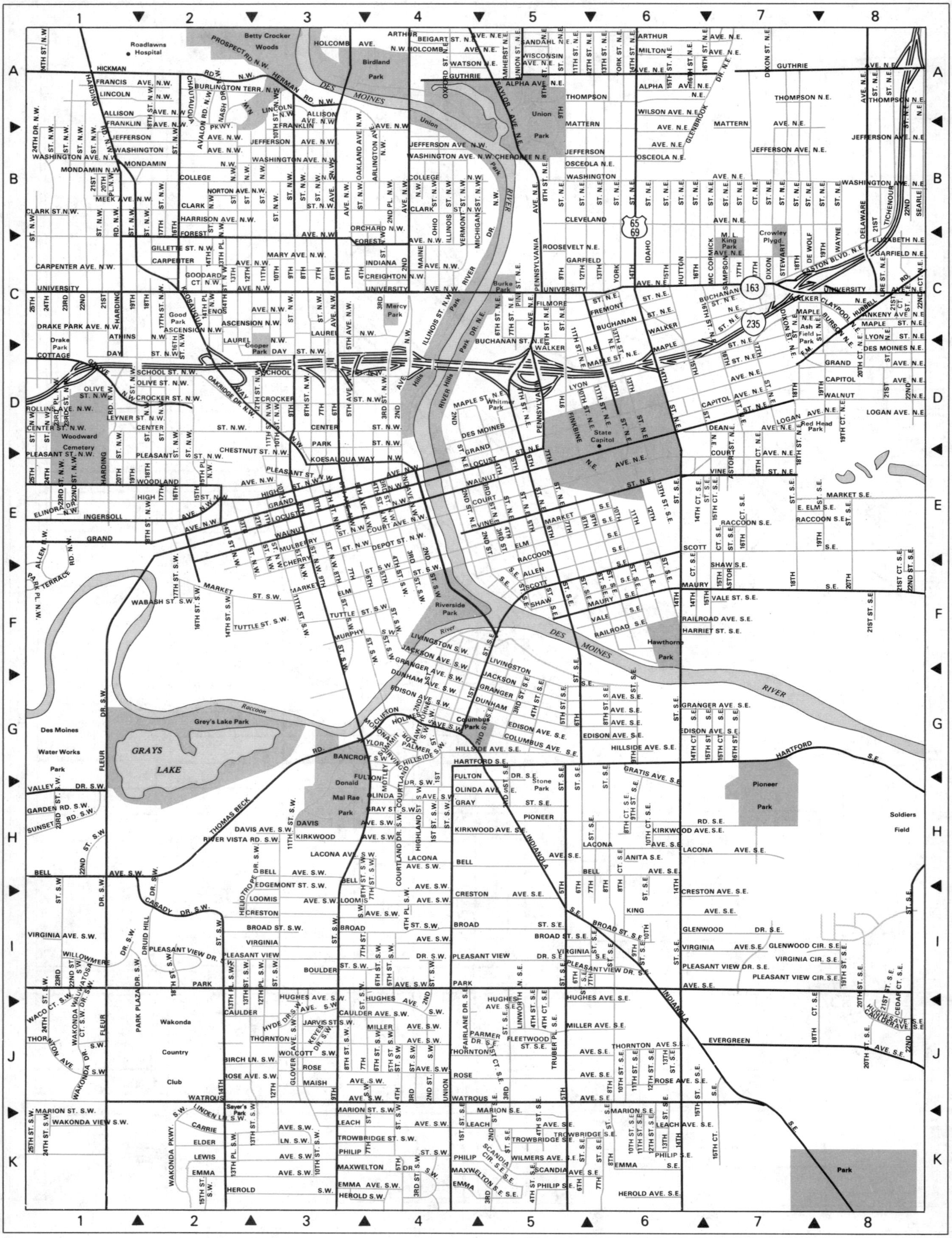

DES MOINES

Allen N.W. E-1,F-1
Allen S.W. E-6,F-5
Allison Ave. N.W. .... A-1 .... A-2,A-3
Alpha Ave. N.E. .. A-5,A-6
Amherst N.E. A-5
Anita S.E. H-6
Ankeny Ave. N.E. C-8
Arlington Ave. N.W. .. B-4
Arthur Ave. N.E. ...... A-4 .... A-5,A-6,A-7
Ascension N.W. .. C-2,C-3
Astor St. N.E. D-7,E-7
Astor St. S.E. E-7,F-7
Athins N.W. C-1,C-2
Avalon Rd. N.W. .. A-2,B-2
Bancroft S.W. G-3,G-4
Bell Ave. S.E. .... H-4 .... H-5,H-6
Bell Ave. S.W. .... H-1 .... H-3,H-4
Biegart St. N.E. A-4
Birch Ln. S.W. J-2,J-3
Boulder St. S.W. I-3
Broad St. S.E. .. I-4,I-5,I-6
Broad St. S.W. I-3,I-4
Buchanan St. N.E. C-6,C-7,D-5
Burlington Terr. N.W. A-2,A-3
Burson N.E. C-8
Capitol Ave. N.E. D-6,D-7,D-8
Carpenter Ave. N.W. C-1,C-2,C-3
Carrie Ave. S.W. .. K-2,K-3
Casady Dr. S.W. I-2
Caulder Ave. S.E. J-8
Caulder Ave. S.W. J-2,J-3,J-4
Cedar Ct. S.E. I-8,J-8
Center St. N.W. D-1,D-2,D-3,D-4
Chautauqua A-2
Cherokee N.E. B-5
Cherry St. N.W. .. E-3,F-3
Chestnut St. N.W. E-2,E-3
Clark St.N.W. .... B-1,B-2 .... B-3,B-4
Claypool N.E. C-8
Cleveland Ave. N.E. B-5,B-6,B-7
Clifton Ave. S.W. G-4
College N.W.B-2,B-3,B-4
Columbus Ave. S.E. .. G-5
Columbus Park .. G-4,G-5
Cottage Grove N.W. .. D-1
Court Ave. N.E. .... E-4 .... E-5,E-6,E-7
Court Ave. N.W. E-4
Courtland Dr. S.W. H-4,G-4
Creighton N.W. C-4
Creston Ave. S.E. I-4,I-5,I-6,I-7
Creston Ave. S.W. I-3,I-4
Crocker St. N.W. D-2,D-3,D-4
Davis Ave. S.W. H-2,H-3,H-4
Day St. N.W.D-1,D-2,D-3
Dean Ave. N.E. D-7
Delware Ave. N.E. A-8,B-8,C-8
Depot St. N.W. E-4
Des Moines ..... D-4,D-5 .... D-7,D-8
DeWolf St. N.E. .. B-7,C-7
Dixon St. N.E. .... A-7 .... B-7,C-7,D-7
Drake Park Ave. N.W. C-1
Druid Hill Dr. S.W. H-2,I-2
Dunham Ave. S.E. G-4,G-5,G-6
Dunham Ave. S.W. .. G-4
Edgemont St. S.W. .. H-3
Edison Ave. S.E. G-5,G-6,G-7
Edison Ave. S.W. G-4
Elder Ln. S.W. K-2,K-3
Elinora Dr. N.W. E-1
Elizabeth N.E. C-8
Elm St. S.W. ..... E-5,E-6 .... E-7,E-8,F-3,F-4
Emma S.E. .. K-4,K-5,K-6
Emma Ave. S.W. ..... K-2 .... K-3,K-4
Enos Ave. N.W. .. C-2,C-3
Evergreen Ave. S.E. J-7,J-8
Fairlane Dr. S.E. I-4,J-4
Faston Blvd. N.E. C-7,C-8
Filmore St. N.E. C-5,C-6
Finkbine N.E. D-5,E-5
Fleetwood St. S.E. J-5
Fleur Dr. S.W. .... G-1 .... H-1,I-1,J-1
Forest Ave. N.W. ..... C-2 .... C-3,C-4
Francis Ave. N.W. A-1,A-2
Franklin Ave. N.W. .. B-1 .... B-2,B-3,B-4
Fremont St. N.E. C-6
Fulton Dr. S.E. H-4,H-5
Fulton Dr. S.W. .. H-3,H-4
Garden Rd. S.W. H-1
Garfield Ave. N.E. C-5,C-6,C-7,C-8
Gillette St. N.W. C-2
Glenbrook Dr. N.E. A-6,A-7,B-6
Glenwood Cir. S.E. I-7,I-8
Glenwood Dr. S.E. I-6,I-7
Glover Ave. S.W. J-3
Goodard Ct. N.W. C-2
Grand Ave. N.E. ...... D-7 .... D-8,E-5
Grand Ave. N.W. ...... E-1 .... E-2,E-3,E-4
Granger Ave. S.E. G-5,G-6,G-7
Granger Ave. S.W. F-4,G-4
Gratis Ave. S.E. G-6,H-6
Gray St. S.E. H-4,H-5
Gray St. S.W. H-4
Guthrie Ave. N.E. ..... A-4 .... A-5,A-6,A-7,A-8
Harding Rd. N.W. ..... A-1 .... B-1,C-1,D-1,E-1
Harriet St. S.E. ... F-6,F-7
Harrison Ave. N.W. .. B-2
Hartford S.E. .... G-4 .... G-5,G-7,G-8
Hawthorne G-4
Heliotrope Dr. S.W. H-3,I-2
Herman Rd. N.W. .... A-1 .... A-2,A-3
Herold Ave. S.E. K-6
Herold S.W. .. K-2,K-3,K-4
High St. N.W. E-2,E-3
Highland St. S.W. H-4
Hillside Ave. S.E. G-4,G-5,G-6
Hillside S.W. G-4
Holcomb Ave. N.E. A-4,A-5
Holcomb Ave. N.W. A-3,A-4
Holmes G-4
Hughes Ave. S.E. ..... I-5 .... I-6,I-8
Hughes Ave. S.W. .... I-3 .... I-4,J-4
Hyde Dr. S.W. J-3
Idaho St. N.E. ... B-6,C-6
Illinois St. N.W. B-4,C-4,D-4
Indiana Ave. N.W. C-4
Indianola S.E. .... H-5 .... I-5,J-6,K-7
Ingersoll Ave. N.W. E-1,E-2
Irving G-4
Jackson Ave. S.E. G-5,G-6
Jackson Ave. S.W. F-4
Jarvis St. S.W. J-3
Jefferson Ave. N.E. B-5,B-6,B-7,B-8
Jefferson Ave. N.W. B-1,B-2,B-3,B-4
Keosauqua Way N.W. C-2,D-2,D-3,E-3,E-4
Keyes Dr. S.W. J-3
King Ave. S.E. I-6,I-7
Kirkwood Ave. S.E. H-4,H-5,H-6,H-7
Kirkwood Ave. S.W. H-3,H-4
Lacona Ave. S.E. H-6,H-7
Lacona Ave. S.W. H-3,H-4
Laurel N.W. .. C-2,C-3,C-4
Leach Ave. S.E. .... K-4 .... K-5,K-6,K-7
Leach Ave. S.W. K-3,K-4
Lewis Ave. S.W. .. K-2,K-3
Leyner St. N.W. .. D-1,D-2
Lincoln N.W.A-1,A-2,A-3
Linden Ln. S.W. J-2,K-2
Linworth Ln. S.E. I-5,J-5
Livingston S.E. ... F-5,G-5
Livingston S.W. F-4
Locust St. N.E. E-4,E-5
Locust N.W. E-3,E-4
Logan Ave. N.E. .. D-7,D-8
Loomis Ave. S.W. .. I-3,I-4
Lyon St. N.E.C-8,D-5,D-7
Maine N.W. B-4,C-4
Maish Ave. S.W. .. J-3,J-4
Maple St. N.E. .... C-7 .... C-8,D-4,D-5,D-6,D-7
Marion S.E. J-5,J-6
Marion St. S.W. ...... J-1 .... J-3,J-4
Market S.E. .. E-5,E-6,E-8
Market St. S.W. ...... F-2 .... F-3,F-4
Mary Ave. N.W. C-3
Mattern Ave. N.E. B-5,B-6,B-7
Maury S.E. ... F-6,F-7,F-8
Maxwelton S.E. .. K-4,K-5
Maxwelton Dr. S.W. K-3,K-4
McCormick St. N.E. B-7,C-7
Meek Ave. N.W. .. B-1,B-2
Michigan St. N.W. B-4,C-4
Miller Ave. S.E. J-5,J-6
Miller Ave. S.W. J-4
Milton Ave.N.E. .. A-6,A-7
Mondamin N.W. .. B-1,B-2
Monona G-4
Morton Ave. N.W. B-2,B-3
Motley G-4,H-4
Mulberry St. N.W. E-3
Murphy S.W. F-3,F-4
Nash Dr. N.W. A-2
Oak Bridge Dr. N.W. D-2,D-3
Oakland Ave. N.W. A-3,B-3
Ohio St. N.W. B-4,C-4
Olinda Ave. S.E. .. H-4,H-5
Olinda Ave. S.W. H-4
Olive St. N.W. ... D-1,D-2
Orchard N.W. B-3,B-4
Osceola N.E. B-5,B-6
Oxford St. N.E. A-4
Palmer St. S.W. G-4
Park Ave. S.E. .. I-4,I-6,I-7
Park Ave. S.W. I-2,I-4
Park Pl. N.W. F-1
Park Plaza Dr. S.W. I-1,J-1
Park St. N.W. D-3,D-4
Parmer Dr. S.E. J-4,J-5
Pennsylvania Ave. N.E. B-5,C-5,D-5
Philip S.E. ... K-4,K-5,K-6
Philip St. S.W. ... K-3,K-4
Pine St. N.E. C-5
Pioneer Rd. S.E. ..... H-5 .... H-6,H-7
Pkwy. B-2
Pleasant St. N.W. E-1,E-2,E-3
Pleasantview Cir. S.E. I-7,I-8
Pleasantview Dr. S.E. I-4,I-5,I-6,I-7
Pleasantview Dr. S.W. I-2,I-3,I-4
Prospect Rd. N.W. A-2,A-3
Pl. N.W. B-1
Raccoon S.E. .. E-5 .... E-6,E-7,E-8
Railroad Ave. S.E. F-6,F-7
River Dr. N.E. C-4,D-4
River Dr. N.W. .... B-5 .... C-4,C-5
River Vista Rd. S.W. H-2,H-3
Rollins Ave. N.W. D-1
Roosevelt N.E. C-5
Rose Ave. S.E. .... J-4 .... J-5,J-6
Rose Ave. S.W. .... J-2 .... J-3,J-4
Sampson St. N.E.B-7,C-7
Sandahl N.E. A-5
Saylor Ave. N.E. .. A-5,B-5
Scandia Ave. S.E.K-5,K-6
Scandia Cir. S.E. K-5
School St. N.W. ..... D-2 .... D-3,D-4
Scott S.E. .... F-5,F-6 .... E-6,E-8
Searle N.E. A-8,B-8
Shaw S.E. F-5,F-7
Stewart St. N.E. .. B-7,C-7
Summit G-4
Sunset Rd. S.W. H-1
Taylor G-3,G-4
Terrace Rd. N.W. E-1,F-1
Thomas Beck Rd. G-3,H-2
Thompson ...... A-5,A-6 .... A-7,A-8
Thornton Ave. S.E. J-4,J-5,J-6
Thornton Ave. S.W. J-1,J-3,J-4
Tichendur St. N.E. A-8,B-8
Trowbridge S.E. K-5,K-6
Trowbridge St. S.W. K-3,K-4
Truber Pl. S.E. J-5
Tuttle St. S.W.F-2,F-3,F-4
Union St. N.E. A-5
Union St. S.W. ... H-4,J-4
University N.E. .... C-5 .... C-6,C-7,C-8
University Ave. N.W. C-1,C-2,C-3,C-4
URE St. N.E. C-8
Vale St. S.E. F-6,F-7
Valley Dr. S.W. H-1
Vermont St. N.W. B-4,C-4
Vine St. N.E. .... E-4 .... E-5,E-6,E-7
Virginia Ave. S.E. I-5,I-6,I-7
Virginia Ave. S.W. I-1,I-2,I-3,I-4
Virginia Cir. S.E. I-7,I-8
Wabash St. S.W. .. F-1,F-2
Waco Ct. S.W. I-1,J-1
Wakonda Ct. S.W. J-1
Wakonda Dr. S.W. J-1
Wakonda Pkwy. S.W. K-2,J-2
Wakonda View S.W. .. K-1
Walker N.E. ..... C-6,C-7 .... C-8,D-5,D-6
Walnut St. N.E. ...... D-7 .... D-8,E-4,E-5
Walnut N.W. E-3,E-4
Washington Ave. N.E. B-5,B-6,B-7,B-8
Washington Ave. N.W. B-1,B-2,B-3,B-4,B-5
Watrous Ave. S.E. .... J-4 .... J-5,J-6
Watrous Ave. S.W. .... J-2 .... J-3,J-4
Watson N.E. A-4,A-5
Wauwatosa Dr. S.W. I-1,J-1
Wayne St. N.E. .. B-8,C-8
Willowmere Dr. S.W. .. I-1
Wilmers Ave. S.E. K-5
Wilson Ave. N.E. A-6
Wisconsin Ave. N.E. .. A-5
Wolcott S.W. J-3
Woodland Ave. N.W. E-2,E-3
York St. N.E.A-6,B-6,C-6
1st Ct. S.E. J-5
1st St. S.E. ... F-5,G-4,K-4
1st St. S.W. G-4,H-4
2nd Ave. N.W. ... B-4,C-4 .... D-4,E-4
2nd Pl. N.W. B-4
2nd St. N.E. D-4,E-4
2nd St. S.E. ...... E-5,F-5 .... G-5,J-5,J-6
2nd St. S.W. ..... E-4,F-4 .... G-4,I-4,J-4
3rd St. N.E. E-5
3rd St.N.W. ...... B-4,C-4 .... D-4,E-4
3rd St. S.E. ...... E-5,F-5 .... G-5,H-5,J-5,K-5
3rd St. S.W. ...... E-4,F-4 .... J-4,K-4
4th Ct. S.E. I-5,J-5
4th Pl. S.W. I-4
4th St. N.E. E-5
4th St. N.W. .. B-3,C-3,E-4
4th St. S.E. ...... E-5,F-5 .... G-5,I-5,J-5,K-5
4th St. S.W. .. E-4,F-4,J-4
5th St.N.E. E-5
5th Ave. N.W. .... B-3 .... C-3,D-3,E-3
5th St. S.E. .... E-5 ..... F-5,G-5,H-5,I-5,J-5
5th St. S.W. .... F-4 .... I-4,J-4,K-4
6th St. N.E. C-5,E-5
6th Ave. N.W. .... B-3,C-3 .... D-3,E-3
6th St. S.E. ...... E-5,F-5 ..... G-5,H-5,I-5,J-5,K-5
6th St. S.W. F-4,I-4,J-4
7th St. N.E. .. C-5,D-5,E-5
7th St. N.W. ..... B-3,C-3 .... D-3,E-3
7th St. S.E. .... E-5,F-5 .... H-5,I-5,K-5
7th St. S.W. ...... F-3,F-4 .... H-4,I-3,J-3,K-4
8th Ct. S.E. H-6,I-6
8th St.N.E. .... A-5,B-5 .... C-5,D-5
8th St. N.W. .... B-3,C-3, ... D-3,E-3
8th St. S.E. .... E-5,F-6 ..... G-6,H-6,I-6,J-6,K-6
8th St. S.W. ...... F-3,H-3 .... I-3,J-3
9th St. N.E. ...... A-5,B-5 .... C-5,D-5,E-5
9th St. N.W. .... B-3 .... C-3,D-3,E-3
9th St. S.E. ...... E-6,G-6 .... H-6,I-6
9th St. S.W. ... F-3,I-3,J-3
10th Ct. S.E. H-6
10th St. N.E. D-5,E-6
10th St. N.W. .... A-3,B-3 .... C-3,D-3,E-3,F-3
10th St. S.E. ..... E-6,F-6 .... H-6,I-6,J-6,K-6
10th St. S.W. K-3
11th St. N.E. ..... A-5,B-5 .... C-5,D-6
11th St. N.W. .... B-3,C-3 .... D-3,E-3
11th St. S.E. .... E-6 .... F-6,J-6,K-6
11th St. S.W. F-3,H-3
12th Pl. S.W. I-3
12th St. N.E. .... A-5 .... B-5,C-5,D-6
12th St. N.W. .... B-2,C-2 .... D-3,E-3,F-3
12th St. S.E. .... E-6 .... F-6,J-6,K-6
12th St. S.W. I-3,J-3
13th Pl. N.W. B-2,C-2
13th Pl. S.W. .. I-2,J-2,K-2
13th St. N.E. .... A-6 .... B-6,C-6,D-6
13th St. N.W. .... B-2 .... C-2,E-2,F-3
13th St. S.E. ..... E-6,F-6 .... I-6,J-6,K-6
13th St. S.W. .. I-2,J-2,K-3
14th Ct. S.E. .. E-6,F-6,G-6
14th Pl. N.W. C-2
14th St. N.E. .... A-6 .... B-6,C-6,D-6
14th St. N.W. .. B-2,C-2,E-2
14th St. S.E. ..... E-6,F-6 .... G-6,H-6,I-6,K-6
14th St. S.W. .... F-2 .... J-2,I-2
15th Ct. S.E. ..... E-7,F-7 .... G-7,J-7,K-7
15th Pl. N.W. E-2
15th St. N.E. .... A-6,B-6 .... C-6,D-6,D-7
15th St. N.W. D-2,E-2
15th St. S.E. ..... E-6,F-6 .... G-6,J-6,K-6
15th St. S.W. K-2
16th Ct. N.E. D-7,E-7
16th Ct. S.E. E-7,G-7
16th St. N.E. .... A-6 .... B-6,C-6,D-7
16th St. N.W. .... B-2 .... C-2,D-2,E-2
16th St. S.W. F-2
17th Ct. N.E. B-7,C-7
17th St. N.E. .. B-7,C-7,D-7
17th St. N.W. .... B-2 .... C-2,D-2,E-2
17th St. S.W. E-2,F-2
18th Ct. S.E. J-7
18th St. N.E. .... B-7 .... C-7,D-7,E-7
18th St. N.W. .... A-2,B-2 .... C-2,D-2,E-2
18th St. S.E. E-7,F-7
18th St. S.W. I-2
19th Ct. N.E. D-8
19th St. N.E. .... B-7 .... C-7,D-7
19th St. N.W. .... B-1 .... C-1,D-1,E-1
19th St. S.E. E-7,I-8
20th Ct. N.E. D-8
20th St. N.W.B-1,D-1,E-1
20th St. S.E. .... E-8 .... F-8,I-8,J-8
21st Ct. C-8,E-8,F-8
21st St. N.E. .... A-8 .... B-8,C-8,D-8
21st St. N.W. B-1,C-1
21st St. S.E. ... F-8,I-8,J-8
22nd Ct. N.E. C-8
22nd St. N.E. .... A-8 .... B-8,C-8,D-8
22nd St. N.W.B-1,C-1,E-1
22nd St. S.E. ..... E-8,F-8 .... I-8,J-8
22nd St. S.W. H-1,I-1
23rd Pl. N.W. D-1
23rd St. N.W. .... B-1,C-1 .... D-1,E-1
23rd St. S.W. H-1,I-1
24th Dr. N.W. A-1,B-1
24th St. N.W. .... A-1,B-1 .... C-1,D-1,E-1
24th St. S.W. .. I-1,J-1,K-1
25th St. N.W. .... B-1 .... C-1,D-1,E-1
25th St. S.W. K-1

POINTS OF INTEREST

Ash Field Park C-7,D-7
Bayer's Park J-3,K-3
Betty Crocker Woods A-3
Birdland Park A-4
Burke Park C-5
Cooper Park D-3
Crowley Plygd C-7
Des Moines River .... A-3 ..... A-4,B-5,F-5,F-6,G-7
Des Moines Waterworks Park G-1
Donald Mal Rae Park H-3
Drake Park C-1,D-1
'Good Park C-2
Gray's Lake G-1,G-2
Grey's Lake Park G-2
Hawthorne Park F-6
Hills Park C-4,D-4
Mercy Park C-4
M. L. King Park C-7
Park K-8
Pioneer Park H-7
Raccoon River ...... G-2 .... G-3,F-4
Red Head Park D-7
Riverside Park F-4
Roadlawns Hospital . A-1
Soldiers Field H-8
State Capitol D-6
Stone Park H-5
Union Park .... A-5 .... B-4,B-5
Wakonda Country Club J-2
Whitmer Park D-5
Woodard Cemetery .. D-1

DETROIT

Abbott J-6
Ackley C-8
Adams E. I-7
Adams W. I-6
Adelaide H-7,I-6
Adele D-6
Alexandrine H-4
Alexandrine E. ... F-7,G-6
Alfred H-7,H-8
Alger C-5,D-4
Alice C-6
Alpena A-7
Amsterdam F-4
Andrus C-6
Anna C-5
Antietam I-7
Antoinette G-2
Arden Park C-3
Ash I-3,I-4,J-2
Atkinson C-3,D-1
Atlas A-4
Atwater E. J-8
Austin K-4
Avalon A-1,B-1
Avery F-3,G-3
Avery Ter. G-3
Bagley J-5,J-6,K-2
Baltimore E-4
Bangor H-1
Bates J-7
Beaubien J-7
Beech J-6
Belmont A-5,B-3
Benham C-7
Bernard B-5
Berres B-6
Bethune D-4,E-3
Blaine D-3,E-2
Boston Blvd. E. C-3
Boston Blvd. W. D-1
Brainard I-4
Brandon K-1
Brewster G-8,H-6
Broadway I-7
Brockton A-7
Brooklyn G-4,K-6
Brush A-3,D-4,J-7
Bryanston H-8
Bryant G-3
Buchanan H-3,I-1
Buena Vista A-1
Buffalo A-7
Burger A-5
Burlingame C-2
Burroughs F-4
Butler B-7
Butternut I-3,J-2
Byron D-2,E-3
California A-3
Calumet H-3
Calvert C-2
Cameron B-4
Campbell K-1
Canfield E. F-7
Canfield W. G-5,H-3
Caniff A-5,B-4
Canton C-8
Cardoni B-4
Carrie B-8,C-8
Carter E-1
Casmer A-5
Cass I-6,J-6
Centre I-7
Chandler D-4
Charest A-6
Charlotte I-5
Chateaufor Pl. I-8
Chene F-7
Cherboneau Pl. I-8
Chicago Blvd. D-1
Chipman K-4
Christopher B-7
Church J-5
Churchill E-2
Civic Center Dr. K-6
Clairmount D-1,D-3
Clark K-2
Clarkdale K-2
Clay C-6,D-5
Clifford I-6
Clinton I-7
Cochiane I-4
Collingwood C-2
Colorado A-3
Columbia E. I-7
Columbia W. I-6
Columbus F-1
Commonwealth . F-3,G-4
Commor A-4
Comstock A-7,B-6
Conant C-7
Concord B-8,C-8
Congress E. J-7
Connecticut B-3
Cortland B-2
Cromwell K-4
Custer E-4
Cymbal C-7
Dallas C-5
Dalzelle J-4
Dane D-7
Danforth C-6
Davenport H-5
Davison Expwy. A-1
Deleware E-2,E-3
Delmar B-4
Deming K-2
Denton C-6
Dequindre G-7
Dodge B-7
Domine B-7
Doremus A-6,A-7
Dorothy B-7
Dubois B-5,C-6
Dunderin F-2
Dunn Rd. C-7
Dwyer B-7
Dyar A-4
Eastern Pl. G-1
East Grand Blvd. D-6,D-8
Edison C-3,D-1
Edsel Ford Frwy. E-6,G-3
Edwin A-6,A-7,B-5
Elijah McCoy Dr. F-3
Eliot H-6
Elizabeth J-5
Elizabeth E. I-7
Elizabeth W. I-6
Ellery A-6,D-8,E-8
Elm I-4
Elmhurst B-2,C-1
Elmwood F-8
Endicott E-4
Englewood B-3
Erskine G-8,H-6
Euclid E. D-4
Euclid W. D-3,E-2
Evaline A-5,A-7
Faber B-6
Farmer I-6
Farnsworth E-7,F-5
Farr C-8
Farrand A-3
Ferry E. E-7,F-5
Ferry Park F-2
Field C-8
Filer B-8
Finley D-6
Fisher Frwy. I-6,J-3
Fleming A-5
Florian B-5
Ford A-1
Fordyce C-6
Forest Ct. G-4
Forest E. F-7,G-5
Forest W. G-5,H-3
Foster B-8
Fort W. K-6
Franklin J-8
Frederick E-7,F-5
Frontenac C-8
Gage F-3
Gallagher A-6
Garfield F-7,G-5
Geimer B-6
Georgia B-7,B-8
Gibson H-4
Gillett C-5
Girardin B-8
Gladstone D-3,E-1
Glendale A-4,B-1
Glynn Ct. C-2
Goldner J-1
Goodson B-6
Goodwin B-4,C-4
Grand A-1
Grand Haven A-4
Grand River G-1,I-6
Grandy C-6,F-8
Gratiot G-8,I-7
Grayling C-6
Greenley C-5
Griffin C-7
Grinnell A-8
Griswold J-7
Guthrie A-8
Hague C-5,D-4
Hale G-8
Hamilton B-2
Hammond K-1
Hancock H-3,I-1
Hancock E. F-7
Hancock W. G-5
Hanley B-6
Hanover F-2
Harmon B-3
Harper E-5
Harrison I-4
Hartwick C-5
Hastings E-5
Hawthorne B-4
Hazelwood D-1,D-3
Heck Pl. E-8
Hecla F-3,G-3
Hedge A-7
Heintz B-7
Helen B-8,C-8
Hendricks H-8
Hendrie E-7
Henry I-5
Hewitt B-6
Highland B-2
Hindle B-4
Hobart F-4
Hobson I-5
Hogarth F-1
Holborn D-8
Holbrook B-6,C-4
Holmes A-5
Hooker G-2
Hope Pl. G-1
Horatio I-1
Horton D-6,E-4
Howard J-6,K-4
Hubbard K-2
Huber A-8
Hudson G-2
Hughes Ter. F-2
Humboldt I-3
Hunt G-8
Huron I-3
Hyde H-8
Illinois G-6,G-8
Jacob B-6
Jay H-8
Jefferson W. K-6
Jeffries I-5
Jeffries Frwy. I-2
John C. Lodge Service Dr. D-3,J-6
John R. E-4,I-6
Joliet Pl. I-8
Jos Campau A-6,F-8
Josephine C-4
Junction K-1
Kanter D-7
Kenilworth C-4
King C-4
Kingsley D-4
Kipling E-3
Kirby F-5,F-6,G-4
Kirby E. E-7,F-5
Kirby W. H-1
Klein C-7
Knox C-5
Konkel K-1
Kopernick J-1
LaBelle A-1
LaBrosse J-5
Lafayette E. I-8
Lafayette W. J-6
Lambert D-8
Lambie Pl. K-3
Lamothe F-2
Lanman I-1
Larned E. J-7
La Salle E-1,F-2
La Salle Gds. N. F-1
La Salle Gds. S. F-1
Lawrence C-2
Lawton E-1,I-3
Ledyard I-5
Lee Pl. E-2
Legrand C-7
Lehman B-6
Leicester Ct. C-4
Leland G-6,G-8
Leverette J-5
Liberty C-6
Lincoln B-1,F-3,G-4
Linwood E-1,G-2
Lockwood J-1
Lodi D-8
Longfellow C-3,D-1
Loraine G-2
Lothorp E-3,F-1
Lovett I-1
Lumpkin A-5,C-5
Lyman D-6
Lynn B-4
Lysander H-3
McDougall A-6,F-8
McGraw G-2
McGregor K-1
McKinley I-2
McLean A-3
Mack G-6,H-8
Macomb I-7
Madison I-7
Magnolia I-2,I-3,J-1
Manhattan B-7
Manson K-1
Mansur E-5
Manuel B-7
Maple I-7
Marantette J-4
Marcus B-8
Marjorie A-8
Mark G-3
Marquette G-2
Marston D-4,D-6
Massachusetts A-3
Mechanic I-7
Medbury D-8,E-7
Melbourne D-4
Melrose D-5
Merrick G-4,H-1
Merrill E-3
Merritt K-1
Michigan J-2,J-6
Middle J-6
Milford H-1
Miller B-7,B-8,C-6
Milwaukee D-7,E-4
Missouri G-2
Mitchell A-5,A-6,F-3
Monning Ct. E-6
Monroe I-7
Montclam E. I-7
Monterey B-2
Montgomery F-1
Moore Pl. G-1
Moran E-8
Morrow C-5
Mt. Elliott B-7,D-8
Mt. Vernon D-4
Mulberry I-3
Myrtle H-5,I-3,J-2
Nagle B-8
N∋ll I-1
Nebraska F-2
Newark K-1,K-4
Newhall B-7
Newton C-6
Nicolet Pl. I-8
Northwestern F-1
Norwalk A-6,A-7,B-5
Oakland A-3
Oliver B-7
Orleans D-6,G-7,I-8
Osborne Pl. E-6
Otis J-1
Owen C-4
Pallister E-2,E-3
Palmer E. E-7,F-5
Palmer W. F-4
Palms K-2
Park Dr. H-8
Parks H-3
Parsons H-5
Pasadena A-1
Pease B-8
Perry I-5,J-3
Peterboro I-5
Philadelphia E. D-4
Philadelphia W. D-3,E-2
Pierce G-8
Pine I-5
Pingree D-3,E-2
Piquette D-7,E-5,E-6
Plaza Dr. J-6
Plum J-5
Plumer K-1
Poe E-3
Poland B-5
Poplar I-2,I-3
Porter K-5
Prentis G-5
Preston G-8
Pulaski A-5
Putnam G-5
Randall K-3
Randolph J-7
Reed Pl. G-4
Rhode Island A-3
Rich I-1
Richardson B-8
Richton B-2
Riopelle .... C-5,D-6 .... F-7,H-7,J-8
Risdon J-2
Rivard H-7,J-8
Roby E-6
Rockwood B-7
Roland A-8
Roosevlet B-6,G-1,I-2
Rosa G-3
Rosa Parks Blvd. B-1
Rose J-3
Rosedale B-3
Rugg B-8
Ruskin K-3
Russell F-7
Saginaw D-8
St. Antone D-5,F-6
St. Aubin. A-4,C-5,F-7,I-8
St. Cyril B-8
St. Hedwig J-1
St. Joseph G-8
St. Thomas C-8
Sallan B-7
Sampson K-4
Sargent D-7
Schewitzer Pl. J-8
Scott G-8
Scotten I-1,K-2
Scovel Pl. G-1
Second B-2,E-4
Selden H-4,H-5
Selkirk B-7
Service H-8
Seward E-2,E-3
Sheehan A-8
Shelby J-7
Sherwood B-8
Sibley I-6
Sloman B-4
Smith C-6,D-4
Sproat I-6
Spruce I-5
Stanley G-2
Sterling F-3
Stimson H-6
Stroh Dr. I-7
Strong C-8
Sturtevant B-1
Superior F-7,G-6
Sycamore I-4
Taylor D-1,D-3
Temple I-5
Tennyson B-3
Theodore F-5,F-7
Third B-2,E-3
Times Square J-6
Toledo K-1
Torrey J-1
Torrey Ct. I-1
Trombly D-6
Trowbridge A-5,B-3
Trumbull .... A-1,F-3 .... G-4,K-5
Tuscola H-5
Tuxedo B-2
Tyler A-1
Varney C-7
Vermont I-4,K-4
Vernor Hwy. E. H-8
Vernor Hwy. W. K-2
Vicksburg F-1
Vincen B-7
Vinewood K-2
Virginia Park D-3,E-2
Walter P. Chrysler Frwy. B-5,F-6
Warren E. F-7
Warren W. G-4,H-1
Washington J-7
Washington Blvd. J-6
Watson G-8,H-6
Waverly A-1
Webb B-2
Weitzel Ct. D-8
Wellington C-5
West Grand Blvd. F-1,G-1,J-2
Westminster C-3
Whalin A-5
Whitney F-1
Widman Pl. D-6
Wildemere E-1
Wilkins G-8,H-7
Willis G-6,H-5
Willis E. F-7
Winder H-7,I-6
Winfield B-8
Wing Pl. K-4
Winkleman B-7
Winona A-1
Witherell I-6
Woodbridge J-8
Woodland B-3
Woodrow Wilson B-1,D-2,E-2
Woodward ... B-2,F-5,J-7
Wreford G-2
Wyandotte B-6
Yemans A-5
Zinow A-5
2nd I-5,J-6
2nd Blvd. E-4
3rd G-5,J-6
4th H-4,J-5
5th J-5
6th K-6
8th H-4,J-5,K-5
10th K-5
14th E-2,I-3,K-4
15th I-3
16th I-3,K-4
17th I-3,K-4
18th I-3,K-4
20th K-3
21st K-3
22nd I-2
23rd I-2
24th I-2
25th I-2,K-3
26th I-2
28th I-1
29th I-1
30th I-1,J-1
31st J-1
32nd J-1

POINTS OF INTEREST

Cass Park I-5
Northwestern Field .. G-1
Roosevelt Field C-1

Scale of Miles
0 .2 .4 .6
N

Scale of Miles
0 .2 .4 .6 .8

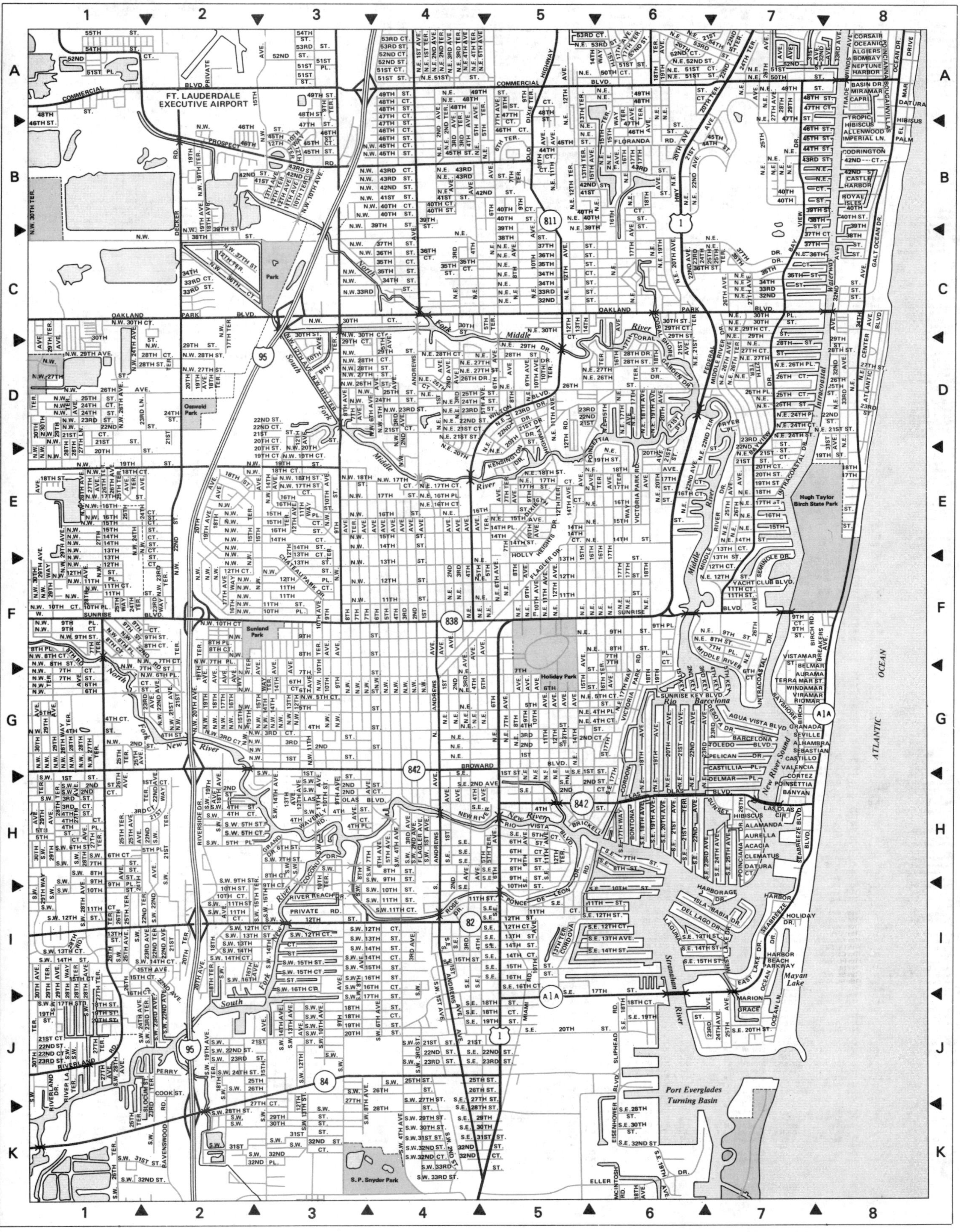

FT. LAUDERDALE

Acacia....H-7
Agua Vista Blvd....G-7
Alamanda....H-7
Algiers....A-8
Alhambra....G-7
Allenwood....B-8
Andrews Ave....D-4
Andrews Ave., N....G-4
Andrews Ave., S..H-4,I-4
Atlantic Blvd....D-8
Aurama....G-7
Aurella....H-7
Banyan....H-7
Barcelona....G-7
Basin Dr....A-8
Bayshore....G-7
Bayview Dr....C-7,E-7
Belmar....G-7
Birch Rd....F-7,G-7
Bombay....A-8
Bontona....H-6
Breakers Ave....F-8
Brickell....H-5
Broward Blvd....G-4
Capri....A-8
Castle Harbor....B-8
Castillia Pl....G-7
Castillo....G-7
Center Ave., N.E....D-8
Chateau Park Dr....F-3
Clematus....H-7
Coconut Dr....H-3
Codrington....B-8
Commercial Blvd. A-1,A-5
Cook St....J-2
Coral Gardens Dr. C-6,D-6
Coral Shore Dr. C-6,D-6
Cordon....H-6
Cordova....I-5
Corsair....A-8
Cortez....H-7
Datura....A-8
Datura Ct....H-7
Decker Rd....B-2
Del Lago Dr....I-6
Delmar Pl....H-7
Desota Dr....G-7
Dixie Hwy....E-5
East Lake Dr....I-7
Eisenhower Blvd....K-6
Eller Dr....K-6
El Mar Dr....B-8
Federal Hwy....D-7
Flagler Ave....H-4
Flagler Dr....F-5
Floranda Rd....B-6
Fryer Pl....D-7
Galt Ocean Dr....C-8
Garden Dr....D-6
Grace....J-7
Granada....G-7
Grand Dr....H-3
Harbor....A-8,I-7
Harborage Dr....I-6,I-7
Harbor Beach Pkwy....I-7
Hibiscus....B-8,H-7
Holiday Dr....I-7
Holly Heights Dr....E-5
Imperial Ln....B-8
Intracoastal Dr. E-7,G-7
Islo Babia Dr....I-6
Kensington Dr....E-5
Kensington St....E-5
Laguna....I-6
Las Clas Blvd....H-3,H-6
Las Olas Cir....H-7
Marion....J-7
McIntosh Rd....K-6
Miami Rd....J-5
Middle River Dr..D-7,F-6
Miramar....A-8
Neptune....A-8
New River....H-4
Oakland Park Blvd. C-1,C-2,C-6,C-7
Ocean Dr....A-8,I-7
Oceanic....A-8
Ocean Ln....J-7
Old Dixie Hwy...A-5,B-5
Palm....B-8
Pelican Dr....G-7
Perry....J-2
Poinciana Bougainvillas....A-8
Poinciana Dr....H-7
Poinsettia....H-7
Poinsettia St....D-6,E-5
Ponce De Leon Dr....I-5
Private....A-2
Private Rd....I-3
Prospect Rd....B-2
Ravenswood Rd....K-2
Riomar....G-7
Rio Vista Blvd....H-5
Riverland Dr....J-1
Riverland Rd....J-1
Riverland Ter....J-1
River Reach Dr....I-5
Riverside Dr....H-2
Rose Dr....I-4
Royal Isles....B-8
Seabreeze Blvd. H-7,I-7
Sebastian....G-7
Seminole Dr....F-7
Seville....G-7
Sliphead Rd....J-6
Slocum St....J-2
Sunrise Blvd....F-6
Sunrise Blvd, W....F-1
Sunrise Key Blvd....G-6
Sunset....H-7
Terra Mar St....G-7
Toledo Blvd....G-7
Tradewinds Ave....A-8
Tropic....A-8
Valencia....G-7
Victoria Park Rd. E-6,G-6
Vistamar St....F-7
Waverly Rd....H-3
West Lake Dr....I-7
Wilton Blvd....D-5
Windamar....G-7
Yacht Club Blvd....F-7
1st Ave. N.E.A-4,D-4,G-4
1st Ave. N.W....F-4,G-4
1st Ave. S.E....H-4,I-4
1st Ave. S.W....H-4,I-4
1st Ct....H-2
1st Key....G-6
1st St. S.E....G-4,G-5
1st St. S.W....G-1,G-3
1st St. N.E....G-4
1st St. N.W....G-2,G-3
1st Ter. N.E....A-4
2nd Ave. N.E....A-4,B-4 ....D-4,F-4,G-4
2nd Ave. N.W....D-4 ....E-4,G-4
2nd Ave. S.E....H-4,I-4
2nd Ave. S.W....H-4
2nd Ct....G-5
2nd Ct. S.E....H-5
2nd Ct. S.W....H-1,H-3
2nd Key....G-6
2nd St. N.E....G-4
2nd St. N.W..G-1,G-2,G-3
2nd St. S.E....H-5
2nd St. S.W....H-1 ....H-2,H-3,K-4
2nd Ter. N.E....A-4,B-4
3rd Ave. N.E....A-4,B-4 ....C-4,D-4,F-4,G-4
3rd Ave. N.W....D-4,G-4
3rd Ave. S.E....I-4
3rd Ave. S.W....H-4,I-4
3rd Ct....H-1
3rd Ct. N.W....G-2,G-3
3rd Key....G-6
3rd St. N.E....G-4
3rd St. N.W....G-3
3rd St. S.W....H-1,J-4
3rd Ter. N.E....A-4,B-4
4th Ave. N.E....A-4,B-4 ....C-4,F-4,G-4
4th Ave. N.W....F-4,G-4
4th Ave. S.E....H-4,I-4
4th Ave. S.W....H-4,K-4
4th Ct....G-1,H-1
4th Ct. N.E....G-5
4th Ct. S.W....H-2,H-3
4th Key....G-7
4th Pl....H-1,H-3
4th Pl. N.E....G-5
4th St....G-1,G-2,H-1
4th St. N.E....G-4
4th St. N.W....G-1,G-2
4th St. S.E....H-4,H-5
4th St. S.W....H-2,H-3
4th Ter. N.E....A-4
5th....H-5
5th Ave....D-4,H-4
5th Ave. N.E....A-5,B-4 ....D-5,F-4,G-5
5th Ave. N.W....D-4,G-4
5th Ct....H-1
5th Ct. N.E....G-5
5th Ct. N.W....G-3
5th Ct. S.E....H-5
5th Ct. S.W....H-2
5th Key....G-7
5th Pl....H-2
5th Pl. S.W....H-2
5th St....H-1
5th St. N.E....G-4
5th St. N.W....G-1,G-2
5th St. S.W....H-2
5th Ter....C-5,H-5
5th Ter. N.E....B-5,F-5
6th Ave. N.E....B-5,C-5 ....D-5,F-5,G-5
6th Ave. N.W.D-4,F-4,G-4
6th Ave. S.E....H-5,I-5
6th Ave. S.W....H-4,J-4
6th Ct....G-3,G-7
6th Ct. N.W....G-1,G-2
6th Ct. S.E....H-4
6th Ct. S.W....H-1
6th Pl. N.W....G-2
6th St....H-3
6th St. N.E....G-4
6th St. N.W....G-1,G-2
6th St. S.E....H-4
6th St. S.W....H-1
6th Ter....B-5
7th S.W....H-3
7th Ave....D-3
7th Ter. N.W....F-3,G-3
7th Ave. N.E....A-5 ....F-5,G-5
7th Ter....B-5,E-5
7th Ave. N.W....F-3,G-3
7th Ct....F-6
7th Ct. N.W....F-1,F-2
7th Pl....F-6,F-7
7th Pl. N.W....F-2
7th St. N.E....G-4
7th St. N.W....F-1 ....G-1,G-2,G-3
7th St. S.E....H-4,H-6
7th St. S.W....H-1,H-3
8th Ave....D-3
8th Ave. N.E....A-5 ....C-5,D-5,F-5,G-5
8th Ave. N.W....F-3,G-3
8th Ave. S.W..H-3,I-3,K-3
8th Ct....F-1,F-2,H-3
8th Ct. N.W....F-1
8th Pl....F-1,F-2
8th Pl. N.W....F-1
8th Rd....F-1
8th St. N.E....F-6,F-7
8th St. N.W....F-1,F-2
8th St. S.E....H-5,H-6
8th St. S.W....H-1,H-3
9th....F-3
9th Ave....H-3
9th Ave. N.E....B-5,D-5 ....E-5,F-5,G-5
9th Ave. N.W....G-3
9th Ave. S.E....H-5
9th Ave. S.W....J-3
9th Ct....F-7,H-3
9th Ct. N.W....F-1,F-2
9th Pl....F-6
9th Pl. N.W....F-1
9th Pl. S.W....H-1
9th St....F-7
9th St. N.E....F-5,F-7
9th St. N.W....E-3,F-3 ....F-1,F-2
9th St. S.E....H-5
9th St. S.W..H-1,H-2,H-4
9th Ter....A-5
9th Ter. N.W....A-3,D-3
10th Ave. N.E....B-5,C-5 ....D-5,E-5,H-5
10th Ave. N.W....B-3 ....D-3,E-3,F-3,G-3
10th Ave. S.E....I-5
10th Ave. S.W....J-3
10th Ct....I-2
10th Ct. N.W....F-1,F-2
10th Pl....F-1
10th Pl. N.W....F-2,F-3
10th St....H-3
10th St. S.E....I-4,I-6
10th St. S.W....I-1,I-2,I-4
10th Ter....B-3,D-5,I-3
10th Ter. N.W....F-3,G-3
10th Way....B-3
11th Ave....B-3
11th Ave. N.E....B-5 ....D-5,F-5,G-5
11th Ave. N.W....G-3
11th Ave. S.E....H-5
11th Ave. S.W....H-3
11th Ct....F-7
11th Ct. N.W..F-1,F-2,F-3
11th Ct. S.E....I-5
11th Ct. S.W....I-1,I-2,I-4
11th Pl. N.W...F-1,F-2,F-3
11th St....F-7,I-4
11th St. N.E....F-5
11th St. N.W....F-1 ....F-2,F-3,F-4
11th St. S.E....I-5,I-6
11th St. S.W....I-2,I-4
11th Way....E-3
12th....C-5,K-3
12th Ave....B-3,D-3,E-3
12th Ave. N.E....A-5 ....C-5,F-5,G-5
12th Ave. N.W...D-3,G-3
12th Ave. S.W....H-3,J-3
12th Ct....F-7
12th Ct. N.W..F-1,F-2,F-3
12th Ct. S.E....I-5,I-6
12th Ct. S.W....I-2,I-3
12th Rd....D-5
12th St. N.E...F-4,F-5,F-7
12th St. N.W....F-1 ....F-2,F-3,F-4
12th St. S.E....I-5,I-6
12th St. S.W...I-1,I-3,K-3
12th Ter....B-3,C-2 ....E-3,H-5
12th Ter. N.E....B-5,E-5
13th....C-5
13th Ave....B-3
13th Ave. N.E....G-5
13th Ave. N.W....G-3
13th Ave. S.E....I-6
13th Ave. S.W....H-3,J-3
13th Ct....E-7
13th Ct. N.W. E-1,E-2,E-3
13th Ct. S.W....I-1,I-2
13th St....F-7
13th St. N.E....F-4,F-5
13th St. N.W....E-1,E-3
13th St. S.E....I-5,I-6
13th St. S.W...I-1,I-2,I-3
13th Ter....A-5,B-5,I-5
14th....C-5,E-5
14th Ave. N.E....E-5,G-5
14th Ave. N.W....E-3,G-3
14th Ave. S.W.H-3,I-3,J-3
14th Ct....E-5
14th Ct. N.W..E-1,E-2,E-3
14th Ct. S.E....I-5
14th Ct. S.W....I-1,I-2,I-3
14th Pl....E-5
14th St....E-5
14th St. N.E....E-6,E-7
14th St. N.W....E-1 ....E-2,E-3,E-4
14th St. S.E....I-5,I-6
14th St. S.W....I-1,I-2,I-3
14th Ter. N.W....G-3
14th Way....A-6
14th Way N.W....G-3
15th S.W....I-3
15th Ave....I-1
15th Ave. N.E....B-6 ....E-5,F-5,G-5
15th Ave. N.W....A-3 ....B-3,E-3,G-3
15th Ave. S.W....J-3
15th Ct....I-1
15th Ct. N.W..E-1,E-2,E-3
15th Ct. S.W....I-3
15th Pl. N.W....E-2,E-3
15th St. N.E...E-6,E-7,E-8
15th St. N.W....E-1 ....E-2,E-3,E-4
15th St. S.E....I-4,I-5,I-6
15th St. S.W....I-3
15th Ter. N.E....B-6,D-6
15th Ter. N.W....E-2,G-2
15th Ter. S.W....I-2
15th Way....G-2
15th Way N.E....B-6
16th....E-3
16th Ave....I-2
16th Ave. N.E....C-6,D-6
16th Ave. N.W....G-2
16th Ct....I-1
16th Ct. N.E...E-4,E-5,E-6
16th Ct. N.W....E-1,E-2
16th Ct. S.E....I-5
16th Ct. S.W....I-3
16th Pl. N.E....E-4
16th St. N.E...E-4,E-5,E-6
16th St. N.W....E-1 ....E-2,E-3,E-4
16th St. S.E....I-5
16th St. S.W....I-2,I-3
16th Ter. N.E....B-6 ....F-6,G-6
16th Way....F-2
17th....E-8
17th S.E....H-6
17th Ave....D-6,G-6
17th Ave. N.E....A-6 ....B-6,C-6,D-6,F-6
17th Ave. N.W....F-2,G-2
17th Ct....E-6
17th Ct. N.E....E-4,E-5
17th Ct. N.W....E-3,E-4
17th St....E-5
17th St. N.E...E-5,E-6,E-7
17th St. N.W..E-1,E-3,E-4
17th St. S.E....I-5
17th St. S.W....J-1,J-3
17th Ter. N.E....A-6 ....B-6,D-6,F-6
17th Ter. N.W....C-2
17th Way N.E....F-6,G-6
17th Way S.E....H-6
18th....D-6,E-8,G-6
18th Ave....B-2
18th Ave. N.E....B-6,C-6 ....D-6,E-5,E-6,F-6,G-6
18th Ave. N.W....E-2,G-2
18th Ave. S.E....H-6 ....J-6,K-6
18th Ave. S.W....H-2,I-2
18th Ct. N.W..E-1,E-2,E-3
18th Ct. S.E....J-4,J-6
18th Ct. S.W....J-3
18th St....E-1,E-2
18th St. N.E....E-5,E-7
18th St. N.W....E-3,E-4
18th St. S.E....J-4
18th St. S.W....J-1,J-3
18th Ter....D-2,I-2
18th Ter. N.E....A-6
18th Ter. S.W....J-2
19th....G-6
19th Ave. N.E....A-6 ....C-6,D-6,G-6
19th Ave. N.W....B-2 ....D-2,E-2,G-2
19th Ave. S.E....H-6,K-6
19th Ave. S.W....H-2,J-2
19th Ct....E-3
19th Ct. N.W....E-3
19th St....E-6,E-7 ....E-8,J-1
19th St. N.W..E-1,E-2,E-3
19th St. S.E....J-4,J-6
19th St. S.W....J-3
19th Ter. N.W....B-2,G-2
20th....D-2
20th N.E....D-4
20th Ave....I-2
20th Ave. N.E....B-6 ....C-6,E-6,G-6
20th Ave. N.W....E-2 ....F-2,G-2
20th Ave. S.E....H-6
20th Ct....D-3,E-7
20th Dr. N.E....D-5
20th St....D-3,E-7,J-1
20th St. N.E....E-6
20th St. N.W.D-1,D-3,E-1
20th St. S.E....J-5,J-7
20th St. S.W....J-3
20th Ter....A-7,I-2
21st....A-7,D-5
21st Ave....D-6
21st Ave. N.E....B-6,G-6
21st Ave. N.W....G-2
21st Ave. S.E....H-6
21st Ct....J-1
21st Ct. N.E....D-4,E-7
21st Ct. N.W....D-1,D-4
21st Dr....D-5
21st St....D-3,D-6 ....E-6,E-7
21st St. N.E..D-4,D-8,E-7
21st St. N.W....D-1
21st St. S.W....J-3,J-4
21st Ter....D-2
21st Ter. N.E....D-6
21st Ter. N.W....G-2
21st Ter. S.E....H-6
21st Ter. S.W....H-2,I-2
21st Way....H-2
22nd....D-5
22nd Ave....I-2
22nd Ave. N.E....B-6 ....C-6,E-6,G-6
22nd Ave. N.W....G-2
22nd Ave. S.E....H-6,J-7
22nd Ave. S.W....H-2 ....I-2,J-2
22nd Ct....D-3,J-1
22nd Dr. N.E....D-5
22nd Rd. N.W....F-1
22nd St...D-3,D-8,E-7,J-1
22nd St. N.E....D-4
22nd St. N.W....D-1,E-2
22nd St. S.E....J-4
22nd St. S.W....J-2,J-4
22nd Ter....H-2,I-2
22nd Ter. N.E....A-7,E-6
23rd....C-6,D-5,G-7
23rd Ave. N.E....G-6
23rd Ave. S.W....G-2 ....I-2,J-2
23rd Dr. N.E....D-5
23rd Ln....D-1
23rd St....D-7,J-1
23rd St. N.E....D-4,D-8
23rd St. N.W....D-1,D-4
23rd St. S.E....J-4
23rd St. S.W....J-2,J-4
23rd Ter. N.W....F-2
23rd Ter. S.W....J-2,K-2
23rd Way....F-2
24th....C-6
24th Ave. N.W....D-1,E-1
24th Ave. S.E....H-7,J-7
24th Ave. S.W....J-1
24th St....D-2
24th Ct. N.E....D-7
24th Ct. N.W....D-1
24th Pl. N.E....D-7
24th St. N.E....D-4,D-7
24th St. N.W.D-1,D-3,D-4
24th St. S.W....J-2
24th Ter....F-1
24th Ter. N.E....A-7
24th Ter. N.W....E-1
25th....C-7
25th Ave..E-1,G-1,H-1,I-1
25th Ave. N.E....B-7,E-7
25th Ave. S.E....H-7,J-7
25th Ct. N.E....D-7
25th Pl....D-7
25th St....D-8
25th St. N.E....D-4,D-7
25th St. N.W.D-1,D-3,D-4
25th St. S.W....J-2,J-4
25th Ter....C-7,E-1 ....G-1,H-1,I-1,K-1
25th Way....F-1
26th....D-8,H-7
26th Ave....H-1
26th Ave. N.E....A-7 ....C-7,D-7,E-7,F-7
26th Ave. N.W....D-1,E-1
26th Ave. S.W....I-1
26th Ct. N.E....D-7
26th Dr. N.E..D-4,D-5,D-6
26th Pl. N.E....D-7
26th St. N.E....D-4,D-5
26th St. N.W....D-3
26th St. S.W..J-2,J-3,J-4
26th Ter....E-1,I-1
26th Ter. N.E....D-7
26th Ter. S.W....K-1
27th....J-3
27th Ave....C-7
27th Ave. N.E....A-7,B-7
27th Ave. N.W....E-1
27th Ave. S.W....H-1,J-1
27th Ct....D-7,J-2
27th Dr. N.E....D-4,D-5
27th Ln....D-1
27th St....D-8
27th St. N.E....D-4 ....D-5,D-6,D-7
27th St. N.W.D-1,D-2,D-3
27th St. S.E....J-4
27th St. S.W....J-4
27th Ter....D-7,H-1 ....I-1,J-1
27th Ter.N.W....G-1
28th Ave. N.E....A-7,B-7
28th Ave. N.W....D-1 ....E-1,F-1,G-1
28th Ave. S.W....H-1 ....I-1,J-1
28th Ct....D-2
28th Ct. N.W....D-3,D-4
28th Rd....I-1
28th St. N.E....D-4,D-5 ....D-6,D-7,D-8
28th Dr....D-6
28th St. N.W....D-1,D-2 ....D-3,D-4
28th St. S.E....K-4,K-6
28th St. S.W....K-2,K-3
28th Ter. N.W....D-1,G-1
28th Ter. S.W.H-1,I-1,J-1
28th Way N.W....G-1
28th Way S.W....I-1,J-1
29th S.E....K-4
29th Ave....D-1,F-1,G-1
29th Ave. N.E....A-7,B-7
29th Ave. N.W....D-1
29th Ave. S.W....H-1,I-1
29th Ct....C-6,D-3
29th Ct. N.E....C-7
29th Dr. N.E....D-4,D-5
29th St....C-6,D-8
29th St. N.E....C-7,D-8
29th St. N.W.D-2,D-3,D-4
29th St. S.W....K-2,K-4
29th Ter. N.W....D-1,G-1
29th Ter. S.W....H-1,I-1
29th Way....F-1,I-1
30th Ave. N.W....D-1 ....F-1,G-1
30th Ave. S.W....H-1,I-1
30th Ct. N.E....C-5
30th Ct. N.W....C-1,C-3
30th Pl. N.E....C-7
30th St....C-1,C-3 ....C-4,C-6
30th St. N.E....C-7
30th St. S.E....K-4,K-6
30th St. S.W..K-2,K-3,K-4
30th Ter. N.W....B-1,E-1
30th Ter. S.W....J-1
31st S.E....K-4
31st Ave....A-7,E-8
31st St. S.W....K-1 ....K-2,K-3,K-4
32nd Ave....A-8,C-8
32nd Ave. N.E....D-8
32nd Ct. S.E....K-4
32nd Ct. S.W....K-2,K-4
32nd Pl....K-2
32nd St. N.E....C-5,C-7
32nd St. S.E....K-4,K-6
32nd St. S.W.K-1,K-3,K-4
33rd Ave....A-8
33rd Ave. N.E....D-8
33rd Ct....C-2
33rd St....C-2
33rd St. N.E....C-5,C-7
33rd St. N.W....C-3,C-4
33rd St. S.W....K-4
34th....C-2
34th Ave. N.E....C-8,D-8
34th Ct. N.E....C-5
34th St. N.E....C-5,C-7
34th St. N.W....C-3,C-4
35th Ct....C-4
35th Ct. N.E....C-7
35th Dr. N.E....C-7
35th St. N.E....C-5,C-7
35th St. N.W....C-3,C-4
36th Ct....C-4
36th Ct. N.W....C-2
36th St....C-6,C-7
36th St. N.E..C-5,C-7,C-8
36th St. N.W....C-3,C-4
37th Ct....C-7
37th Dr. N.E....C-7
37th St....C-7
37th St. N.E....C-5
37th St. N.W.C-2,C-3,C-4
38th....C-8
38th St....B-7
38th St. N.W....C-1 ....C-2,C-4,C-5
39th....B-8
39th St....B-4,B-5,B-7
39th St. N.E....B-5,B-6
39th St. N.W.B-2,B-3,B-4
40th....B-8
40th Ct....B-4,B-5 ....B-6,B-7
40th Ct. N.W....B-4
40th St....B-5,B-5 ....B-7,B-8
40th St. N.E....B-5,B-6
40th St. N.W....B-3,B-4
41st St....B-3,B-4 ....B-5,B-6
41st St. N.W....B-3,B-4
42nd Ct....B-3,B-8
42nd St....B-2,B-3,B-5
42nd St. N.E....B-4 ....B-5,B-8
42nd St. N.W....B-3,B-4
43rd Ct. N.E....B-4,B-5
43rd Ct. N.W....B-3,B-4
43rd St....B-3
43rd St. N.E..B-4,B-6,B-7
43rd St. N.W....B-3,B-4
44th Ct....B-5
44th St....B-6
44th St. N.E....B-7
45th Ct....B-3
45th Ct. N.W....B-4
45th St....B-3,B-4 ....B-5,B-7,B-8
45th St. N.W....B-4
46th Ct....B-4,B-5
46th St....A-1,A-2 ....B-2,B-4,B-7
46th St. N.E....B-5,B-6
46th St. N.W....B-2
47th Ct....A-4,A-5,A-7
47th St....B-3,B-4
47th St. N.E....A-7,B-6
48th Ct....A-4
48th Ct. N.E..A-4,A-5,A-6
48th St....A-1,A-3 ....A-4,A-5,A-7
49th St....A-3,A-4
49th St. N.E..A-4,A-6,A-7
50th Ct. N.E..A-5,A-6,A-7
51st Ct....A-4
51st Ct. N.E....A-6
51st Pl....A-1,A-3
51st St....A-3,A-4,A-6
51st St. N.E....A-4 ....A-6,A-7
52nd Ct....A-1,A-4,A-6
52nd St....A-3,A-4 ....A-6,A-7
52nd St. N.E....A-6
53rd Ct....A-4,A-5
53rd St....A-3,A-4
53rd St. N.E....A-5 ....A-6,A-7
54th St....A-1,A-3
54th St. N.E....A-6,A-7
55th St....A-1

POINTS OF INTEREST

Ft. Lauderdale Executive Airport...A-2
Holiday Park....F-5,G-5
Hugh Taylor Birch State Park....E-7,E-8 ....F-7,F-8
Osswald Park....D-2
S.P. Snyder Park K-3,K-4
Sunland Park....F-2,F-3

FORT WORTH

A Ave....G-7
Abney....J-5
Ada St....H-7
Adams St....G-3,I-3,K-3
Adolph....E-2
Adrian....E-1
Akers....D-5
Alabama....F-3
Alcannon St....K-7
Alice St....K-3
Allen Ave....H-3,H-5
Alloway....J-6
Alston Ave....G-3
Alta View....A-6
Alvin....K-7
Alvord....E-6
Amont....J-4
Amspoker....K-5
Amy....H-6
Andy Ave....F-8
Angle....B-1
Ann....G-6
Anna St....J-6
Annabell....J-6
Annglenn....J-6
Annie St....G-4,G-5
Arch St....G-8,H-8
Arch Adams....E-1
Arizona....G-4,H-4
Arlington...H-3,H-5,H-6
Armour....C-4
Arnold....D-7
Arthur....E-2
Ash Crescent....G-6,I-6
Aster....B-5,B-6
Atkins St....J-5
Aurline....E-5
Austin....D-6,E-2
Aval....F-8
Avenue....B-3
Avondale....H-1
Ayers Ave....F-8,G-8
Azalea....E-1
B Ave....G-6,G-7
Bailey....E-1
Baker Lane....B-8
Baker St....I-4
Baldwin St....J-3,K-3
Ballinger....F-3
Balsam....B-5
Baltimore Ave. H-3,H-5
Barbella....B-6
Barclay....C-6
Barden....E-1
Baylor St....J-7
Beach St....A-6 ....D-6,D-7,E-7,G-7
Beckham....G-2
Bedsoe....F-1
Belford Ct....F-8
Belknap....A-8,D-5,E-3
Belmead St....K-4
Belmont....C-1
Belzise....G-6
Belzise Terr....I-6
Benbrook Dr....J-1,J-2
Benhal Ct....H-2
Benjamin....C-2
Berke Rd....K-5
Berner....A-5
Bernice....B-7
Berry St....I-7,I-8 ....J-3,J-4
Berryhill....H-6
Bessie....F-5
Betty....C-7
Beverly Ave....H-5
Bewick....J-1,J-3
Biddison....J-1,J-2,J-4
Bideker Ave....H-7
Binkley St....G-7,H-7,I-7
Bird....C-5
Birdville....C-8
Bishop....I-8
Blanch....E-1
Blandin....B-5,C-5
Blalock Ave....K-4,K-5
Blevins....D-6
Blitton....K-5
Blodgett Ave....K-5
Blue....C-5
Bluebird....B-4
Blue Grove....D-6
Blue Smoke Ct....F-6
Boland....E-1
Bolt....K-1
Bomar....F-6,F-7
Bonnett....B-5,C-5
Bonnie Brae....B-6,C-6
Booker....E-5
Boston Ave....F-8,G-8
Bowie St....I-1,I-3,I-4
Boyd Ave....I-1,K-1
Brady....K-1
Brandies....E-6
Bransford....G-5
Braswell....A-4
Brenning....B-3
Brents....D-4
Bright....I-8
Bristol....E-4
Brittian....B-6
Broadway....F-2,F-3 ....F-5,F-6
Brookshire....E-4
Brown....D-6
Bruce....A-5
Bryan Ave....G-4,I-4,K-4
Buck St....G-2
Bundie St....K-7
Burchill....H-7
Burchill Ct....H-7
Burnett....E-3,F-3
Burson....J-4
Burton St....I-8
Buster Ct....C-6
Butler....J-1,J-2 ....K-2,K-4,K-5
Buxton....G-5
Calhoun....B-2,D-3 ....E-3,F-4
Calvert....E-2
Calvin....I-6
Camilla....G-6
Campbell St....G-8 ....H-8,I-8
Canberra....H-6
Cannon....G-3,G-5
Cantey....I-1,I-3 ....I-4,I-5
Canyon Ct....G-8
Capps St....I-3
Cardinal....B-4
Carlock St....H-3
Carnation....B-5,B-6
Carnes....K-5
Carrol....E-2
Carter....F-6
Carter Park Dr....K-5
Carver....C-4
Casablanca....E-1
Castleman....I-8
Catalpa....B-8,C-7
C Ave....G-6,G-7
Cedar....F-5
Central....C-2
Chambers....E-4
Chandler....C-5,E-6
Chandler Dr....B-6
Chenault....D-5
Cherry....F-3
Cheryl....B-6
Chase Ct....H-3
Chester....B-4,F-6
Chester Boyer Rd....A-6
Chestnut....B-1
Chicago Ave....F-8,G-8
Chickasaw Ave....J-8
Childress....J-7
Christin....H-7
Circle....D-7
Circle Park. Blvd....C-2
Circle Pkwy....H-1
Clairemont Ave..F-8,G-8
Clara St....G-1
Clarence....C-7,D-7
Clary....C-6
Clearview....K-6
Cleckler....C-6
Clement....G-6,G-7
Cleveland....F-4
Cleyburn....J-2
Clinton....A-2,B-2,C-2
Cloer....K-1
Cobb....F-5
Cobb Park Dr....H-6
Cockerell Ave.I-1,J-1,K-1
Cole St....K-4
Cole Spring Rd. C-4,D-4
Collard....I-7
College St....G-3 ....I-3,J-3
Collier....F-3
Collin....J-7,J-8
Collins....H-1
Colonial....D-6
Columbus....B-1
Colvin Ave....I-4,I-5
Comanche....I-7
Commerce....B-2
Commercial....E-2
Concord....C-6
Congress....E-2
Conkling....A-7
Conway....D-6,D-7
Cook....D-4
Cooper....G-2
Corner Ave....G-7
Corpus Ct....J-3
Cosgrove Ct....A-8
Cottonwood....D-6
Court....G-7
Covella....D-6
Coventry....E-1
Crawford St....G-4
Creach Rd....B-7
Crenshaw St....H-7
Crest....J-6
Crockett....E-1
Cromwell....F-6
Crump....E-4
Cullen....D-2
Cummings....E-3
Currie....E-1
Cutter St....K-7
Cypress....F-5
D Ave....G-6,G-7
Daggett....F-2-4
Dakota....E-2
Daisy La....B-5
Dalford....C-5
Dallas-Ft. Worth Tpk....F-5
Damon....D-6
Darby....H-8
Darcy....E-1
Dashwood....G-3,G-4
David....B-6
Davis Blvd....H-5
Dayton....B-8,C-5
Debbie St....K-5
Decatur....A-3
Decosta....D-6,E-6
Degar....G-1
Delaware St....H-5
Delga....C-4
Dell....B-7,C-5
Denair....E-6
Denman St....K-7
Denver....C-1
Devitt....J-2,J-4,J-5
Dewey....A-3,A-4
Dickson....K-1,K-2,K-4
Donalee St....H-8,I-8
Donna St....J-4
Dooling....A-5
Dowell....J-8
Drew St....K-1,K-2,K-4
Duell St....H-6
Dundee....B-4
Dunford....I-6
Dunlap dr....K-6
E Ave....G-6,G-7
E Dr....F-1
Eagle....B-6,C-6
Earl....B-6
Eastland....I-7
Eastline Dr....J-6,K-6
East Ridge....A-7,B-7
Eden Ave....B-8
Edith....A-7
Edwin....H-2
Elinor....A-6
Elizabeth Blvd....I-3
Ella....E-4
Elliot....D-7
Ellis....A-2,B-2,C-2
Elm....A-2,E-4
Elmwood Ave...H-5,H-6
El Paso....F-3
El Rancho Rd....K-6
Elsie....G-7
Elton....B-8
Elva Warren St....K-5
Embry....C-5
Emerson....I-7
Enneca....F-2
Ennis....E-6
Eoch....E-1
Erath St....K-8
Ernst....G-6
Essex....G-6
Esthill....I-7
Etsie....C-8
Eugene....K-5
Evans St....H-4,I-4,J-4
Exchange....B-2
Exeter....F-5,G-5
Faett Ct....J-6
Fain....C-7
Fairfax....K-8
Fairline....K-8
Fairmont Ave....I-3
Fair Park Blvd....K-5
Fair View....A-6,B-6 ....C-6,D-6
Fairway....J-7
Fairway Rd....J-7
Felcher-Andrews....A-8
Field....A-8
Fincher....B-8
Finley....E-5
First Ave. East....D-5
First St. East....D-7
Fisher....E-6
Fitzhugh....I-7,I-8
Flint....K-1,K-2
Florence....F-3
Foard....K-7
Fogg....K-3,K-4
Forbes....I-8
Forby Ave....F-8
Forest Blvd....H-2,I-2
Forest Park Blvd. F-2
Fossil....A-8
Fouriner....F-2
Fox....C-7
Frazier Ave....I-2,K-2
Freddie....I-8,J-8
Freman....G-5
Fry St....K-4
Fulton....F-3
G Ave....H-7,H-8
Gage....B-8
Galves....D-5,D-6
Galveston....H-4
Gardina St....K-7
Garvey....D-4
Gibson....C-7,E-5
Gilcrest....C-6
Gillis....D-5
Gilmore....D-7
Glen....J-6
Glencoe Terr....H-2
Glenda....A-7
Glendale....B-3
Glengarden Dr....I-4
Glenhaven....B-8
Glenmore....C-4
Goldenrod....B-5
Goldie....B-7
Goddard....D-7
Gorden Ave....I-2,K-2
Gould....B-1,C-1
Gounah....D-5
Grace....B-5
Grainge....G-3
Grand....D-1,D-2
Grant....D-4
Grapewood....D-5
Grayson....J-7
Greene Ave....I-1,J-1
Greenfield....D-4
Greenleaf....E-2
Greer....D-3
Gross....D-7
Grover....A-4,B-4
Grove St....C-2,E-4 ....J-4,K-4
Gunther....B-3
H Ave....H-7,H-8
Hale....A-4,B-3
Hall....G-6
Haltom Rd....A-8,B-8
Hampshire....G-8
Hampton....A-3,D-4,E-4
Hanger Ave....H-7
Harding....A-3,D-4,E-4
Hardy....A-3
Harper....C-7
Harrington....D-1
Harris....G-2
Harris Lane....B-7
Harrison....G-2
Harrold....E-2
Harrow....A-8
Harvey....H-5
Harwent Terr....J-1
Harwood St....F-7
Hathcox....K-5
Hattie....G-5
Hawthorne....H-2,H-3
Haynes Ave....F-8,G-8
Hazeline....G-8
Heath Ct. E....E-5
Hedrick....A-6
Hemlock....C-8
Hemphill St...G-3,I-3,K-3
Henderson St....F-3 ....G-3,J-3
Hendricks....G-6
Hickory....C-8
Higgens....B-7
Highcrest....A-5
Highland....C-1
High Point Rd....J-6
Hill Dr....I-2
Hill Place....C-1
Hillview....J-6
Hoffman....E-5
Hollis St....B-7
Holmes....G-6
Holtzer....H-1
Homan....D-1
Honey Suckle...B-5,B-6
Houston....B-2,C-2 ....D-2,D-3,F-3
Howard....A-8,J-7
Hudgins....D-6
Humboldt....G-2,G-4
Hunting Dr....K-7
Huntington....H-2
Hutchinson....A-3
I Ave....H-7,H-8
Illinois....F-5,J-5
Inderly....H-2
Inderly Pl....H-2
Industrial Blvd....F-4
Irion....B-4,E-7
Irma....G-4
Irwin....G-2
Ivey....B-5,B-7
J Ave....H-7,H-8
Jackson....J-7
Jamaica....F-6,G-8
James Ave....J-2,K-2
Jane Ln....K-7
Janis St....F-3
Jarvis St....F-2
Jeanette....J-1,K-1
Jefferies....A-7
Jefferson Ave...H-3,H-5
Jennings Ave....F-3,G-3 ....H-3,I-3
Jerome....F-2,G-2
Jessamine St....H-3,H-5
Jones St....C-2,D-2 ....I-4,K-4
Joplin....C-7
Juanita....D-5
Judd St....I-4,I-6
Juniper....B-8
K Ave....H-7,H-8
Kansas....E-2
Karnes....C-6,D-6
Kearby....B-7
Kellis....K-8
Kennedy St....F-5
Kent....I-1
Kentucky Ave....G-4
Kerry....A-8
Killian....J-8
Kimble St....H-6
Kimbo Ct....A-6
King....B-8,C-7,D-7
King Oaks....D-7
Kingsdale....J-6
Knoll....B-7
Knox Dr....K-8
L Ave....H-7,H-8
Lagonia....C-1
Lake....F-3,G-3
Lakeland....A-6
Lames....J-1
Lancaster Ave....F-1 ....F-3,F-4,F-6
Lane....A-7
Lasalle....E-5
Laughton....J-3
Lawnwood....E-6
Layton....B-7
Lee....B-1,C-2
Leming....A-4
Leona....B-7
Leon Ave....G-5
Leota....C-4
Leslie....G-2
Leuda....G-3,G-5
Lewis St....F-8
Lexington....E-3,F-3
Lilac St....H-3
Lillian....C-5
Lincoln....B-1,C-2
Linda Ln....K-6
Lipscomb St..G-3,I-3,K-3
Lisbury....B-4
Little St....H-8,I-8
Little John St....H-7,H-8
Live....D-4
Livingston....I-2,J-2,K-2
Locust....D-3
Loeton Terr....H-1
Logan....H-6
Lois St....I-8
Lola....B-6
Lollita Ct....J-6
Lomita....J-7
Lomo....K-4
Loney St....G-5
Loraine....A-1,A-4,A-7
Lotus....B-5
Louisiana....H-4
Loving....B-1
Lowden....I-1,I-3,I-4
Lowe St....J-3
Lower Birdville Rd....B-8,C-7,E-7
Lowriemore....I-6
Lucinda....K-7
Lucy....G-4
Ludell....F-6
Lulu....A-3
Lynch....D-7
Lynfield....G-8
M Ave....H-7,H-8
Macon....F-3
Maddox Ave....H-3,H-5
Magnolia Ave....G-2-4
Main St..D-3,E-3,J-4,K-4
Malone....B-3
Malta St....K-3,K-4
Malvern....I-6
Mandell....F-7
Mansfield Ave....G-5
Maple....D-4
Maple Leaf....B-5
Marigold....C-6
Marion Ave....I-5
Market....B-1
Marsalis....C-7
Marshall....D-5
Martin St....K-8
Mason St....K-3,K-4
Maurice....C-6
Maxine St....C-7
May St....H-3,J-3 ....J-3,K-4
Mayfield....D-3
McCart....I-2,K-2
McComas....H-6
McCurdy....G-6,H-6
McIvey....E-5
McKenzie St....G-7,H-7
McLean St....F-7
McLemore Ave....C-5
McLennon....B-3
McNutt....C-7
McPherson Ave...I-1,I-2
Meadowbrook Dr....F-7
Mecca St....J-7
Medford Ct....H-1
Menzer....E-8
Menzer Ct....E-8
Mercedes....E-1
Mercury....B-7
Merida Ave....I-1,J-1
Meriwether....K-5
Merrimac....E-1
Mesquite....A-6
Midland....G-7
Millet Ave....H-7
Mills....E-3
Milton....F-6
Minden....J-2,J-5
Minnie....B-7
Mission....J-1
Mississippi Ave....H-5
Missouri Ave....G-4,H-4
Mistletoe....G-1
Mistletoe Ave....G-2
Mistletow Blvd....G-2
Mitchell Blvd....H-6,I-7
Mitchell St....H-3
Moberly St....K-8
Moline....B-8
Monda St....J-2
Montague....J-7
Moore....B-4
Moreby....I-6
Morgan....E-4
Morning Glory....B-4
Morningside Dr. I-3,I-4
Morphy....G-3,G-5
Morrison....D-3
Morton....F-1
Mt. Vernon St....F-7,F-8
Mt. View....F-8
Mulke St....I-3,I-5
Murphy....C-5
Myrtle St....H-3,H-5
N Ave....H-7,H-8
Nashville....G-7
Neal....B-3
Nebraska....E-2
Nelson....B-5
Newman....A-7
Newton....B-8
New York....F-5,J-4
New York Ave....H-5,I-4
Nichols....A-3,E-4
Nixon....C-4
Noble....D-5,D-6
Noe St....I-8
Nolan St....K-8
Normandy....F-8
North....C-2
North Glen Dr....J-6
Northside Dr....C-2
Norwood....E-1
Oak....C-7,D-4
Oak Grove St....G-4
Oak Hurst Scenic Dr....C-4,E-5
Oak Ridge....B-8
Oak View....C-7
Oakwood....B-7
Odessa Ave....J-1
Old Mansfield Rd....J-6
Oleander....G-3
Ollie St....K-7
Orange St....J-2,J-3
Orr....G-2
Oscar....A-3
Otto St....H-8
Owens....B-8
Oxford....B-4
Pafford St...K-1,K-2,K-3
Page St....I-3
Panola....G-8
Paradise....E-5
Park....C-1,C-3,I-1
Parkdale....G-7
Park Dr....D-1
Parkins St....F-8
Park Place Ave....H-3
Park Place Dr....H-2
Park Ridge Blvd....J-1
Parrish....C-7
Patton Ct....H-2
Pavillion....C-3
Peach....E-3
Peak....B-3
Pearl....B-1
Pecan St....A-2,E-4,J-4
Pecos....K-6-8
Pembroke Dr....H-2
Penn....F-2
Pennsylvania Ave....G-3
Perry....A-7
Petersmith....F-2,F-3
Pharr....D-4
Photo St....G-1
Pine....F-5
Pioneer....K-7,K-8
Pittsburgh....D-5
Plumwood....D-5
Poindexter....C-3
Poplar....F-4
Porter St....G-6
Portland....C-4
Post....B-7
Powell Ave....H-3,H-5
Prairie....B-1
Pratcher....K-6
Premier....A-6
Presidio....F-3,F-5
Prince....J-6
Primrose....C-5
Prospect....B-1
Pruitt....G-2,G-3
Pulaski....G-3,G-4
Quentin Ct....A-4
Quinn....H-7
Race....C-5
Ramey....H-8,I-8
Ramsey....H-4,I-6
Ranch Ter....J-6
Rapurt....A-4
Rattikin....I-6
Ravin....G-7
Ray....K-7
Raynor....D-5
Reaford....A-7
Refugid....B-1
Retta....E-5
Riardale Rd....J-6
Richmond...H-3,H-5,H-6
Ridgeview....J-6
Riley St....J-5
Rio Grand....F-3
Ripy St...J-2,J-3,J-4,J-5
Riverridge....C-6
Riverside Dr..G-6,I-5,K-6
Roberts....I-2-5
Robert Burns Dr....J-6
Robinwood....B-6
Rodeo St....K-7
Rogers Ave....H-1,I-1
Rolling Hills Dr....J-6
Roosevelt....B-1
Rosedale St..G-3,G-5,G-7
Ross....A-2,B-2
Rouse....D-5
Rufus....I-8
Runnels....A-4
Rupert....E-2
Rusty....B-6
Rutan....K-8
Ryan Ave....J-2,K-2
Ryan Place Dr....I-3
St. Louis Ave....J-4,K-4
St. Louis St....G-4
Samuels....C-3
Sanborn....F-7
Sandage....I-1
Sanders....B-7
Sanderson St....F-8
Sandgate....I-6
Santa Rosa....B-8
Sarah....K-6
Sargent....E-7
Seaman....C-6,D-6
Seaman Ave....D-6
Selk....B-6
Selma....B-5,B-6
Scenery Hill Ct....E-8
Scenic Ct....C-5
Schadt....A-3
Schwartz....A-3
Scott....E-4,F-6
Shackelford....K-8
Shadow....C-7
Shamrock....D-2
Shane....A-7
Shaw St....J-2-5
Shirley Way....I-1
Shotts....E-1
Shropshire....I-6
Simpson....F-5
Smilay....C-4
South Freeway....I-4
South Hill....J-1
Southland St....G-2
Spiller....I-6
Spring St....G-1
Springdale Rd....B-6
Stadium Dr....I-1,J-1
Stanley....H-2,I-2 ....J-2,K-2
Stephen Lee....J-6
Stardust....J-6
Stayton....E-2
Stearnes....G-6
Stella....F-5
Stephenson....F-4
Stratford Dr....F-8
Strong....I-7
Stuart Dr....I-4,K-4
Summit....F-2
Sunday....A-7
Sunset....F-2
Surrey....K-1
Swayne....E-6
Swift....C-4
Sycamore....G-6
Sydney....I-8
Sylvania....D-5
Tallman St....K-8
Taylor....E-3
Templeton....E-1
Tennessee....G-5
Terrace....D-1
Terrell....G-2,G-3,G-4
Terry....A-2,E-4
Thanntson....I-7
Thockmorton....D-3,E-3
Thrall St....G-7,H-7,I-7
Tillar....E-1
Timberline Dr....K-5,K-6
Todd Ave....J-5
Tom Ellen....A-6
Townshend Dr....I-2,K-2
Transcontinental Cutoff....A-5
Travis St....G-3,I-3,K-3
Troost....G-5
Trueland Dr....J-7,K-7
Tucker St....G-5
Ubbock Ave..I-1,J-1,K-1
University Dr....F-1 ....I-1,J-1
Uvalde....H-6
Vacek....E-2
Valley....E-3
Vance....C-7
Van Horn....E-5
Vaughn Blvd....I-7
Vaughn St....J-8
Vera Cruz....A-4
Verben E....G-4
Vickery Blvd....F-3,F-6
Vicki Ln....I-4
View....F-7
Vinetta....K-8
Viola....E-2
Virginia....C-5,G-5
Vogt St....H-8
W Dr....F-1
Wabash....I-1
Wabash Ave....J-1
Waggoman St....K-1 ....K-3,K-4
Waits Ave....I-1,J-1
Waldemar....B-7,B-8
Walker....B-4
Wall....D-4
Wallace St....E-7,H-8
Ward Pkwy....H-2
Ward St....F-7
Warner....H-2
Warwick....B-4
Washington Ave....G-3
Watauga Rd....B-5
Waterman....D-4
Wathal....A-8
Wayne....B-7,C-7,D-7
Wayside Dr....I-2,K-2
Weatherbee St....H-2
Weatherford....E-3
Weber....A-3
Weisenberger St. E-1,J-5
Wesley....A-6
Wesleyan Dr....G-7,H-7
Westbrook....C-5
Westchester....B-8
Wheeler....C-7
White Ave....G-5
White Settlement Rd....E-1
Whitmore....E-1
Wichita St....K-7
Wilbarger St....J-7
Wilkinson....F-7
William....F-4
Williams....A-6
Williams Pl....B-6
Willing Ave....J-2,K-2
Wilshire....H-2
Wimberly....E-1
Windham....F-6
Windmill....C-4
Winfield....K-1
Wingate....E-1
Winslow Pl....H-2
Winston Rd....J-1
Winston Terr....H-1
Withers St....G-6
Woodland....J-3
Woodrow St....G-6
Woods....B-8
Woodward....E-2
Worth St....G-2
Worthills....J-1
Wyatt Ct....J-6
Wynne....C-6
Young....F-7
Yucca....C-6
Yuma St....H-5,I-5,J-5
Zelma....B-8
1st St....D-5,E-3
2nd....E-3
3rd....E-3
4th St....D-3,D-5,D-6 ....E-1,E-3
5th St....D-3,E-1-3
5th Ave.D-3,E-1-3,I-3,K-3
6th....D-3,E-1-3
6th Ave....I-3,K-3
7th....D-3,E-1,E-3
8th....E-3
8th Ave....H-2,J-2,K-2
9th....D-3,E-3
10th....C-2,C-3
11th St....C-3,F-2,G-2
12th St....E-5,G-2
13th St....C-3,G-2
14th St....C-1,F-2,F-4
15th....C-1,F-4
16th....C-1,C-3,F-4
17th....C-3,F-4
18th....C-1,C-3,F-5
19th St....C-1,F-4
20th....C-1,C-2
21st....C-1,C-2
22nd....B-1,B-2
23rd....B-1,B-2
24th....B-1
25th....B-1
26th....B-1
27th....B-1,B-2
28th....A-1,A-2,A-5
29th....A-1,A-3,A-6
30th....A-1,A-2,A-3
31st....A-1,A-2,A-3
32nd....A-1,A-2,A-3

Scale of Miles
0. .1 .2 .3 .4 .5

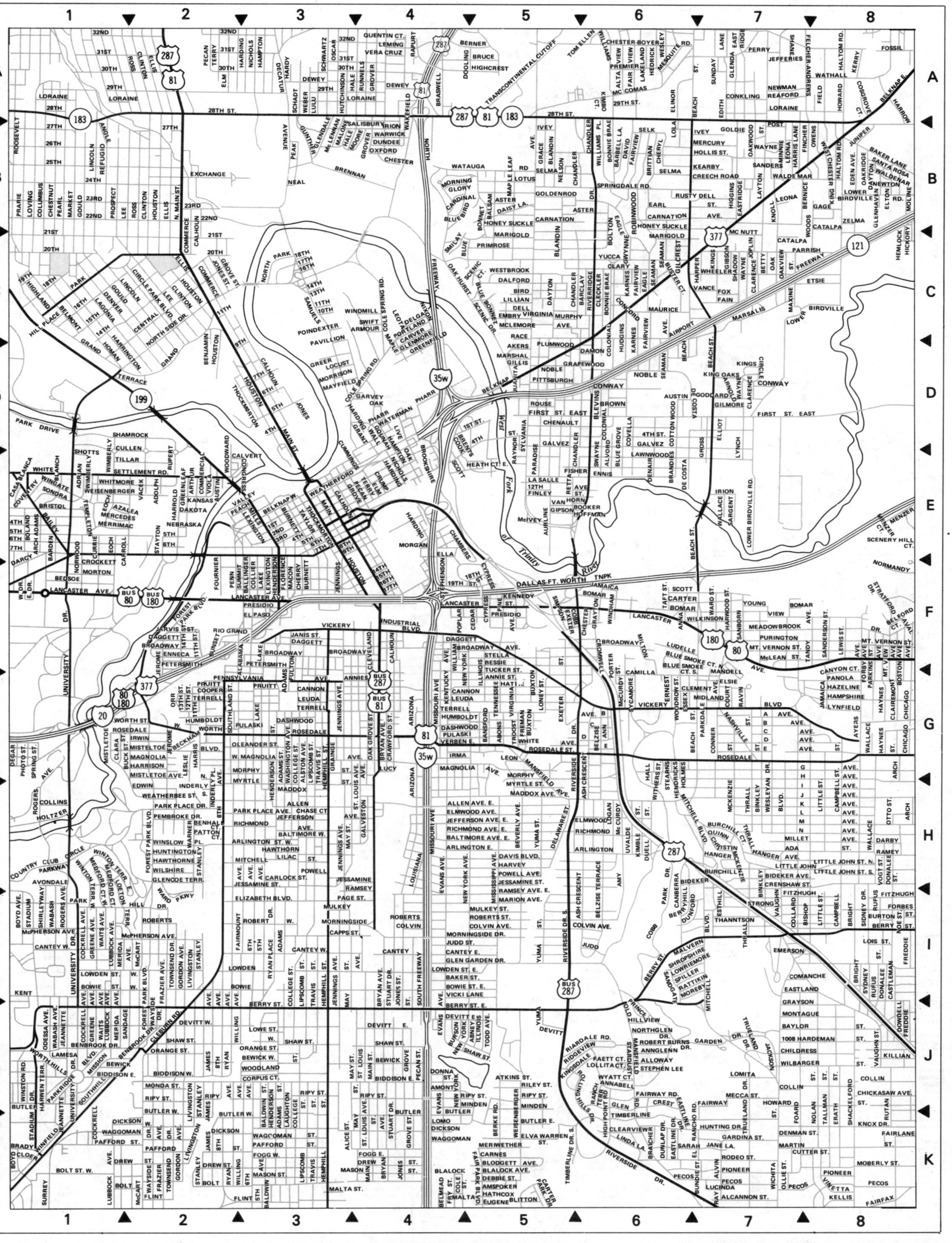

Fort Wayne, IN

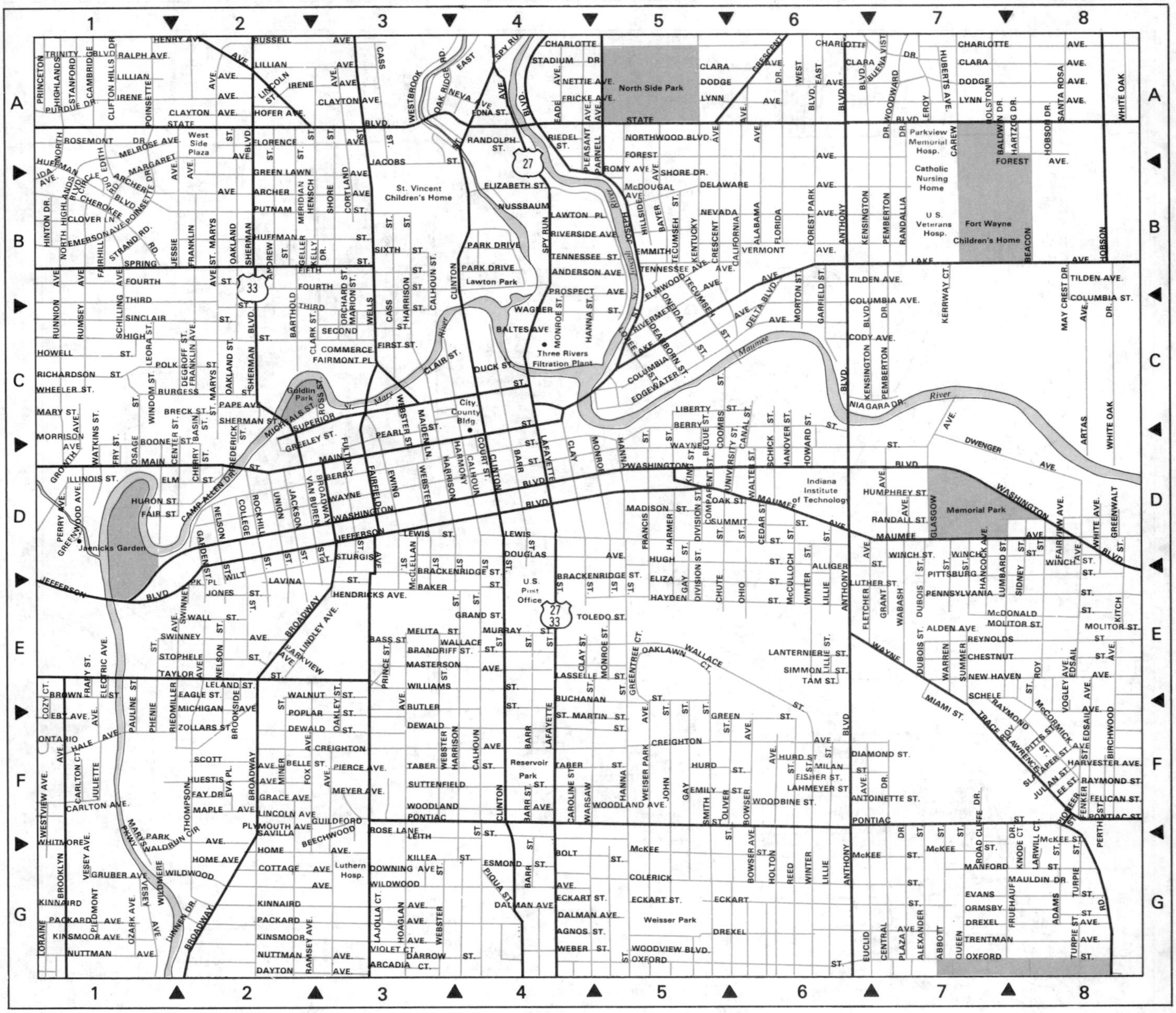

FORT WAYNE

POINTS OF INTEREST

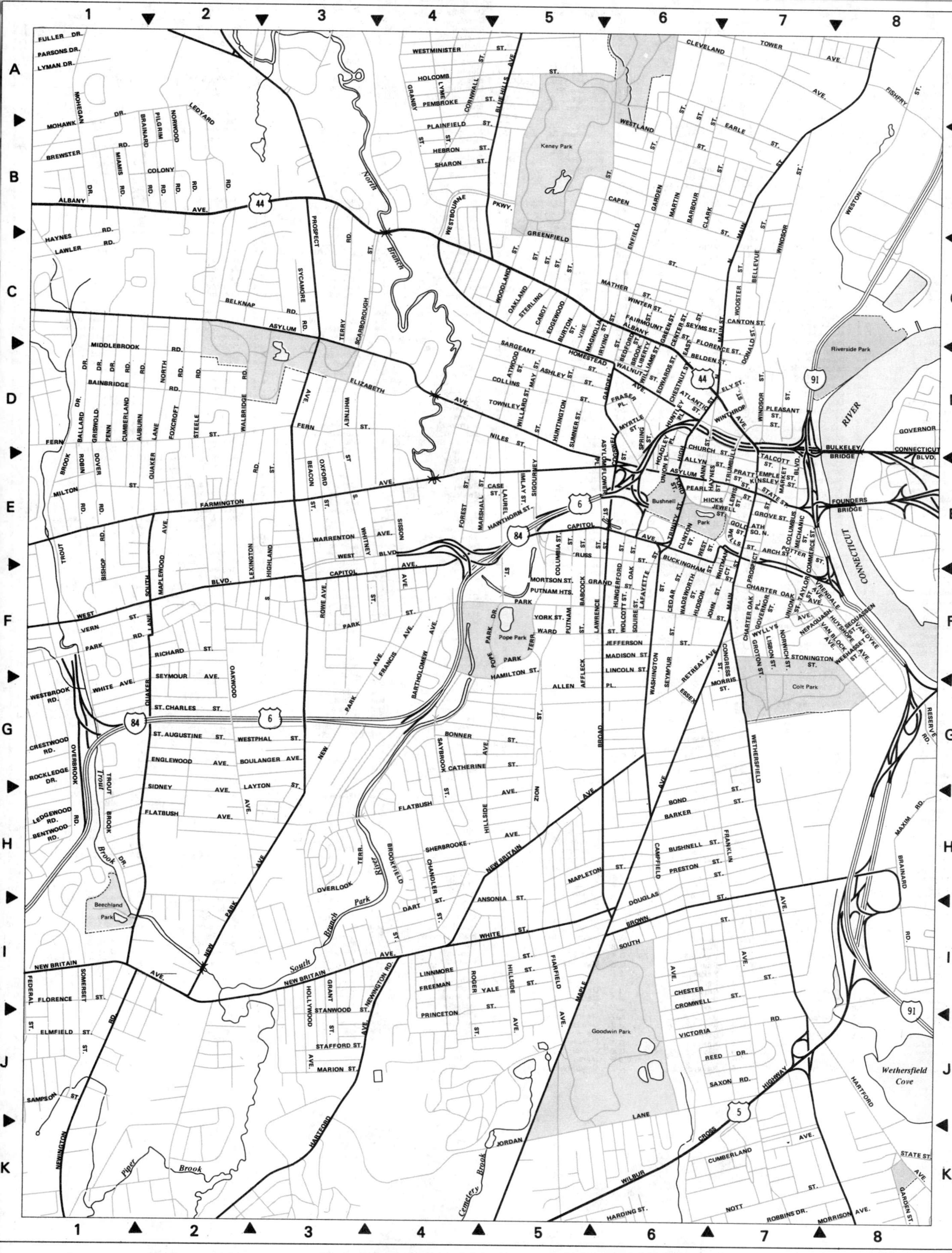

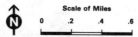

N
Scale of Miles
0 .2 .4 .6
1 2 3 4 5 6 7 8
A B C D E F G H I J K
FULLER DR.
PARSONS DR.
LYMAN DR.
MOHEGAN
MOHAWK DR.
BRAINARD
PILGRIM
NORWOOD
LEDYARD
BREWSTER RD.
MIAMIS RD.
COLONY
ALBANY AVE.
HAYNES RD.
LAWLER RD.
PROSPECT
SYCAMORE RD.
BELKNAP RD.
ASYLUM
MIDDLEBROOK RD.
BAINBRIDGE RD.
BALLARD DR.
GRISWOLD
PENN
CUMBERLAND
AUBURN
LANE
FOXCROFT
STEELE
WALBRIDGE RD.
NORTH
FERN
BROOK
ROBIN
DOVER
QUAKER
MILTON
FARMINGTON AVE.
TROUT
BISHOP RD.
SOUTH
MAPLEWOOD AVE.
LEXINGTON
HIGHLAND
WEST BLVD.
VERN
PARK
RICHARD ST.
SEYMOUR AVE.
OAKWOOD
WHITE AVE.
WESTBROOK RD.
ST. CHARLES ST.
ST. AUGUSTINE ST.
WESTPHAL ST.
ENGLEWOOD AVE.
BOULANGER AVE.
SIDNEY AVE.
LAYTON ST.
FLATBUSH AVE.
CRESTWOOD RD.
ROCKLEDGE DR.
OVERBROOK
LEDGEWOOD RD.
BENTWOOD RD.
Trout Brook
Beechland Park
NEW BRITAIN AVE.
FEDERAL
FLORENCE ST.
SOMERSET
ELMFIELD ST.
SAMPSON ST.
NEWINGTON
Piper Brook
WESTMINISTER ST.
HOLCOMB
LYME
GRANBY
PEMBROKE
CORNWALL
BLUE HILLS AVE.
PLAINFIELD ST.
HEBRON ST.
SHARON ST.
WESTBOURNE PKWY.
North Branch
TERRY
SCARBOROUGH
ELIZABETH
WHITNEY
BEACON
OXFORD
WARRENTON AVE.
SISSON
CAPITOL AVE.
ROWE AVE.
NEW PARK
FRANCIS AVE.
BARTHOLOMEW AVE.
Keney Park
GREENFIELD
WOODLAND
OAKLAND
STERLING
CABOT
EDGEWOOD
BURTON
VINE
MAGNOLIA
IRVING
SARGEANT
ATWOOD
COLLINS
ASHLEY
TOWNLEY
WILLARD ST.
NILES ST.
HUNTINGTON
SUMNER ST.
FOREST
MARSHALL
CASE
LAUREL
IMLAY ST.
SIGOURNEY
HAWTHORN ST.
COLUMBIA ST.
RUSS
MORTSON ST.
PUTNAM HTS.
Pope Park
YORK ST.
WARD
HAMILTON ST.
ALLEN
AFFLECK
BONNER ST.
SAYBROOK
CATHERINE
FLATBUSH
HILLSIDE AVE.
ZION
SHERBROOKE
CHANDLER
BROOKFIELD
OVERLOOK
DART
ANSONIA ST.
South Branch Park River
WHITE ST.
NEWINGTON RD.
HOLLYWOOD
GRANT
STANWOOD
STAFFORD ST.
MARION ST.
HARTFORD
LINNMORE
FREEMAN
ROGER
YALE
PRINCETON
FAIRFIELD AVE.
Cemetery Brook
JORDAN
CLEVELAND
TOWER AVE.
WESTLAND
EARLE
CAPEN
GARDEN
MARTIN
BARBOUR
CLARK
ENFIELD
MATHER ST.
WINTER ST.
FAIRMOUNT
ALBANY
HOMESTEAD
WALNUT
SEYMS ST.
FLORENCE ST.
BELDEN ST.
CANTON ST.
WOOSTER
BELLEVUE
WINDSOR
WESTON
FISHFRY ST.
MAIN
Riverside Park
ATLANTIC ST.
WINTHROP
ELY ST.
PLEASANT ST.
GOVERNOR
CONNECTICUT BLVD.
BULKELEY BRIDGE
CHURCH ST.
ALLYN
PRATT
TALCOTT
TEMPLE
KINSLEY
PEARL
HICKS
Bushnell Park
JEWELL
FOUNDERS BRIDGE
GROVE ST.
GOLD
CAPITOL
BUCKINGHAM ST.
ARCH ST.
CHARTER OAK
CONNECTICUT RIVER
HUNGERFORD
WOLCOTT
OAK
LAFAYETTE
BABCOCK
GRAND
LAWRENCE
SQUIRE ST.
JEFFERSON
MADISON ST.
LINCOLN ST.
WASHINGTON
SEYMOUR
CEDAR
WADSWORTH
HUDSON
RETREAT AVE.
CONGRESS
MORRIS
ESSEX
WYLLYS
GROTON ST.
LISBON
NORWICH ST.
STONINGTON ST.
Colt Park
VAN DYKE
RESERVE RD.
BROAD
BOND
BARKER
BUSHNELL
PRESTON
CAMPFIELD
FRANKLIN
WETHERSFIELD AVE.
MAPLETON
DOUGLAS
BROWN
SOUTH
MAPLE
Goodwin Park
CHESTER
CROMWELL
VICTORIA
REED DR.
SAXON RD.
LANE
WILBUR CROSS HIGHWAY
CUMBERLAND
HARDING ST.
NOTT
ROBBINS DR.
MORRISON AVE.
MAXIM RD.
BRAINARD RD.
Wethersfield Cove
HARTFORD
STATE ST.
GARDEN ST.
44
84
6
91
5

HARTFORD

Affleck St. F-5
Albany Ave. B-1,C-6
Allen Pl. G-5
Allyn St. E-6
Ann St. E-6
Arch St. E-7
Ashley St. D-5
Asylum Ave. C-3
Asylum Pl. D-6
Asylum St. E-6
Ath Sq. N. E-7
Atlantic St. D-6
Atwood St. D-5
Auburn Rd. D-1
Babock St. F-5
Bainbridge Rd. D-1
Ballard Dr. D-1
Barbour St. B-6
Barker St. H-6
Bartholomew Ave. F-5,G-4
Beacon St. E-3
Bedford St. C-6,D-6
Beldeno St. D-6
Belknap Rd. C-2
Bellevue St. C-7
Bishop Rd. F-1
Blue Hills Ave. A-5
Bond St. H-6
Bonner St. G-4
Boulanger Ave. G-2
Brainard Rd. A-1
Brainard Rd. ——— H-8
Brentwood Rd. H-1
Brewster Rd. B-1
Broad St. G-6
Brookfield St. H-4
Brook St. D-6
Brown St. I-6
Buckingham St. E-6
Burton St. C-5
Bushnell St. H-6
Cabot St. C-5
Campfield Ave. H-6
Canton St. C-7
Capen St. B-6
Capitol Ave. E-5,F-3
Case St. E-5
Catherine St. G-4
Cedar St. F-6
Center St. C-6
Chandler St. H-4
Charter Oak Ave. F-7
Charter Oak Pl. F-7
Chester St. I-6
Chestnut St. D-6
Church St. D-6
Clark St. B-6
Cleveland Ave. A-6
Clinton St. E-6
Cogswell St. D-6
Collins St. D-5
Colony Rd. B-2
Columbia St. E-5
Columbus Blvd. E-7
Commerce St. E-7
Congress St. F-7
Connecticut Blvd. D-8
Cornwall St. A-4
Crestwood Rd. G-1
Cromwell St. I-6
Cumberland Ave. K-7
Cumberland Rd. D-1
Dart St. I-4
Donald St. D-7
Douglas St. I-6
Dover Rd. E-1
Earle St. B-7
East St. C-6
Edgewood St. C-5
Edwards St. D-6
Elizabeth D-3
Elmfield St. J-1
Ely St. D-7
Enfield St. C-6
Englewood Ave. G-2
Essex G-6
Fairfield Ave. I-5
Fairmount St. C-6
Farmington Ave. E-2
Federal St. I-1
Fern St. D-1,D-3
Fishery A-8
Flatbush Ave. H-2,H-4
Florence St. C-6,I-1
Flower St. E-6
Ford St. E-6
Forest St. E-4
Foxcroft Rd. D-2
Francis Ave. F-4
Franklin Ave. H-7
Fraser Pl. D-6
Freeman St. I-4
Fuller Dr. A-1
Garden St. B-6,D-6,K-8
Gold St. E-7
Governor St. F-7
Granby St. A-4
Grand St. F-6
Grant St. I-3
Green St. C-6
Greenfield St. B-5
Griswold Dr. D-1
Groton St. F-7
Grove St. E-7
Hamilton St. F-5
Harding St. K-6
Hartford Ave. J-8,K-3
Hawthorn St. E-5
Haynes Rd. C-1
Haynes St. E-6
Hebron St. B-4
Hicks E-6
High St. D-6
Highland St., S. F-3
Hillside Ave. I-5
Hoadley Pl. D-6
Holcomb St. A-4
Hollywood Ave. I-3
Homestead Ave. D-5
Hudson St. F-6
Hungerford St. F-6
Huntington St. D-5
Huntley Pl. D-6
Huyshope Ave. F-8
Imlay St. E-5
Irving St. D-6
Jefferson St. F-6
Jewell St. E-7
John St. F-6
Jordan Ln. K-5
Keney Park B-5
Kinsley St. E-7
Lafayette St. F-6
Laurel St. E-5
Lawler Rd. C-1
Lawrence St. F-6
Laxton St. G-2
Ledgewood Rd. H-1
Ledyard Rd. A-2
Lewis St. E-7
Lexington Rd. F-2
Liberty D-6
Lincoln St. F-6
Linnmore St. I-4
Lisbon St. F-7
Lyman Dr. A-1
Lyme St. A-4
Madison St. F-6
Magnolia St. C-5
Main St., N. B-7,D-7
Maple Ave. I-5
Mapleton St. H-5
Maplewood Ave. F-2
Marion St. J-3
Market St. E-7
Martin St. B-6
Marshall St. E-4
Mather St. C-6
Maxim Rd. H-8
May St. D-5
Mechanic St. E-7
Miamis Rd. B-1
Middlebrook Rd. D-1
Milton St. E-1
Mohawk Dr. B-1
Mohegan Dr. A-1
Morrison Ave. K-8
Morris St. G-7
Mortson St. F-5
Myrtle St. D-6
Nepaquash F-7
New Britain Ave. H-5,I-1,I-3
Newington Rd. K-1
New Park Ave. G-3,I-2
Niles St. D-5
Norwich St. F-7
Norwood Rd. B-2
Nott St. K-7
Oak St. F-6
Oakland St. C-5
Oakwood Ave. G-2
Overbrook Rd. G-1
Overlook Terr. H-3
Oxford St. E-3
Park Rd. F-1
Park St. F-3,F-5
Park Terr. F-5
Parsons Dr. A-1
Pearl St. E-6,E-7
Pembroke St. A-4
Penn Dr. D-1
Pilgrim Rd. B-2
Plainfield St. A-4
Pleasant St. D-7
Pope Park Dr. F-5
Potter St. E-7
Pratt St. E-7
Preston St. H-6
Princeton St. J-4
Prospect Ave. B-3
Prospect St. E-7,F-7
Putnam Hts. F-5
Putnam St. F-5
Quaker Lane, N. D-2,E-2
Quaker Lane, S. F-2,G-2
Reed Dr. J-7
Reserve Rd. G-8
Retreat Ave. F-6
Richard St. F-2
Robbins Dr. K-7
Robin Rd. E-1
Rockledge Dr. G-1
Roger St. I-4
Rowe Ave. F-3
Russ St. E-5
St. Augustine St. G-2
St. Charles St. G-2
Sampson St. J-1
Sargeant St. D-5
Saxon Rd. J-7
Saybrook St. G-4
Scarborough St. C-3
Sequassen St. F-8
Seymour St. F-6,G-6
Seyms St. C-6
Sharon St. B-4
Sherbrook Ave. H-4
Sidney Ave. G-2
Sigourney St. E-5
Sisson Ave. E-4
Somerset St. I-1
South St. I-6
Spring St. D-6
Squire St. F-6
Stafford St. J-3
State St. E-7,K-8
Steele Rd. F-2
Sterling St. C-5
Stonnington St. F-7
Sumner St. D-5
Sycamore Rd. C-3
Talcott St. E-7
Taylor St. F-6
Temple St. E-7
Terry Rd. C-3
Tower Ave. A-7
Townley D-5
Trinity St. E-6
Trout Brook Dr. E-1,H-1
Trumbull St. E-7
Union Pl. E-6
Union St. F-7
Van Block Ave. F-8
Van Dyke F-8
Vern St. F-1
Victoria Rd. J-6
Vine C-5
Vrendale Ave. F-7
Wadsworth St. F-6
Walbridge Rd. D-2
Walnut St. D-6
Ward St. F-5
Warrenton Ave. E-3
Washington St. F-6,G-6
Weehasset St. F-8
Wells St. E-7
West Blvd. E-3,F-1
West St. E-6
Westbourne Pkwy. B-4
Westbrook Rd. G-1
Westland St. A-6
Westminster St. A-4
Weston St. B-8
Westphal St. G-2
Wethersfield Ave. G-7
White Ave. G-1
White St. I-5
Whitney St. D-3
Whitney St., S. E-3
Wilbur Cross Hwy. K-6
Willard St. D-5
Williams St. D-6
Windsor St. C-7,D-7
Winter St. C-6
Winthrop St. D-7
Wolcott St. F-6
Woodland St. C-5
Wooster St. C-7
Wyllys Ave. F-7
Yale St. I-5
York St. F-5
Zion St. H-5

POINTS OF INTEREST

Beechland Park I-1
Bulkeley Bridge D-8
Bushnell Park E-6
Coh Park G-7
Founders Bridge E-8
Goodwin Park J-6
Pope Park F-5
Riverside Park C-8

HOUSTON

Alabama St. J-5,J-7
Alabama St. W. H-1
Alamo C-4
Albany G-3
Alber St. A-7
Allen D-1
Allen Parkway E-2
Allston St. B-1
Alpha St. F-1
Andrews St. F-3
Angelia F-1
Anita St. H-4,I-7
Ann St. F-8
Arbor St. J-4,K-6
Arch E-7
Archer A-4
Arlington St. B-2
Arthur St. F-4
Ashby J-1
Attucks J-7
Audobon H-3
Austin J-3
Austin St. G-5,J-3
Autrey I-2
Averill A-6
Avondale St. G-3
Baer D-8
Bagby St. F-5,G-4
Bailey G-3
Baker E-6
Baldwin F-4
Banks I-2
Banks St. J-1
Barbee St. J-5
Bardwell A-7
Barkdull J-2
Barnes D-1
Bass St. D-1
Bastrop St. G-6, H-6,J-5
Bayard J-2
Bayland St. B-3
Beach D-5
Bell H-8
Bell, W. F-3
Bell Ave. G-6
Bering F-8
Berry I-5
Berthea J-2
Beverly St. B-2
Bigelow St. A-7
Billingsley St. A-6
Bingham St. D-4
Binz St. J-3,K-4
Bishop C-5
Bissonnet St. J-1
Blair St. A-1
Blodgett St. J-5,K-6
Bolsover K-1
Bomar G-2
Bonnie Brae I-1
Boone B-8
Booth St. B-6
Boswell St. A-7
Boundary B-6
Bradley B-4
Brailsfort St. I-6
Branard St. I-1
Brandt I-3
Brazos St. F-5
Bremond G-4
Bremond St. I-7
Briley St. I-6
Brooks Pl. C-8
Brooks St. D-6
Bruce A-4
Buckner St. F-4
Buel G-3
Buffalo Terrace E-3
Bunton St. A-7
Burkett J-6
Burkett St. K-6
Burnett St. D-6
Bute St. I-3
Butler St. E-2
Calendar A-5
Calhoun Ave. G-5
California H-2
Calle J-8
Calumet St. J-3
Campbell St. C-7
Canal F-8
Canfield St. I-7
Capitol E-4
Capitol Ave. F-5
Carl C-5
Caroline St. G-5,J-3
Carr A-8
Castle Ct. I-2
Catherine A-5
Cetti B-6
Chapman C-7
Chartres K-3
Chase St. C-7
Chelsea I-3
Chenevert St. G-6,J-4
Cherokee J-1
Cherry A-8
Churchill B-5
Clay, W. F-3
Clay Ave. G-6
Clay St. H-7
Cleburne St. J-5
Cleveland F-3
Cline St. E-8
Clinton Dr. E-7
Cobb St. K-6
Cochran St. B-6
Collingsworth St. A-7
Collins D-6
Colorado St. D-4
Colquitt I-1
Columbia St. B-2
Columbus F-2
Commerce St. E-6
Common B-6
Common St. C-6
Congress Ave. E-6
Conti D-8
Cook G-4
Cordell A-4
Cordier F-7
Cortland St. B-2
Cottage A-3
Court St. D-2
Courtland Pl. H-3
Coyle St. H-7
Cranberry C-2
Crawford J-4
Crawford St. F-6
Crocker St. F-3
Crockett D-4
Crosby St. F-4
Cullen St. K-7
Cushing St. F-4
Dallas, W. F-2
Dallas Ave. F-5
Daly D-6
D'Amico St. F-1
Damon G-2
Dart St. D-4
Davis St. C-8
Day I-3
Decatur E-4
De George A-4
DeLano St. H-7,I-6
Dell A-4
Dennis Ave. H-5
Denver H-8
De Pel C-4
Dewey D-4
Diesel D-3
Dora J-2
Douglas St. I-7
Dowling St. G-7,J-4
Drew G-4,H-5
Drew St. G-4
Driscoll St. G-1,I-1
Dunlavy St. H-1
Dunstan K-1
Eagle St. J-5
Eberhard F-2
Edison St. A-6
Edmundson St. I-8
Edwards St. D-4
Elder D-4,D-5,E-5
Elgin H-4
Eli St. D-1
Elmen St. G-1
Elser B-6
Elysian C-7,E-7
Embry B-6
Emerson H-3
Engeike St. F-8
Enid A-4
Ennis, N. F-8
Ennis St. H-7,J-6
Erin St. A-7
Euclid St. B-3
Eunice B-5
Evella A-8
Ewing St. J-3
Fairview St. G-1
Fannin St. G-5,I-3
Fargo St. G-3
Fletcher St. C-6
Flora H-3
Florence St. B-4
Flynn F-8
Foote E-8
Fowler E-1
Fox F-8
Francis H-4,J-7
Franklin Ave. E-6
Frasier C-2
Freund E-8
Fugate St. A-3
Fulton St. A-5,B-6
Gano C-7
Gardner, W. A-3
Gargan C-5
Garrott I-3
Garrow St. G-8
Garvin Ct. D-4
Genese St. G-3
Gilette G-3
Gillespie E-8
Givens D-2
Gladys C-4
Glaser D-6
Goldenrod B-5
Golf Links F-3
Goliad St. D-5
Grant G-2
Gravstark J-2
Gray Ave. W. F-3
Gray St. G-4,G-5
Grayson E-8
Greeley St. I-3
Greenle C-4
Grigsby B-8
Gross F-1
Gulf Freeway I-8
Haddon Ave. G-1
Hadley Ave. G-4
Hain A-5
Hamilton St. G-6,H-5
Hammock B-6
Hardy C-7
Harold St. H-1
Harrington St. D-6
Harrisburg G-8
Harvard St. B-2,D-2
Hathaway St. H-3
Hawkins G-8
Hawthorne St. H-2
Hays St. B-6
Hazard St. H-1
Hazel F-2
Heights Blvd. B-2,D-2
Helen St. B-4
Helena G-3
Hemphill St. E-4
Henderson St. E-4
Herkimer St. B-1
Hermann St. K-3
Hickory D-5
Hiensley D-5
Highland St. B-3
Hill St. E-1
Hogan St. C-6
Hogg C-8
Holman Ave. H-4,J-7
Holy D-5
Home D-2
Honsin D-2
Hopkins St. G-3
Hopson F-3
Houston St. D-5
Howe F-4
Hussion St. I-8
Hutcheson St. H-8
Hutchins St. G-6,J-4
Hyacinth B-5
Hyde St. G-3
Ideal B-5
Indiana Ave. G-1
Ingborg I-8
Institute J-2
Isabella St. J-5
Jack St. I-3
Jackson J-4
Jackson St. F-6
James St. C-6
Jasmine F-1
Jefferson Ave. G-5
Jensen E-8
Jensen St. C-8
Jessamine A-5
Joe Anne St. F-2
Johnson St. D-4
Jones B-8
Joseph St. H-8
Julian C-3
Kane E-4
Karnes A-5
Keating St. H-8
Keene C-6
Kennedy F-8
Kent J-1
Key St. A-3
Kipling St. H-1
Koehler St. D-1
Kolb St. C-1
Kuester H-1
Kyle I-2
La Branch J-4
La Branch St. F-6
Lamar F-2
Lamar, W. F-3
Lamar Ave. F-5
Larkin D-2,E-2
La Rue F-2
Lee St. C-7
Leek St. J-8
Leeland Ave. G-6, H-8,I-8
Leona D-8
Leonidas St. F-1
Leverkuhn E-4
Lewis St. D-6
Lexington I-1
Lincoln F-2
Live Oak, N. F-8
Live Oak St. G-7,K-4
Loretto St. I-2
Lorraine St. C-7
Lottmann St. E-8
Louisiana St. F-5,H-4
Lovett St. H-2
Lubbock E-4
Lucinda St. J-7
Luzon St. B-7
Lyle E-7
Lyons Ave. D-7,D-8
MacGregor K-4
Maggie B-6
Main, N. A-4
Main St. G-5,I-3
Main St. W. I-1
Mandell H-1,J-1
Marconi St. F-2
Marie St. C-5
Marigold B-5
Marina C-1
Marshall St. H-1
Marstow F-1
Mary St. C-8
Maryland Ave. G-1
Mason St. G-3
Matthews F-4
Maury St. C-7
Maverick A-5
Maylor D-6
McGowen G-4
McGrower St. I-7
McKee C-7
McKenney, W. F-3
McKinney Ave. F-5
McLIhenney G-4
McLIhenney Ave. I-7
McMillan St. E-2
McNeil St. B-7
Melwood St. A-3
Menefee C-1
Merrill St. B-3
Michaux B-3
Michigan Ave. G-1
Milam St. F-5
Milby St. I-8
Milford St. J-1
Miller St. I-8
Mills C-8
Mills St. C-7
Mirimar I-2
Missouri G-2
Montana St. D-1
Montrose I-2
Moore B-6
Mop C-7
Morgan G-3
Morris B-6,B-8
Morrison St. B-4
Morse St. G-1
Moss St. A-4
Mt. Vernon St. I-2
Mulberry St. H-2
Nagle Alley F-8
Nagle St. G-7,I-6
Nagle St. N. F-8
Nance St. D-7
Napoleon St. J-7
Nettletor J-6
Nevada G-1
Newhoff B-8
Newhouse F-1
Nicholson B-1
Noble St. C-7
Norfolk I-1
Norhill A-3
North B-3
North Blvd. J-1
Northwood B-4
Oak St. G-4
Oak Dr. C-4
Oakdale J-3
Oakley I-3
Oak Ridge St. B-3
Odin D-8
Olive St. D-1
Omar St. B-3
O'Neil St. F-4
Opelousas St. D-7
Orr St. B-7
Oxford B-2
Ovid C-4
Pacific G-3
Paige F-8
Paige St. H-7,I-6
Palm J-3
Palmer H-7,K-5
Palmer, N. F-8
Panama St. B-6
Park B-6,G-1
Parkview B-5
Paschall C-6
Patterson E-1
Payne B-5
Pease H-7
Pease Ave. G-5
Peden Ave. F-2
Peveto F-2
Pierce, W. F-3
Pierre Ave. G-5
Pinckney St. C-6
Pinedale J-3
Pineridge B-3
Polk F-5
Polk, W. F-3
Polk Ave. G-6
Portland J-3
Portsmouth I-1
Prairie Ave. E-6
Preston Ave. E-6,G-8
Prospect St. J-3
Providence D-7
Quinn A-4
Quitman C-6
Race E-7
Railey A-4
Rains E-7
Ralph H-1
Raymond D-2
Reagan B-4
Redan B-4
Reeves J-7
Rein B-6
Relsner E-5
Renfro F-1
Renner Ct. E-4
Reynolds B-6
Rice Blvd. K-1
Richmond Ave. I-1
Ridge St. B-4
Ridgewood G-1
Riverside Dr. K-4
Roanoke E-7
Roberts H-8
Robertson B-6
Robila St. F-3
Robin St. F-3
Rochow F-1
Rockwood St. K-8
Rosalie St. H-4,I-7
Rose D-1
Rosedale J-3,K-5
Roseland I-3
Rosewood J-5
Rosine F-2
Rossmoyne St. I-2
Ruiz St. E-7
Rusk Ave. F-5
Ruth St. J-5,K-7
Ruthven F-3
Rutland Pl. C-1
Rylis F-2
Ryon St. B-7
Sabine St. C-4,E-4
Sachs St. E-2
St. Charles St. G-7,I-6
St. Charles St. N. F-8
St. Emmanuel St. G-6,J-4
Saltus F-8
Sampson H-8,K-5
Sampson St. K-6
Sanders J-7
San Jacinto St. G-5,I-3
Sauer St. I-5,K-5
Saulnier, W. F-3
Sawyer St. D-3
Scott K-7
Scott St. J-7
Schulan St. D-1
Schwartz D-8,E-8
Searle A-5
Sellers D-2
Semmes St. C-7
Shaw F-5
Shearn St. D-4
Shelby St. A-6
Shelley A-4
Sherman St. F-8
Shiloh E-8
Silver St. E-4
Simmons J-7
Sledge C-3
Smith St. F-5
Snover E-1
South Blvd. J-1
Southmore St. J-3
Southwest Freeway I-1
Spencer C-1
Spring C-4
Spruce St. E-7
Stalker D-2
Stanford St. I-3
State St. E-4
Stevens St. C-8
Stout B-7
Stuart H-4,J-7
Stude C-3
Studenmont D-3
Studewewood B-3
Sul Ross St. H-1
Summer D-4
Sumpter St. C-7
Sun Ct. F-7
Sunset Blvd. K-2
Sutton St. G-3
Sweetwood F-1
Sydnor D-8
Tabor A-4
Tackaberry B-6
Taft St. G-3
Taylor St. E-3
Temple A-4
Temple St. W. A-3
Terrell F-1
Terry C-7
Texas Ave. E-6,G-8
Thelma C-4
Thomas C-5
Thompson D-1
Threlkeld C-3
Tierwester St. K-6
Top E-7
Travis I-3
Travis St. G-5,I-3
Tretham D-6
Trimble A-5
Trinity E-4
Trulley H-6
Truxillo J-5
Tuam St. H-4,I-5
Tulane St. B-1
Union St. D-3
Usener Blvd. C-3
Valentine St. F-4
Van Buren F-2
Varsity K-8
Vassai I-2
Velasco G-8,K-5
Vermont Ave. G-1
Vick E-1
Victor F-3
Vincent A-4
Violet F-1
Voight C-3
Wagner St. D-2,E-2
Walker Ave. F-5
Walker, W. F-3
Walton A-4
Watson A-3
Waugh Dr. F-2
Waverly Ct. J-2
Waverly St. B-1
Weber C-4
Weber Ave. G-4
Webster G-4,H-6
Welch Ave. G-1
Wendel C-3
Wentworth St. J-4,K-6
West Blvd. J-2
West St. C-8
Westmoreland H-3
Wheeler Ave. J-5,K-7
White St. E-4
White Oak Dr. C-2
Whitney H-3
Wichita St. J-3
Wilkenson St. F-2
Wilkes B-6
Willard Ave. G-2
Wilson G-4
Winbern J-5
Winnie C-5
Woodhead St. H-1
Woodland St. B-3
Wood Leigh H-8
Wood Row I-3
Wrightwood A-5
Yale St. B-1,D-1
Yoakum G-2,J-2
York H-8
Yupon St. G-2,H-2
2nd D-2
4th W. C-2
4th St., E. C-2
4½ E. C-2
5th, E. C-2
5th, W. C-2
6th St., W. C-2
6½ St., E. B-2
7th St., E. B-2
7½ St., E. B-2
8th St., E. B-2
8th St., W. B-2
8½ St. E. B-2
9th St. E. B-2
9th St. W. B-2
9½ E. B-2
10th, E. B-2
10th St., W. B-2
10½ St., E. A-2
10½ St., W. A-1
11th St., E. A-2
11th St., W. A-2
11½ St., E. A-2
12th St., E. A-2
12th St., W. A-1
13th St., E. A-2
13th St., W. A-1
13½ St., E. A-2
14th St., E. A-2
14th St., W. A-1

POINTS OF INTEREST

Hermann Park K-2,K-3
Moody Park A-6
Stude Park C-3
Woodlawn Park C-5

Scale of Miles
0 .2 .4 .6

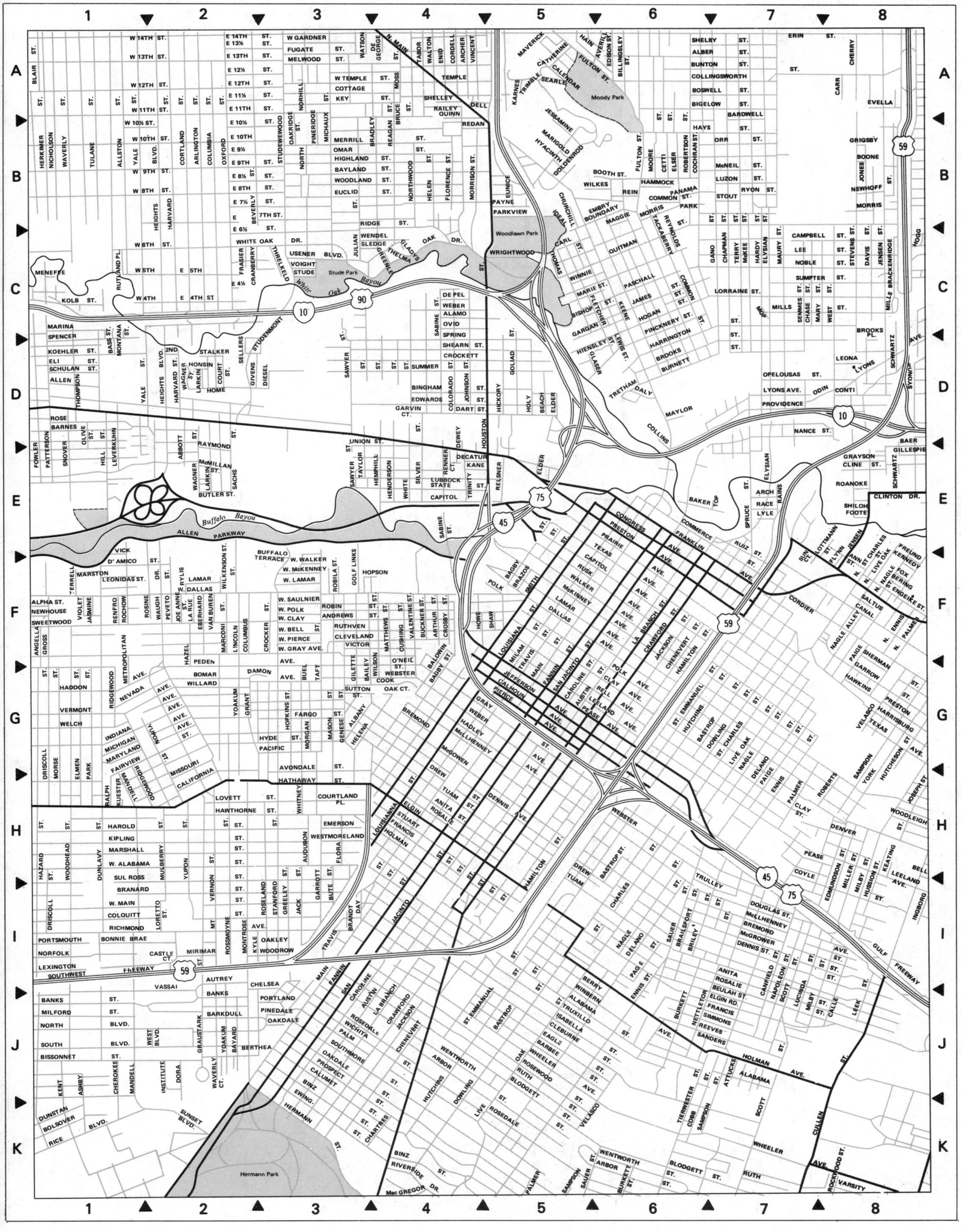

Scale of Miles

0 .1 .2 .3

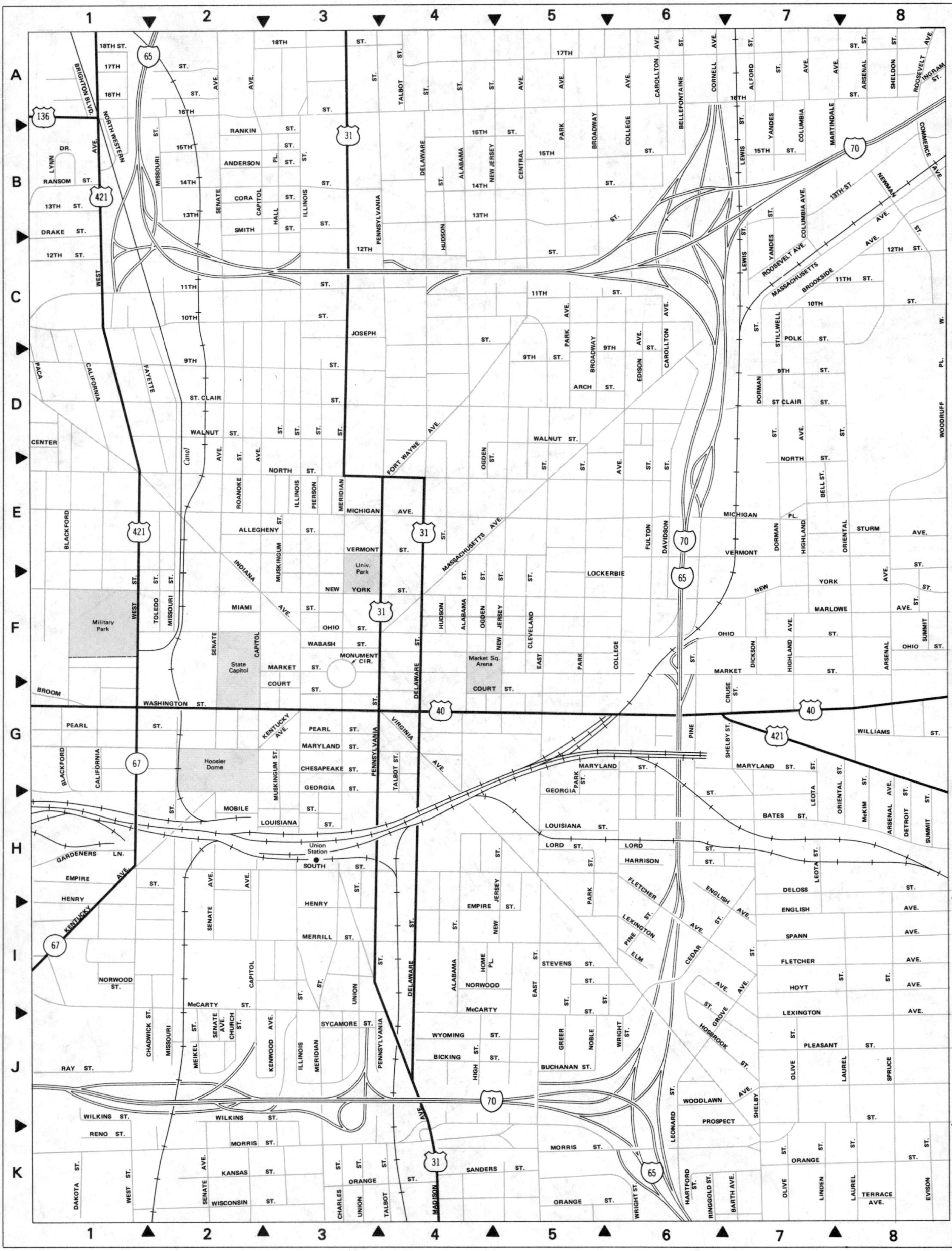

INDIANAPOLIS

Alabama St. ... B-4,F-4,I-4
Allegheny St. ... E-2
Alford St. ... A-7
Anderson St. ... B-2
Arch St. ... D-5
Arsenal St. ... A-8,F-8,H-8
Barth Ave. ... K-7
Bates St. ... H-7
Bell St. ... E-7
Bellefontaine St. ... A-6
Bicking St. ... J-4
Blackford ... E-1,G-1
Brighton Blvd. ... A-1
Broadway ... B-5,D-5
Brookside Ave. ... C-7
Broom ... G-1
Buchanar St. ... J-5
California ... D-1,G-1
Capitol Ave. ... B-2,F-2,I-2
Carollton Ave. ... A-6,D-6
Cedar St. ... I-6
Center ... D-1
Central Ave. ... B-5
Chadwick St. ... J-1
Charles St. ... K-3
Chesapeake St. ... G-3
Church St. ... J-2
Cleveland St. ... F-5
College Ave. ... B-6,F-6
Columbia Ave. ... B-7,C-7
Commerce Ave. ... B-8
Cora St. ... B-2
Cornell Ave. ... A-6
Court St. ... G-4
Cruse St. ... G-7
Dakota St. ... K-1
Davidson St. ... E-6
Delaware St. ... B-4,G-4,I-4
DeLoss St. ... H-7
Detroit St. ... H-8
Dickson ... F-7
Dorman St. ... D-7,E-7
Drake St. ... B-1
East St. ... F-5,I-5
Edison Ave. ... D-6
Elm St. ... I-6
Empire St. ... H-1,I-4
English Ave. ... H-6,I-7
Evison St. ... K-8
Fayette ... D-2
Fletcher Ave. ... H-6,I-7
Fort Wayne Ave. ... E-4
Fulton St. ... E-6
Gardeners Ln. ... H-1
Georgia St. ... G-3,H-5
Greer St. ... J-5
Grove Ave. ... J-6
Hall Pl. ... B-3
Harrison St. ... H-6
Hartford St. ... K-6
Henry ... H-1,I-3
Highland Ave. ... E-7,F-7
High St. ... J-4
Home Pl. ... I-4
Hosbrook St. ... J-6
Hoyt Ave. ... I-7
Hudson St. ... C-4,F-4
Illinois St. ... B-3,E-3,J-3
Indiana Ave. ... E-2
Ingram St. ... A-8
Joseph St. ... C-3
Kansas St. ... K-2
Kentucky Ave. ... G-3,I-1
Kenwood Ave. ... J-3
Laurel St. ... J-8,K-8
Leonard St. ... K-6
Leota St. ... H-7
Lexington Ave. ... I-6,J-7
Lewis St. ... B-7,C-7
Linden St. ... K-7
Lockerbie St. ... F-5
Lord St. ... H-5,H-6
Louisiana St. ... H-3,H-5
Lynn Dr. ... B-1
McCarty St. ... I-2,I-4
McKim St. ... H-8
Madison St. ... K-4
Market St. ... F-3,F-7
Marlowe Ave. ... F-7
Martindale Ave. ... B-7
Maryland St. G-3,G-5,G-7
Massachusetts Ave. ... C-7,E-4
Meikel St. ... J-2
Meridian St. ... E-3,J-3
Merrill St. ... I-3
Miami St. ... F-2
Michigan Ave. ... E-3
Michigan Pl. ... E-7
Missouri St. ... B-2,F-2,J-2
Mobile St. ... H-2
Monument Cir. ... F-3
Morris St. ... K-2,K-5
Muskigum St. ... E-3,G-3
New Jersey St. ... B-5,F-5,I-5
Newman St. ... B-8
New York St. ... F-3,F-7
Nobel St. ... J-5
North St. ... Ep3,E-7
Northwestern ... A-1
Norwood St. ... I-1,I-4
Ogden St. ... E-4,F-4
Ohio St. ... F-3,F-7
Olive St. ... J-7,K-7
Orange St. ... K-2,K-5,K-7
Oriental St. ... E-8,H-8
Paca ... D-1
Park Ave. ... B-5,C-5 ... F-5,G-5,I-5
Pearl St. ... G-1,G-3
Pennsylvania St. ... B-4,G-3,J-4
Pierson St. ... E-3
Pine St. ... G-6,I-6
Pleasant St. ... J-7
Polk St. ... C-7
Prospect St. ... J-6
Rankin St. ... B-2
Ransom St. ... B-1
Ray St. ... J-1
Reno St. ... K-1
Ringgold St. ... K-6
Roanoke St. ... E-2
Roosevelt ... A-8,B-7
St. Clair St. ... D-2,D-7
Sanders St. ... K-4
Senate Ave. ... B-2,F-2 ... I-2,K-2
Shelby St. ... G-7,J-7
Sheldon St. ... A-8
Smith St. ... B-2
South St. ... H-3
Spann Ave. ... I-7
Spruce St. ... J-8
Stevens St. ... I-5
Stillwell ... C-7
Sturm Ave. ... E-8
Summit St. ... F-8,H-8
Sycamore St. ... J-3
Talbot St. ... A-4,G-4,K-4
Terrace Ave. ... K-8
Toledo St. ... F-2
Union St. ... I-3,K-3
Vermont St. ... E-3,E-7
Virginia Ave. ... G-4
Wabash St. ... F-3
Walnut St. ... D-2,D-5
Washington St. ... G-2
West Ave. ... C-1
West St. ... F-1,K-1
Wilkins St. ... J-1,J-2
Williams St. ... G-8
Wisconsin St. ... K-2
Woodlawn Ave. ... J-6
Woodruff Pl. ... D-8
Wright St. ... J-6,K-6
Wyoming St. ... J-4
Yandes St. ... B-7,C-7
9th St. ... D-2,D-5,D-7
10th St. ... C-2,C-7
11th St. ... C-2,C-5,C-8
12th St. ... C-1,C-3,C-8
13th St. ... B-1.B-2,B-4
14th St. ... B-2,B-4
15th St. ... B-2,B-4,B-5,B-7
16th St. ... A-1,A-2,A-7
17th St. ... A-1,A-5
18th St. ... A-1,A-3

POINTS OF INTEREST

Military Park ... F-1
Univ. Park ... E-3

JACKSONVILLE

Acosta Bridge ... H-3
Adams St. ... F-1,F-3,G-5
Alvarez St. ... J-5
Arch St. ... A-3
Ashley St. ... E-4,F-6,G-8
Bay St. ... F-1,G-3,G-6
Beaver St. ... D-1,E-4,F-6
Blanche St. ... D-1
Broad St. ... B-4,D-4,F-4
Bugbee St. ... J-6
Catherine St. ... H-7
Cemetery St. ... F-8
Chelsea St. ... H-1
Church St. ... E-2,F-5,G-8
Clay St. ... B-5,F-4
Cleveland St. ... D-2,F-1
Crothe St. ... B-1
Dante Pl. ... K-4
Davis St. ... C-3,F-3
Dewdrop North ... E-4
Dewitt St. ... E-1
Dora St. ... H-1
Duval St. ... F-2,F-5,G-8
Eaverson St. ... B-1,D-1
Edison Ave. ... I-1
Elm St. ... G-1
Flagler St. ... J-5,K-5
Forest St. ... H-1
Forsyth St. ... F-1,G-4,G-6
Francis St. ... C-2
Fuller Warren Bridge ... J-2
Gary St. ... K-4
Gilmore St. ... J-1
Gulf Life Dr. ... I-5
Hart St. ... C-1
Hendricks Ave. ... K-6
Hogan St. ... E-5,G-4
Home St. ... J-6
Illinois ... B-4
Ionia St. ... B-8,D-8
Jackson St. ... H-1
Jefferson St. ... D-4,F-3
Jessie St. ... E-8
Johnson St. ... C-2,F-2
Julia St. ... E-5,G-4
Kings Ave. ... K-6
Kings Rd. ... D-2
Kipp St. ... J-6
Laura St. ... B-6,F-5
Lee St. ... C-2,F-2
Leila St. ... H-2
Liberty St. ... B-7,G-7
Lisbon St. ... K-5
Louisa St. ... K-6
Louisiana ... B-3
Madison St. ... F-3
Magnolia St. ... H-1
Main St. ... B-6,F-5
Main St. Bridge ... I-5
Market St. ... B-7,E-7,G-6
Mars ... A-3
Mary St. ... J-5
May St. ... H-1
McConihe St. ... A-1
McCoy St. ... H-3
Minnie St. ... D-1
Monroe St. ... F-3,G-6
Mt. Herman St. ... C-2
Myrtle Ave. ... B-1,E-1
Nadia ... B-3
Newman St. ... G-6
Nira St. ... K-4
Oak St. ... H-1
Ocean St. ... H-5,F-6
Odessa St. ... E-8
Orange St. ... E-5
Palm St. ... K-4
Park St. ... H-1
Pearl St. ... B-5,E-4,G-4
Phelps St. ... E-6,E-8
Pippin St. ... F-8
Price St. ... H-1
Prudential Dr. ... J-4
Reiman ... A-2
Riverside Ave. ... H-2,J-1
Roselle St. ... I-1
San Marco Blvd. ... J-5
Schofield St. ... E-7
Spruce St. ... H-1
State St. ... E-4,E-6
Steele St. ... B-1
Stonewall St. ... H-2
Stuart St. ... F-2
Union St. ... D-1,E-4,F-6,F-8
Venus ... A-3
Walnut St. ... B-8,E-7
Washington St. ... G-7
Water St. ... G-3
Wilcox St. ... B-1,D-1
1st St. ... D-5,D-7
2nd St. ... D-5,D-7
3rd St. ... C-1,C-5,D-7
4th St. ... C-1,C-5,C-7
5th St. ... B-1,C-5,C-7
6th St. ... B-1,B-5,B-7
7th St. ... B-1,B-3,B-5,B-7
8th St. ... A-1,A-5,B-7
9th St. ... A-1,A-5,A-7
10th St. ... A-1,A-5,A-7

POINTS OF INTEREST

Baptist Hospital ... J-4
Cemetery ... E-7
St. Lukes Hospital ... A-4
Springfield Park ... C-4

Scale of Miles
0 .1 .2 .3
N

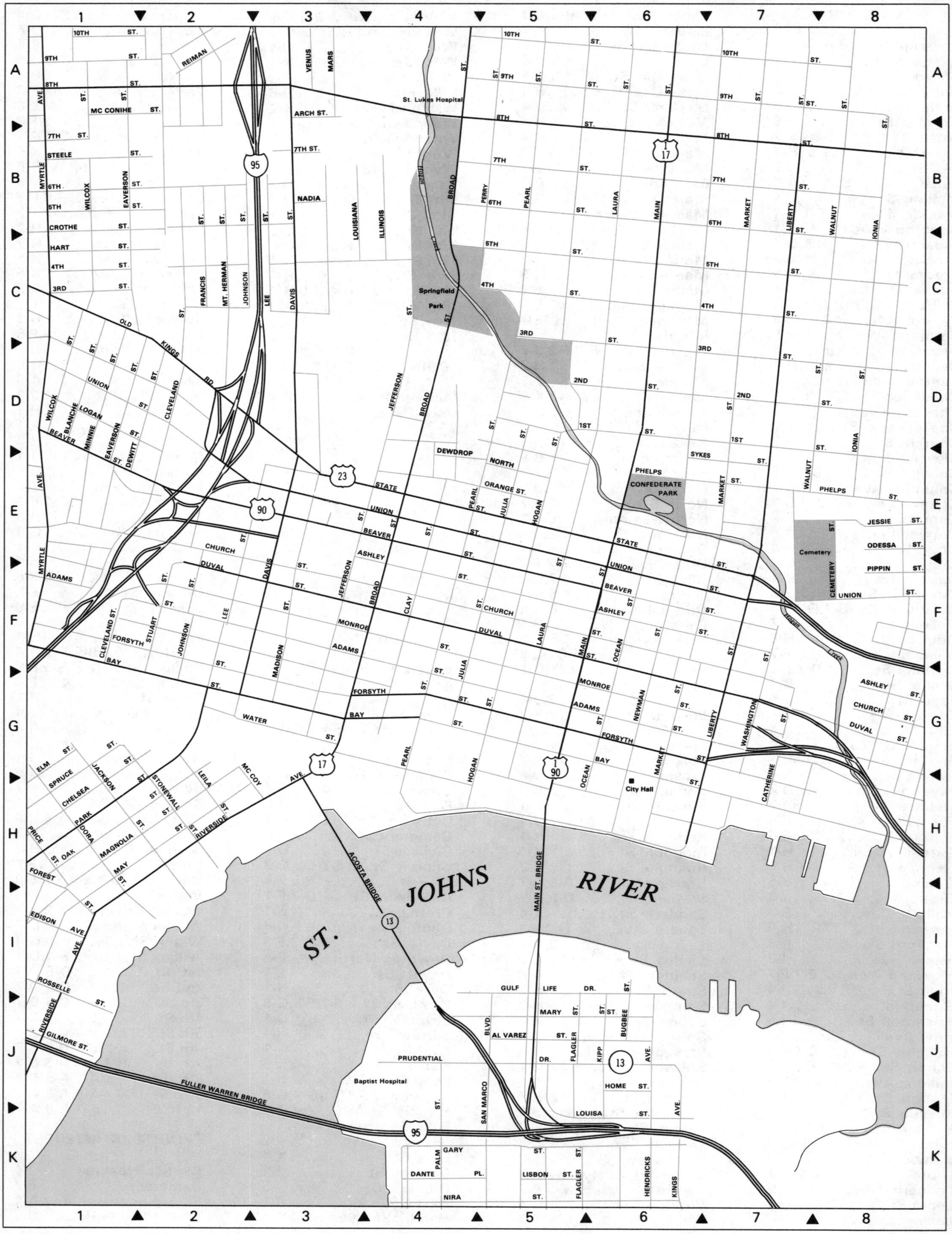

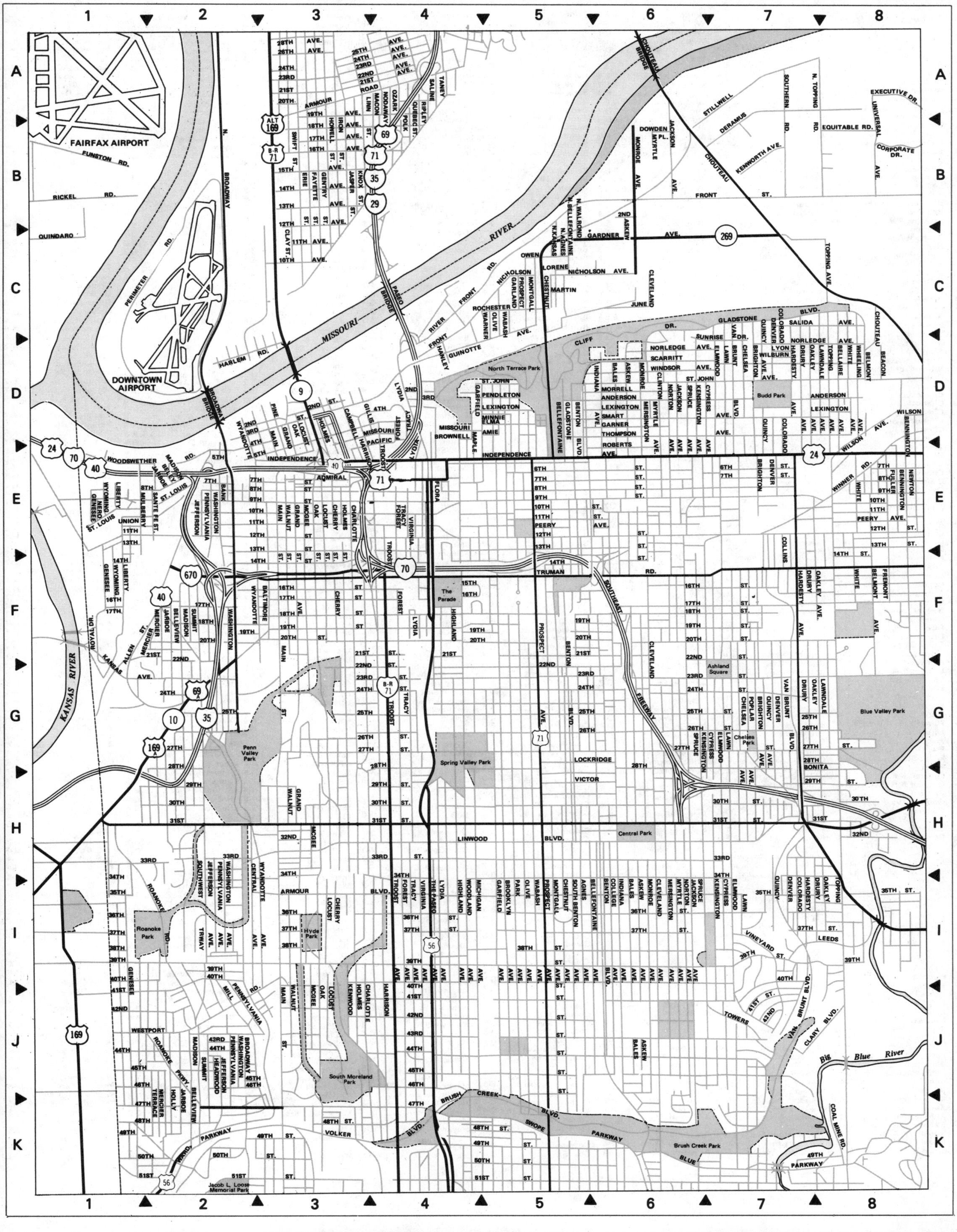
Scale of Miles
0 .2 .4 .6 .8
N
FAIRFAX AIRPORT
DOWNTOWN AIRPORT
MISSOURI RIVER
KANSAS RIVER
Big Blue River
CHOUTEAU BRIDGE
BROADWAY BRIDGE
PASEO BRIDGE
North Terrace Park
Budd Park
The Parade
Penn Valley Park
Spring Valley Park
Ashland Square
Chelsea Park
Blue Valley Park
Central Park
Roanoke Park
Hyde Park
South Moreland Park
Brush Creek Park
Jacob L. Loose Memorial Park
INDEPENDENCE AVE.
TRUMAN RD.
LINWOOD BLVD.
SOUTHEAST FREEWAY
BRUSH CREEK BLVD.
SWOPE PARKWAY
BLUE PARKWAY
WARD PARKWAY
FRONT ST.
GARDNER AVE.
CLIFF DR.
GLADSTONE BLVD.
WOODSWETHER RD.
PROSPECT AVE.
TROOST AVE.
MAIN ST.
BROADWAY
VAN BRUNT BLVD.
COAL MINE RD.
1 2 3 4 5 6 7 8
A B C D E F G H I J K

KANSAS CITY, MO.

Admiral....E-3
Agnes, N....C-5
Allen St....F-1
Amie....D-5
Anderson....D-6,D-8
Armour Blvd....I-3
Armour Rd....A-3
Askew....B-6,D-6
Askew Ave....I-6,J-6
Bales....D-6
Bales Ave....I-6,J-6
Baltimore....F-3
Bank....E-2
Beacon....D-8
Beley....E-2
Bellaire Ave....D-8
Bellefontaine....D-5
Bellenfontaine, N....B-5
Bellefontaine Ave....I-6
Belleview....F-2
Bellview Ave....J-2
Belmont....D-8
Belmont Ave....F-8
Bennington....D-8
Bennington....E-8
Benton Blvd....D-5
Benton Blvd....F-5
Benton Blvd....I-6
Blue Parkway....K-6
Broadway, N....B-2
Broadway Ave....J-2
Broadway Bridge....D-2
Brooklyn Ave....I-5
Brownell....D-4
Brighton....D-7
Brighton....E-7
Brighton Ave....G-7
Brush Creek Pkwy....J-4
Campbell....D-3
Central Ave....H-2
Charlotte....E-3
Charlotte....I-3
Chelsea....D-7
Chelsea Ave....G-7
Cherry....F-3,I-3
Cherry St....E-3
Chestnut....C-5
Chestnut Ave....I-5
Chouteau....B-7,C-8
Chouteau Bridge....A-6
Clary Blvd....J-7
Clay St....B-3
Cleveland....C-6
Cleveland Ave....F-6,I-6
Cliff Dr....D-5
Clinton....D-6
Coal Mine Rd....K-8
College Ave....I-6
Colorado....C-7,D-7
Colorado Ave....I-7
Collins....E-7
Corporate Dr....B-8
Cypress....G-7
Cypress Ave....D-7,I-7
Denver....C-7,E-7,G-7
Denver Ave....I-7
Deramus....A-7
Dowden Pl....B-6
Drury....F-8,G-7
Drury Ave....D-7,I-8
Elma....D-5
Elmwood....D-7,G-7
Elmwood Ave....I-7
Equitable Rd....B-8
Erie St....B-3
Executive Dr....A-8
Fayette St....B-3
Flora....E-4
Forest....D-4,E-4,F-4
Forest Ave....I-4
Fremont....F-8
Front....D-4
Front St....B-6
Fuller....E-8
Funston Rd....B-1
Gardner Ave....C-6
Garfield....D-5
Garfield Ave....I-5
Garland....C-5
Garner....D-6
Genesee....E-1,F-1,I-1
Gentry St....B-3
Gillis....D-4
Gladstone....D-5
Gladstone Blvd....C-7
Grand....D-3,H-3
Grand St....E-3
Guinotte Ave....D-4
Hanley....D-4
Hardesty Ave.D-7,F-8,I-7
Harlem Rd....D-2
Harrison....D-3
Harrison Ave....J-4
Headwood Ave....J-2
Highland....F-4
Highland Ave....I-4
Holly Ave....J-2
Holmes....D-3,I-3
Holmes St....E-3
Howell St....A-3
Independence Ave....E-5
Indiana Ave....D-6,I-6
Iron St....A-3
Jackson Ave..B-6,D-6,I-6
Jarboe....E-2,F-2
Jarboe Ave....J-2
Jasper St....B-3
Jefferson....E-2
Jefferson Ave....H-2,J-2
June....C-6
Kansas, N....C-5
Kansas Ave....F-1
Kensington....G-6
Kensington Ave..D-6,I-7
Kenwood....I-3
Kenworth Ave....B-7
Knox St....B-3
Lawn....D-7,G-7
Lawn Ave....I-7
Lawndale....G-8
Lawndale Ave....D-8
Leeds Ave....I-8
Lexington...D-5,D-6,D-8
Liberty....E-1,F-1
Linn St....A-4
Linwood Blvd....H-4
Lockridge....G-5
Locust....D-3,I-3
Locust St....E-3
Lorene....C-5
Lydia....D-4,F-4
Lydia Ave....I-4
Lyon....D-7
Macon....A-4
Madison....E-2,F-2
Madison Ave....J-2
Main....D-3
Main St....E-3,F-3,J-3
Maple....D-4
Martin....C-5
McGee....E-3,H-3,I-3
Mercier....F-2
Mercier Ave....J-2
Mersington....D-6
Mersington Ave....I-6
Michigan Ave....I-4
Mill....I-2
Minnie....D-5
Missouri....D-4
Monroe....D-6
Monroe Ave....B-6,I-6
Montgall....C-5
Montgall Ave....F-5,I-5
Morrell....D-6
Mulberry....E-2
Myrtle....B-6
Myrtle Ave....D-6,I-6
Nero....E-1
Newton....E-8
Nodaway....A-4
Norledge Ave....D-6,D-7
Norton Ave....D-6,I-6
Nicholson Ave....C-5
Oak....D-3,I-3
Oak St....E-3
Oakley....G-8
Oakley Ave...D-8,F-8,I-8
Olive....C-5
Olive Ave....I-5
Owen....C-5
Ozark....A-7
Pacific....D-4
Park Ave....I-5
Paseo Bridge....C-4
Peery Ave....E-5,E-8
Pendleton....D-5
Pennsylvania....E-2,I-2
Pennsylvania Ave....H-2
....J-2
Perimeter Rd....C-1
Pine....D-3
Polk....A-4
Poplar Ave....G-7
Prospect....C-5
Prospect Ave....I-5
Quebec St....A-4
Quincy....C-7,D-7
Quincy Ave....G-7,I-7
Quindaro....B-1
Rickel Rd....B-1
Ripley....A-4
River Front Rd....C-4
Roanoke Pkwy....J-2
Roanoke Rd....I-2
Roberts....D-6
Rochester....C-5
Royal Dr....F-1
St. John....D-5
St. John Ave....D-7
St. Louis....E-1
St. Louis....E-2
Salida Ave....C-7
Saline....A-4
Sante Fe St....E-2
Scarritt....D-6
Smart Ave....D-6
South Benton Ave....I-5
Southeast Freeway....F-6
Southern Rd....A-7
Southwest Trway....H-2
Spruce....G-6
Spruce Ave....D-6,I-6
Stillwell....A-7
Summit....F-2
Summit Ave....J-2
Sunrise Dr....C-7
Swift St....B-3
Swope Pkwy....K-5
Taney....A-4
Terrace Ave....J-2
The Paseo Ave....I-4
Thompson Ave....D-6
Topping Ave..C-8,D-8,I-8
Topping Rd., N....A-8
Towers....J-7
Tracy....D-4,E-4,G-4
Tracy Ave....I-4
Troost....E-4,G-4
Troost Ave....I-4
Truman Rd....F-5
Union....E-1
Universal Ave....B-8
Van Brunt Blvd....C-7
....G-7,J-7
Victor....H-5
Vineyard Ave....I-7
Virginia....E-4
Virginia Ave....I-4
Volker Blvd....K-3
Wabash....C-5
Wabash Ave....I-5
Walnut....H-3,I-3
Walnut St....E-3
Walrond, N....B-5
Ward Pkwy....K-2
Warner....C-5
Washington....E-2,F-2
Washington Ave.H-2,J-2
Westport Rd....J-1
Wheeling Ave....D-8
White....E-8,F-8
White Ave....D-8
Wilburn....D-7
Wilson Ave....E-8
Windsor Ave....D-6
Winner Rd....E-8
Woodland Ave....I-4
Woodswether Rd....E-1
Wyandotte....D-2,F-3
Wyandotte Ave....H-3
Wyoming....E-1,F-1
2nd St....B-6,D-3,D-4
3rd St....D-3,D-4
4th....D-3,D-4
5th....D-3,E-2
6th St....E-5,E-7
7th....E-2,E-3,E-5,E-7,E-8
8th St....E-2,E-3,E-5,E-8
9th St....E-3,E-5,E-8
10th....C-3,E-3,E-5,E-8
11th..C-3,E-1,E-3,E-5,E-8
12th St....B-3,E-3,E-5,E-8
13th St....B-3,E-1,E-3
....E-5,E-8
14th St....B-3,E-1,E-3
....F-5,F-8
15th....B-3,F-4
16th St....B-3,F-1,F-3
....F-4,F-6
17th St....B-3,F-1-3, F-6
18th St....A-3,F-2,F-3,F-6
19th St....A-3,F-2-6
20th St....A-3,F-2-6
21st St....A-3,A-4
....F-2-5
22nd St....A-4,F-2,F-3
....F-6,G-5
23rd St....A-3,A-4,G-3
....G-5,G-6
24th St....A-3,A-4,G-2
....G-3,G-5,G-6
25th St....A-4,G-2,G-3
....G-5,G-6,G-7
26th St....A-3,G-3
....G-5-7
27th St....G-2,G-3
....G-4,G-6,G-8
28th St....A-3,G-2
....G-4,G-6,G-7
29th St....H-2,H-4,H-7
30th St..H-2,H-4,H-7,H-8
31st St....H-2-8
32nd St....H-3,H-8
33rd St..H-1,H-2,H-4,H-7
34th St....H-1,H-3,H-4-7
35th St....I-1,I-7,I-8
36th St....I-1,I-3,I-4,I-6
37th St....I-1,I-3,I-4
....I-6,I-7
38th St....I-1,I-3,I-5
39th St....I-1-8
40th St....I-1,I-2,I-4,I-7
41st St....I-1,I-4,I-7
42nd St....J-1,J-4,J-7
43rd St....J-2,J-4
44th St....J-1,J-2,J-4
45th St....J-1,J-2,J-4
46th St....J-1,J-2,J-4
47th St....K-1,K-4
48th St....K-1,K-3,K-4
49th St....K-1,K-3
....K-4,K-7
50th St....K-1,K-2,K-4
51st St....K-1,K-2,K-4

POINTS OF INTEREST

Ashland Sq....G-7
Blue Valley Park....G-8
Broadway Bridge....D-2
Brush Creek Park....K-6
Budd Park....D-7
Central Park....H-6
Chelsea Park....G-7
Chouteau Bridge....A-6
Downtown Airport..D-1
Fairfax Airport....B-1
Hyde Park....I-3
Jacob L. Loose
Memorial Park....K-2
North Terrace Park
....D-5
Penn Valley Park....G-2
Roanoke Park....I-1
South Moreland
Park....J-3
Spring Valley
Park....G-4
The Parade....F-4

KNOXVILLE

Acker St....B-6
Adair Ave....B-6
Adams Ave....D-8
Adcock St....D-1
Agee St....I-7
Ailor Ave....H-4,I-2
Alabama Ave....E-2
Albert Ave....B-6
Alexander Ave....E-5
Alpha Ave....H-3
Amber St....B-8
Ambrister St....H-2
Ambrose St....D-2
Anderson Ave....E-5,F-4
Andy Holt Ave....J-4
Arcade St....C-8
Armstead St....E-5
Armstrong Ave....D-6
Arthur St....H-4
Ashwood St....C-5
Atchley St....I-7
Atlantic Ave....C-4
Atlantic St....C-3
Augusta Ave....J-6
Austin St....F-8
Avondale Ave....A-7
Bales St....F-5
Bank Ave....C-4
Barber St....I-8
Barton St....B-6
Battery Ave....J-1
Baxter Ave...F-4,F-5,G-3
Bearden Pl....F-5
Beaumont Ave....F-2
Belleaire Ave....F-3
Bell St....G-7
Bellevue St....A-6
Belmont Hts....G-1
Belvoir....B-6
Bernard St....F-5
Bertrand St....E-8
....F-8,G-8
Bethel Ave....G-8
Blount Ave....I-7,K-6
Bluff St....D-6
Boggs Ave....I-8
Bond St....D-3
Bonnyman Dr....F-2
Booker St....G-3
Bookwalter Dr....B-1
Boone St....C-8
Booth St....I-1
Boright Ave....A-7
Boright Place....A-7
Boruff St....E-7
Bowling Ave....G-1
Boxwood Ln....B-7
Boyd St....F-3,G-4
Bradley Ave....G-5
Bragg St....E-1
Brandau St....G-3
Branner St....E-4
Branson Ave....C-6
Breda Dr....A-3
Brice St....B-7
Bridalwood Dr....A-8
Bridge Ave....H-5
Brigham Ave....G-7
Brisco St....F-7
Britton Hts....J-8
Broadview Rd....A-1
Broadway....E-6,G-6
....H-6,I-6,J-6
Brock Ave....I-2
Brookside Ave...F-3,G-3
Brown Ave....D-7
Browning Ave....H-1
Brown St....D-6
Bruhin Rd....A-1
Brunswick St....A-7
Buchanan Ave....A-5
Buck St....G-1
Buffalo Ave....H-3
Buffat Mill Rd....B-7,B-8
Burge Dr....G-8
Burgess Ave....G-4
Burnside St....E-1
Burwell Ave....D-3
Byrd Ave....B-4
Caldwell Ave....D-4
Caledonia St....J-4
Callaway Ave....G-4
Cambridge St....J-6
Cammichael St....I-7
Campbell Ave....G-7
Canary St....K-8
Cansler Ave....G-4
Capella....A-5
Carrick St....H-4
Carson St....C-8
Carus Rd....B-2
Cary St....J-1
Caswell Ave....E-6
Cecil....C-8,D-6
Cedar St....C-2
Central....C-2,D-3
....E-5,H-6
Century St....H-2
Chamberlain Blvd....K-7
Chapman St....J-7
Charles Pl....H-6
Cherry St....C-8
Chicago St....C-6
Chickamauga Ave.
....B-4,C-3
Chilhowee Ave....F-7
Chipman....D-7
Church Ave....H-6,H-8
Churchwell....D-4
Citico St....H-3
Citrus St....C-8
Claiborne Pl....B-5
Clancy St....J-6
Clark St....G-4
Claude St....I-8
Claudius....B-2
Clay St....C-8
Clearview St....A-6
Cleveland St....F-5
Clifford St....G-8
Clinch Ave....I-4
Clyde St....H-3
Coker Ave....C-6
College St....G-3
Colonial Ave....B-5
Colter St....I-8
Columbia St....D-4
Commerce Ave....H-5
Common Ave....G-6
Cooper St....F-5
Concord St....I-2
Connecticut Ave....E-1
Copeland St....B-6
Coram....C-3
Cornelia....D-3,D-4
Coster St....A-1
Cottage Pl....D-6
Council Pl....I-7
Cowan St....H-4
Cox St....D-5
Cristine Ave....I-8
Crockett St....C-8
Cruze St....E-8,F-8
Cumberland Ave....J-3
Dale Ave....H-4
Dameron Ave....F-4
Dandridge Ave....G-8
Davanna St....E-4
Davenport Rd....I-8
Davison Ave....J-6
Dawn St....G-1
Dawson St....I-7
Deadrick Ave....G-4
Deery St....F-6
Delaware Ave....E-1
Delden Dr....A-4
Dell St....G-3
Dempster St....B-6
Denson Ave....H-1
Depot Ave....G-6
Derieux St....B-7
Dill St....C-2
Dinwiddie St....D-1
Division St....I-1
Dixie St....I-8
Dodson Ave....D-8
Dora St....G-4
Douglas Ave....G-4
Dow Dr....K-8
Drive One....F-2
Drive Three....F-2
Drive Two....F-2
Druid Dr....K-8
Dunbar St....G-4
Dundee St....D-7
Durbin....B-1
Dutch Rd....A-2
Edgewood St....B-6,B-7
Edmonds Ave....I-8
Eleavor Ave....F-6
Ellis St....K-8
Elm Ave....E-3
Ely Ave....E-1
Emerson St....I-6
Emerald St....E-4,F-3
Emmett St....I-1
Emoriland Blvd....A-6
Eubanks Ave....H-1
Euclid Ave....H-3,H-4
Exeter Ave....G-3
Ezell St....C-7
Fairfax....A-4
Fairmont Blvd....B-5
Fairview St....B-6
Fairwood....B-6
Farragut....B-3
Felts St....C-4
Fillmore Ave....H-1
Fine Ave....C-7
Flagg Ave....E-8
Flamingo St....K-8
Flemming St....C-7
Folsom Ave....D-5,E-5
Fontana....A-7
Forest Ave....H-4,I-3
Forestdale Ave....A-8
Forsythe St....B-4
Fort Ave....J-7
Fort Dickerson Rd....K-7
Fort Hill Rd....J-8
Fox St....C-2
Francis St....J-4
Fraternity Park
Dr....J-5,K-5
Frazier St....F-6
Freemason St....B-4
Fremont Ave....D-5
Front Ave....I-6
Fulton Pl....F-5
Galba Rd....B-2
Galbraith St....D-1
Gale St....C-8
Galway St....D-8
Gap Rd....E-1
Gaston Ave....B-8
Gay St....G-5,H-6
Georgia St....F-6,G-7
Geraldine St....E-4
Gerson Dr....K-8
Gertrude Ave....I-8
Geta Rd....B-2
Gibbsons St....F-7
Gill....F-5
Gillespie Ave....D-7
Gladstone....B-4
Glen Ave....H-1
Glen Oaks St....A-1
Glenview Dr....C-6
Glenwood St....C-4
....D-4,E-6,E-7
Glider Ave....D-7
Godrrey St....B-6
Goldfinch Ave....K-8
Goins Dr....F-1
Gordon St....F-2
Grace St....B-5
Grainger....D-6
Grand Ave....H-4,I-3
Gratz St....E-6,F-6
Greenfield Ln....C-7
Griffin St....G-2
Grove St....B-3
Hague, The....A-5
Hall St....J-8
Hancock St....C-4
Hannah Ave....H-4,H-5
Hanover ST....B-4
Hardin Hill Rd....B-8
Harp St....D-8
Harriet Tubman St....F-7
Harris Ave....H-1
Hart Ave....I-3
Hartford St....J-7
Harvey St....C-4,D-4
Hatton Ave....F-4
Haun Dr....A-8
Hawkins St....F-1
Hawthorne St....J-6
Haynes Pl....E-6
Hays Dr....A-1
Hazel Pl....F-5
Hazen St....G-8
Heins Ct....A-2
Heiskell....D-1
Helen St....C-5
Helland Ave....E-5
Henegar St....C-5
Henley St....H-6
Henrietta Ave....F-8
Hickley Pl....H-5
Hickman St....I-8
High Ave....J-8
Highland Ave....I-3,I-4
High School St....A-1
Hill Ave....H-7
Hill St....I-6
Hiwassee Ave....B-4
Hiwassee St....C-3
Hoitt Ave....D-7
Holland Dr....A-4
Holly St....F-7
Hooker St....F-2
Hooray Ln....C-2
Howard St....C-6
Humes St....G-6
Huron St....B-4,D-5
Hutchinson Ave....C-6
Hutton Dr....A-1
Iredell Ave....G-3
Irene Ave....I-8
Irwin St....E-5
Isabella Cir....H-8
Islington Ave....F-8
Jackson Ave....G-6
James Ave....G-4
Jefferson Ave....E-7
Jenkins St....D-1
Jennings Ave....F-5
Jersey Ave....J-2
Jessamine St....F-7
Johnston St....D-1,D-2
Jonathan Ave....J-8
Jones St....I-7
Jordan St....G-2
Jourolman Ave....F-2
Kanterbury Dr....B-8
Karns Ave....A-5
Katherine Ave....D-2
Keith Ave....G-1
Keller St....F-8
Kenilworth Ln....B-7,B-8
Kennington Rd....B-8
Kentucky St....F-7
Kenyon St....C-4,D-5
Kern Pl....E-5
Keystone Ave....B-7
King St....G-6
Kingland Ave....J-8
Krohn St....C-5
Kuhlman St....A-5
Kyle St....F-8
Lake Ave....J-4
Lake Loudoun Blvd....J-5
Lamar St....F-6
Langford Ave....I-8
Langland St....F-8
Larkwood Ln....G-1
Laurel Ave....I-3,I-4
Laurens Ave....G-8
Lawson Ave....C-6
Lee St....F-4
Ledgerwood Ave....C-5
Leinard Ln....K-5
Leland St....C-4
Lemon St....D-8
Leonard Pl....D-6
Leslie Ave....H-3
Lincoln St....I-8
Linden Ave....F-7,F-8
Lindsay St....J-2
Link St....F-4
Lippincott St....J-8
Locust St....H-6
Logan Ave....H-4
Lonsdale Ave....E-2
Loraine Ave....H-1
Louisiana Ave....E-1
Lovenia Ave....F-6
Ludlow....I-2
Luck St....D-6
Luttrell....D-6,F-6
Lynn Ave....G-4
Magnolia....F-8,G-6
Major Ave....G-2
Main Ave....I-6
Mall St....H-1
Maria Ave....G-3
Marietta Ave....A-5
Marion St....E-3,F-4
Market St....H-6
Martin Mill....J-7
Maryland....F-1
Massachusetts Ave.
....E-2,F-1
Matthews Pl....E-5
Maxwell St....A-7
May St., N.W....F-5
Maynard....B-4
McCalla Ave....F-7
McClellan St....F-1
McCroskey Ct....C-7,D-6
McElroy Ave....J-1
McGhee Ave....G-4
McGuffey St....D-5
McKinley St....A-5
McMillan....D-3
McMinn St....C-7
McMurry St....B-2
McNutt St....A-7
McPherson St....F-1
McSpadden St....F-3
McTeer St....G-1
Mead Ave....E-3
Melbourn St....C-5
Melrose Ave....I-5,J-4
Melrose Pl....J-4
Melrose St....J-4
Mercer St....F-3
Metler St....C-3
Miami St....A-6
Middle St....G-4
Middlebrook Pike Ave.
....H-1,H-2
Midway St....D-1
Millers Ave....J-7
Milton St....A-5
Mimosa St....J-7
Mingle Ave....H-1
Minnesota Ave....E-1
Mississippi Ave....G-2
Mitchell Ave....D-7
Mitchell St....A-1,E-7
Money Pl....B-7
Monmouth....B-5
Monroe St....E-7
Monticello....B-5
Morelia St....D-3
Morgan St....F-6,G-6
Morris Ave....H-1
Moses Ave....G-4
Mount Castle St....J-4
Mulvan St....G-7
Murphy St....E-3
Myers St....G-2
Mynatt Ave....J-1
Myrtle St....F-7
Nadine Ave....C-6
Nelson Ave....G-7
Nerva Rd....B-2
New St., West....G-7
New College Hill Dr..G-2
Newman St....C-7
New York Ave....E-1
Neyland Dr....J-3,K-5
Nickerson Ave....B-6
Nolan Ave....G-3
North Ave....D-3
Oak St....G-4,G-5
Oakhill Ave....E-3
Oakhill St....E-4
Oakota Ave....D-1
Ocoee Trail....B-5
Oglewood St....D-4
Ohio St....E-1
Oldham Ave....E-4
Oldham, West....F-3
Old Vine Ave....G-8
Olive St....E-8
Oklahoma Ave....E-5
O'Neal St....D-1
Orange Ave....H-2
Orchard Dr....A-8
Orlando St....A-6
Oswald St....B-5
Overton Pl....E-6
Pacific St....E-5
Paige St....C-5
Painter Ave....J-2
Palmer St....J-6
Park Circle....J-5
Patton St....G-7
Pedigo Ave....I-8
Pembrokelinciad....A-5
Pershing St....C-4
Pertinax Dr....B-2
Phillips Ave....I-8
Pickett Ave....G-3
Pike St....B-7,E-2
Pitner Pl....K-6
Polk St....E-8
Poplar St....I-6
Portland St....I-1
Potter St....C-8
Powers Ave....A-5,A-6
Pratt St....E-6,E-7
Probus Rd....B-2
Pruitt St....F-5
Quincy Ave....D-4
Rader Ave....E-5
Radford Pl....C-3,C-4
Raleigh Ave....A-4,B-5
Ramona Ave....H-1
Randolph St....F-6
Rector St....D-1
Redwine St....K-6
Reed St....F-3
Reverse Curve Ave....I-8
Reynolds St....G-2
Richmond Ave....G-1
Rider Ave....B-5
Rim St....C-7
Riverside Ave....H-7
Rogers St....C-6
Rosedale Ave....G-8
Rosemond Dr....C-6
Ross St....C-6
Roy St....E-5
Ruckart Ln....B-1
Rudy St....D-1
Russell St....G-3
St. Mary St....D-5
St. Paul St....J-6
Salem St....I-1
Salvus St....H-7
Sam Houston St....J-7
Sandra St....A-6
Sanford St....C-5
Schade Ave....G-8
Schofield St....G-1
Scott Ave....E-5
Scott, West....F-3
Scottish Pike....K-5
Seaman St....I-1
Sevier Ave....I-7
Seymour Ave....B-6
Shamrock Ave....C-4
Sharp Ln....A-1
Sharps Ridge Park
Rd....B-2,B-3
Shaw Dr....A-6
Shawmut Ave....I-2
Shea St....G-3
Shepard Pl....E-5
Sheridan St....E-2
Sherman St....E-1
Sherrod St....J-7
Silver St....E-5,F-5
Southwood Dr....K-8
Spencer St....B-8
Spring Ave....E-8
Springs Rd....B-7
Springdale Ave....D-3
Spruce St....E-8
Stadium Dr....J-5
Stair Ave....F-3
State St....G-6,H-6
Stephenson St....K-4
Sterchi St....G-1
Stewart St....E-5
Stone St....F-5
Stonewall St....E-1,F-2
Sunrise St....F-3
Susanne Ave....I-8
Sutherland Ave....I-2
Sullins St....J-2
Tecoma Dr....A-6
Teeple St....B-7
Tellico St....H-3
Temple St....J-4
Tennessee....F-1
Terrace Ave....J-4
Testerman St....F-2
Texas....E-1
Thomas St....E-1
Thompson Pl....D-6
Tiberius Rd....B-2
Tillery St....C-7
Tims Rd....A-2
Tindell St....E-3
Tipton Ave....K-8
Titus Way....B-2
Toms St....G-2
Topaz St....B-8
Town View Dr....G-7
Truman St....G-1
Tulip Ave....H-4
Tulip St....H-5
Tyson St....F-5
Unaka St....H-3
Union Ave....H-5
University Ave....H-3
U of T Rd....J-4
Upland Ave....A-6
Valley Ave....I-8
Valley Rd....A-2
Val St....F-4
Vandeventer Ave....J-8
VanGilder St....F-8
Vermont Ave....F-2
Vincent St....B-7
Vine Ave....G-8,H-6
Vine St....G-7
Virginia Ave....F-2
Volunteer Blvd....J-4
Walker Blvd....A-5
Walker St....F-3
Wall Ave....H-5
Wall St....H-5
Wallace St....G-4
Walnut St....H-6
Walnut Grove, West.A-2
Warren St....D-4
Washington Ave.C-6,E-7
Washington Pike....A-3
Watauga Ave....B-3
Watson Ave....G-4
Waycross St....H-1
Weaver....A-5
Webster Ave....H-3
Wells Ave....E-5,E-7
Western Ave....G-1,H-3
Westover Ave....A-4
Westview Ave....H-2
Wheeler St....D-7
White Ave....I-4
Whitney Pl....A-7
Whittle St....A-7
Wilkins St....G-3
Willow Ave....G-7
Winona St....F-7
Woodbine Ave....E-7
Woodland....E-4,F-3
Woodlawn Dr....A-1,K-7
Woodmont....A-8
Worth St....E-4
Wray St....F-5
Wynderse Ave....F-1
Yale Ave....J-5
Yarnell Ave....J-8
3rd Ave....F-6
4th Ave....D-6,E-6,F-6,G-4
5th St....F-6,F-7,G-4,G-6
6th, North....D-6
7th, North....D-7
8th, North....D-7
9th, North....D-7
10th St....H-5
11th St....H-5
12th St....H-5
13th St....H-5
14th St....I-5
15th St....H-5
16th St....H-4
17th St....I-4
18th St....I-4
19th St....I-4,J-4
20th St....I-4
21st St....H-3,I-3,J-4
22nd St....I-3,I-4
23rd St....I-2
24th St....H-2

POINTS OF INTEREST

Caswell Park....E-7
Chevans Park....B-6
City Hall....H-5
Court House....I-6
East Tenn. Baptist
Hospital....I-6
Ft. Saunders Presb.
Hospital....I-4
Knoxville College....G-3
Leslie Street Park
....H-2
Linden Park....F-8
Lonsdale Park....E-1
Morning Side Park....G-8
Post Office....I-6
Preston Park....F-8
Sharps Ridge Park....B-3
Tom Dickerson Park.K-6
Tyson Park....J-3
University of
Tennessee....I-5
University of
Tennessee Agriculture
Center....K-2

Scale of Miles
0. .1 .2 .3 .4 .5

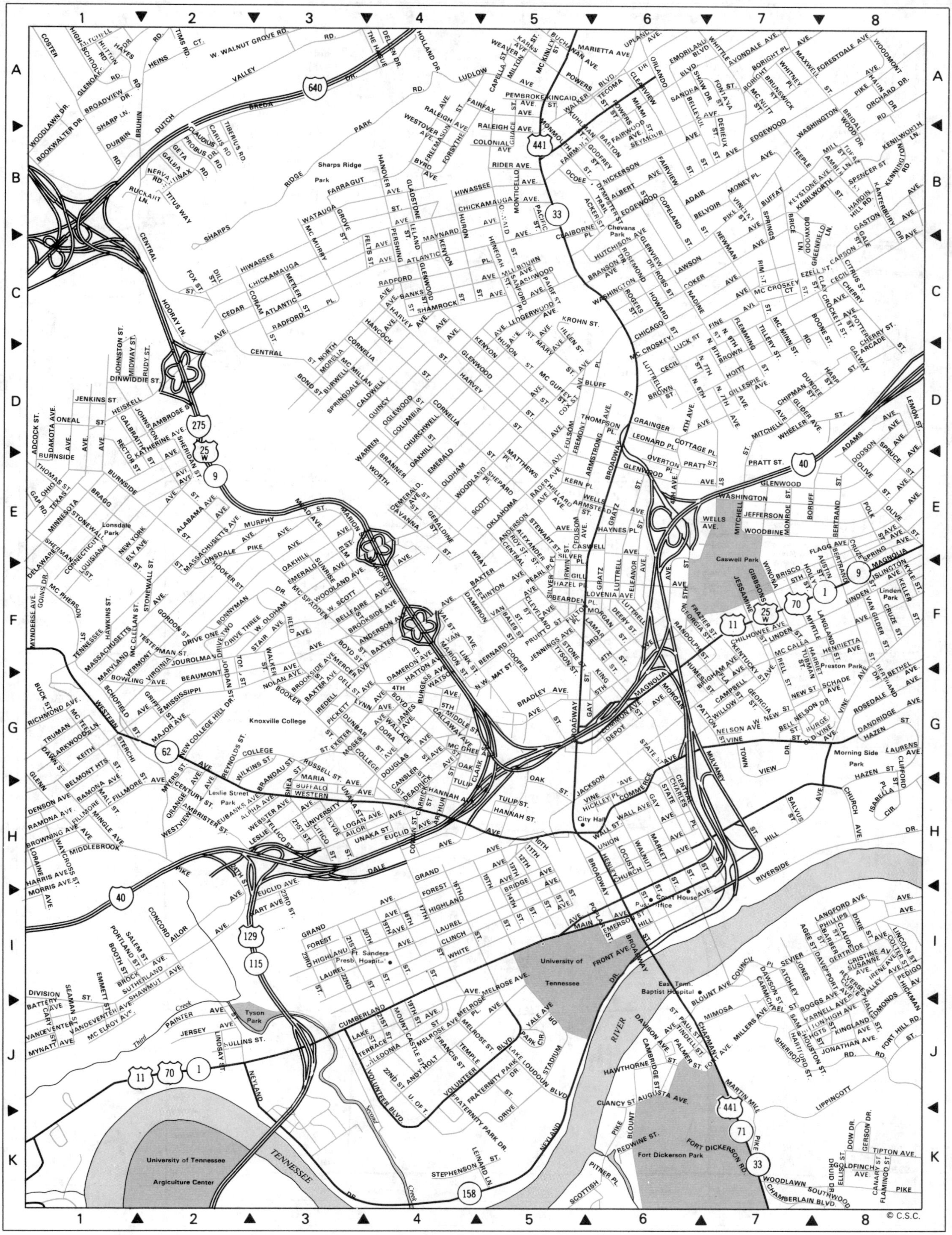

Scale of Miles

0 .2 .4 .6 .8

N

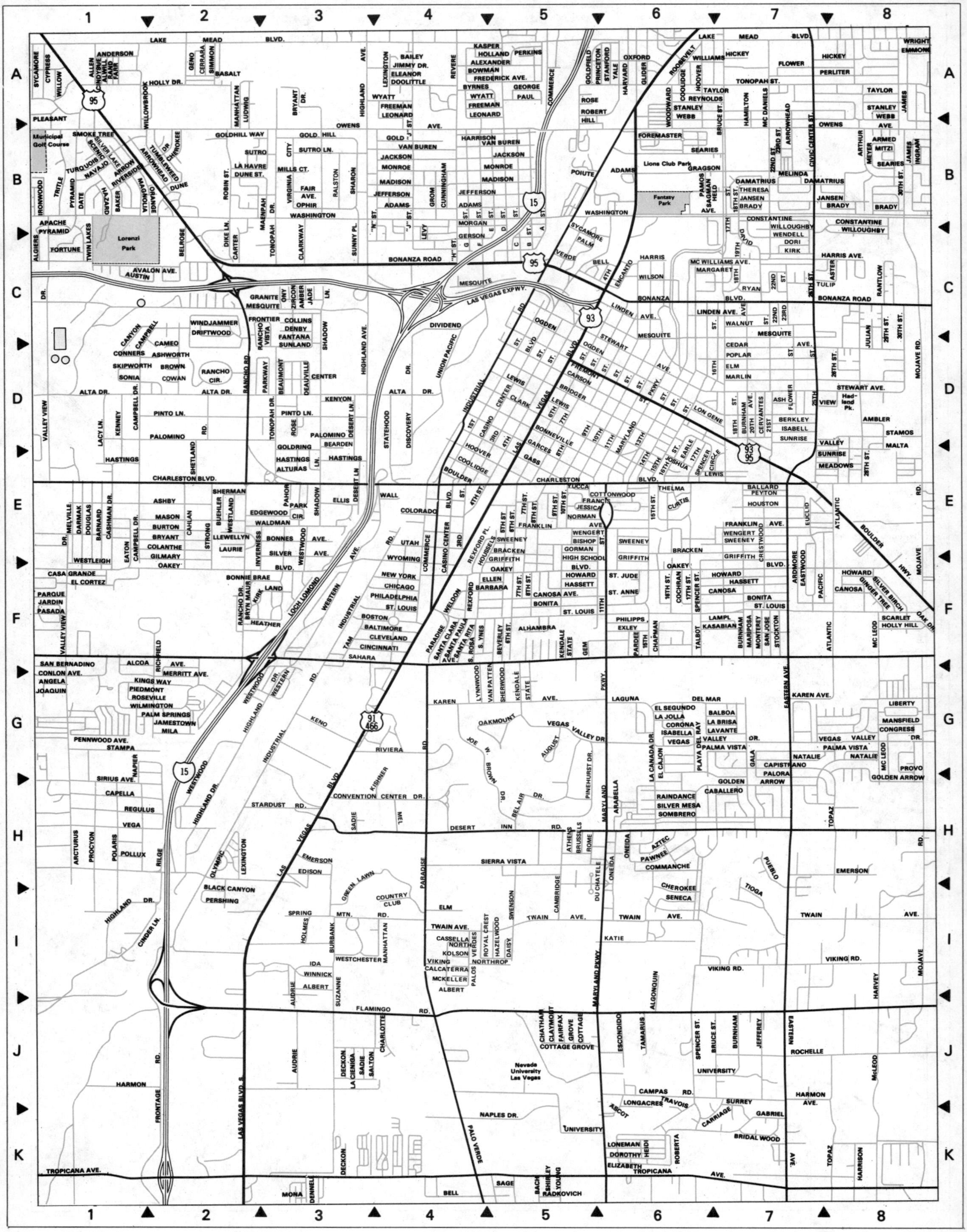

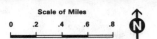

LAS VEGAS

A St. ... B-5
Adams ... B-4,B-6
Albert ... I-3,I-4
Alcoa Ave. ... F-1
Alexander ... A-5
Algiers ... C-1
Algonquin ... I-6
Alhambra ... F-5
Allen ... A-1
Alta Dr. ... D-1,D-2,D-4
Alturas ... E-3
Alwill ... A-1
Amber ... C-3
Ambler ... D-8
Anderson ... A-1
Angela ... G-1
Apache ... B-1
Arabella ... H-6
Arcturus ... H-1
Ardmore ... F-7
Armed ... B-8
Arrow ... B-1
Arrowhead ... B-2,B-7
Arthur ... B-8
Ascot ... K-6
Ash ... D-7
Ashby ... E-2
Ashworth ... D-2
Aster ... C-8
Athens ... H-5
Atlantic ... E-8,F-8
Audrie ... J-3
August ... G-5
Austin ... C-1
Avalon ... C-1
Aztec ... H-6
B St. ... C-5
Bach ... K-5
Bailey ... A-4
Baker ... B-1
Balboa ... G-6
Ballard ... E-7
Baltimore ... F-3
Barnard ... E-1
Barbara ... F-4
Basalt ... A-2
Beardee ... D-3
Beaumont ... D-3
Bel Air Dr. ... H-5
Bell ... C-5,K-4
Belrose ... C-2
Berkley ... D-7
Beverly ... F-5
Bishop ... E-5
Black Canyon ... I-2
Bonanza Blvd. ... C-6
Bonanza Rd. ... C-4,C-8
Bonita ... F-5,F-7
Bonnie Brae ... F-2
Bonnes Ave. ... E-3
Bonneville ... D-5
Boston ... F-3
Boulder ... E-4
Boulder Hwy. ... E-8
Bowman ... A-5
Bracken ... E-5,E-6
Brady ... B-7,B-8
Bridal Wood ... K-7
Bridger ... D-5
Brown ... D-2
Brown, Joe W. Dr. ... G-4
Bruce St. ... A-7,J-6
Brussels ... H-5
Bryant ... E-2
Bryant Dr. ... A-3
Burbank ... I-3
Bryn Mawr ... F-2
Buehler ... E-2
Burnham ... F-7,J-7
Burnham Ave. ... D-7
Burton ... E-2
C St. ... C-5
Caballero ... H-7
Cahlan ... E-2
Calcaterra ... I-4
Campbell ... C-1
Campbell Dr. ... D-1,E-1
Cameo ... C-2
Campas Rd. ... J-6
Canosa ... F-7,F-8
Canosa Ave. ... F-5
Canyon ... C-1
Capella ... H-1
Capistrano ... G-7
Carrara ... A-2
Carriage ... K-6
Carson ... D-5
Carter ... C-2
Casa Grande ... F-1
Cashman Dr. ... E-1
Casino Center Blvd. ... D-5,E-4
Cassella ... I-4
Cedar Ave. ... D-7
Center ... D-3
Cervantes ... D-7
Chapman ... F-6
Charleston Blvd. ... E-2,E-5
Charlotte ... J-4
Chatham ... J-5
Cherokee ... B-2,I-6
Chicago ... F-4
Cincinnati ... F-3
Cinder Ln. ... I-1
Cindysue ... A-1
Circle ... E-6
Clark ... D-5
Claymont ... J-5
Cleveland ... F-3
Cochran ... F-6
Colanthe ... E-2
Collins ... C-3
Colorado ... E-4
Commanche ... H-6
Commerce ... A-5,F-4
Congress ... G-8
Conlon Ave. ... G-1
Conners ... D-1
Constantine ... B-7,B-8
Convention Center Dr. ... H-3
Coolidge ... A-6,E-4
Corona ... G-6
Cottage ... J-5
Cottage Grove ... J-5
Cottonwood ... E-5
Country Club ... I-4
Cowon ... D-2
Crestwood ... E-7
Cunningham ... B-4
Curtis ... E-6
Cypress ... A-1
D St. ... B-5
Daisy ... I-5
Dale ... B-1
Damatrius ... B-7
Darmak ... E-1
David ... C-7
Deauville ... D-3
Deckon ... J-3,K-3
Del Mar ... G-6
Denby ... C-3
Dennell ... K-3
Desert Inn Rd. ... H-5
Desert Ln. ... D-3,E-3
Dike Ln. ... C-2
Discovery Dr. ... D-4
Dividend ... C-4
Doolittle ... A-4
Dori ... C-7
Dorothy ... K-6
Douglas ... E-1
Dune ... B-2
Dune St. ... B-2
E St. ... B-5
Earle ... E-6
Eastern Ave. ... G-7,J-7
Eastwood ... F-7
Eaton ... E-1
Edgewood ... E-3
Edison ... H-3
El Cajon ... H-6
El Cortez ... F-1
El Segundo ... G-6
Eleanor ... A-4
Elizabeth ... K-6
Ellen ... F-4
Ellis ... E-3
Elm ... D-7,I-4
Emerson ... H-3,H-8
Emmone ... A-8
Encanto ... C-6
Escondido ... J-6
Euclid ... E-7
Exley ... F-6
F St. ... C-4
Fair Ave. ... B-3
Fairfax ... J-5
Farr ... A-1
Flamingo Rd. ... J-3
Flower ... A-7
Flower St. ... D-7
Fontana ... C-3
Foremaster ... B-6
Fortune ... C-1
Francis ... E-5
Franklin Ave. ... E-5,E-7
Frederick Ave. ... A-5
Freeman ... A-4,A-5
Fremont St. ... D-5
Frontage Rd. ... K-2
Frontier ... C-2
G St. ... C-4
Gabriel ... K-7
Gala ... G-7
Garces ... D-5
Gass ... E-5
Gem ... F-5
Geno ... A-2
George ... A-5
Gerson ... C-4
Gilmary ... E-2
Glider ... A-6
Gold ... B-4
Gold Hill ... B-3
Golden Arrow ... H-7,H-8
Goldfield ... A-5
Goldhill Way ... B-2
Goldring ... D-3
Gorman ... E-5
Gragson ... B-6
Granite ... C-2
Green Lawn ... I-3
Griffith ... F-5--7
Grom ... B-4
Grove ... J-5
H St. ... C-4
Hamilton ... A-7
Harmon ... J-1
Harmon Ave. ... J-7
Harris ... C-6
Harris Ave. ... C-8
Harrison ... B-4,K-8
Harvard ... A-6
Harvey ... J-8
Hassett ... F-5,F-7
Hastings ... E-1,E-3
Hazard ... B-1
Hazelwood ... I-5
Heather ... F-2
Heidi ... K-6
Held ... B-7
High School ... F-5
Highland Ave. ... A-3,D-3
Highland Dr. ... G-2,H-2,I-1
Hickey ... A-7,A-8
Hill ... A-5
Holly Dr. ... A-2
Holly Hill ... F-8
Holmes ... I-3
Hoover ... A-6,E-4
Houssels ... E-4
Houston ... E-7
Howard ... F-5,F-7,F-8
Ida ... I-3
Industrial Rd. ... D-4,F-3,G-3
Ingram ... B-8
Inverness ... E-2
Ironwood ... B-1
Isabell ... D-7
Isabella ... G-6
J St. ... B-4
Jade ... C-3
Jackson ... B-4,B-5
James ... A-8,B-8
Jamestown ... G-2
Jansen ... B-7,B-8
Jefferson ... B-4
Jeffery ... J-7
Jessica ... E-5
Jimmy Dr. ... A-4
Joaquin ... G-1
Joshua ... E-6
Julian ... C-8
Karen ... G-4
Karen Ave. ... G-4,G-7
Kasabian ... F-6
Kasper ... A-4
Katie ... I-5
Kendale ... F-5,G-5
Kenney ... D-1
Keno ... G-3
Kenyon ... D-3
Kings Way ... G-1
Kirk ... C-7
Kirkland ... F-2
Kishner ... H-3
Kolson ... I-4
La Brisa ... G-6
La Canada Dr. ... H-6
Lacy Ln. ... D-1
La Cienega ... J-3
Laguna ... G-6
La Havre ... B-2
La Jolla ... G-6
Lake Mead Blvd. ... A-2,A-6
Lampl ... F-7
Las Vegas Blvd. ... D-5,H-3
Las Vegas Blvd. S. ... K-2
Las Vegas Expwy. ... C-4
Laurie ... E-3
Lavante ... G-6
Leonard ... A-4,A-5
Levy ... C-4
Lewis ... D-5,E-6
Lexington ... A-4,H-2
Liberty ... G-8
Linden Ave. ... C-6,C-7
Llewellyn ... E-2
Loch Lomond ... F-3
Lon Gene ... D-6
Loneman ... K-6
Longacres ... J-6
Ludwig ... A-2
Lynnwood ... G-4
Madison ... B-4,B-5
Maenpah ... B-3
Magnolia ... B-1
Malta ... E-8
Manhattan ... A-2,I-4
Mansfield ... G-8
Margaret ... C-6
Mariposa ... F-7
Marlin ... D-7
Maryland Pkwy. ... D-6,H-6,J-5
Mason ... E-2
McDaniels ... A-7
McKeller ... I-4
McLeod ... F-8,G-8,J-8
McWilliams Ave. ... C-6
Meadows ... E-8
Mel ... H-4
Melinda ... B-7
Melville ... E-1
Merritt Ave. ... G-2
Mesquite ... C-2,C-4 ... C-6,C-7
Meyer ... B-8
Mila ... G-2
Mills Ct. ... B-3
Mitzi ... B-8
Mojave Rd. ... D-8,F-8,I-8
Mona ... K-3
Monroe ... B-4,B-5
Monterey ... F-7
Morgan ... B-4
N St. ... B-4
Napier ... G-1
Naples Dr. ... K-4
Natalie ... G-7,G-8
Navajo ... B-1
New York ... F-4
Norman ... E-5
North ... I-4
Northrop ... I-4
Oak Dr. ... F-8
Oakey Blvd. ... F-2,F-5,F-6
Oakmont ... G-4
Ogden ... C-5,D-5
Olympic ... H-2
Oneida ... H-6
Ony ... I-5
Ophir ... B-3
Orange ... B-2
Owens Ave. ... A-3,B-8
Oxford ... A-6
Pacific ... F-7
Pahor ... E-3
Pamos ... B-6
Palm ... C-5
Palm Springs ... G-1
Palma Vista ... G-6,G-8
Palo Verde ... K-4
Palomino ... D-2,D-3
Palora ... H-7
Palos Verdes ... I-4
Paradise ... F-4
Paradise Rd. ... I-4
Pardee ... F-6
Park Cir. ... E-3
Parkway ... D-3
Parque ... F-1
Pasada ... F-1
Paul ... A-5
Pawnee ... H-6
Pennwood Ave. ... G-1
Perkins ... A-5
Perliter ... A-8
Pershing ... I-2
Peyton ... E-7
Philadelphia ... F-4
Phillips ... F-6
Piedmont ... G-1
Pinehurst Dr. ... H-5
Pinto Ln. ... D-2,D-3
Playa Del Ray ... G-6
Pleasant ... A-1
Poiute ... B-5
Polaris ... H-1
Pollux ... H-1
Poplar ... D-7
Princeton ... A-6
Procyon ... H-1
Provo ... G-8
Pueblo ... H-7
Pyramid ... B-1
Radkovich ... K-5
Raindance ... H-6
Ralston ... B-3
Rancho ... C-3
Rancho Cir. ... D-2
Rancho Dr. ... F-2
Rancho Rd. ... D-2
Rand ... A-1
Rantlow ... C-8
Regullis ... H-1
Revere ... A-4
Rexford ... F-4
Rexford Pl. ... E-4
Reynolds ... A-6
Richfield ... F-2
Rilge ... H-2
Riverside Dr. ... B-1
Riviera ... G-4
Robert ... A-5
Roberta ... K-6
Robin St. ... B-2
Rochelle ... J-7
Rome ... H-5
Roosevelt ... A-6
Rosa ... F-4
Rosa, S. ... F-4
Rose ... A-5,D-3
Roseville ... G-1
Royal Crest ... I-4
Ryan ... C-7
Sadie ... H-3,J-3
Sage ... K-5
Sagman ... B-6
Sahara Ave. ... F-3
St. Anne ... F-6
St. Jude ... F-6
St. Louis ... F-4,F-5,F-7
Salton ... J-3
San Bernadino ... F-1
San Jose ... F-7
Santa Clara ... F-4
Santa Paula ... F-4
Santa Rita ... F-4
Scarlet ... F-8
Scenic ... B-1
Searles ... B-6,B-8
Seneca ... I-6
Shadow Ln. ... C-3,E-3
Sharon ... B-3
Sherman ... E-2
Sherwood ... G-5
Shetland Rd. ... E-2
Shirley ... K-5
Sierra Vista ... H-4
Silver ... B-1
Silver Ave. ... E-3
Silver Mesa ... H-6
Simmon ... A-2
Sirius Ave. ... H-1
Skipworth ... D-1
Smoke Tree ... B-1
Sombrero ... H-6
Sonia ... D-1
Spencer ... E-6
Spencer St. ... F-6,J-6
Spring Mtn. Rd. ... I-3
Stamos ... D-8
Stampa ... G-1
Stanford ... A-6
Stanley ... A-6
Stardust Rd. ... H-2
State ... F-5,G-5
Statehood ... D-4
Stewart Ave. ... D-6,D-8
Stockton ... F-7
Strong ... E-2
Sunny Pl. ... C-3
Sunrise ... D-7,E-8
Surrey ... J-7
Sutro ... B-2
Sutro Ln. ... B-3
Suzanne ... J-3
Sweeney ... E-5-7
Swenson ... I-5
Sycamore ... A-1,C-5
Talbot ... F-6
Tam ... F-3
Tamarus ... J-6
Taylor ... A-6
Thelma ... E-6
Theresa ... B-7
Tioga ... I-7
Tonapah Dr. ... C-3,D-3
Tonopah St. ... A-7
Topaz ... H-8,K-8
Tritle ... B-1
Tropicana Ave. ... K-1,K-6
Tulip ... C-8
Tumbleweed ... B-2
Turquois ... B-1
Twain Ave. ... I-4-7
Twin Lakes ... B-1
Union Pacific ... D-4
University ... J-6,K-5
Utah ... E-4
Valley ... D-8
Valley View ... D-1
Valley View Dr. ... F-1
Van Buren ... B-4,B-5
Van Patten ... G-5
Vega ... H-1
Vegas Valley Dr. ... G-5,G-6,G-8
Verde ... C-5
View ... D-7
Viking ... I-4
Viking Rd. ... I-6,I-8
Virginia City ... B-3
Vista ... C-3
Waldman ... E-3
Wall ... E-4
Walnut ... C-1
Washington ... B-3
Washington AVe. ... B-6
Webb ... A-6,A-8
Weldon ... F-4
Wendell ... C-7
Wengert ... E-5,E-7
Westchester ... I-3
Western ... F-3,G-2
Westland ... E-2
Westleigh ... E-1
Westwood ... E-3,G-2,H-2
Williams ... A-6
Willoughby ... B-7,C-8
Willow ... H-1
Willow Brook ... A-2
Wilmington ... G-1
Wilson ... C-6
Windjammer ... C-2
Winnick ... I-3
Woodward ... A-6
Wright ... A-8
Wyatt ... A-4,A-5
Wyoming ... E-4
Yucca ... E-5
Ynes, S. ... F-4
Young ... K-5
Zircon ... C-3
1st St. ... D-4
3rd St. ... D-5,E-4
4th St. ... C-6,D-5,E-4
5th St. ... E-5
6th St. ... D-5,E-5,F-5
7th St. ... D-5,E-5,F-5
8th St. ... E-5,F-5
9th St. ... D-5,E-5
10th St. ... D-6,E-5
11th St. ... D-6,F-6
13th St. ... D-6
14th St. ... E-6
15th ... E-6,F-6
16th St. ... D-7,E-6,F-6
17th ... E-6
17th St. ... B-7,F-6
18th ... C-7
18th St. ... B-7,D-7
19th ... C-7
20th Ave. ... D-7
21st St. ... D-7
22nd ... C-7
22nd St. ... B-7
23rd St. ... B-7,C-7
25th St. ... C-7,D-7
26th St. ... D-8
28th St. ... E-8
29th St. ... C-8
30th St. ... B-8,C-8

POINTS OF INTEREST

Fantasy Park ... B-6
Hadland Pk. ... D-8
Lions Club Park ... B-6
Lorenzi Park ... C-1
Municipal Golf Course ... B-1
Nevada University Las Vegas ... J-5

LITTLE ROCK

Allen ... B-6
Allis ... H-1,I-1,J-1
Appianway ... G-1
Arch ... H-6,J-5
Augusta ... B-4
Barber ... I-8,K-8
Barton ... F-2
Battery ... H-3,J-3
Berry ... E-1
Bishop ... H-4,K-4
Booker ... G-1,H-1,J-1
Bragg ... J-8
Branch Dr. ... E-2
Broadway ... E-8
Broadway ... H-6,J-6
Brookwood Dr. ... C-1
Cantrell Rd. ... D-1,D-2
Cantrell, N. ... E-2,E-3
Capitol, W. ... F-1,G-5
Cedar Hill Dr. ... C-1
Centennial Park ... H-3
Center ... H-6,J-6
Chandler ... B-6
Charles ... E-1
Chester ... H-5,J-5
Coates ... G-2
College Cir. ... A-6
College Pk. ... A-6
Collins ... G-8
Commerce ... G-7,H-7,J-7
Coolwood Dr. ... E-2
Cottondale La. ... D-1,D-2
Crest ... C-4
Cross ... H-4,J-4
Crutcher ... B-4
Cumberland ... H-7,J-7
Cypress ... B-8,D-8
Denison ... F-2,H-2,J-2
Division ... B-5,C-5
Dunbar Park ... I-4,I-5
Fairfax ... E-1
Fern ... F-1
Ferry ... G-8
Flora ... B-4
Fort Roberts Dr. ... A-3
Fountain ... F-2
Frank ... B-4,C-4
Franklin ... B-5,C-5
Gaines ... H-5,J-5
Garland ... F-3
Gill ... E-3
Grove ... F-2
Gum ... B-6,E-6
Harold ... B-3
High ... H-4,J-4
Howard ... J-2
Izard ... H-5,J-5
Jessie Rd. ... D-2
Johnson ... G-1,H-1,J-1
Jones ... G-2,H-2
Julian ... B-3
Karrot ... E-6
Lamar ... G-1
Linden ... F-1
Little ... E-1
Lloyd Ct. ... E-3
Locust ... D-8
Long 17th, W. ... B-5
Louise ... E-1
Louisiana ... H-6,J-6
Magnolia ... B-7,D-7
Main ... B-7,D-7,H-6,J-6
Maple ... B-7,D-7
Marion ... B-6
Markham, E. ... F-7,F-8
Markham, W. ... F-1,F-2,F-5
Marshall ... H-3,J-3
Maryland ... G-2
McAlmont ... I-8,J-8
McGowan ... H-8,I-8
Melrose Cir. ... C-6,C-7
Melrose Dr. ... C-6,D-6
Midland ... E-1,F-1
Moss ... B-5
Nanette ... B-3
Nona ... B-4
North ... E-3,E-4,E-5,F-5
Oak ... A-2
Oak ... D-6,E-6
Olive ... B-8,D-8
Orange ... B-7,D-7
Ozark ... E-1
Park ... F-3,J-3,H-2
Park Dr. ... C-4
Parker ... B-5,C-5
Park La. ... J-7
Pearl ... F-1
Phyllis ... B-3
Pike Ave. ... A-5,B-5C-5
Pine ... B-8,D-8,E-8
Poplar ... B-7,D-7
Pulaski ... H-4,J-4
Recton ... G-8
Rice ... F-2,H-2,J-2,K-2
Ringo ... H-5,J-4
River ... C-3,D-4
Riverdale Rd. ... B-1
Riverfront Dr. ... C-1
Riverside ... E-4
Riverview ... E-3
Rock ... H-7,J-7
Roosevelt Rd., E. ... K-7
Roosevelt Rd., W. ... K-4,K-5
Rosetta ... F-1
Schaer ... B-5
Schiller ... F-3,H-3,J-3
Scott ... H-7,J-6,J-7
Sherman ... G-8,K-7
Short 17th, W. ... B-5
Spring ... H-6,J-6
State ... H-5,J-5
Summit ... F-3,H-3,J-3
Summit Ave. ... E-3
Sycamore ... B-6
Terrace Dr. ... E-2
Thayer ... F-2,H-2,J-2
Turtle Creek La. ... B-1
Tuxedo Ct. ... K-7
Vance ... J-8
Vernon ... F-1
Vestal ... C-4
Victory ... G-4,H-4
Vine ... B-8,D-8,E-8
Water Works Rd. ... D-2,E-2
Willow ... B-6,D-6
Wolfe ... H-3,J-3
Wood Ln. ... G-4
Woodrow ... E-1,F-1 ... G-1,H-1,K-1
Wright Ave. ... I-5
W. Wright Ave. ... I-2,I-3
2nd ... A-2
2nd, E. ... E-8
2nd, E. ... F-7
2nd, W. ... D-5,E-6
2nd, W. ... F-3,F-5
3rd ... A-2
3rd, E. ... G-7
3rd, W. ... D-5,D-6
3rd, W. ... F-1,F-5
4th ... A-2
4th, E. ... D-8
4th, E. ... G-7
4th, W. ... D-5,D-6
4th, W. ... F-1,F-5
5th, E. ... D-8
5th, E. ... G-7
5th, W. ... D-7
6th, E. ... D-8
6th, E. ... G-7
6th, W. ... D-7
6th, W. ... G-1,G-5
7th, E. ... D-8
7th, E. ... G-7
7th, W. ... D-5,D-7
7th, W. ... G-1,G-5
8th, E. ... D-8
8th, E. ... H-7
8th, W. ... D-5,D-7
8th, W. ... G-5
9th, E. ... C-7,C-8
9th, E. ... H-7
9th, W. ... C-5,C-7
9th, W. ... G-5
10th, E. ... C-7,C-8
10th, E. ... H-7
10th, W. ... C-5
10th, W. ... G-2,H-5
11th, E. ... C-7
11th, E. ... H-7
11th, W. ... C-5
11th, W. ... H-2,H-5
12th, E. ... C-7
12th, E. ... H-7
12th, W. ... C-5,C-6
12th, W. ... H-2,H-4,H-5
13th, E. ... C-7
13th, E. ... H-7
13th, W. ... C-5,C-6
13th, W. ... H-2,H-4,H-5
14th, E. ... B-7
14th, E. ... I-7
14th, W. ... B-6
14th, W. ... H-2,H-4,H-5
15th, E. ... B-7
15th, E. ... I-7
15th, W. ... B-5
15th, W. ... H-4,I-5
16th, E. ... B-7
16th, E. ... I-7
16th, W. ... B-5
16th, W. ... I-2,I-4
17th, E. ... B-7
17th, E. ... I-7
17th, W. ... B-6
17th, W. ... I-2,I-4
18th, E. ... B-7
18th, W. ... A-5
18th, W. ... I-2,I-4
19th, E. ... A-7
19th, E. ... I-7,J-7
19th, W. ... A-5
19th, W. ... I-4
20th, E. ... A-7
20th, E. ... J-7
20th, W. ... A-5,A-6
20th, W. ... J-4
21st, E. ... A-7
21st, E. ... J-7
21st, W. ... A-5,A-6
21st, W. ... J-4
22nd, E. ... A-7
22nd, E. ... J-7
22nd, W. ... A-5
22nd, W. ... J-4
23rd, W. ... J-4
24th, E. ... J-7
24th, W. ... J-4
25th, W. ... J-1
26th, E. ... K-7
26th, W. ... J-1,K-4
27th, E. ... K-7
27th, W. ... J-1,K-4
28th, E. ... K-7
28th, W. ... K-4
32nd, W. ... K-1

POINTS OF INTEREST

Ark. Baptist College ... I-4
Arkansas Livestock Show Grounds ... K-2
Arkansas River ... D-3,E-5
Arkansas School for the Blind and the Deaf ... E-2
Barton Park ... J-2
Calvary Cemetery ... I-1,J-1
Central Baptist Hospital ... H-3
City Hall ... E-7,F-6
County Hospital ... K-1
Court House ... F-6
David D. Terry Lake ... E-6,E-7,F-6,F-7
Fletcher Park ... H-1
Fort Roots Veterans Hospital ... A-2
Little Rock Central H.S. ... H-2
MacArthur Park ... H-8
Missouri Pacific Hospital ... E-4
Mt. Holly Cemetery ... H-5,H-6
Pettaway Park ... J-7
Philander Smith College ... H-5
Riverview Park ... B-2,B-3
Roselawn Cemetery ... J-1,J-2
Shorter College ... D-8
State Capitol ... F-4
Vestal Park ... B-4
Veterans Hospital ... K-7

Scale of Miles
0 .1 .2 .3 .4
N

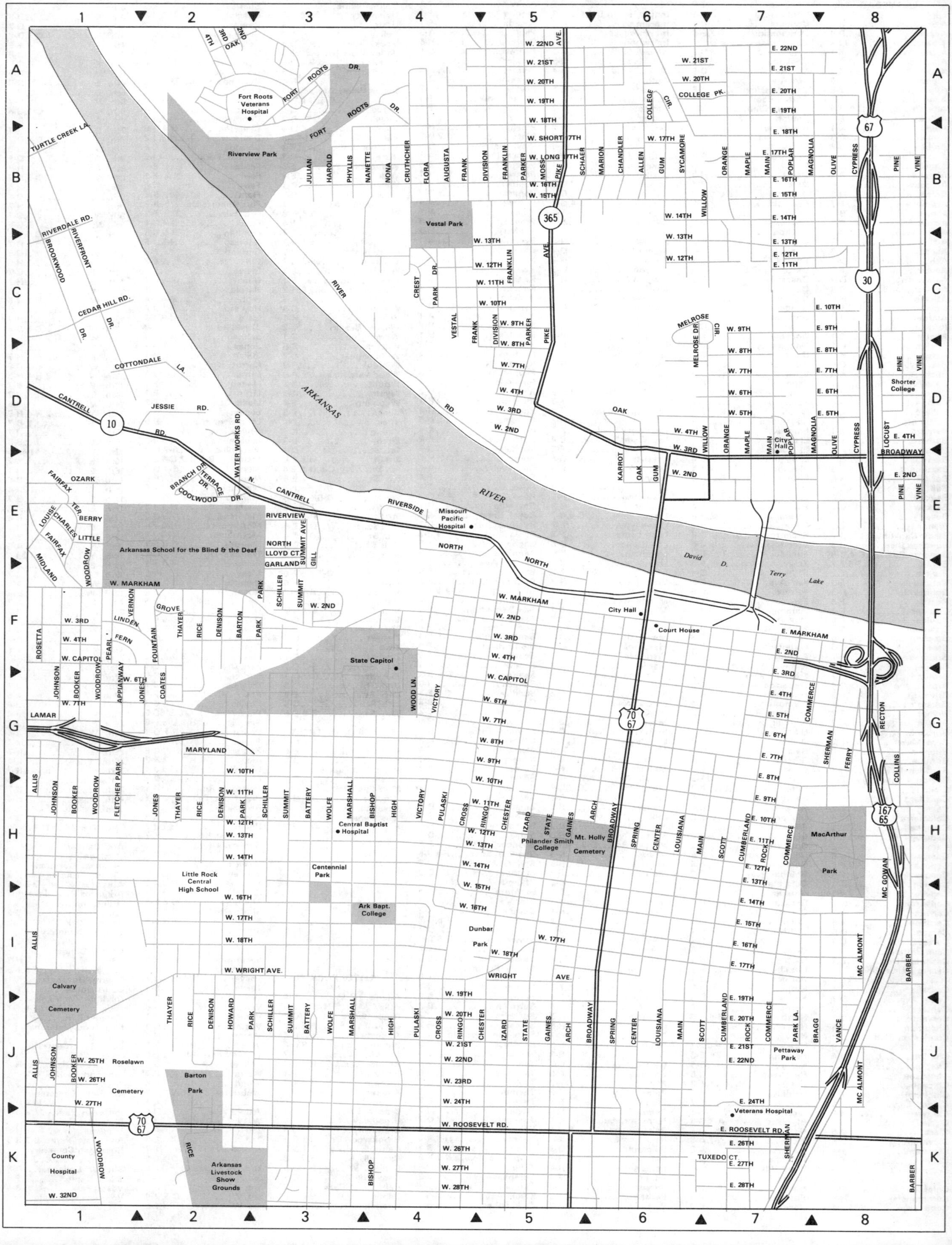

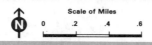

Scale of Miles
0 .2 .4 .6

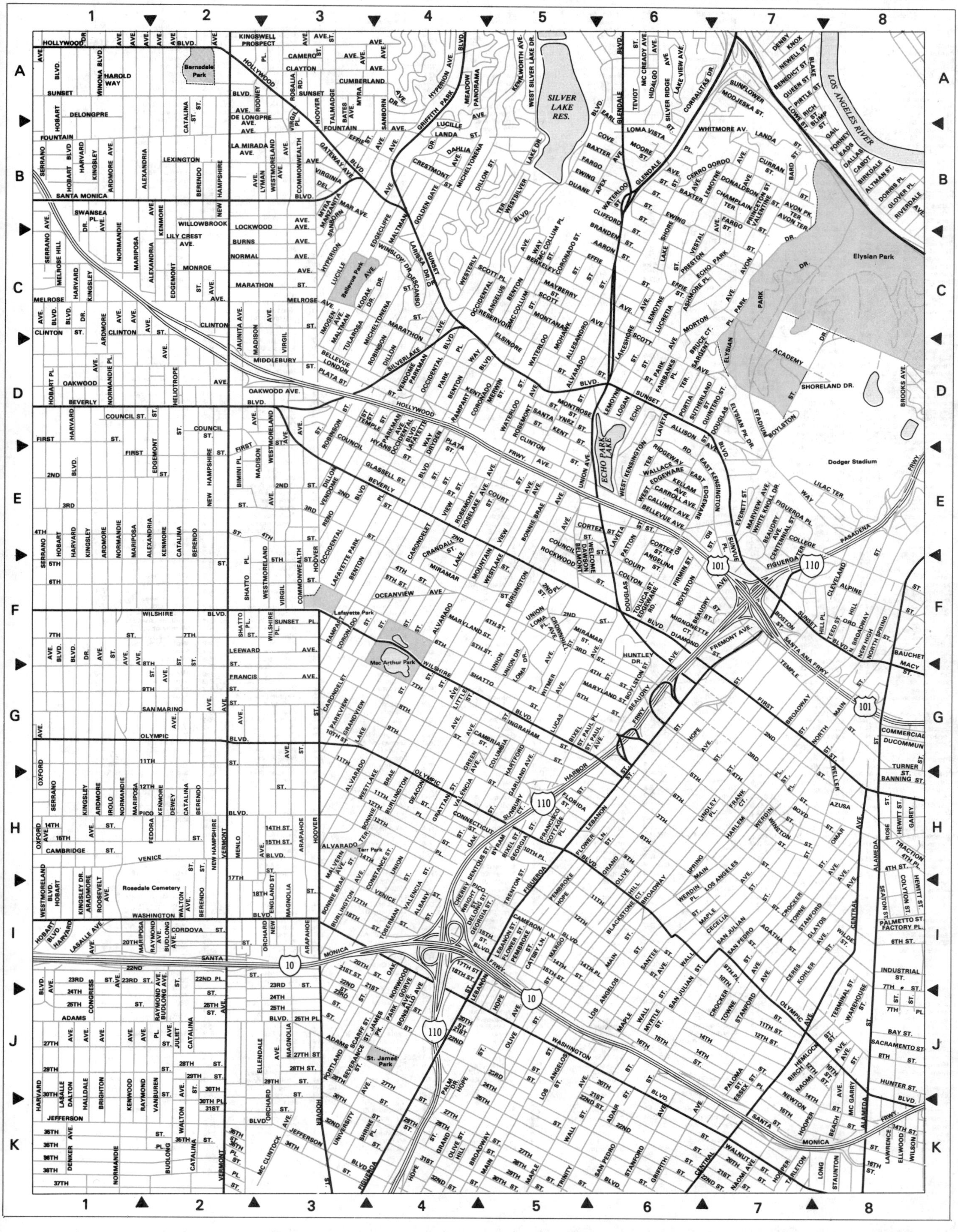

LOS ANGELES

Aaron St. C-6
Academy D-7
Adair St. K-6
Adams Blvd. J-1,J-3
Agatha St. I-7
Alameda St. H-8,K-8
Albany St. I-4
Alexandria Ave. B-2 C-2,E-2
Allesandro St. C-5,D-5
Allison Ave. D-6
Alpine St. F-8
Alvarado St. D-5,F-4,H-3
Altman St. B-8
Angelina St. F-6
Angelus Ave. C-5
Apex Ave. B-6
Arapahoe St. H-3,I-3
Ardmore Ave. B-1,C-1 E-1,H-1,I-1
Ashmore Pl. C-6
Avon Terr. B-7
Avon Pk. Ter. B-7
Azusa H-8
Banning St. H-8
Bard St. B-7
Bates Ave. A-3
Baxter St. B-6
Bay St. J-8
Beaudry Ave. E-7,F-6,G-6
Bellevue Ave. D-3,E-6
Belmont F-5
Benedict St. A-7
Berendo St. B-2 E-2,H-2,I-2
Benton Way C-5,D-4,F-3
Berkeley Ave. C-5
Beverly Blvd. D-1,E-4
Bimini Pl. E-2
Birch St. J-7
Birkdale B-8
Bixel St. G-5,H-5
Blackstone Ct. I-6
Blake Ave. A-7
Blimp St. A-8
Bonniebrae E-5,H-4,I-3
Bonsallo Ave. J-4
Boston St. F-7
Boyd St. H-7
Boylston Dr. D-7
Boylston St. F-6,G-6
Branden St. C-6
Brighton Ave. J-1
Broadway G-7,I-6,K-4
Broadway, N. F-8
Brooks Ave. D-8
Bruce Ct. D-8
Budlong Ave. I-2,J-2,K-2
Burlington Ave. F-5 H-4,I-3
Burns Ave. C-3
Byram H-5
Cabot B-8
Calumet Ave. E-6
Cambridge St. H-1
Cambria St. G-5
Camero Ave. A-3
Cameron Ln. I-5
Carroll Ave. E-6
Carondelet St. E-4,G-3
Catalina St. A-2,E-2 H-2,J-2,K-2
Catsby Ln. I-5
Cecelia St. I-7
Centennial St. E-7
Central Ave. I-8,K-6,K-7
Ceres Ave. I-7
Cerro Gordo St. B-7
Cherry I-4
Clayton Ave. A-3
Cleveland F-8
Clifford St. C-6
Clinton St. C-1,C-2,D-5
College St. E-7
Colton St. F-6
Columbia Ave. G-5
Colyton St. I-8
Commercial G-8
Commonwealth Ave. B-3,F-3
Congress Ave. J-1
Connecticut St. H-4
Constance St. H-4
Cordova St. I-2
Coronado St. C-5 D-5,F-3
Corralitos Dr. A-6
Cortez St. E-6
Cottage Pl. H-5
Council St. D-1-3,5
Court St. E-5,F-6
Cove Ave. B-6
Crandall St. E-4
Crestmont St. B-4
Crocker St. I-7,J-7
Crownhill Ave. F-5
Cumberland Ave. A-3
Curran St. B-7
Dahlia B-4
Dallas B-8
Dalton Ave. J-1
Dawson F-5
Deacon Ave. H-4
Delong St. I-4
Delongpre Ave. A-1,A-2
Denby A-7
Denker Ave. K-1
Descanso C-4
Dewey Ave. H-2
Diamond St. F-6
Dillon St. B-5,D-4,E-3
Donaldson St. B-7
Douglas St. D-7,F-6
Dorris Pl. B-8
Duane St. B-6
Ducommun G-8
Eads B-8
Earl St. B-6
East Edgeware E-6
Echo Park Ave. C-7,D-6
Edgecliffe Dr. B-4,C-4
Edgemont Ave. C-2
Edgemont St. E-2
Effie St. C-6
Ellendale J-3
Ellwood St. K-8
Elsinore D-5
Elyian Park Dr. C-7,C-8,D-7
Essex St. J-7
Everett St. E-7
Ewing St. B-6
Factory Pl. I-8
Fairbanks Pl. D-6
Fargo St. B-6,B-7
Fedora St. H-2
Figueroa Pl. E-7
Figueroa St. I-5,K-3
Figueroa Ter. F-7
Firmin St. F-6
Florida St. H-5
Flower St. H-5,I-5
Forney B-8
Fountain Ave. B-1,B-3
Francis Ave. G-3
Francisco H-5
Frank Ct. H-7
Fremont Ave. F-7
Gail B-8
Garey St. H-8
Garland Ave. H-5
Gateway Ave. B-3
Georgia St. H-5,I-4
Glassell St. E-4
Gladys Ave. I-8
Glendale B-6
Glendale Blvd. A-6
Glover Pl. B-8
Golden Gate Ave. B-4
Grand Ave. H-6,K-4
Grandview St. G-3
Grattan St. H-4
Green Ave. H-4
Griffith Ave. K-6
Griffith Park Blvd. A-4
Halldale Ave. J-1
Harbor Frwy. H-5
Harlem Pl. H-7
Harold Way A-1
Hartford Ave. G-5
Harvard B-1
Harvard Blvd. C-1 D-1,E-1,I-1,J-1
Heliotrope D-2
Hemlock St. J-7,J-8
Hewitt St. H-8,I-8
Hidalgo Ave. A-6
Hill St. F-8,I-6,K-4
Hobart Blvd. A-1 B-1,E-1,I-1
Hobart Pl. D-1
Hollywood Blvd. A-1,A-2,A-3
Hooper Ave. K-7
Hoover St. A-3,F-3 H-3,K-3
Hope St. G-6,I-5 J-4,J-5,K-4
Hunter St. J-8
Huntley Dr. F-6
Hyans St. E-4
Hyperion Ave. A-4,C-3
Imogen Ave. C-3
Industrial St. I-8
Ingraham St. G-5
Irolo St. H-1
Jaunita Ave. C-2
Jefferson Blvd. K-1-3
Juliet St. J-2
Kellam Ave. E-6
Kenilworth Ave. A-5
Kenmore Ave. B-2 E-2,H-2
Kensington Rd., E. E-7
Kensington Rd., W. E-6
Kent St. D-4,D-5
Kenwood Ave. J-1
Kingsley Dr. B-1,C-1 E-1,H-1,I-1
Kingswell Ave. A-2
Knox A-7
Kodak Dr. C-3
Kohler St. I-7
Lafayette Park Pl. F-3
Lake St. F-4,G-3
Lakeshore Ave. C-6,D-6
Lake View Ave. A-6
La Mirada Ave. B-2
Landa St. B-4,B-7
Larissa Dr. C-4
Lasalle Ave. I-1,J-1
Laveta Terr. D-6,E-6
Lawrence St. K-8
Lebanon St. H-6,I-5
Leeward Ave. F-2
Lemoyne St. C-6,D-6
Lexington Ave. B-2
Lilac Ter. E-8
Lily Crest Ave. C-2
Lindley Pl. H-7
Little St. G-4
Lockwood Ave. B-3
Logan St. D-6
Loma Dr. G-5
Loma Vista Pl. B-6
London St. D-3,D-4
Long Beach Ave. K-8
Los Angelos St. I-7,J-5,J-6
Lucas Ave. G-5
Lucile Ave. A-4,C-3
Lucretia C-6
Macy St. G-8
Madison Ave. D-2,E-3
Magnolia Ave. I-3,J-3
Main St. H-6,I-6,K-5
Maltman Ave. C-3
Malvern Ave. H-3
Manzanita St. B-3
Maple Ave. I-7,J-6,K-5
Mar Ave. B-3
Marathon St. C-3,C-4
Mariposa Ave. C-1 E-1,H-1,I-1
Margo I-5
Marview Ave. E-7
Maryland St. F-4,G-6
Mayberry St. C-5
McClintock Ave. K-3
McCollum Pl. C-5
McCready Ave. A-6
McGarry St. K-8
Meadow A-4
Melrose Ave. C-1,C-3
Melrose Hill C-1
Menlo Ave. H-2
Merwin St. D-5
Micheltonena B-4,C-4
Middlebury St. D-3
Mignonette Ct. F-6
Miramar St. F-4
Modjeska St. A-7
Mohawk St. C-5
Moore St. B-6
Monroe Ave. C-2
Montana St. C-5
Morton Ave. C-6
Montrose St. D-5
Mountainview Ave. E-5,F-5
Myra Ave. A-3,B-3
Myrtle St. J-6
Naomi Ave. J-7,K-7
New England St. I-3
New Hampshire Ave. B-2,E-2,H-2
New High F-8
Newell St. A-7
Newton St. K-7
Normal Ave. C-3
Normandie Ave. C-1 E-1,H-1,K-1
Normandie Pl. D-1
North Main St. G-8
North Spring F-8
Norwood I-4
Oak St. H-4,I-4
Oakwood Ave. D-1,D-3
Occidental Blvd. C-5,D-4,E-3
Oceanview Ave. F-4
Olive St. H-6,J-5,K-4
Olympic Blvd. G-2 H-4,J-7
Omar H-8
Orchard Ave. I-3,K-3
Ord St. F-8
Oxford Ave. G-1,H-1
Palm Dr. J-4
Palmetto St. I-8
Paloma St. J-7
Panorama A-4
Park Dr. C-7
Park Pl. D-4
Parkman Ave. D-4
Parkview St. G-3
Park Grove Ave. J-4
Patton St. E-6
Pembroke Ln. I-5
Pico Blvd. H-1,H-2,I-4
Pirtle St. A-7
Plata St. D-3,D-4
Portland St. J-3
Preston Ave. C-6
Princeton St. B-7
Prospect Ave. A-2,A-3
Queen St. A-7
Quintero St. D-7
Rampart Blvd. D-4,F-3
Raymond Ave. I-2,J-1
Reno St. E-3
Reservoir St. C-5
Rich St. A-7
Ridgeway E-6
Riverdale B-8
Robinson St. D-3,D-4
Rockwood St. F-5
Rosalia Rd. A-3
Rose St. H-8
Roselake Ave. E-4
Rosemont Ave. D-5,E-4
Roosevelt Ave. I-1
Sacramento St. J-8
St. James Pk. J-4
St. Paul Ave. G-6
St. Paul Pl. G-5
Sanborn Ave. A-4,B-3
San Julian St. I-6 I-7,J-6
San Marino St. G-1,G-2
San Pedro I-7,K-6
Santa Ana Frwy. F-7,G-8
Santa Monica Blvd. B-1
Santa Monica Frwy. I-2,I-3,I-5,K-7,K-8
Santa Ynez St. D-5
Santee St. I-6
Sargent Pl. D-6
Scarff St. J-3
Scott Ave. C-5,D-6
Scott Pl. C-5
Scout Way E-5
Seaton St. I-8
Sentous St. H-4
Serrano Ave. B-1,E-1,H-1
Severance St. J-3
Shatto Pl. F-2
Shatto St. G-4
Shoreland Dr. D-8
Shrine Pl. K-3
Silverlake D-4
Silver Ridge Ave. A-6
Spring St. H-6
Stadium Way D-7,E-7,E-8
Stanford Ave. I-7 I-8,J-7,K-6
Staunton K-8
Sunbury Ct. H-5
Sunflower A-7
Sunset Dr. A-3
Sunset Blvd. A-1 C-4,D-6,F-7
Sunset Pl. F-3
Sutherland St. D-6
Sunvue Pl. E-7
Swansea Pl. B-1
Talmadge St. A-3
Tarleton K-7
Teed St. F-8
Temple St. G-7
Terminal St. J-8
Teviot St. A-6
Toberman St. I-4
Toluca St. F-6
Towne Ave. I-7,J-7
Traction H-8
Trenton St. I-5
Trinity St. K-5
Tularosa Dr. C-3,C-4
Turner St. H-8
Union F-5
Union Ave. G-4
Union Dr. G-5
Union Pl. F-5
University Ave. K-3
Valencia St. I-4,H-4
Valentine B-7
Van Buren Pl. J-2
Vendome D-4,E-3
Venice Blvd. H-2,I-4
Vermont Ave. H-2,K-2
Vestal Ave. B-7,C-6
View St. E-4
Virgil Ave. C-3,F-3
Virgil Pl. A-3
Virginia B-3
Wall St. I-6,J-6,K-5
Wallace E-6
Walnut St. K-7
Walton Ave. I-2,K-2
Warehouse St. J-8
Washington Blvd. I-1,I-2,K-5
Waterloo St. B-6,D-5
Welcome F-6
Weller H-8
Werdin Pl. H-7,I-5
West Edgeware E-6
Westmoreland Ave. B-3,D-3,F-3
Westmoreland Blvd. I-1
Westerly Ter. C-4
Westlake Ave. F-5
Westlake St. H-3
West Silver Lake Dr. A-5,B-5
White Knoll Dr. E-7
Whitmore Av. B-7
Wilde St. I-8
Willowbrook Ave. B-2
Wilshire Blvd. F-2,G-4
Wilshire Pl. F-3
Wilson K-8
Winona Blvd. A-1
Winslow Dr. C-4
Winston St. H-7
Witmer St. G-5
Wright St. I-4
1st St. D-1,D-2,G-7
2nd St. E-1,E-3,E-4 F-5,G-7
3rd St. E-1,E-3,F-5,G-7
4th Pl. H-8
4th St. E-1,E-3,F-4 F-5,G-6,H-7,H-8
5th St. E-1,E-3,F-4,G-6
6th St. E-1,F-4,H-6,I-8
7th Pl. J-8
7th St. F-1,F-2 G-4,H-6,J-8
8th St. F-2,G-4,H-6,J-8
9th Pl. I-7
9th St. G-1,G-4,H-6
10th Pl. H-5
10th St. G-3,I-7,J-8
11th Pl. H-4
11th St. G-3,I-6,J-7
12th St. H-4,I-5,J-7
14th Pl. I-5,J-6,J-7
14th St. H-1,H-3 I-4,I-5,J-7,K-8
15th St. H-1,H-3 I-5,J-6,K-7
16th St. J-6,K-8
17th St. H-2,I-3
18th St. I-3,I-4
20th St. I-1,I-3 J-4,J-6,K-7
21st St. I-3,J-4,J-5,K-7
22nd Pl. I-2
22nd St. I-1,I-3 J-4, K-6, K-7
23rd St. I-1,I-3,J-3,J-5
24th St. I-1,J-3,J-5
25th Pl. J-3
25th St. J-1,J-2,J-3,K-5
27th St. J-1,J-3 J-4,K-4,K-5
28th St. J-2,J-3,K-4,K-5
29th St. J-1,J-2 J-3,K-4,K-5
30th Pl. K-2
30th St. J-1,J-3,K-5
31st St. K-2,K-4
32nd St. K-3,K-4
34th St. K-3
35th Pl. K-1,K-2
35th St. K-1,K-2
36th Pl. K-1,K-2
36th St. K-1
37th St. K-1

POINTS OF INTEREST

Barnsdale Park A-2
Bellevue Park C-3
Dodger Stadium E-8
Lafayette Park F-3
MacArthur Park F-4
Rosedale Cemetery I-1,I-2
St. James Park J-4
Terr Park H-3

LOUISVILLE

Abraham B-6
Adams St. A-8
Adelia Ave. F-2
Adair St. I-6
Airview Dr. J-8
Algonquin Pkwy. E-2
Alley A-3
Alleycourt Pl. B-5
Alliston Ave. E-1
Alma Ave. J-2
Almond Ave. J-5
Anna Lane J-1
Ann Ct. F-2
Appleton Ct. G-1
Appleton Ln. G-1
Arcade Ave. G-3
Ardmore Dr. F-7
Argonne Ave. G-1
Arling Ave. K-3
Arling Ct. K-2
Armory B-5
Ash St. E-7
Ashbury Rd. K-4
Ashland Ave. I-3,I-5
Ashton Ave. I-6
Auburndale Ave. K-4
Audobon Parkway G-7
Auery Ave. E-5
Bachman Dr. H-1
Badger Ave. J-5
Ballard Ct. G-7
Bancroft St. C-6
Bank St. A-4
Barbee Ave. F-6
Barbee Way F-6
Barkwood Rd. H-2
Baroness St. D-7
Barret Ave. C-7
Bardstown C-8
Barret C-8
Barrowdale Dr. K-1
Barton Ave. I-7
Bates Ct. D-8
Baxter St. B-8
Beacher St. I-3
Becker Ct. F-1
Beech Ave. I-2
Beech St. E-1
Beecher St. I-3
Beeler K-4
Bedgravia Ct. E-5
Bellevue J-4
Bellevue Ave. J-4
Belmar Ave. H-8
Bergman St. E-6
Berkley Sq. J-8
Bernheim Ave. E-2
Berry Blvd. H-2
Bicknell Ave. J-3
Bloom E-5
Blue Grass J-3
Bobolink Rd. F-8
Bohannon St. G-3
Bolling Ave. D-2
Bourban Ave. H-8
Boxley Ave. G-6
Boyle St. D-7
Brandies F-5
Breckinridge St. C-4,C-7
Brent St. D-8
Brentwood Ave. H-3
Briden Ave. H-2
Broadway B-1,C-6
Brook C-6,F-5,I-5
Brookline Ave. J-3
Buchanan A-7
Buckner Ave. K-4
Burnett Ave. D-2,E-5,E-7
Burwell E-1
Byrne Ave. G-5
Cable St. A-8
Caldwell C-7
Camden Ave. I-2
Campbell St. C-7
Camp St. D-6
Cardinal Dr. H-8
Carl Ct. I-1
Carlisle Ave. H-2
Carrico I-3
Cassin Ave. E-5
Castlevale Dr. E-8
Castlewood Ave. D-8
Catalpa St. D-1
Cawthan St. C-4
Cayuga I-2
Cedar St. A-2
Center Cliff I-4
Central Ave. G-3
Chalmer F-2
Chapel St. A-4
Charles St. D-7
Cherokee C-8
Chester Rd. H-1
Chestnut B-1,B-4,B-7
Cheyenne Ave. H-6
Chickadee Rd. G-8
Chicopee I-5
Christopher Pl. J-4
Churchman Ave. J-2
Clara Ave. H-2
Clarks Lane F-7
Clay C-7
Clay St. E-6
Cliff Ave. J-4
Clover Hills Dr. J-1
College St. C-5
Colgan St. B-3
Collins Ct. H-5
Colorado Ave. G-3
Columbia St. A-2
Compton St. F-4
Concord Dr. G-6
Conestoga Ave. E-1
Congess A-2,A-5
Conlin Ave. F-7
Conn St. H-2
Conrad C-6
Cooper St. B-8
Cornette Way J-1
Craig Ave. I-2
Crittenden Dr. G-6,J-6
Crop St. A-2
Crossbill Rd. G-8
Crown St. D-8
Cumberland Ave. K-4
Curry Dr. I-7
Cypress St. D-2,E-1
Dahlia Dr. E-8
Dakota Ave. H-6
Dale Ave. G-3,K-4
Dana Dr. I-1
Dandridge D-7
Date St. C-2
Davies Ave. E-4
Dearcy H-3
Dellwood Dr. J-1
Del Mar Ave. K-1
Delmar Ct. J-1
Delmar Ln. J-1
Delor Ave. F-7
Del Park B-1
Dena Dr. I-1
Denmark Ave. H-3
Dixdale Ave. E-1
Dixie St. F-8
Dixie Hwy. E-2,H-1
Dixon St. E-7
Doerr Dr. H-1
Dove Ln. G-8
Dove Rd. G-8
Dresden Ave. H-3
Dubourg Ave. G-1
Dumesnil D-2
Durrett Lane I-8
Duvall G-6
Eagan Ave. J-6
Eagle Pass F-8
Earl Ave. G-3
Eastern Pkwy. F-7
Edward St. C-8
Eicher Rd. H-1
Eigelbach Ave. E-8
Elderwood Way I-1
Elliot Ave. B-2
Ellison Ave. D-8
Elm St. A-6
Emil Ave. F-4
English Ave. G-8
Estate Dr. K-1
Euclid F-4
Euclid Ave. F-4
Evelyn Ave. H-4
Expressway St. B-6
Fairmount Ave. H-5
Falcon Dr. G-8
Farmdale Ave. I-8
Farmington Ave. H-5
Farnsley Rd. H-1
Fayette Ave. H-8
Faywood Way G-2
Federal Pl. B-5
Fern Dr. E-7
Finzer St. C-6
Fischer Ave. D-7
Fitzgerald Dr. G-1
Flexner Way B-6
Floral Terr. D-5
Florence Ave. I-4,I-5
Floyd C-6,G-5
Fontaine Ave. H-7
Forest Ave. E-7
Forum Ave. K-4
Foster St. E-5
Fountain Ct. E-5
Francis Ave. J-3
Franklin Ave. H-8
Franklin St. A-8
Fust Ave. F-2
Gagel Ave. K-1
Garden Row J-8
Garey Ln. G-2
Garland Ave. C-2,C-4
Garrett St. H-4
Garvey Ct. J-1
Garvey Dr. J-1
Garvin Pl. D-5
Gaulbert Ave. D-2,E-5
Geiger St. A-7
Georgetown Ave. H-2
Gillette Ave. G-1,I-5
Glenafton Ln. G-7
Glendale Ave. H-2
Glenrock Rd. K-1
Glenview Rd. F-2
Goddard Ave. D-8
Goss St. D-7
Grand Ave. C-1,C-2
Grant H-5
Gray B-6
Greenleaf Rd. G-7
Green St. A-2
Greenup I-2
Greenwood Ave. C-2
Gregg St. E-2
Guthrie St. B-5
Hale C-2
Hamilton Ave. A-7
Hancock St. C-6,E-6
Hannah Ln. I-8
Hardesty Ave. F-1
Harding Ave. I-6
Harold Ave. F-2
Harrison Ave. F-6
Hartwell K-5
Harwell G-6
Haskin Ave. K-3
Hathaway Ave. H-3
Hawes Ln. I-6
Hawthorne E-8
Hazel St. D-1
Hazelwood Ave. J-2
Hazelwood Ct. K-2
Hdertz Ave. E-7
Helm St. G-6
Hemlock St. D-1
Hepburn Ave. C-8
Herbert Ave. I-1
Herr F-4
Hess Lane G-8
Heywood Ave. G-4
Hickory St. E-7
Highland Ave. C-8
Highway H-8
High Pine Dr. K-1
Hill Ave. D-2,E-1
Hill Top Ct. I-4
Hobart Dr. J-1
Homeview Dr. F-3,G-4
Hopkins Ave. F-4
Howard St. C-2
Hull St. B-8
Huntoon Ave. K-3
Huron Dr. H-5
Innis Ct. C-8
Inverness K-4
Iowa Ave. G-4
Iroquois Ave. K-3,K-4
Ivy Ct. J-1
Jackson St. C-6,E-6
Jacob St. C-5,C-6
Jefferson A-1,A-4
Jefferson Ct. G-7
Johnson St. B-7
Jordan E-4
Joseph St. I-1
Julia Ave. D-8
Kahlert Ave. J-3
Kathleen Ave. I-4
Kelland Way H-1
Keller Ave. I-7
Kennedy Dr. F-2
Kenton St. H-5
Kentucky St. C-1,C-4,C-6
Kenwood Way J-4
Keswick F-7
Kings K-2
Kingston K-4
Knight Ave. J-2
Knight Rd. K-1
Krieger St. E-7
Lafayette H-2
Lammers D-8
Lampton St. C-6
Lancaster Ave. K-2
Lance Dr. J-1
Lansing Ave. I-5
Larchmont Ave. G-3
Larue Ave. H-8
La Salle Ave. J-2
Lawrence H-2
Lawrie Ln. K-2
Lee Dr. J-8
Lee St. E-5,E-6
Lehigh Ave. J-3
Lennox St. H-5
Lentz Ave. I-3
Leroy Ave. H-1
Lester G-7
Lewis Ave. B-2
Lexington Rd. B-8
Libertybell H-2
Liberty St. B-5
Lillian Ave. F-3
Lily Ave. F-6
Lindberg G-2
Lindberg Dr. F-3
Lincoln Ave. F-4
Linnet Rd. G-8
Linwood Ave. E-1
Livingston Ave. I-5
Locust Lane G-7
Logan St. C-7
Lone Oak Ave. K-4
Loney Ln. F-2,G-2
Longfield H-2
Loretta Ave. H-2
Lou Gene Way J-1
Louisville J-6
Lucas Ave. I-8
Lukin Dr. H-1
Lupino Ct. H-8
Lydia St. F-3
Lynnhurst Ave. J-3
Lynn St. F-6
Lyttle A-4
Madelon St. B-1
Madison St. B-1,B-6
Magazine B-3
Magnolia Ave. D-2,D-4
Main A-1,A-4
Malcom Rd. J-1
Malcome Pl. J-2
Manitau Ave. I-3
Mann Ave. I-3
Manning Rd. H-7
Manor Rd. H-7
Manslock Ct. I-1,
Maple B-2
Maple Ct. I-4
Mapleton I-3
Market St. A-1,A-4
Marrett Ave. D-6
Mary St. D-7
Mary Catherine Dr. H-1
Mason Ave. C-7
Mathias Ln. H-1
Mayer Ave. E-8
May Lawn Ave. G-6
McAtee B-1
McCloske Ave. F-1
McCoy G-3
McKinley Ave. F-8
Meade St. F-8
Meadowlark G-8
Mellwood Ave. B-8
Merhoff St. G-6
Merriweather St. E-6
Merwin G-6
Mill St. A-7
Millers Lane F-1
Milton Ave. E-7
Mission Dr. H-7
Mitscher Ave. K-4
Mix Ave. E-4
Model Dr. F-2
Mohawk Ave. I-5
Molter Ave. G-7
Montana Ave. G-3
Morgan Ave. E-7
Morgan St. H-8
Morrison Ave. K-3
Morton Ave. C-8
Mulberry Ave. E-7
Myrtle St. D-4
Nancy Lee Dr. J-8
Naneen Dr. J-1
Narraganset Dr. E-1
Navaho Ave. I-3
Nelson Ave. F-1
New High St. G-6
Nichols Dr. H-2
Nobel H-1
Nobel Pl. H-1
North-South St. B-6
Oak St. C-2,D-5,D-7
Oakwood Ave. J-3
Oehrle Dr. H-1
Ohio St. A-8
Oldham St. D-4
Oleanda Ave. G-3,H-3
Oleanda Ct. G-3
Olenda Ave. G-1
Olive St. D-1
Oneida Ct. I-2
Oregon Ave. E-1
Oriole Dr. G-8
Ormsby Ave. D-3,D-6
Osage Ave. C-2
Ottawa Ave. I-5
Packard Ave. G-7
Park Ave. D-5,H-1
Park Rd. H-1
Parkway Dr. F-7
Parthenina I-2
Parthenive Ave. I-2
Paul Ave. H-3
Payne St. B-8
Peachtree H-3
Peachtree St. I-3
Peck Ave. I-3
Peerless Ct. D-3
Penquin G-8
Penway Ave. E-1
Phillips Lane I-6
Phyllis Ave. G-3
Picadilly Ave. G-3
Pidgeon Ave. G-8
Pikeview Rd. H-7
Pindell Ave. F-7
Pine St. B-8
Piper Ct. G-7
Place St. B-5
Plantation Dr. F-1
Plover F-8
Plymouth Ct. B-2
Pocahontis I-3
Poplar Level Rd. F-8
Powell Ave. I-2
Preston C-6,G-7
Prosperity Ct. B-1
Pylon Ct. I-7
Queen Ave. G-3
Quincy St. A-8
Racine Ave. G-4
Ralph Ave. G-1
Rammers D-7
Ramser Ave. G-1
Ratcliffe Ave. E-2
Rawlings Ave. E-6
Reasor Ave. E-7
Reutlinger St. D-7
Rhonda Dr. J-1
Rhonda Way J-1
Rice Ave. H-6
River Rd. A-6
Robin Dr. H-1
Robin Rd. G-7
Rochester Dr. K-4
Rodman St. G-4
Rondean Dr. J-1
Roosevelt H-8
Rosa Ter. H-1
Roselane Ave. C-6
Rosemary Dr. G-7
Rowan A-2,A-4
Royal Ave. E-8
Rubel Ave. C-8
Ruffer Ave. D-8
Rutland I-3
Sadie Ave. J-1
St. Bertand St. D-5
St. Catherine C-4,D-7
St. James Ct. E-5
St. Louis Ave. D-2
St. Michael D-7
St. Paul St. D-6
Sale Ave. H-3
Samuel St. D-7
Sanders Ln. K-1
Scanlon St. G-5
Schaffner F-3
Schiley St. J-2
Schiller C-7
Schneiter Ave. G-3
School K-2
School Way K-4
Seelbach Ave. I-2,I-3
Seneca I-5
Sharp Ave. F-5
Shelby St. C-7
Sherry Dr. G-6
Shingo Ave. H-8
Short K-2
Sioux Ave. H-6
Skyway Dr. J-8
Sonne Rd. F-2,F-3
Southcrest Dr. J-4
Southern Ave. D-1
Southern Pkwy. K-3
Southern Heights I-2,I-4
Southgate Ave. H-3
Southland Blvd. K-3
South St. F-3
Speckert Ct. C-7
Spratt St. E-7
Spring St. B-8
Springdale I-8
Squires Dr. I-3
Standard Ave. D-2
Stanford Ave. J-8
Stanford Lane J-8
Stanley Ave. I-3
Stephan Lane K-1
Story Ave. B-7
Strader I-2
Strader Ave. I-2
Stratter Alley C-6
Summit Ave. E-8
Swako Ln. K-1
Swan St. C-7
Sylvia Ave. E-7
Tallulah Ave. I-6
Talmadge Way J-1
Taylor Ave. J-3
Teal Ave. G-8
Tennessee Ave. F-3
Tenny Ave. J-4
Terry K-5
Texas Blvd. F-7
Theresa K-5
Theresa Ave. H-1
Thornberry Ave. G-4
Thrush Rd. G-8
Thruston Dr. F-7
Tokay Ave. G-6
Towne Way J-5
Tuberose Ave. K-8
Tuscarora Way J-3
Utah G-3
Valley Forge H-2
Valley Rd. D-8
Valley View Dr. I-1
Vine C-7
Virginia Ave. C-1
Vorster Ave. E-2
Wabasso Ave. J-6
Wagner Ave. E-7
Wainwright F-6
Wallie F-2
Walnut St. A-1,B-4
Walter Ave. J-3
Wampum Ave. I-5
Warnock F-5
Warren Ave. H-4,I-3
Washington St. A-7
Wathens Ln. F-2
Watkins Ave. C-8
Wawa I-5
Weaver Ct. D-1
Webster A-8
Weyler G-3
Weller Ave. F-3
Wellington Ave. I-5
Wenatchee I-2
Wenona Ave. I-6
Wenzel St. B-7
Wetterau E-7
Wheeler J-2
Wheeler Ave. I-2
Whitewood Dr. I-6
Whitney Ave. H-5
Wilson I-2
Wilson Ave. D-3
Wingfield F-1
Wingfield Ave. E-3
Winkler Ave. F-4
Winter St. D-8
Wirth G-7
Wolfe Ave. H-8
Woodbine D-5
Woodlawn Ave. D-1 D-2,J-4,J-6
Woodruff I-3
Woody Ave. I-3
Wren Rd. G-7
Wue St. F-2
Wurtele Ave. Fp3,G-1
Wyandotte Ave. E-1
Yolanda Dr. J-1
York St. C-4
Youngland Ave. F-1
Zane St. C-5
Ziegler E-6
1st St. C-5,E-5,J-5
2nd St. C-5,E-5,J-5
3rd St. C-5,G-5,J-4
4th St. C-5,G-4,J-4
5th St. C-5,G-4,I-4,J-4
6th St. C-5,E-5,G-4,J-4
7th St. C-5,G-2
8th St. C-4,E-4,I-4
9th St. C-4,E-4,G-4
10th St. B-4,E-4
11th St. D-4,E-4
12th St. B-4,E-3
13th St. B-4,E-3
14th St. B-4,E-3
15th St. B-4,E-3
16th St. B-3,D-3,E-3
17th St. B-3,D-3,E-3
18th St. B-3
19th St. B-3
20th St. B-3,E-2
22nd C-2,E-2
23rd A-2,B-2,C-2,E-2
24th St. A-2,B-2,C-2,E-2
25th St. A-2,C-2,E-2
27th St. B-2
28th St. A-2,C-1,D-1
29th St. A-2,C-1
30th St. A-1,B-1,C-1
31st St. B-1,D-1
32nd D-1
33rd St. C-1
34th St. C-1
35th St. B-1
36th St. A-1

POINTS OF INTEREST

Standiford Field Airport J-6
Algonquin Park E-1
Boone Park A-3
Central Park D-5
Elliot Park B-1
George Rogers Clark Park F-8
Iroquois Park K-3
Shelby Park D-6
Sheppard Park B-3
South Central Park F-3
Victory Park C-2
Westonia Park A-1
Wyandotte Park I-3

N

Scale of Miles

0 .2 .4 .6

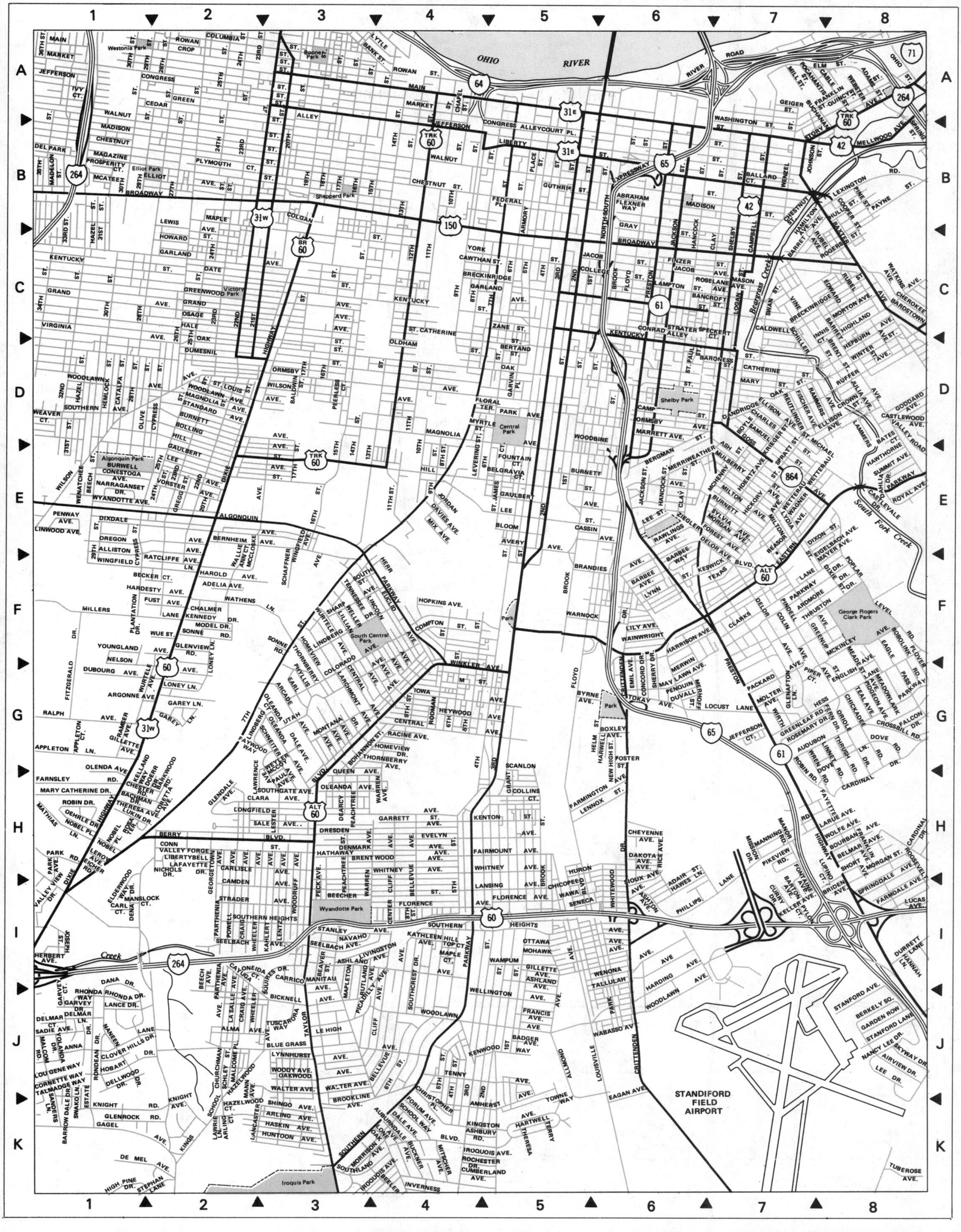

Scale of Miles

0 .1 .2 .3 .4

N

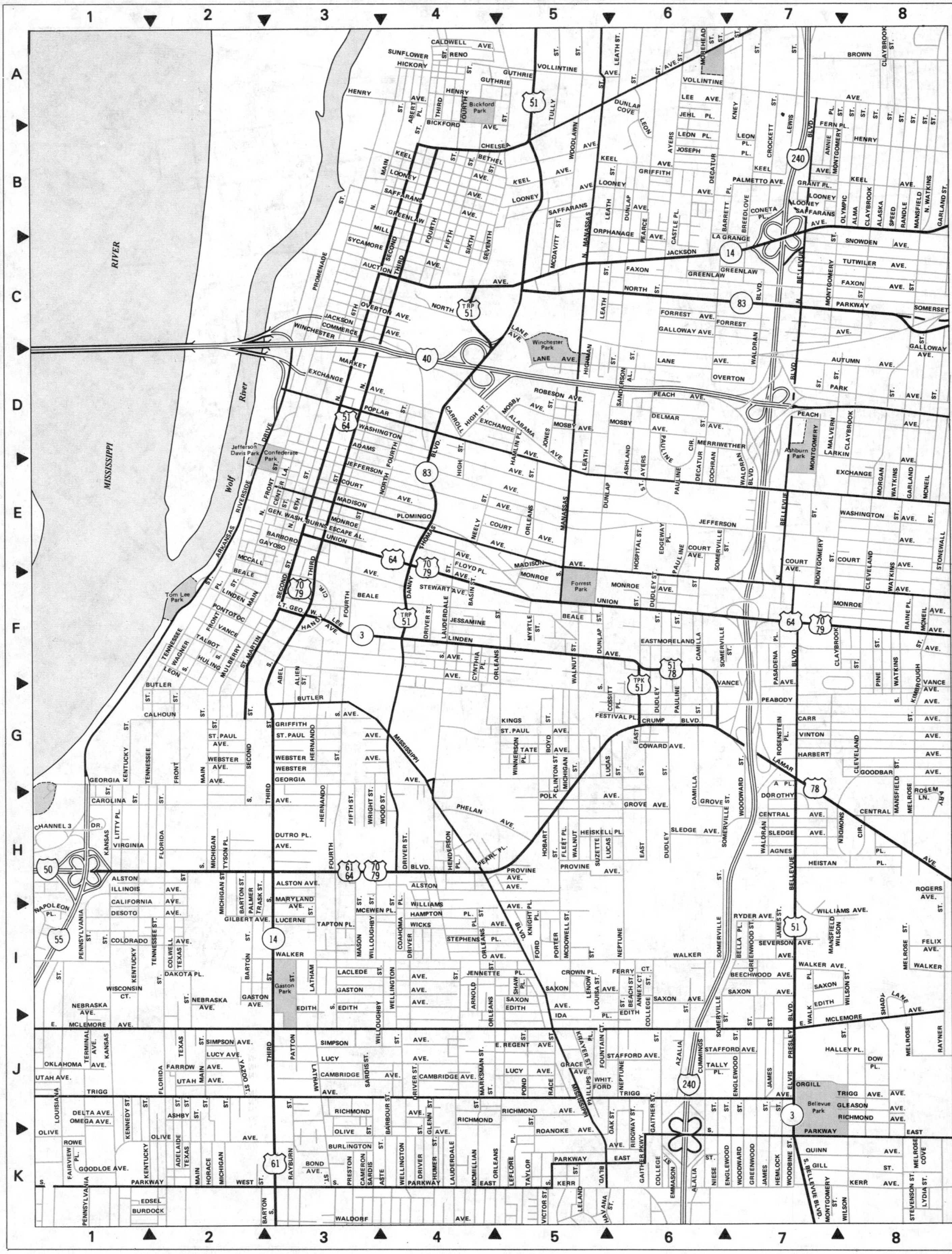

MEMPHIS

A Pl. ... G-7
Abel ... F-3
Abert Pl. ... A-4
Adams Ave. ... D-3
Adolph ... J-3
Agnes Pl. ... H-7
Alien St. ... F-3
Alma St. ... B-8
Alston Ave. ... H-1,H-4
Alabama Ave. ... D-5
Alalia St. ... K-6
Alaska St. ... B-8
Annex Ct. ... I-6
Annie Pl. ... B-7
Arkansas Riverside Dr. ... E-2
Arnold Pl. ... I-4
Ashburn Park ... D-7
Ashby ... J-2
Ashland St. ... D-6
Aste St. ... K-3
Auction Ave. ... C-3
Autumn Ave. ... D-8
Ayers St. ... B-6,E-6
Azalia St. ... J-6
Barboro ... E-3
Barbour St. ... J-4
Barrett Pl. ... B-7
Barton St. ... H-2,K-2
Basin St. ... F-4
Beach St. ... I-6
Beachwood Ave. ... I-7
Beale ... F-2,F-3,F-5
Bellevue Blvd. ... H-7
Bellevue Blvd., N. ... C-7,E-7
Bellevue Blvd., S. ... K-7
Bethel Ave. ... B-4
Bickford Ave. ... A-4
Bond Ave. ... K-3
Boyd St. ... G-5
Breedlove St. ... B-7
Brown Ave. ... A-8
Burdock ... K-1
Burlington Ave. ... K-3,K-5
Butler ... G-1,G-3
Caldwell Ave. ... A-4
Calhoun Ave. ... G-1
California Ave. ... H-1
Cambridge Ave. ... J-3
Cameron ... K-3
Camilla St. ... F-6,H-6
Carolina Ave. ... H-1
Carr Ave. ... G-7
Carroll ... D-4
Castle Pl. ... B-6
Center La. ... E-3
Central Ave. ... H-7,H-8
Channel 3 Dr. ... H-1
Chelsea Ave. ... A-6,B-4
Claybrook St. ... A-8 ... D-8,F-7
Cleveland St. ... F-8
Clinton St. ... G-5
Coahoma Pl. ... I-4
Cochran ... E-6
College St. ... I-6,K-6
Colorado Ave. ... I-1
Colwell ... I-2
Commerce ... C-3
Coneta Pl. ... B-7
Cossitt Pl. ... G-6
Court Ave. ... E-3,E-6,E-8
Coward Ave. ... G-6
Crockett St. ... A-7
Crown Pl. ... I-5
Crump Blvd. ... G-6,H-1
Cummings ... J-6
Cynthia Pl. ... F-4
Dakota Pl. ... I-2
Danny Thomas Blvd. ... E-4
Decatur St. ... B-6,E-6
Delmar Ave. ... D-6
Delta Ave. ... J-1
Desota Ave. ... I-1
Dorothy ... H-7
Dow Pl. ... J-8
Driver St. ... F-4 ... H-4,J-4,K-4
Dudley St. ... F-6,H-6
Dunlap Cove ... A-6
Dunlap St. ... B-6,E-5
Dunlap St., S. ... F-5
Dutro Pl. ... H-3
East St. ... G-6
Eastmoreland Ave. ... F-6
Edgeway Pl. ... E-6
Edith Ave. ... I-3,I-7,J-6
Edsel ... K-1
Elvis Presley Blvd. ... J-7
Emmason St. ... K-6
Englewood St. ... J-7,K-7
Exchange Ave. ... D-3 ... D-5,E-8
Fairview Pl. ... K-1
Farrow Ave. ... J-2
Faxon Ave. ... C-6,C-8
Felix Ave. ... I-8
Fern Pl. ... B-7
Ferry Ct. ... I-6
Festival Pl. ... G-6
Fifth St. ... C-4,H-3
Fleet Pl. ... H-5
Florida St. ... H-2
Floyd Pl. ... E-4
Ford Pl. ... I-5
Forrest Ave. ... C-6
Fountian Ct. ... J-5
Fourth St. ... A-4,B-4
Fourth St., N. ... E-4
Fourth St., S. ... F-3,H-3
Front St. ... G-2
Front St., N. ... E-3
Front St., S. ... F-2
Gaither Pkwy. ... K-6
Gaither St. ... J-6
Galloway Ave. ... C-6,D-8
Garland St. ... B-8,E-8
Gaston Ave. ... I-2,I-3
Gayoso Ave. ... E-3
Gen Wash.-Burns Escape Al. ... E-3
Georgia Ave. ... G-1,G-3
Gilbert Ave. ... I-2
Gill St. ... K-7
Gleason Ave. ... J-8
Glenn St. ... K-4
Goodbar Ave. ... G-8
Goodloe Ave. ... K-1
Grace Ave. ... J-5
Grant Pl. ... B-7
Greenlaw ... B-4,C-6
Greenwood St. ... I-7,K-7
Griffith ... B-6,G-3
Grove Ave. ... H-6
Guthrie Ave. ... A-4
Halley Pl. ... J-7,J-8
Hamlin Pl. ... D-5,E-5
Hampton Pl. ... I-4
Handy Cir. ... F-3
Hanover ... K-1
Harbert Ave. ... G-7
Havana St. ... K-5
Heiskell Pl. ... H-5
Heistan Pl. ... H-7
Hemlock St. ... K-7
Henderson Pl. ... H-4
Henry Ave. ... A-3,B-8
Hernando ... G-3,H-3
Hickory Ave. ... A-4
Highman ... D-5
High St. ... D-4,E-4
Hobart ... H-5
Horace St. ... K-2
Hospital St. ... E-6
Huling ... F-2
Humer St. ... K-4
Ida Pl. ... J-5
Illinois Ave. ... H-1
Jackson Ave. ... C-3,C-6
James St. ... I-7,K-7
Jefferson Ave. ... E-3,E-6
Jehl Pl. ... A-6
Jennette Pl. ... I-4
Jessamine ... F-4
Jones ... D-5
Joseph Pl. ... B-6
Kansas St. ... H-1,J-1
Keel Ave. ... B-4,B-8
Kennedy St. ... K-1
Kentucky St. ... G-1,I-1,K-1
Kerr Ave. ... K-5,K-8
Kings ... G-5
Kiney St. ... A-7
Krayer St. ... J-5
Laclede Ave. ... I-3
La Grange ... C-6,C-7
Lamar Ave. ... G-7
Lane Ave. ... C-5,D-6
Larkin Ave. ... E-8
Latham St. ... I-3,J-3
Lauderdale ... K-4
Lauderdale St., S. ... F-4
Leath St. ... A-6,B-6,E-5
Lee Ave. ... A-6
Leflore Pl. ... K-5
Leland St. ... K-5
Lenow St. ... I-5
Lewis St. ... B-7
Leon ... F-2
Leon Pl. ... B-6,B-7
Leon St. ... B-6
Lt. Geo. W. Lee Ave. ... F-3
Linden Ave. ... F-2,F-4
Litty Pl. ... H-1
Looney Ave. ... B-4,B-7
Lucerne ... I-3
Lucy Ave. ... J-2,J-3,J-5
Lydia St. ... K-8
Madison Ave. ... E-3,E-5
Main St. ... J-2,K-2
Main St., N. ... B-4
Main St., S. ... F-2,G-2
Malvern St. ... D-7
Manassas St., N. ... C-5
Manassas St., S. ... E-5
Mansfield St. ... B-8 ... H-8,I-7
Market ... D-3
Marksman St. ... J-4
Mars Hall Ave. ... E-4,F-5
Maryland Ave. ... H-3
Mason ... I-3
McCall ... E-2
McDavitt St. ... C-5
McDowell St. ... I-5
Mcewen Pl. ... I-3
McLemore Ave., E. ... I-1,J-8
McMillian St. ... K-4
McNeil St. ... E-8,F-8
Melrose Cove ... K-8
Melrose St. ... H-8,J-8
Merriwether ... D-6
Michigan ... G-5
Michigan St. ... H-2,K-2
Mill ... B-4
Mississippi Blvd. ... G-4,J-5
Monroe Ave. ... E-3,F-5,F-8
Montgomery St. ... B-7 ... C-7,E-7,K-7
Morehead St. ... A-6
Morgan ... E-8
Mosby Ave. ... D-5
Mulberry ... F-2
Myrtle St. ... F-5
Napoleon Pl. ... I-1
Nebraska Ave. ... I-1,I-2
Neeley St. ... E-4
Neptune St. ... I-6,J-6
Niese St. ... K-6
North ... C-4
Oklahoma Ave. ... J-1
Olive Ave. ... K-1-3
Olympic St. ... B-8
Omega Ave. ... J-1
Orgill Ave. ... J-7
Orleans St. ... E-5,F-5 ... J-4,K-4
Orphan Ave. ... A-4
Orphanage Ave. ... B-5,C-6
Overton Ave. ... C-3,D-6
Palmer ... I-2
Palmetto Ave. ... B-7
Park Ave. ... D-7
Parkway ... C-6
Parkway East, S. ... K-4,K-8
Parkway West, S. ... K-1
Pasadena Pl. ... F-7
Patton St. ... J-3
Pauline Cir. ... D-6
Pauline St., ... F-6,G-6
Peabody Ave. ... G-7
Peach Ave. ... D-6,D-7
Pearce St. ... C-6
Pearl Pl. ... H-4
Pennsylvania St. ... I-1,K-1
Phelan Ave. ... H-4
Phillips Pl. ... J-5
Pine St. ... G-8
Plomingo ... E-4
Polk Ave. ... H-5
Pond St. ... J-5
Pontotoc Ave. ... F-2
Poplar Ave. ... D-3,E-8
Porter St. ... I-5
Preston ... K-3
Promenade St. ... C-3
Provine Ave. ... H-5
Quinn Ave. ... K-7
Race St. ... J-5
Raine Pl. ... F-8
Randle St. ... B-8
Rayburn St. ... K-3
Rayner St. ... J-8
Regent Ave., E. ... J-5
Reno Ave. ... A-4
Richmond Ave. ... J-3 ... J-5,J-8
Ridgway St. ... K-6
Roanoke Ave. ... K-5
Robeson Ave. ... D-5
Rogers Ave. ... H-8
Rosemary Ln. ... H-8
Rosenstein Pl. ... G-7
Rowe ... K-1
Ryder Ave. ... I-7
Louisa St. ... I-5
Louisiana St. ... J-1
Lucas St. ... G-5,H-5
Saffarans Ave. ... B-4,B-5,B-7
St. Kimbrough St. ... G-8
St. Martin ... F-2
St. Paul Ave. ... G-2,G-5
Sanderson Al. ... D-6
Sardis St. ... J-3,K-3
Saxon Ave. ... I-5,I-7
Second St. ... F-3
Second St., N. ... C-4
Second St., S. ... G-2
Seventh St. ... C-4
Severson Ave. ... I-7
Shady Lane ... I-8
Shaw Pl. ... I-5
Simpson ... J-2,J-3
Sixth St. ... C-4
Sledge Ave. ... H-6,H-7
Snowden Ave. ... C-8
Snowden Cir. ... H-8
Somerset ... C-8
Somerville St. ... E-6 ... F-6,H-6,I-6,J-6
Speed St. ... B-8
Stafford Ave. ... J-6
Stephens Pl. ... I-4
Stevenson St. ... K-8
Stewart Ave. ... F-4
Stonewall ... E-8
Sunflower Ave. ... A-4
Suzette ... H-5
Sycamore Ave. ... C-3
Talbot ... F-2
Tally Pl. ... J-6
Tapton Pl. ... I-3
Tate Ave. ... G-5
Taylor St. ... K-5
Tennessee St. ... F-2 ... G-1,I-2
Terminal Ave. ... J-1
Texas St. ... I-2,K-2
Third St., N. ... A-4,C-4
Third St., S. ... E-3 ... H-3,J-3
Trask St. ... I-2
Trigg Ave. ... J-1,J-8
Tully St. ... A-5
Tutwiler Ave. ... C-8
Tyson Pl. ... H-2
Union Ave. ... E-3,F-5
Utah Ave. ... J-1,J-2
Vance Ave. ... F-2,G-6,G-8
Victor St. ... K-5
Vinton Ave. ... G-7
Virginia Ave. ... H-1
Vollintine Ave. ... A-5,A-6
Wagner Pl. ... F-2
Waldorf Ave. ... K-3
Waldran Blvd. ... D-7 ... E-7,H-7
Walker Ave. ... I-3,I-8
Walk Pl. ... I-7,J-7
Walnut St. ... F-5,H-5
Washington Ave. ... D-3,D-4,E-8
Watkins ... E-8,F-8
Watkins St., N. ... B-8
Watkins, S. ... F-8,G-8
Webster Ave. ... G-2,G-3
Wellington St. ... I-4,K-4
Whitford ... J-5
Wicks Ave. ... I-4
Williams Ave. ... I-4,I-7
Willoughby St. ... J-3
Wilson St. ... I-7,I-8,K-8
Winchester ... C-3
Winnerson Pl. ... G-5
Wisconsin Ct. ... I-1
Woodbine St. ... K-7
Woodlawn St. ... B-5
Wood St. ... H-4
Woodward St. ... H-7,K-7
Wright St. ... H-3
Yazoo St. ... J-2
6th St., N. ... C-3,E-3

POINTS OF INTEREST

Ashburn Park ... D-7
Bellevue Park ... J-7
Bickford Pk. ... A-4
Confederate Park ... D-3
Forrest Park ... F-5
Gaston Park ... I-3
Jefferson Davis Park ... D-2
Tom Lee Park ... F-2
Winchester Park ... C-5

MIAMI

Airport Expwy. ... A-1
Bay Shore Dr., N. ... F-7,G-7
Biscayne Blvd. ... A-6 ... B-6,H-6
Chopin Plaza ... J-7
East-West Expwy. ... G-2,G-5
Flagler St. E. ... I-6
Flagler St. W. ... I-2,I-5
Flagler Ter. ... J-1
Herald Plaza ... F-7,G-7
Julia Tuttle Causeway ... B-8
McArthur Causeway ... G-7,G-8
Miami Ave. N. ... C-5,H-5
Miami Ave. S. ... K-5
Palm ... A-7
River Dr. N.W. ... H-2
River Dr. S. ... H-2
Sabal ... A-7
Venetian Causeway ... F-7,F-8
1st Ave. N.E. ... A-6,H-6
1st Ave. N.W. ... C-5,H-5
1st Ave. S.E. ... J-6
1st Ave. S.W. ... K-5
1st Ct. N.W. ... E-5,F-5
1st Pl. N.W. ... E-5,F-5
1st St. N.E. ... I-6
1st St. N.W. ... I-2,I-5
1st St. S.E. ... J-6
1st St. S.W. ... J-2
2nd Ave. N.E. ... A-6,D-6,H-6
2nd Ave. N.W. ... C-4,H-5
2nd Ave. S.E. ... K-6
2nd Ave. S.W. ... K-5
2nd St. N.E. ... I-6
2nd St. N.W. ... I-2,I-4,I-5
2nd St. S.E. ... J-6
2nd St. S.W. ... J-2
3rd Ave. N.W. ... H-4
3rd Ave. S.E. ... J-6
3rd Ave. S.W. ... K-4
3rd St. N.E. ... I-6
3rd St. N.W. ... I-2,I-4,I-5
3rd St. S.E. ... J-6
3rd St. S.W. ... J-2
4th Ave. N.W. ... C-4,F-4 ... G-4,H-4
4th Ave. S.W. ... J-4
4th St. N.E. ... I-6
4th St. N.W. ... I-2,I-4,I-5
4th St. S.E. ... J-6
4th St. S.W. ... J-2,J-5
5th Ave. N.W. ... C-4,F-4,H-4
5th Ave. S.W. ... J-4
5th Pl. N.W. ... E-3
5th St. N.E. ... H-6
5th St. N.W. ... H-3,H-5,I-2
5th St. S.E. ... K-6
5th St. S.W. ... J-2
6th Ave. N.W. ... C-3,I-3
6th Ave. S.W. ... J-3
6th St. N.W. ... H-2,H-3,H-5
6th St. S.E. ... K-6
6th St. S.W. ... K-2,K-4
7th Ct. ... C-3,D-3
7th Ave. N.W. ... C-3,H-3,I-3
7th Ave. S.W. ... J-3
7th Pl. ... C-3,D-3
7th Ct. S.W. ... J-3
7th St. N.E. ... H-6
7th St. N.W. ... H-2 ... H-3,H-5
7th St. S.E. ... K-6
7th St. S.W. ... K-2,K-5
8th Ave. N.W. ... A-2 ... C-3,F-3,I-3
8th Ave. S.W. ... J-3
8th Ct. S.W. ... J-3,K-3
8th St. N.E. ... H-6
8th St. N.W. ... H-2,H-3,H-5
8th St. S.E. ... K-6
8th St. S.W. ... K-2,K-5
8th St. Rd. N.W. ... G-2
9th Ave. ... H-3
9th Ave. N.W. ... B-2,F-2,I-2
9th Ave. S.W. ... J-2
9th Ct. N.W. ... H-2
9th St. N.E. ... H-6
9th St. N.W. ... H-5
9th St. S.E. ... K-6
9th St. S.W. ... K-2,K-5
10th Ave. ... H-2
10th Ave. N.W. ... A-2 ... C-2,G-2,I-2
10th Ave. S.W. ... J-2
10th Ct. ... E-2,H-2
10th St. N.W. ... G-3,G-5
11th Ave. ... G-2
11th Ave. N.W. ... C-2,I-2
11th Ave. S.W. ... J-2
11th Ct. ... C-2,E-2,H-2
11th Pl. ... C-2
11th St. N.E. ... G-6
11th St. N.W. ... G-2 ... G-3,G-5
11th St. Rd. N.W. ... G-3
12th Ave. N.W. ... B-1 ... C-1,I-1
12th Ave. S.W. ... J-1
12th Ct. ... H-1
12th St. N.E. ... G-6
12th St. N.W. ... G-3 ... G-4,G-5
13th Ave. N.W. ... A-1 ... C-1,I-1
13th Ave. S.W. ... J-1
13th Ct. N.W. ... F-1,H-1
13th St. N.E. ... G-6
13th St. N.W. ... G-3,G-5
14th Ave. N.W. ... A-1 ... C-1,F-1,I-1
14th Ave. S.W. ... J-1
14th Ct. N.W. ... H-1
14th St. N.E. ... G-6
14th St. N.W. ... G-1,G-5
14th Ter. ... F-1,F-2,F-4
15th Ave. N.W. ... C-1,I-1
15th Ave. S.W. ... J-1
15th St. ... F-1
15th St. N.E. ... F-6
15th St. N.W. ... F-3,F-5
15th St. Rd. ... E-1
15th Ter. ... F-6
16th St. ... F-1,F-2
16th St. N.E. ... F-6
16th St. N.W. ... F-5
17th St. N.E. ... F-6
17th St. N.W. ... F-3-5
17th Ter. N.E. ... F-6
18th St. N.E. ... E-6
18th St. N.W. ... F-3,F-5
18th Ter. ... H-1
18th Ter. N.W. ... E-3
19th St. N.E. ... E-6
19th St. N.W. ... E-1,E-3-5
19th Ter. N.E. ... E-6
20th St. N.E. ... E-6
20th St. N.W. ... E-2,E-4
20th Ter. N.E. ... E-6
21st St. N.E. ... E-6
21st St. N.W. ... E-2,E-5
22nd Ln. N.W. ... D-4
22nd St. N.E. ... D-6
22nd St. N.W. ... D-2,E-4
22nd Ter. N.W. ... D-2,D-4
23rd St. N.E. ... D-7
23rd St. N.W. ... D-2,D-4
24th St. N.E. ... D-6
24th St. N.W. ... D-2,D-4
25th St. N.E. ... D-6
25th St. N.W. ... D-2,D-4
26th St. N.E. ... D-6
26th St. N.W. ... D-2,D-4
27th St. N.E. ... D-6
27th St. N.W. ... D-2
27th Ter. ... D-4
28th St. N.E. ... C-6
28th St. N.W. ... C-2,C-4
29th St. N.E. ... C-6
29th St. N.W. ... C-2,C-4
29th Ter. N.W. ... C-2
30th St. N.E. ... C-6
30th St. N.W. ... C-2-4
31st St. N.E. ... C-6
31st St. N.W. ... C-2,C-4
32nd St. N.E. ... C-6
32nd St. N.W. ... C-1,C-3,C-4
33rd St. N.E. ... B-7
33rd St. N.W. ... B-1,C-4
34th St. N.E. ... B-7
34th St. N.W. ... B-1,B-3-5
34th Ter. ... B-5
35th St. N.E. ... B-6
35th St. N.W. ... B-1,B-3-4
35th Ter. N.E. ... B-6
36th St. N.E. ... B-6
36th St. N.W. ... B-2,B-4
37th St. N.W. ... B-2,B-4
38th St. N.E. ... B-6,B-7
38th St. N.W. ... B-2,B-5
39th St. N.E. ... A-6,A-7
39th St. N.W. ... A-2,A-4
40th St. N.E. ... A-6
40th St. N.W. ... A-2,A-4
41st St. N.E. ... A-6
41st St. N.W. ... A-2,A-4
42nd St. N.E. ... A-6
42nd St. N.W. ... A-2,A-4
43rd St. N.E. ... A-6
43rd St. N.W. ... A-2,A-4
44th St. N.E. ... A-6
44th St. N.W. ... A-2,A-4

POINTS OF INTEREST

Bay Front Park ... I-7
Moore Park ... B-2

Scale of Miles
0 .1 .2 .3 .4

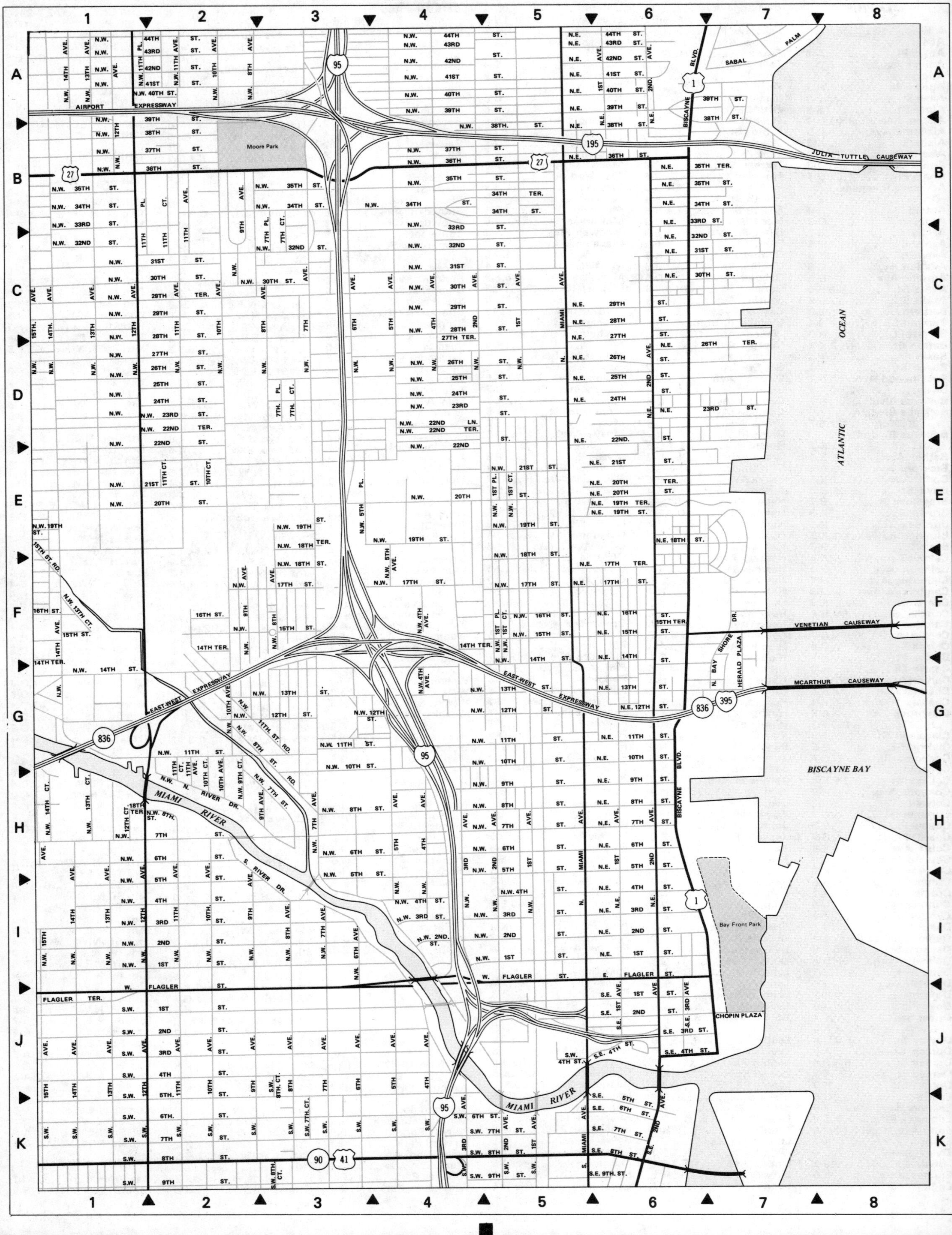

Scale of Miles 0 .2 .4 .6 .8

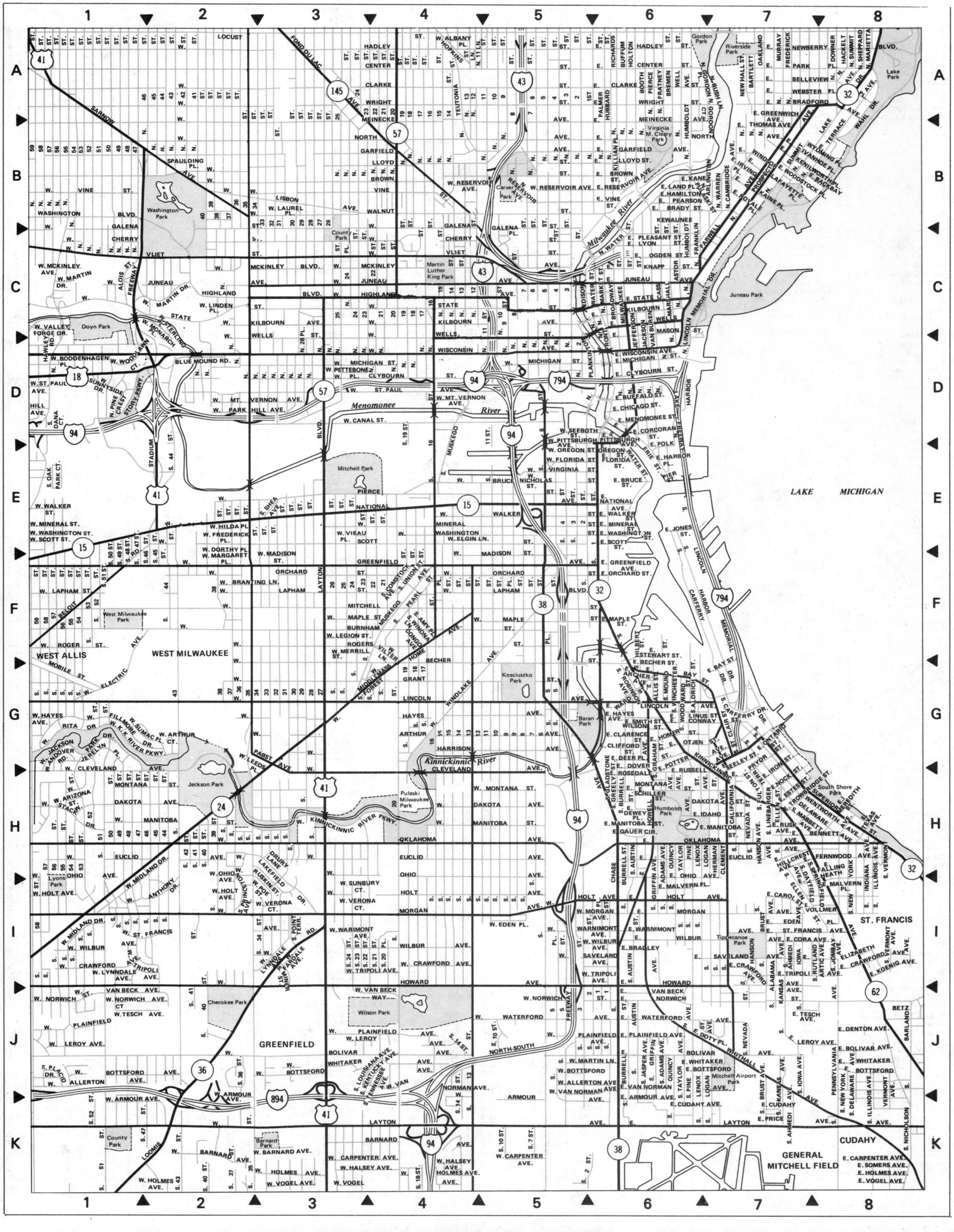

MILWAUKEE

Adams Ave., S...H-6,J-6
Ahmedi Ave., S...I-7,K-7
Alabama Ave., S...I-7
Albany Pl., W...A-4
Aldrich St., S...G-6
Allerton Ave., W...J-1,J-5
Allis St., S...G-6
Alois St...C-1
Amy Pl., S...F-4
Andover Rd., W...G-1
Anthony Dr., W...I-2
Archer Ave., E...G-6
Arizona St., W...H-1
Arlington...B-7
Armour Ave., E...K-6
Armour Ave., W...J-1,K-1,K-5
Arthur Ave., W...G-4
Arthur Ct., W...G-2
Artic Ave...I-8
Astor St., N...C-6
Austin St., S...H-6,I-6,J-6
Backbay, E...B-8
Barland Ave., S...J-8
Barnard Ave., W...K-2,K-3,K-4
Bartlett, N...A-7
Bay St., E...G-6,G-7
Becher St., E...G-6
Becher St., W...F-4,G-4
Belleview, E...A-7
Beloit Rd...F-1
Bennett Ave., E...H-8
Betz...J-8
Blue Mound Rd., W...D-2
Boddenhagen Pl., W...D-1
Bolivar Ave., E...J-6,J-8
Bolivar Ave., W...J-3
Bombay Ave., S...I-8
Booth St., N...A-6
Bottsford, E...J-6,J-8
Bottsford Ave., W...J-1,J-3,J-5
Bradford Ave., E...A-7
Bradley Ave., E...I-6
Brady St., E...B-6
Branting Ln., W...F-2
Bremen St., N...A-6
Broadway St., N...C-6
Brown St., E...B-6
Brown St., W...B-4
Bruce St., E...E-6
Bruce St., W...E-5
Brust Ave., S...I-7,J-7
Buffalo St., E...D-6
Buffum St., N...A-6
Burnham St., W...F-3
Burrell St., S...H-6,J-6
Bush Ln., N...A-7
California St., S...H-7
Cambridge, N...B-7
Canal St., W...D-3
Carferry Dr., S...F-6,G-7
Carol St., E...I-7
Carpenter Ave., E...K-8
Carpenter Ave., W...K-3,K-5
Cass, N...C-6
Center St., E...A-6
Center St., W...A-4
Chase Ave., S...H-6
Cherry St., W...C-1,C-4
Chicago St., E...D-6
Clarence St., E...G-6
Clark St., E...A-6
Clarke St., W...A-4
Clement Ave., S...H-7
Cleveland Ave., W...G-1,H-4
Clifford St., E...G-6
Clybourn St., E...D-6
Clybourn St., W...D-4
Comstock Ave., S...F-4
Congo Ave...F-4
Conway St., E...G-6
Cora Ave., E...I-7
Corcoran St., E...D-6
Crawford Ave., E...I-7,I-8
Crawlford Ave., W...I-1,I-4
Cudahy Ave., E...K-6,K-7
Dakota Ave., W...H-1,H-5
Dakota St., E...H-7
Dana Ct., S...D-1
Dayfield St., S...I-7
Deer Pl., E...G-6
Delaware Ave., S...H-7,H-8,J-8,K-8
Denton Ave., E...J-8
Dewey Pl., E...H-6
Dorothy Pl., W...E-2
Doty Pl., E...J-7
Dover St., E...G-6
Downer, N...A-8
Drury Lane...H-3
Eden Pl., E...I-7
Eden Pl., W...I-5
Edison, N...C-5
Electric Ave., W...G-1
Elgin Ln., W...E-4
Elizabeth...I-8
Ellen St., S...H-7,I-7
Erie St., E...E-6
Estes St., E...H-7
Euclid Ave., E...H-6,H-7
Euclid Ave., W...H-1,H-4
Falling Heath, E...H-8
Fardale Ave., W...I-3
Farwell Ave., N...C-7
Fernwood Ave., E...H-8
Fillmore Dr., W...G-1
Florida St., E...E-6
Florida St., W...E-5
Fond Du Lac Ave...A-3
Forest Home Ave., W...F-4,G-4
Franklin, N...C-6
Fratney St., N...A-6
Frederick, N...A-7
Frederick Pl., W...E-2
Front St., N...D-6
Fulton St., S...H-7
Galena Pl...C-5
Galena St., W...B-1,B-4
Garfield Ave., E...B-6
Garfield Ave., W...B-4
Gauer Cir., E...H-6
Gladstone, S...H-6
Gordon Ct., N...A-7
Gordon Pl., N...A-7,B-7
Graham St., S...D-6,G-6
Grant St., W...G-4
Greeley St., S...H-6
Greenfield Ave., E...F-6
Greenfield Ave., W...F-4
Greenwich Ave., E...A-7
Griffin Ave., S...I-6,J-6
Hackelt, N...A-8
Hadley St., E...A-6
Hadley St., W...A-4
Halsey Ave., W...K-3,K-4
Hamilton, E...B-6
Hansen Ave., S...H-7
Harbor, N...D-6
Harbor Dr., S...F-7
Harbor Pl., E...E-6
Harrison Ave., W...G-4
Hawley Rd...D-1
Hayes Ave., E...G-6
Hayes Ave., W...G-1,G-4
Herman St., S...H-7
Highland Blvd...C-2,C-4
Hilbert St., S...F-6
Hilda Pl., W...E-2
Hill Ave...D-1
Hillcrest Ave., E...H-7
Holmes Ave., E...K-8
Holmes Ave., W...K-2,K-3,K-4
Holt Ave., W...I-1,I-2,I-4,I-6
Holton St., N...A-6
Homer St., E...G-6
Hopkins, W...A-4
Howard Ave., E...I-6
Howell Ave., S...H-6
Howard Ave., W...I-4
Hubbard St., N...A-6
Humboldt Blvd, N...A-6,B-6,C-6
Illinois Ave., S...K-8
Indiana Ave., S...I-8
Iowa Ave., S...I-7,J-7
Iron St., E...H-7
Irving Ave., E...B-7
Ivanhoe Pl...B-8
Jackson St., N...C-6
Jackson Park Dr., W...G-1
Jasper Ave., S...J-6
Jefferson St., N...C-6
Jerelyn Pl...G-1
Jones St., E...E-6
Juneau Ave., E...C-6
Juneau Ave., W...C-2,C-4
Kaine Pl., E...B-7
Kane, E...B-6
Kansas Ave., S...J-7
Kenilworth Pl., E...B-7,B-8
Kentucky Ave., S...J-4
Kewaunee...B-6
Kilbourn Ave., E...C-6
Kilbourn Ave., W...C-3,C-4
Kinnickinnic River Pkwy., W...G-1,H-3
Kinnickinnic Ave., S...G-7,H-7
Knapp St., E...C-6
Koenig Ave., E...I-8
La Fayette Pl., E...B-7
Lake Dr., N...B-8
Lake Freeway...D-6
Lakefield Dr., W...H-3
Land Pl., E...B-6
Lapham St., W...F-1,F-3,F-5
Laurel Pl., W...B-3
Layton Ave., E...K-7
Layton Blvd...F-3
Leeds Pl., W...G-2
Legion St., W...F-3
Lenox St., S...H-6,J-6
Leroy Ave., E...J-7
Le Roy Ave., W...J-1,J-3
Lincoln Ave., E...G-6
Lincoln Ave., W...G-4
Lincoln Memorial Dr. N...C-6
Lincoln Memorial Dr. S...F-7
Linden Pl., W...C-2
Linebarger Terr., S...H-7
Linus St., E...G-6
Lisbon Ave., W...B-3
Lloyd Ave., W...B-4
Lloyd St., E...B-6
Locust St., W...A-2
Logan Ave., S...H-7,J-7
Loomis Rd...K-2
Louisiana Ave., S...J-4
Lynndale Ave., W...I-1,I-3
Lyon St., E...C-6
Mabbett Ave., S...H-7,H-8
Madison St., W...F-5
Malvern Pl., E...I-6,I-8
Manitoba St., E...H-6,H-7
Manitoba St., W...H-2,H-5
Maple St., E...F-6
Mapel St., W...F-3,F-5
Marietta, N...A-8
Market St., N...C-6
Marshall St., N...C-6
Martin Dr., W...C-1,C-2
Martin Ln., W...J-5
Mason St., E...C-6
McKinley Blvd., W...C-3,C-4
McKinley Ave., w...C-1
Meinecke Ave., E...B-6
Meinecke Ave., W...A-4
Meinecke St., E...A-6
Menomonee St., E...D-6
Meredith St., E...H-8
Merrill St., W...F-3
Michigan St., E...D-6
Michigan St., W...D-3,D-5
Middlemass, W...G-4
Midland Dr., W...H-2,I-1
Milwaukee St., N...C-6
Miner St., S...I-3
Mineral St., E...E-6
Mineral St., W...E-1,E-4
Mitchell St...F-3
Mobile St...G-1
Monarch Pl...W...C-2
Montana St., E...H-6
Montana St., W...H-1,H-5
Morgan Ave., W...I-4,I-6
Mound, S...G-6
Mt. Vernon Ave., W...D-3,D-4
Murray, N...A-7
Muskego Ave., S...E-4,F-4
National Ave...E-4
National Ave., E...E-6
New Hall St., N...A-7
Newberry Blvd., E...A-7
New York, S...I-8,J-8
Nevada St., S...H-7,J-7
Nicholas St., W...E-5
Nicholson, S...K-8
Nock St., E...H-7
North Ave., E...B-6
North Ave., W...B-4
North-South Frwy...J-5
Norwich Ave., W...J-1
Norwich Ct., W...J-1
Norwich St., E...J-6
Norwich St., W...J-1,J-5
Oak Park Ct., S...E-1
Oakland, N...A-7
Ogden St., E...C-6
Ohio Ave., E...I-6
Ohio Ave., W...H-1,H-2,H-4
Oklahoma Ave., E...H-6
Oklahoma Ave., W...H-4
Ontario St., E...G-7
Orchard St., E...F-6
Orchard St., W...F-3,F-5
Oregon St., E...E-6
Oregon St., W...E-5
Otjen St., E...G-6
Pabst Ave., S...G-3
Palmer St., N...A-6
Park Pl., E...A-7
Park Hill Ave., W...D-2
Pearl St., S...F-4
Pearson, E...B-6
Pennsylvania Ave., S...J-8
Petibone Pl., W...D-3
Pier St...E-6
Pierce St...E-4
Pierce St., N...A-6
Pine Ave., S...H-6,J-6
Pine Crest, N...D-1
Pittsburgh Ave., W...D-5,D-6
Placid Dr., S...J-1
Plainfield Ave., E...J-6
Plainfield Ave., W...J-1,J-3,J-4,J-5
Plankinton, N...D-6
Pleasant St., E...C-6
Poe St., W...I-3
Point Terr., S...I-3
Polk, E...E-6
Potter Ave., E...G-6
Price Ave., E...K-7
Princeton Ave., S...I-2
Prospect Ave., N...B-7
Pryor St...H-7
Pryor St., E...G-7
Pulaski St., N...B-6
Quincy Ave., S...H-6,J-6
Reservoir Ave., E...B-6
Reservoir Ave., N...B-5
Reservoir Ave., W...B-4
Richards St., N...A-6
Rita Dr., W...G-1
Robinson, S...G-6
Rogers St., W...F-1,F-3
Rosedale, E...H-6
Royale Pl., E...B-7
Rusk Ave., E...H-7
Ruskin St...I-3
Ruskin St., W...H-3
Russell, E...H-6
Rutland, S...H-8
St. Clair St., S...G-7
St. Francis Ave...I-7
St. Francis Ave., W...I-1,I-2
St. Paul Ave., W...D-1,D-4
Sarnow Ave...A-1
Saveland Ave., E...I-7
Saveland Ave., W...I-6
Schiller St., E...H-6
Scott St., E...E-6
Scott St., W...E-1,E-4
Seeboth St., W...D-5
Seeley St., E...G-7
Shea Ave., S...E-3
Sheppard, N...A-8
Smith St., E...G-6
Somers Ave., E...K-8
Spaulding Pl...B-2
Springfield, S...I-8
Stadium Frwy...C-1,E-2
Stark Dr., W...H-1
State St., E...C-6
State St., W...C-2,C-4
Sterling Pl., W...C-2
Stewart St., E...F-6
Story Pkwy...D-1
Sumac Pl., W...G-2
Summit Ave., N...A-8,B-7
Sunbury Ct., W...I-3
Sunnyside Dr., W...D-1
Superior St., S...H-8
Taylor Ave., S...H-6,J-6
Tennessee Ave., S...J-4
Terrace Ave., N...B-8
Tesch Ave., E...J-7
Tesch Ave., W...J-1
Teutonia St., N...A-4
Texas Ave., E...H-8
Thomas Ave., E...B-7
Tripoli Ave., E...I-7
Tripoli Ave., W...I-1,I-3,I-6
Trowbridge St., E...H-7
Union St., S...F-4
Valley Forge Dr., W...C-1
Van Beck Ave., E...J-6
Van Beck Ave., W...J-1,J-3
Van Buren St., N...C-6
Van Norman Ave., E...J-6
Van Norman Ave., W...J-4,J-5
Vermont, S...H-8,I-8,J-8
Verona Ct., W...I-3
Vieau Pl., W...E-3
Vilter Ln., W...F-4
Virginia St., W...E-5
Vine St., E...B-6
Vine St., W...B-1,B-4
Vliet St., W...C-2,C-4
Vogel Ave., E...K-8
Vogel Ave., W...K-3
Vollmer, E...I-8
Wahl Dr...B-8
Walker St., E...E-6
Walker St., W...E-1,E-5
Walnut St., W...B-4
Ward St...G-6
Warnimont Ave., E...I-6
Warnimont Ave., W...I-3,I-6
Warren N...B-7
Washington Blvd., W...B-1
Washington St., E...E-6
Washington St., W...E-1,E-4
Water St., N...C-6
Water St., S...E-6
Waterford Ave., E...J-6
Waterford Ave., W...J-5
Webster Pl., E...A-7
Wells St., E...C-6
Wells St., N...A-6
Wells St., W...C-3,C-4
Wentworth Ave., S...H-8
Whitaker Ave., E...J-6,J-8
Whitthall Ave., S...J-7
Wilbur Ave., E...I-6
Wilbur Ave., W...I-1,I-4,I-6
Wilson St...G-6
Winchester, S...G-6
Windlake Ave., W...G-4
Windsor, E...B-7
Winona Ln., S...F-4
Wisconsin Ave., E...D-6
Woodlawn Ct., W...D-1
Woodstock Pl., E...B-7
Woodward St., S...G-6
Wright St., E...A-6
Wright St., W...A-4
Wyoming Pl...B-6
1st Pl., S...J-6
1st St., N...A-6
1st St., S...J-6
2nd St., N...A-5,D-5
2nd St., S...E-5,J-6,K-5
3rd St., N...A-5,C-4
3rd St., S...E-5,J-5
4th St., N...A-5,C-5
4th St., S...E-5
5th Pl., S...G-5,J-5
5th St., N...A-5,C-5
5th St., S...G-5,J-5
6th St., N...A-5,C-5
6th St., S...D-5,G-5
7th St., N...A-5,C-5
7th St., S...G-5,K-5
8th St., N...A-5,C-5
8th St., S...G-5
9th Pl., S...G-5
9th St., N...A-5,C-5
9th St., S...G-5
10th St., N...A-5,C-5
10th St., S...G-5,K-5
11th Ln., N...A-5
11th St., N...A-5,C-5
11th St., S...D-5,G-5
12th Ln., N...A-4
12th St., N...C-4
12th St., S...G-5
13th St., N...A-4,C-4
13th St., S...G-4,J-4
14th St., N...A-4,C-4
14th St., S...G-4,J-4
15th St., N...A-4,C-4
15th St., S...G-4
16th St., N...A-4,C-4
16th St., S...G-4
17th St., N...A-4,C-4
17th St., S...G-4
18th St., N...A-4,C-4
18th St., S...G-4,K-4
19th St., N...A-4,C-4
19th St., S...D-4,G-4
20th St., N...A-4,C-4
21st St., N...A-4,C-4
21st St., S...F-4,I-4
22nd St., N...A-4,C-4
22nd St., S...F-4,I-3
23rd St., N...A-4,C-3
23rd St., S...F-3,I-3
24th Pl., N...C-3
24th St., N...A-3,C-3
24th St., S...F-3,I-3
25th St., N...A-3,C-3
25th St., S...F-3
26th St., N...B-3
26th St., S...F-3
27th St., N...B-3
28th Pl., N...D-3
28th St., N...B-3
28th St., S...G-3
29th St., N...B-3
29th St., S...G-3
30th St., N...B-3
30th St., S...G-3
31st St., N...B-3
31st St., S...G-3
32nd St., N...B-3
32nd St., S...G-3
33rd St., N...B-3
33rd St., S...G-3
34th St., N...B-3
34th St., S...G-3,I-3
35th St., N...B-2
35th St., S...G-2
36th St., N...B-2
36th St., S...G-2,J-2
37th St., N...B-2
37th St., S...G-2,K-2
38th St., N...B-2
38th St., S...F-2,G-2
39th St., N...B-2
39th St., S...H-2
40th St., N...B-2
40th St., S...H-2,J-2,K-2
41st St., N...A-2
41st St., S...H-2,J-2
42nd St., N...A-2
42nd St., S...H-2
43rd St., N...A-2
43rd St., S...G-2,K-2
44th St., N...A-2
44th St., S...E-2,F-2,H-2
45th St., N...A-2
45th St., S...E-2,H-2
46th St., N...A-2
46th St., S...E-2,H-2
47th St., N...B-1
47th St., S...E-1,H-1,K-1
48th St., N...B-1
48th St., S...B-1
49th St., N...B-1
49th St., S...E-1,H-1
50th St., N...B-1
50th St., S...E-1,H-1
51st St., N...B-1
51st St., S...F-1,H-1,K-1
52nd St., N...B-1
52nd St., S...F-1,H-1,K-1
53rd St., N...B-1
53rd St., S...F-1,H-1
54th St., N...B-1
54th St., S...F-1,H-1
55th St., N...B-1
55th St., S...F-1,H-1
56th St., N...B-1
56th St., S...F-1,H-1
57th St., N...B-1
57th St., S...F-1,H-1
58th St., N...B-1
58th St., S...F-1,I-1
59th St., N...B-1
59th St., S...F-1

POINTS OF INTEREST

Baran Park...G-5,G-6
Barnard Park...K-3
Carver Park...B-5
Cherokee Park...J-2
County Park...C-3
County Park...K-1
Doyn Park...C-1
Grodon Park...A-6
Humboldt Park...H-6
Jackson Park...H-2
Juneau Park...C-7
Kosciuszko Park...G-5
Lake Park...A-8
Lyons Park...I-1
Martin Luther King Park...C-4
Mitchell Airport Park...J-7
Mitchell Park...E-3
Pulaski Milwaukee Park...H-4
Riverside Park...A-7
South Shore Park...H-8
Tippecanoe Park...I-7
Virginia M. Cleary Park...B-6
Washington Park...B-2
West Milwaukee Park...F-1
Wilson Park...J-4

MINNEAPOLIS

Aldrich...B-3
Aldrich Ave. S...E-3,I-3
Arthur Ave...D-8
Bedford St...D-8
Belmont...I-3
Blaisdell Ave...E-3,H-3
Bloomington...E-5
Bloomington Ave...J-5
Border Ave...B-3
Bossen Ter...K-7
Bradford...B-3
Bryant Ave. N...B-2
Bryant Ave. S...D-2,J-2
Calhoun Pkwy...G-2
Cecil St...D-8
Cedar Ave...F-6,J-6
Cedar Lake Rd...C-1
Central Ave...B-5
Chateau Pl...J-5
Chestnut Ave...C-1,C-3
Chicago...C-4
Chicago Ave...E-5,H-4,K-4
Clarence...D-8
Clifton...D-3
Clinton Ave...D-4,H-4,K-4
Colfax...C-2
Colfax Ave. S...D-2,J-2
Columbus Ave...E-4,H-4
Como Ave...B-7
Currie Ave...B-3
Delaware...C-7
Diamond Lake Rd...J-3
Dight Ave...F-7
Dorman Ave...E-8
Douglas Ave...D-2
Dupont Ave. N...B-2
Dupont Ave. S...D-2,J-2
Edgewater Blvd...J-5
Elm Ave...B-7
Elmwood Pl. W...I-3
Emerson Ave. N...B-2
Emerson Ave. S...D-2,J-2
Erie St. S.E...D-7
Essex St...C-7
Fairmount Ave...B-7
Farwell Ave...A-1
Floyd B. Olson Mem. Hwy...B-2
Franklin Ave. E...D-5
Franklin Ave. W...D-3
Fremont Ave...F-2
Fremont Ave. N...B-2
Fremont Ave. S...D-2,F-2,J-2
Fulton St...C-7
Garfield Ave...E-3,I-3
Girard Ave...F-2
Girard Ave. S...J-2
Girard Ter...B-2
Glenwood Ave...B-2
Grand Ave...E-3,H-3,K-3
Grant St...C-3
Grass Lake...K-2
Groveland Ave...D-3
Groveland Ter...C-2
Harding...A-7
Harmon Pl...C-3
Harriet Ave...E-3,I-3
Harvard...C-7
Hawthorne Ave...C-1,C-3
Hennepin Ave...B-4,E-2,F-2
Hennepin Ave. E...A-7,B-5
Hiawatha Ave...G-7
Holmes...F-2
Hoover St...A-8
Humboldt Ave. N...B-2
Humboldt Ave. S...F-2,K-2
Irving Ave. N...A-2,C-2
Irving Ave. S...F-2,J-2
James Ave. N...A-2,C-2
James Ave. S...F-2,J-2
Kasota Ave...B-8
Keewaydin Pl...I-7
Kennedy St...A-7
Kenwood...D-1
Kenwood Pkwy...C-2,D-1
Knox Ave. N...A-2
Knox Ave. S...J-2
Lagoon Ave...E-2
Lake Pl...E-2
Lake St. E...F-5
Lake St. W...F-2
Lake Harriet Pkwy. E...I-2
Lake Harriet Pkwy. W...H-1
Lakeside Ave...B-3
Lasalle Ave...C-3
Laurel Ave...C-1,C-3
Lincoln Ave...D-2
Linden Ave...C-3
Linden Hill Blvd...H-1
Logan Ave. N...A-2
Logan Ave. S...D-2,J-2
Longfellow Ave...G-6
Luverne Ave...J-4
Lyndale AVe. S...E-3,I-3
Main St. S.E...B-5
Malcom Ave...C-8,D-8
Marquette Ave...C-4
Melbourne Ave...D-8
Minneapolis Ave...D-7
Minnehaha Ave...D-6,F-7
Minnehaha Pkwy...I-5
Mondamin St...J-7
Morgan Ave. N...A-1
Morgan Ave. S...J-1
Mt. Curve Ave...D-2
Newton Ave. N...A-1
Newton Ave. S...D-1,J-1
Nicollet Ave...E-3,H-3
Nokomis Ave...H-7
Nokomis Ct...K-5
Nokomis Ln...K-5
Nokomis Pkwy...J-5
Oak St...C-7
Oak Grove St...D-3
Oakland Ave...E-4,H-4
Oak Park...A-1
Oliver Ave. N...A-1
Oliver Ave. S...D-1,J-1
Ontario St.S.E...D-7
Orlin Ave...D-8
Park Ave...C-4,E-4,H-4
Park Dr...I-2
Penn Ave. N...A-1
Penn Ave. S...D-1,J-1
Pickfield...G-1
Pillsbury Ave...D-3,H-3
Pleasant Ave...E-3,H-3
Pleasant St...C-6
Plymouth Ave. N...A-2
Portland Ave...C-4,E-4,H-4,K-4
Prospect Ave...I-3
Queen Ave. N...A-1
Queen Ave. S...D-1,J-1
River Rd...D-8
River Ter...D-8
Riverside Ave...D-6
Roosevelt...A-7
Royalston...B-3
Russell Ave. N...A-1
Russell Ave. S...K-1
Rustic Lodge Ter...I-3
St. Mary's...C-8
Sander...K-7
Seabury Ave...E-8
Seymour...D-8
Sharon Ave...D-8
Sheridan Ave. N...A-1
Sheridan Ave. S...D-1,K-1
Shore View Ave...J-6
Snelling...D-7
Snelling Ave...F-7
Spring St...A-5,A-8
Stevens Ave...D-4,H-4
Summit Ave...D-2
Sunrise Dr...K-2
Taft St...A-7
Talmadge Ave...A-7
Thomas Ave. N...A-1
Thomas Ave. S...D-1,J-1
University Ave...B-5
University Ave. N.E...A-5
Upton Ave. N...A-1
Upton Ave. S...E-1,J-1
Valley View Pl...J-3
Vincent Ave. N...A-1,C-1
Vincent Ave. S...J-1
Walnut...C-7
Warwick St...D-8
Washburn Ave. N...A-1,C-1
Washburn Ave. S...J-1
Washington Ave. N...A-3
Washington Ave. S.E...C-6
Wayzata...C-2
Weeks...B-8
Weenonan Pl...I-7
Wentworth...H-3,K-3
Williams...D-8
Wilson St...A-7
Winter St...A-6,A-8
Woodlawn Blvd...I-7,J-6
Yale Pl...C-3
Yndale Ave. N...B-3
1st Ave. N...B-4
1st Ave. N.E...A-5
1st Ave. S...E-3,H-3,K-3
1st St. N...A-4
1st St. S...B-5
2nd...F-2
2nd Ave. N...B-1,B-2,B-4
2nd St. N.E...A-5
2nd Ave. S...C-4,D-4
2nd Ave. S.E...B-5
2nd St. N...A-3,A-4
2nd St. S...B-4
2nd St. S.E...B-5
3rd Ave. N...B-1,B-3,B-4
3rd Ave. N.E...A-5
3rd Ave. S...C-4,D-4,H-4
3rd Ave. S.E...B-5
3rd St...A-3
3rd St. N...A-3
3rd St. S...C-5
4th...C-5
4th Ave. N...B-1,B-2
4th Ave. N.E...A-5
4th Ave. S...C-4,E-4,H-4
4th Ave. S.E...B-5
4th St. N...A-3,B-3
4th St. N.E...A-5
4th St. S...C-5,C-6
4th St. S.E...B-5,C-8
5th...C-5
5th Ave. N...B-1-3
5th Ave. N.E...A-4
5th Ave. S...C-4,E-4,H-4
5th Ave. S.E...B-6
5th St. N...A-3,B-3
5th St. N.E...A-5
5th St. S...C-4,C-6
5th St. S.E...B-5
6th...B-3,C-5
6th Ave. N...B-1,B-3
6th Ave. N.E...A-4
6th Ave. S.E...B-6
6th St. N...A-3,B-4
6th St. S...C-4,D-6
6th St. S.E...A-5
7th Ave. N...B-3
7th Ave. N.E...A-4
7th Ave. S.E...B-6
7th St. N...B-3
7th St. S...C-4,D-6
7th St. S.E...B-6
8th...A-3
8th Ave. N...A-1
8th Ave. N.E...A-4
8th Ave. S.E...B-6
8th St. S...C-4,D-7
8th St. S.E...A-6
9th...A-3
9th Ave. S...C-5
9th St. S...C-4
9th St. S.E...A-6
10th Ave...E-5
10th Ave. N...B-3
10th Ave. S...C-5
10th Ave. S.E...B-6
10th St. S...C-4
11th Ave...E-5
11th Ave. S...C-5
11th Ave. S.E...B-6
11th St. S...C-4
12th Ave...E-5
12th Ave. N...A-2
12th Ave. S...C-5
12th Ave. S.E...B-6
12th St. S...C-4
13th...C-4
13th Ave...E-5
13th Ave. S...D-5
13th Ave. S.E...B-6
14th Ave. N...A-2
14th Ave. S...E-5,H-5
14th Ave. S.E...B-7
14th St. E...C-4
14th St. W...C-3
15th...D-5
15th Ave. N...A-2
15th Ave. S...D-5
15th Ave. S.E...B-7
15th St. E...D-4
16th...B-7,C-5
16th Ave. N...A-2
16th Ave. S...D-5
16th Ave. S.E...A-7
16th St. E...D-4
16th St. W...D-3
17th...C-7
17th Ave. S...E-5
17th Ave. S.E...B-7
17th St. E...D-4
18th...C-7
18th Ave. S...E-5,K-5
18th Ave. S.E...B-7
18th St. E...D-4,D-5
19th...C-7
19th Ave. S...D-6,F-6
19th Ave. S.E...B-7
19th St. E...D-5
20th...K-6
20th Ave. S...D-6,F-6
20th Ave. S.E...B-7
21st Ave. S.E...B-7
21st St. E...D-5
21st Ave. S...D-6,F-6
22nd Ave. S...D-6,F-6
22nd Ave. S.E...B-7
22nd St. E...D-5,D-7
22nd St. W...D-2
23rd Ave. S...D-6,F-6
23rd Ave. S.E...B-8
24th...B-8
24th Ave. S...D-6,F-6,K-6
24th Ave.S.E...B-8
24th St. E...D-7,E-5
24th St. W...D-1,D-2
25th...C-7
25th Ave. S...D-6,F-6
25th Ave. S.E...B-8
25th St. E...E-5,E-7
25th St. W...E-2
26th...C-7
26th Ave. S...D-6,G-6
26th Ave. S.E...B-8
26th St. E...E-5,E-7
26th St. W...E-2
27th Ave. S...D-7,G-7,K-7
27th Ave. S.E...B-8,D-7
27th St. E...E-5,E-7
27th St. W...E-2
28th Ave. S...D-7,G-7,K-7
28th St. E...E-5,E-7
28th St. W...E-2
29th...B-8,C8
29th Ave. S...F-7,G-7
29th Ave. S.E...B-8
29th St. E...E-5
29th St. W...E-2
30th...B-8,C-8
30th Ave. S...F-7,G-7
30th Ave. S.E...B-8
31st Ave. S...F-7,H-7
31st St. E...F-5
31st St. W...F-2
32nd Ave. S...F-7,H-7
32nd St. E...F-5
32nd St. W...F-2
33rd Ave. S...F-7,H-7
33rd St. E...F-5
33rd St. W...F-2
34th Ave. S...F-7,H-7
34th St. E...F-5
34th St. W...F-2
35th Ave. S...F-7,H-7
35th St. E...F-5
35th St. W...F-2
36th Ave. S...F-8
36th St. E...G-5
36th St. W...G-2
36½ St. E...G-6
37th Ave. S...F-8
37th St. E...G-5
37th St. W...G-3
38th St. E...G-5
38th St. W...G-1,G-3
38th St. S...F-8,J-8
39th Ave. S...F-8
39th St. E...G-5
39th St. W...G-1,G-3
40th Ave. S...F-8
40th St. E...G-5
40th St. W...G-1,G-3
41st E...H-5
41st Ave. S...F-8
41st St. W...H-1,H-3
42nd E...H-5
42nd Ave. S...F-8,J-8
42nd St. W...H-1,H-3
43rd W...H-1
43rd Ave. S...H-8
43rd St. E...H-5
43rd St. W...H-1,H-3
44th W...H-1
44th Ave. S...H-8
44th St. E...H-5,H-8
44th St. W...H-2
45th W...H-1
45th Ave. S...H-8
45th St. E...H-5,H-8
45th St. W...H-2
46th W...H-1
46th Ave. S...H-8,J-8
46th St. E...H-5,H-8
46th St. W...H-2
47th W...I-1
47th St. E...I-5,I-7
47th St. W...I-2
48th W...I-1
48th St. E...I-5,I-7
48th St. W...I-2
49th W...I-1
49th St. E...I-5,I-7
49th St. W...I-2
50th St. E...I-4,I-7
50th St. W...I-2
51st St. E...I-5,I-7
51st St. W...I-1,I-2
52nd W...J-3
52nd St. E...J-5,J-7
52nd St. W...J-1,J-3
53rd St. E...J-5,J-7
53rd St. W...J-1,J-2
53rd Ter...J-5,J-7
54th St. W...J-3
55th St. E...J-5,J-7
55th St. W...J-3
56th St. E...J-5,J-7
56th St. W...J-3
57th St. E...J-5,J-7
57th St. W...J-2
58th St. E...K-5,K-8
58th St. W...K-3
59th St. E...K-4,K-6,K-8
59th St. W...K-2
59½ St. E...K-7
60th St. E...K-4
60th St. W...K-1,K-3
61st St. E...K-4
61st St. W...K-1,K-3

POINTS OF INTEREST

Bryn Mawr Meadows...C-2
Dorilus Morrison Park...E-4
Dr. Martin Luther King Park...H-3
Elliot Park...C-5
Kenwood Park...D-1
Loring Park...C-3
McRae Park...I-5
Minnehaha Park...I-8
Pearl Park...J-4
Powder Horn Lake Park...F-5

Scale of Miles
0 .2 .4 .6 .8

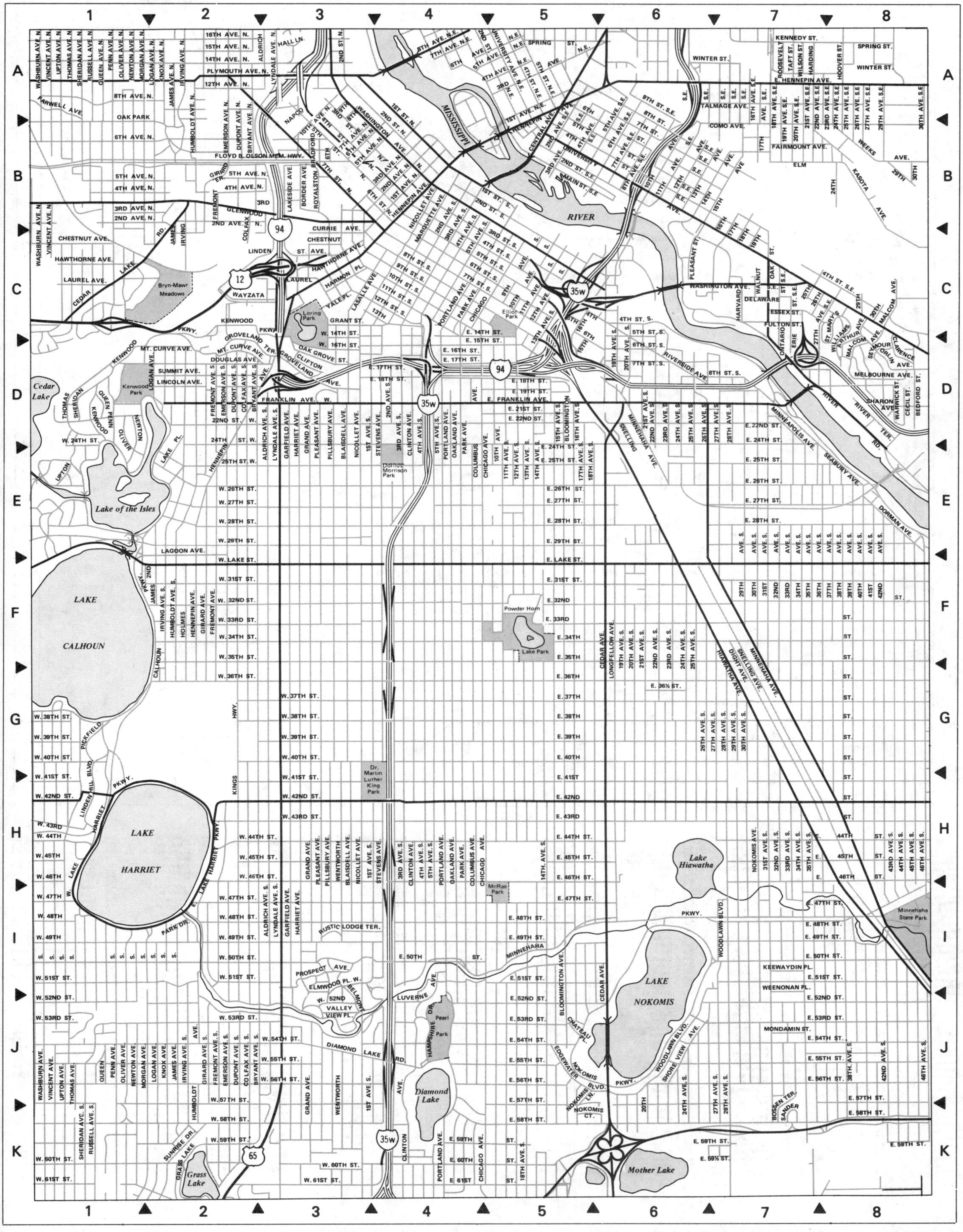

Montgomery, AL

Scale of Miles
0. .1 .2 .3 .4 .5
N

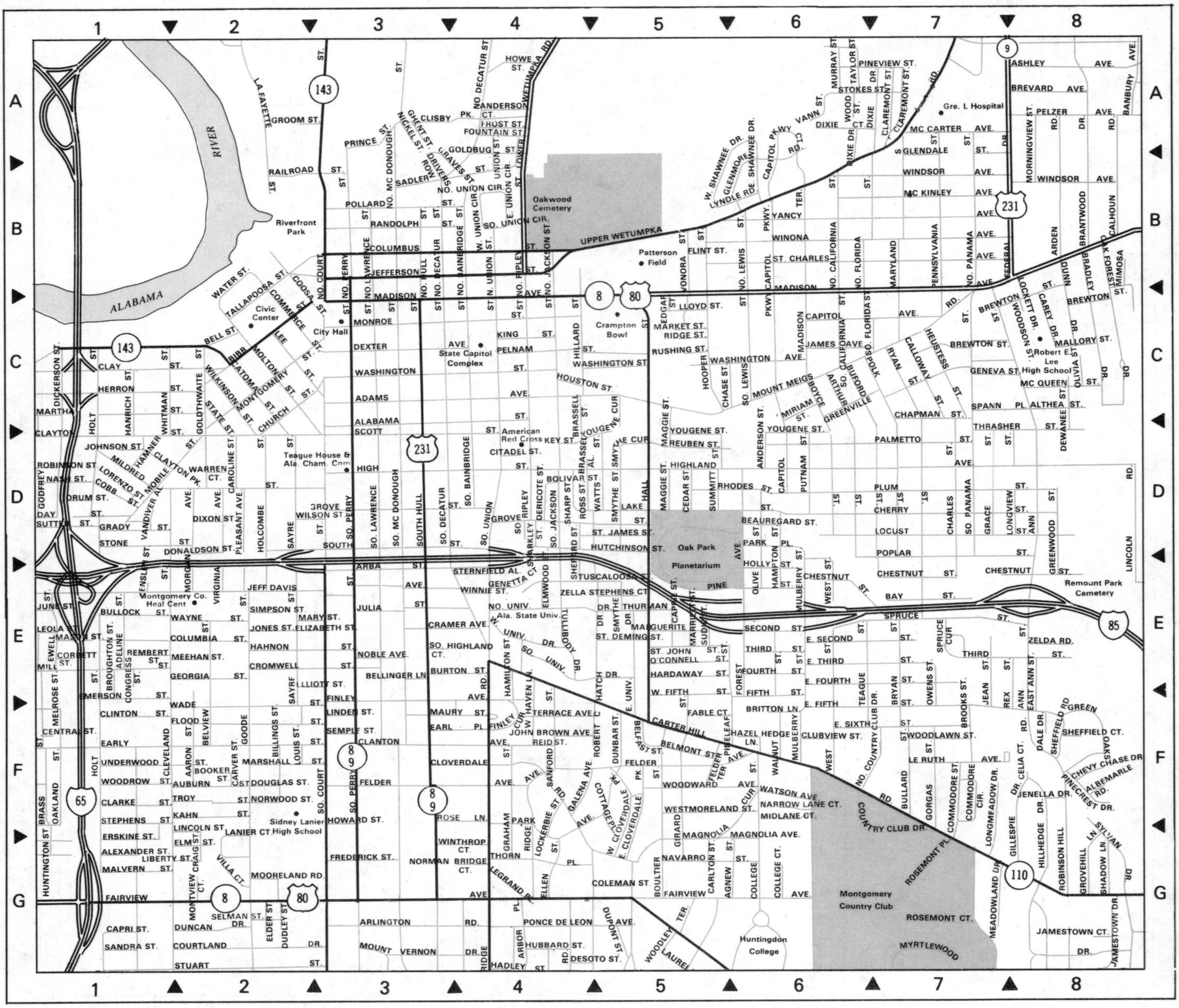

Scale of Miles
0 .2 .4 .6 .8

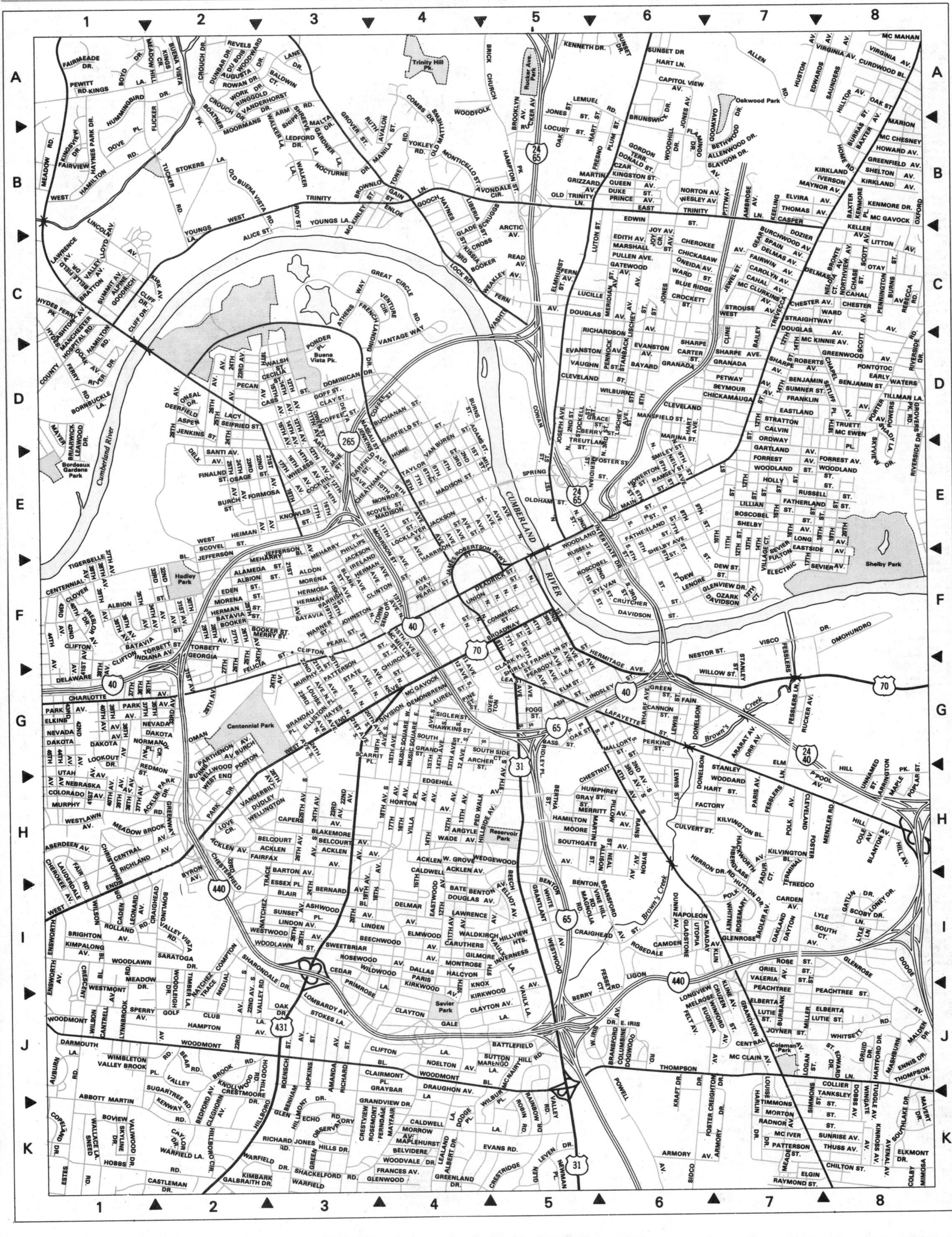

NASHVILLE

Abbott Martin Rd. J-1
Aberdeen Ave. H-1
Acklen Ave. H-2-4
Acklen Park Dr. H-1
Adams St. D-5
Alameda St. F-2
Albert Dr. K-4
Albion St. F-1,F-2
Aldon F-3
Allen Rd. A-7
Allenwood Dr. B-7
Alice St. B-2
Allison H-5
Alpine C-1
Amanda Av. J-3
Ambrose Av. B-7
Ararat Ave. G-6
Archer St. G-4
Arctic Av. B-5
Argyle H-4
Arm Rd. A-3
Armory Ave. K-6
Arrington H-8
Arthur Ave. D-3
Ash St. G-5
Ashton Av. C-1
Ashwood Av. I-3
Aspen D-2
Athens Way C-3
Auburn La. J-1
Augusta Dr. A-2
Avalon St. B-4
Avenal Ave. K-8
Avondale Cir. B-5
Bailey C-7
Baldwin Ct. A-3
Barton Ave. H-3
Bass St. G-5
Batavia F-3
Batavia St. F-1,F-2
Bate I-4
Battlefield J-5
Baxter B-8
Baxgter Av. B-8
Bayard D-6
Bear Rd. J-2
Bedford Av. K-2
Beechwood Av. I-3
Belcourt Ave. H-3
Belle Field Dr. C-1
Bellwood H-2
Belvidere K-4
Benham Av. K-3
Benjamin D-7
Benton I-5
Benton Av. I-4
Bernard Av. I-3
Berry Rd. J-5
Berry St. D-5
Bertha St. H-5
Bethwood Dr. B-7
Beuna Vista Pk. A-2
Blair I-3
Blakemore H-3
Blank St. F-3
Blanton H-8
Blue Ridge C-6
Boatner A-2
Boensch St. J-3
Booker C-4,F-2
Booker St. F-2
Bornbuckle Ln. D-1
Boscobel St. E-7
Boview K-1
Bowling Av. I-2
Boyd Dr. A-1
Brandau Pl. G-3
Bransford Av. I-6,J-6
Bratton C-1
Briarwick D-1
Brick Church Pk. A-5
Brighton Av. I-1
Broadway F-5
Brooklyn Av. A-5
Bronte Av. C-8
Brownlon B-3
Brunswick Dr. A-6
Buchanan St. D-4
Burbank Av. J-7
Burch G-2
Burch St. E-2
Burchwood Av. B-7
Burns Av. G-2
Burns St. C-8,D-4
Burras St. B-8
Byron Ave. H-2,H-6
Caden Dr. I-1
Cahal Av. C-7,C-8
Caldwell H-4
Calvin D-7
Camden I-6
Canaday I-6
Cannon St. G-6
Cantrell Av. I-1
Capers Ave. H-3
Capitol View Av. A-6
Carden Av. I-7
Carolyn Av. C-7
Carter St. D-6
Caruthers I-4
Casper B-7
Cass D-3
Castleman Dr. K-1
Caylor Dr. D-2
Cecilia St. D-3
Cedar Ln. I-3
Centennial Blvd. F-1
Central J-7
Central Ave. H-1
Chapel Av. D-8
Charlotte Av. G-1
Chase St. C-8
Cheatham Pl. E-3
Cherokee Av. C-6,H-1
Chester C-8
Chesterfield H-2
Chestnut St. G-6
Chester Av. C-7
Chickamauga D-7
Chickasaw C-6
Chilton St. K-8
Christopher H-1
Church St. F-4
Cladwell Ln. K-4
Clairmont Pl. J-3
Clay St. D-3
Clayton J-4
Clayton Av. J-4
Cleghorn Av. K-2
Cleveland D-6
Cleveland Ave. H-7
Cleveland St. D-5
Cliff Dr. C-1
Clifton F-1,F-3
Clifton Ln. J-3
Cline C-7
Clinton St. F-3
Clover F-1
Cockrill St. E-3
Coffee St. D-3,D-4
Colby K-8
Cole Ave. H-8
Collier J-4
Colorado Ave. H-1
Columbine J-6
Combs Dr. A-4
Commerce St. F-5
Compton I-2
Copeland Dr. K-1
County Hospital Rd. D-1
Cowan St. D-5
Craighead I-1
Craighead St. I-5
Crescent I-1
Crestmore Dr. J-2
Crestridge Dr. K-5
Crestview K-3
Crockett St. C-6
Cross C-4
Crouch Dr. A-2
Crutcher St. F-6
Cruzen St. J-7
Culvert St. H-6
Curdwood Blvd. A-8
Czar B-6
Dakota Av. G-1
Dakota Pl. G-1
Dallas I-4
Darmouth J-1
Davidson F-7
Davidson St. F-6
Dayton I-7
Deadrick St. F-4
Deerfield D-2
Delaware G-1
Delk Av. E-2
Delmar I-4
Delmas C-7
Delmas Av. C-7
Delta D-3
Demonbrenn St. G-4
Dew F-6
Dew St. F-7
Division G-4
Doak Av. D-1
Dobbs Av. J-8
Dodge I-8
Dodge Pl. I-8
Dogwood J-6
Dominican Dr. D-3
Donald St. B-6
Donelson G-6
Douglas Av. C-5,C-7,I-4
Dove Pl. B-1
Dozier B-7
Draughon Av. J-4
Druid Dr. J-8
DuBois A-2
Dudley H-2
Duke St. B-8
Dunbar Dr. A-2
Dunn Av. I-6
Early D-8
Eastland Av. D-7
Eastside Av. E-7
East Trinity Ln. B-6
Eastwood I-4
Eden St. F-2
Edith Av. C-6
Edwards Av. A-8
Edwin St. B-6
Elberta J-7
Eletric Av. F-7
Elgin K-7
Elkins Av. G-1
Elkmont Dr. K-8
Elliot Av. I-5
Elliston Pl. G-3
Elm St. G-5
Elm Hill G-6
Elmhurst St. C-5
Elmwood I-4
Elvira Av. B-7
Enloe B-4
Ennis Dr. H-2
Ensworth I-1
Ensworth Av. I-1
Essex Pl. H-3
Estes Rd. H-1
Eugenia Av. J-6
Evans Rd. K-5
Evanston Av. D-5,D-6
Factory H-6
Fadur Ct. H-7
Fain G-8
Fairfax Ave. H-2
Fairmeade Dr. A-1
Fair Rd. H-1
Fairview B-1
Fairwin Av. C-7
Fatherland St. E-6,E-7
Felicia St. G-2
Felt Av. J-6
Fern Av. C-5
Ferndale I-6
Fessey Ct. I-6
Fesslers F-7
Fiberglass Rd. H-7
Frances Ave. K-4
Finland St. E-2
Fisk St. F-3
Flamingo Dr. B-6
Flicker A-2
Forest Av. E-7,E-8
Formosa E-2
Foss St. G-5
Foster Ave. H-7
Foster St. E-6
Foster Creighton
Dr. K-6
Franklin Av. D-7
Franklin St. F-5
French Landing Dr. C-3
Fresno B-6
Fulton F-7
Gain St. A-4
Galbraith Dr. K-2
Gale Ln. J-4
Gardner Ln. B-3
Garfield St. D-4,E-3
Gartland Av. D-7
Gatewood Av. C-6
Gatlin Dr. I-8
Gay F-4
Gear C-7
Georgia F-2
Gilmore I-4
Glade B-4
Gladstone I-6
Glen Echo Rd. K-3
Glen Leven Dr. I-5
Glenrose Av. I-7,I-8
Glenview Dr. F-7
Glenwood K-3
Goff St. D-3
Golf Club Ln. J-2
Gooch E-6
Goodrich C-1
Gordon Terr. B-6
Grace D-6
Gray St. H-5
Granada D-6
Granada Av. D-7
Grand St. G-4
Grandview Av. J-7
Grandview Dr. K-3
Grantlant I-5
Graybar Ln. J-4
Great Circle Rd. C-4
Green St. G-6
Greenfield Av. B-8
Green Hills Dr. K-3
Greenland Dr. K-4
Greenway H-2
Greenwood Av. D-8
Grizzard Av. B-5
Grove, W. H-4
Grover St. A-3
Grovers Pk. Rd. B-8
Hackworth H-7
Halcyon I-4
Hamilton Ave. H-5
Hamilton Rd. C-1
Hampton Av. J-2
Hampton St. B-5
Harlin Dr. K-7
Harrison St. E-4
Hart Ave. D-6
Hart Ln. A-6
Hart St. B-6,H-6
Hartford Dr. J-8
Hawkins St. G-4
Haynes Park Dr. B-1
Haynes St. B-4,G-3
Herman F-3
Herman St. F-2,F-3
Hermitage Ave. F-6
Hermosa F-3
Herron Dr. H-6
Hill Ave. H-8
Hillboro K-2
Hillboro Cir. K-2
Hillmont Dr. J-3
Hillside Ave. H-4
Hilltop Av. A-8
Hillview Hts. I-5
Hobbs Rd. K-1
Holly St. E-7
Home Rd. B-8
Home St. D-4
Hoodhill Rd. J-2
Hopkins St. J-3
Horton Ave. H-4
Houston Av. A-7
Howard Av. B-8
Howerton St. E-2
Hummingbird Dr. A-1
Humphrey H-5
Hutton Dr. I-7
Hydes Ferry Pk. C-1
Hydes Ferry Rd. C-1
Indiana Av. F-1
Interstate Dr. E-6
Inverness I-5
Ireland St. F-3
Iris Dr., W. J-5
Iris Rd., E. J-5
Iverson B-8
Jackson St. E-3,E-4
James Robertson
Pkwy. F-4
Jane St. E-3
Jefferson E-2
Jefferson Blvd. E-3
Jenkins Ave. D-3
Jenkins St. D-2
Jewel St. C-7
Johnston Ave. F-3
Jones Av. A-6,C-6
Jones St. A-5
Joseph Ave. D-5
Joy Av. B-6
Joy Cir. C-6
Joyner St. J-7
Keeling B-7
Kenmore B-8
Keller Av. K-6
Kenmore Dr. B-8
Kenneth Dr. A-5
Kenway K-2
Kilvington Blvd. H-7
Kimbark K-2
Kimpalong Ave. I-1
Kings Cr. A-2
Kings Ln. A-1
Kingston St. B-6
Kingsview Dr. B-1
Kinross Ave. K-8
Kirk Av. C-2
Kirkland B-8
Kirkland Av. B-8
Kirkwood Av. I-4,J-4
Kissia C-7
Klin I-7
Kline Av. I-7
Knollwood J-2
Knowles E-3
Knox I-4
Kraft Rd. K-6
Lacy D-2
Lafayette St. G-6
Lane A-3
Lauderdale H-1
Laurel St. G-4
Lawrence I-4
Lawrence Av. I-4
Lea St. G-5
Lealand Ln. K-4
Leawood Dr. D-1
Ledford Dr. B-3
Lemuel Rd. A-5
Lenore St. F-6
Leonard Av. I-1
Lewis St. G-6
Liberia St. B-4
Ligon I-8
Lillian St. E-7
Lincoln Av. B-1
Linden Av. I-3
Linden Ave. I-3
Lindsley St. G-5
Lischey Ave. D-6
Litton Av. C-8
Lloyd Av. C-1
Lock Rd. C-4
Locklayer St. E-4
Locust St. B-5
Logan St. J-7
Lombardy Av. J-3
Loney Dr. I-8
Long Av. E-7
Longview J-6
Lookout Dr. G-1
Louise Ave. G-3
Louise Dr. J-7
Love Cir. H-2
Lucille C-5
Lutie St. J-7
Luton St. C-8
Lyle Ln. I-7,I-8
Lynnbrook Rd. J-1
Madison St. E-3
Magnolia Rd. I-5
Main St. E-6
Malden Dr. I-7
Mallory St. G-6
Malta Dr. A-3
Manchester C-1
Manila B-4
Mansfield St. D-6
Maple H-8
Maplehurst K-4
Marina St. D-5
Marion A-8
Marion Av. J-4
Marshall St. E-5
Martin B-5
Martin St. H-5
Mashburn J-8
Mavert Dr. K-8
Mayer D-1
Mayfair K-4
Maynor Av. B-7
McChesney B-8
McClain J-7
McClurkins Av. C-7
McEwen D-8
McGavock B-8
McGavock St. G-4
McIver K-7
McKinley St. B-3
McKinnie Av. C-7
McMahan A-8
McMilin F-4
McNairy J-5
Mead Ave. K-7
Meadow Dr. I-1
Medow Rd. B-1
Meadowbrook H-1
Meadow Hill A-2
Medial I-2
Meharry F-2
Meharry Pl. E-3
Melrose J-6
Menzler Rd. H-8
Meridian St. C-6,E-5
Merritt Ave. H-5
Merry St. F-2
Mill St. E-4
Miller St. J-7
Mimosa K-8
Monticello St. B-4
Montrose I-4
Moore H-5
Morena F-3
Morena St. F-2
Morrison St. E-4
Morrow Av. K-4
Mortons St. K-7
Murphy Rd. H-1
Murphy St. G-3
Music Square E. G-4
Music Square W. G-4
Napoleon I-6
Nassau St. D-3
Matchez Trace I-2
Neal H-6
Nebraska A-1
Neldia Ct. C-8
Nestor St. F-6
Nevada G-1
Nevada Av. G-1
Newman Pl. K-5
Niel Ave. E-6
Nocturne Dr. B-8
Nolton Av. J-4
Norton Av. B-6
Northview Av. C-8
Normandy Cir. G-1
Oak Dr. J-3
Oak St. A-8,B-5,G-5
Oakland I-7
Oakwood Av. A-7
Observatory K-3
Old Buena Vista
Rd. B-2
Oldham St. E-5
Old Matthews B-4
Old Trinity Ln. B-5
Oman G-2
Omohundro F-8
Oneal Dr. D-2
Oneida Av. C-6
Ordway Pl. D-7
Oriel St. I-7
Orr Ave. G-6
Osage E-2
Otay C-8
Overton G-5
Owen St. D-3
Oxford B-8
Ozark F-7
Paris I-4
Paris Ave. H-7
Parish St. F-3
Park Av. G-1
Parthenon Av. G-2
Patterson St. G-3,I-6
Peachtree I-7
Peachtree St. I-7
Peabody St. G-5
Pearl St. F-3,F-4
Pecan D-2
Pennington C-8
Pennock D-6
Perkins St. G-6
Petway Av. D-7
Pewitt Rd. A-1
Phillips St. E-3
Pillow St. H-6
Pine St. G-4
Pittway B-7
Plum St. B-6
Polk Ave. H-7
Ponder Pl. C-3
Pontotoc D-8
Poplar St. H-8
Porter Rd. D-8
Poston G-2
Powell Av. J-6
Powers D-8
P'Pool Ave. H-1
Preslor Dr. F-1
Primrose B-6
Prince Av. B-6
Pullen Ave. C-6
Queen Av. B-6
Radnor St. K-7
Rainbow K-5
Rains Ave. H-6
Ramsey St. E-6
Raymond St. K-7
Read Av. C-5
Rebecca Rd. C-8
Redmon St. G-1
Red Walk H-4
Revels Dr. A-2
Richard St. B-3
Richland Jones Rd. K-3
Richardson Av. C-5
Richland Ave. H-1
Ridley Pl. G-5
Ringgold A-2
River Dr. D-1
Riverside Dr. D-8,E-8
Robin Rd. K-5
Roberts D-7
Rolland Rd. I-1
Roscobel St. F-5
Rose St. I-7
Rosedale Av. I-6
Rosemary I-7
Rosemont K-3
Rosewood Av. I-3
Rowan Dr. A-2
Roy St. B-3
Rucker Ave. A-5,G-6
Russell St. E-5,E-7
Ruth A-3
Sadler Av. I-7
St. Edward Dr. J-8
Santi Av. D-2
Saratoga I-2
Saunders Av. A-8
Scarrt Pl. G-3
Scott Ave. C-8
Scovel St. E-2,E-4
Scruggs B-5
Setliff Pl. D-8
Sevier E-7,F-7
Seymour Av. D-7
Shackelford Rd. K-3
Shady Ln. D-8
Sharondale Dr. J-2
Sharpe Av. D-6,D-7
Shelby Ave. E-6,E-7
Shelton Av. B-8
Shifried St. D-2
Shipp A-3
Shirley St. G-5
Shreeve Ln. A-3
Sidco Dr. K-6
Sigler St. G-4
Simmons St. K-7
Skyline Dr. K-1
Skyview Dr. D-8
Slaydon Dr. B-7
Smiley St. E-6
Sneed Rd. K-1
South Ct. I-7
South St. G-4
Southgate Ave. H-5
Southlake Dr. K-8
South Side Ct. G-4
Spain Av. C-7
Sperry J-1
Spring St. E-5
Stanback Av. D-6
Stanley St. F-7
State St. G-3
Stockell St. D-5
Stokers Ln. B-2
Stratton D-7
Strokes Ln. J-3
Strouse Av. C-7
Sugartree Rd. J-1
Summit Av. C-1
Sumner St. D-7
Sunrise Ave. A-8
Sunset Dr. A-2
Sunset Pl. I-3
Sutton Hill Rd. J-5
Sweetbriar Av. I-3
Sylvan St. F-6
Tanksley J-7
Taylor St. E-4
Terminal Blvd. H-7
Thomas Av. B-7
Thomson Ln. J-6,J-8
Thuss Ave. K-8
Tigerbelle F-1
Tillmania D-8
Timber Ln. I-2
Timons St. K-7
Toney Rd. B-4
Torbett E-2
Torbett St. F-1
Town Send Dr. F-4
Trace B-2
Tredco I-7
Treutland St. D-5
Trevecca C-7
Truett D-8
Tucker Rd. B-2
Tuggle Av. J-8
Unamed St. H-8
Union St. F-4
Utah Av. G-1
Utopia I-6
Valeria St. I-7
Vallwood Dr. K-1
Valley Av. C-1
Valley Brook Pl. J-1
Valley Brook Rd. J-2
Valley Vista Rd. J-2
Van Buren St. D-4
Vanderbilt H-2
Vanderhorst Dr. A-2
Vantage Way C-4
Vashti C-5
Vaughn St. D-5
Vaulx Ln. I-5,J-5
Venture Cir. C-4
Villa Pl. H-4
Village Ct. F-7
Vine Hill Rd. I-4
Virginia Av. K-2
Visco Dr. F-7
Wade Ave. H-4
Waldkirch I-4
Walker Ln. A-3,B-3
Wallace Ln. K-1
Walsh St. D-3
Ward C-6
Ward St. C-6
Warfield K-3
Warfield Dr. K-2
Warfield Ln. K-2
Warner St. F-3
Waters D-8
Weakley Av. C-5
Wedgewood H-4
Westmont I-1
Wellington H-2
West C-7
Westend I-2
West End Ave. G-3
West End Dr. I-1
West Hamilton Rd. B-1
West Heiman St. E-2
Westlawn Av. H-1,I-2
Westley Av. B-6
West Trinity Ln. B-3
Westwood Av. I-2
Westwood I-2
Wharf Ave. G-6
White Av. I-5
Whitney J-7
Whitsett Rd. J-8
Wilbur Pl. K-4
Wilburn D-6
Wildwood I-3
Willow St. H-5
Wilson Bl. I-1,J-1
Wimbleton Rd. J-1
Winford Av. J-6
Wingate Ave. J-8
Woodfolk A-4
Woodhill Dr. B-8
Woodland St. E-5,E-7,E-8
Woodlawn Dr. I-1
Woodleigh Dr. I-1
Woodmont Blvd.
.... J-1,J-2,J-4
Woodvale Dr. K-4
Woodward A-2,H-7
Work Dr. A-2
Yokley Rd. B-4
Youngs Ln. B-2,B-3
1st Ave. N. E-4
1st Ave. S. F-5
1st St. F-5
1st St. N. E-5
2nd Ave. N. E-4
2nd Ave. S. F-5,G-6
2nd St. F-6
2nd St. N. D-5,E-5
3rd C-4
3rd Ave. E-4
3rd Ave. S. F-5,G-6
3rd St. S. F-6
4th Ave. N. E-4
4th Ave. S. F-5.G-6
4th St. S. E-6
5th Ave. N. E-4
5th Ave. S. F-5
5th St. D-6
5th St. S. E-6
6th Ave. N. E-4
6th Ave. S. F-5
6th St. D-6
6th St. N. E-6
6th St. S. E-6
7th Ave. N. E-4
7th Ave. S. F-5
7th St. S. E-6
8th Ave. N. E-4,E-6
8th Ave. S. F-5
8th St. E-6
9th Av. I-4
9th Ave. N. E-4,E-6
9th St. E-6
10th Av. I-4
10th Ave. N. E-4
10th St. E-7
11th Av. D-3,H-4,I-4
11th Ave. N. E-4
11th St. E-7
12th Ave. D-3,E-3,H-4
12th Ave. S. G-4
12th St. C-7,D-7,E-7
13th Av. E-3
13th Ave. S. G-4
13th Ct. F-7
13th St. F-7
14th Ave. D-3,E-3,H-4
14th St. D-7,E-7
14th Ave. S. G-4
15th Av. D-3,E-3,H-4
15th Ave. N. F-4
15th Ave. S. G-4
15th St. E-7
16th Ave. E-3,H-4
16th St. E-7
17th Ave. E-3,H-4
17th St. F-7
18th Av. D-3,E-3,J-3
18th Ave. N. F-3,F-4
18th Ave. S. G-4,H-4
18th St. D-8,E-8
19th Ave. H-3
19th Ave. N. F-3
19th Ave. S. G-4,H-4
19th St. E-8
20th Ave. I-3
20th Ave. N. F-3
20th Ave. S. G-3
20th St. E-8
21st Ave. E-3,F-3
21st Ave. N. F-3
21st Ave. S. G-3
22nd Av. E-2,H-3
22nd Ave. N. F-3
22nd Ave. S. J-2
23rd Av. D-2,E-2,H-3
23rd Ave. N. G-3
23rd Ave. S. J-2
24th D-2,F-2
24th Ave. D-2,E-2,G-3
24th Ave. S. G-3,H-3
25th F-2
25th Ave. D-2,E-2
.... F-2,H-3,I-3
26th F-2,G-2
26th Ave. D-2,H-3,I-3
27th F-2,G-2
28th F-2
28th Ave. D-2,G-2,G-3
29th F-2
30th F-2
31st Ave. F-2,G-2
32nd Ave. F-2
33rd Ave. F-2
34th Ave. F-2
35th Ave. F-1
36th G-1
37th Ave. E-1,G-1,H-1
38th Ave. F-1,G-1,H-1
39th F-1,G-1,H-1
40th Ave. F-1,G-1,H-1
41st Ave. G-1,H-1
42nd Ave. F-1,G-1
43rd Ave. F-1,G-1
44th Ave. F-1,G-1
45th Ave. G-1

NEWARK

Abington Ave., E. B-6
Abington Ave., W. A-4
Academy St. F-5
Adams St. H-7
Afton C-8
Alexander St. E-1
Alpine St. J-1,K-1
Alpine St., E. I-4
Alpine St., W. I-4
Algea H-8
Amherst St. C-1
Ampere Pkwy. B-4
Ann St. H-8
Argyle G-3
Arlington G-3
Arlington, N. B-3
Arlington Ave., S. D-2
Ashland B-2
Astor St. I-5
Austin St. I-5
Avenue A I-5
Avenue B I-6
Avenue C I-6
Avon Ave. H-2
Badger Ave. I-3
Baldwin Ave. H-3
Ballantine B-6
Bank St. F-6
Barclay St. H-3
Bayview Ave. J-1
Beacon St. G-5
Beardsley Ave. A-4
Bedford C-1,G-4
Beech St. C-2
Belgrove Dr. D-8
Belmont H-3
Bergen Ave. C-4
Bergen St. F-8,G-4,K-2
Berkeley G-1
Berkeley Ave. A-5
Berwyn B-1
Beverley St. H-1
Bigelow St., E. I-4
Bigelow St., W. I-3
Bleeker St. F-6
Bloomfield Ave. C-6
Bock Ave. I-2
Boston St. F-5
Boyd St. H-4
Boyden St. E-6
Boylan E-1
Bragaw Ave. I-1
Branford I-4
Branford Pl. G-6
Breckenridge F-1
Brenner St. G-3
Bridge St. E-7
Brighton C-8, G-1
Briley Ave. K-1
Broad St. D-7,G-6
Broadway C-7
Brookside D-4
Brookwood St. E-1
Broone St. G-5
Bruce St. F-4
Bruen St. G-7
Brunswick St. H-5
Burnet, N. B-2
Burnet St., S. C-1
Cabinet St. E-4
Calumet I-7
Camden G-4
Camp St. H-6
Carlton St. B-2
Carnegie Ave. C-1
Central Ave. C-1,E-4,E-8
Center St. A-1,F-7
Chadwick Ave. J-3
Chancellor Ave. J-1
Charlton St. H-4
Chelsea Pl. A-1
Chester Ave. B-7
Chestnut C-2
Chestnut St. H-6
Clark Ave. D-8,K-1
Clark St. D-7
Clay St. E-7
Clifford St. I-7
Clifton Ave. D-6
Clifton St. I-8
Clinton Ave. H-2,H-4
Clinton Pl. J-1
Clinton St. F-6
Clinton St., N. B-2
Clinton St., S. C-1
Clover St. G-8
Columbia St. G-7
Commerce St. F-7
Concord St. J-4
Congress St. H-7
Conklin Ave. K-1
Court G-5
Crane St. D-6
Crawford C-1
Crawford St. H-5
Crescent Ave. J-1
Cross St. E-8
Custer Ave. J-2
Cutler St. D-6
Cypress St. H-1
Davenport Ave. A-5
Davis D-8
Dawson St. I-7
DeLancy St. I-8
Delavan Ave. A-7
Delmar G-1
Devon D-8
Dewey St. J-1
Dickerson St. E-4
Division St. E-7
Dorer Ave. K-1
Downing St. G-8
Duryea E-5
Eagles E-6
Earl St. I-5
Eastwood A-2
Edgar St. D-1
Edgerton Terr. A-3
Edison A-3,A-5
Edison Pl. G-6
Elizabeth Ave. I-4,K-2
Ellington St. B-4
Elliott A-3
Ellis Ave. G-1,H-1
Elm St. A-1,G-6
Elmwood Ave. D-1
Elwood Ave., E. A-7
Emmet St. I-5
Empire J-4
Essex St. F-8
Evergreen C-1
Fabyan Pl. I-1
Fairmount G-4
Fairmount Terr. E-1
Fairview Ave. G-4
Farley Ave. H-3
Ferguson St. H-8
Ferry St. G-7
Franklyn G-6
Freeman Ave. A-4
Frelinghuysen Ave. K-4
Fuller Pl. G-1
Fulton F-7
Garden H-7
Garden State Pkwy.
.... C-3,D-2,E-2
Garrison St. I-8
Garside St. D-6
Gillett H-5
Glenwood Ave. B-1
Goble St. I-6
Goldsmith Ave. J-1
Goodwin Ave. J-2
Gotthart St. I-8
Gould Ave. D-4
Gouverneur D-7
Grafton Ave. A-7
Grand Ave. E-1
Grant E-7
Grant Ave. D-8
Gray St. D-4
Green St. G-6
Greenwood Ave. C-3
Grove St. F-2,H-11
Grove St., N. A-4,C-3
Grove St., S. D-3
Grove Terr. F-1
Grumman Ave. K-1
Halleck St. K-4
Halsey St. G-6
Halstead St. C-1
Hamilton Ave. A-2
Hamilton St. G-7
Hampton Terr. B-1
Harding Terr. J-2
Harrison Ave. E-8
Harrison Pl. H-1
Harrison St., S. C-1
Harper St. I-6
Hartford St. E-5
Harvey St. C-7
Hawthorne D-2
Hawthorne Ave. I-1,J-4
Hayes St. F-4
Heckel St. D-1
Hecker St. E-5
Hedden Terr. I-3
Heller Pkwy. A-7
Hensler H-8
Herbert Pl. B-7
Hickory St. B-1
Highland G-1
Highland Ave. C-6,D-8
High St. D-6,F-6,H-5
Hill St. G-6
Hillside Ave. I-4
Hinsdale Pl. B-7
Hobson St. J-1
Hoffman Blvd. A-4
Holland St. G-3
Hollywood D-3
Hopkins Pl. H-1
Hose D-8
Houston St. I-8
Howard St. G-5
Hoyt St. D-8
Hudson St. K-5
Humboldt D-4
Hunter St. E-1
Hunterdon St. J-3
Huntington Terr. J-2
Irving J-2
Irving Turner
Blvd. H-4
Isabella Ave. F-1
Jabez St. I-8
Jacob St. E-4
James St. E-6
Jay St. E-5
Jefferson St. H-7
Jelliff Ave. I-3
Jersey St. E-1
John St. E-8
Johnston Ave. D-8,I-4
Johnson St. H-6
Jones St. F-5
Kearney Ave. D-8
Kearney St. C-6
Keer Ave. J-1
Kellor St. F-7
Kent St. H-6
Kinney St., E. H-6
Kinney St., W. G-4
Lafayette St. G-6,H-7
La France A-4
Lake St. C-6
Lang St. H-8
Lehigh Ave. J-2
Lenox Ave. C-2
Leslie St. B-4,J-1
Liberty St. G-7
Lincoln Ave. B-7
Lincoln St. B-2,G-5
Linden Ave. D-1,G-1
Littleton Ave. G-3
Livingston St. H-4
Lock St. F-5
Lombardy J-1
Longworth H-5
Lyons Ave. A-1
Madison G-8
Madison Ave. G-1
Magnolia St. G-3
Main St. B-1,C-3
Malvern St. H-7
Mapes Ave. J-2
Maple Ave. H-1,K-1
Maple Ave., N. A-4,C-3
Maple Ave., S. D-3
Maple St. D-8
Market St. F-6
Market St., W. E-4,F-5
Marshall D-8
May St. B-7
McCarter Hwy. D-7,H-6
McNary D-8
McWhorter St. H-7
Meeker Ave. J-3
Melmore Gardens B-2
Melrose F-1
Mercer St. G-5
Merchant St. H-8
Middlesex St. F-8
Milford Ave. I-4
Miller St. B-1,I-5
Millington Ave. I-2
Milton St. E-8
Mohammad Ali Ave. H-5
Monroe H-8
Montgomery G-5
Montgomery Ave. H-1
Montrose F-2
Morris A-3,E-5,F-4
Morton H-5
Mountainview Ave. E-1
Mt. Prospect AVe. D-6
Mulberry St. H-6
Munn Ave., N. C-3
Munn Ave., S. E-2
Murray St. H-5
Myrtle D-4
Myrtle Ave. F-1
Nairin Pl. I-2
Napoleon St. F-8
Nesbitt Ave. E-6
Nevada St. D-8
New St. A-1,E-5,F-6
Newfield St. B-4
New York Ave. H-7
Newark St. F-5
Nobel K-4
Norfolk St. F-5
Norwood St. D-1
Nursery C-7
Nye Ave. H-1
Oak Ave. F-2
Oak St. D-1
Oakwood Ave. B-1
Oakwood Pl. B-1
Oliver St. H-7
Orange St. D-4,E-6,E-7
Orange Ave., S.
.... E-1,F-4
Oraton St. B-7
Oriental St. C-7
Osborne Terr. J-2
Park Ave. A-1
Park Pl. A-1,F-7
Park St. E-1
Parker St. C-6
Parkhurst St. H-6
Parkview Terr. K-1
Patterson H-8
Peabody B-8
Peddle St., E. I-6
Peddle St., W. I-3
Pennington St. H-6
Peshine Ave. J-3
Poinier St. I-5
Polk St. H-8
Pomona Ave. J-1
Prince St. H-5
Prospect St. B-2,H-7
Pulaski St. I-8
Quitman St. H-5
Randolph I-2
Rankin J-5
Raymond Blvd. F-6,G-8
Raymond Plaza E. G-7
Raymond Plaza W. G-7
Renner Ave. J-2
Richmond F-5
Ridge St. D-6
Ridgewood Ave. I-4
Rhode Island Ave. D-1
Roosevelt Ave. A-4
Rose St. G-3,H-4
Rose Terr. H-3
Roseville Ave. D-4
Rutledge Ave. A-3
Runyon St., E. I-4
Runyon St. W. I-3
St. Agnes Lane D-2
Sanford St. C-1
Saybrook F-7
Scheerer Ave. J-2
Schley St. J-1
Seymour Ave. J-2
Shanley Ave. H-3
Shepard D-1
Shephard Ave. I-8
Sherman Ave. D-8,I-5
Shipman G-5
Snyder A-1
Somerset St. F-8,H-5
South St. H-6
Springdale Ave. A-2
Springfield Ave. G-2
Spruce St. G-4
Standard G-2
Stanton St. I-5
State St. A-1,E-6
Stengel J-2
Sterling St. F-5
Stockton C-3
Stockton Pl. F-1
Stone St. D-6
Stratford Pl. H-4
Stueben D-3
Summit B-2
Summit St. F-6
Sunnyside E-1
Sunset Ave. E-1
Sussex E-8
Sussex Ave. D-4
Taylor C-6
Telford St. D-1
Thomas St. H-6
Tichenor F-1
Tichenor St. H-6
Tillinghast St. I-2
Treacy Ave. H-3
Tremont D-1,G-1
Union St. G-7
University F-1
University Ave. G-6
Van Buren St. H-8
Vanderpool St. I-5
Vanness I-2
Vassar Ave. J-1
Vernon H-2
Vernon Terr. C-3
Vermont Ave. F-1
Victoria J-4
Wainwright St. J-1
Wall H-8
Wallace A-1
Walnut St. G-6
Walnut St., N. A-3,B-2
Ward St. A-1
Warren St. E-8,F-5
Warrington Pl. B-3
Warwick St. B-4
Washington St. A-1
.... F-6,G-6
Washington Terr. B-2
Watson J-3
Watson Ave. D-2
Waverly Ave. G-3
Webster Pl. B-1
Webster St. D-6
Webster Pl. B-1
White Terr. I-2
Wickliffe St. F-5
William St. B-1,E-8,G-6
Williamson Ave. K-1
Willow St. J-1
Wilsey St. F-5
Wilson H-8
Wilson Ave. C-8
Winans Ave. G-3,K-1
Winans St. C-2
Woodland C-8
Woodland Ave. A-2,D-8
Woodside B-7,C-7
Wright St. I-5
Yates Ave. I-3
1st Ave. W. B-5
1st St. D-5,F-8
2nd Ave. E. C-6
2nd Ave. W. B-5
2nd St. D-5,F-8
2nd St., N. E-8
3rd Ave. E. C-6
3rd Ave., W. B-4
3rd St. B-6,D-5,F-8
4th Ave. B-3
4th Ave., E. D-6
4th St. C-5,D-5,F-8
5th St. F-8
5th St., N. C-5
6th Ave., E. D-6
6th Ave., W. C-6
6th St., N. B-5
7th Ave., E. D-6
7th Ave., W. D-4
7th St., N. B-5
8th A-5
8th Ave. E-6,E-7
9th A-5
9th Ave. D-3
10th St., N. B-5
10th St., S. H-3
11th Ave. E-4
12th Ave. E-4
12th St., N. B-4
13th Ave. E-2,E-3,E-5
14th Ave. F-3
14th St., S. D-4,H-2
15th Ave. F-3
15th St., N. A-5,C-4
15th St., S. H-3
16th Ave. F-3
16th Ave. E-2
16th St., S. H-2
16th St., N. A-5,C-4
17th Ave. F-2,G-4
17th St. H-2
17th St., N. A-4,C-4
18th Ave. G-3
18th St. F-1
18th St., N. C-4
18th St., S. J-3
19th Ave. G-2
19th St., N. C-3
20th St. B-4
21st St. B-4,H-1
22nd St. B-4,G-1

POINTS OF INTEREST

Branch Brook Park A-6
Hayes Park North C-7
Independence Park H-7
Lincoln Park H-6
Newark International
Airport K-7
Riverbank Prk. G-8
Stickle Bridge E-7
Vailsburg Park E-1
Wahington Park F-7
Weequahil Park K-3
West Side Park G-2

Scale of Miles
0. .1 .2 .3 .4 .5

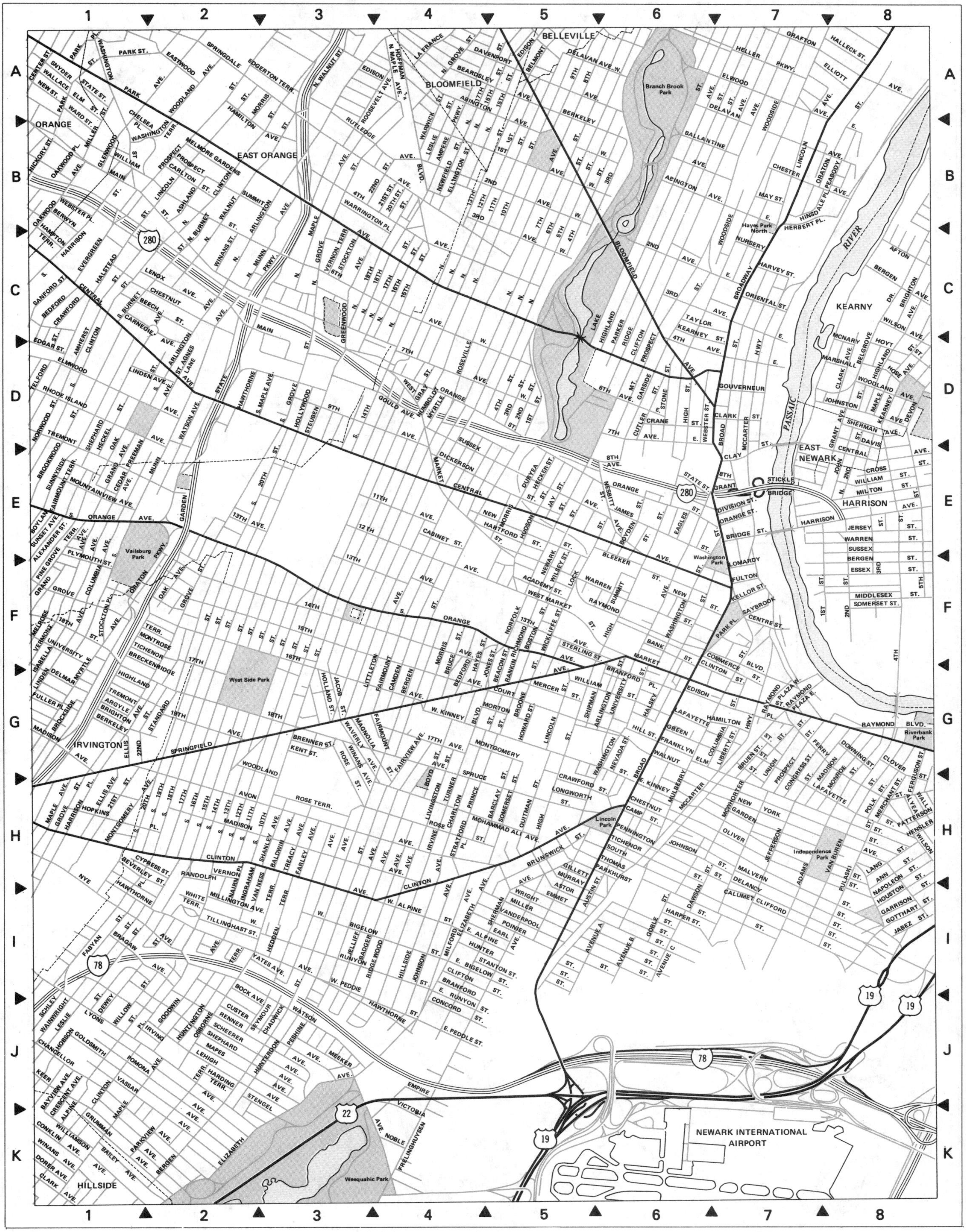

New Orleans, LA

Scale of Miles
0 .1 .2 .3 .4

NEW ORLEANS

Abundance ... A-2
Adele ... J-8
Agriculture ... A-2
Alix ... E-8
Allen ... C-3
Almonaster Ave. ... A-5
Alvar ... A-7
Annette ... C-4
Annunciation ... K-7
Anthony ... C-4
Arts ... A-4
Aubry ... C-3
Banks ... G-3
Baronne ... K-5
Barracks ... D-2,D-4
Bartholomew ... A-7
Basin ... F-4
Bayou Rd. ... D-2
Belfort Ave. ... C-1
Bell ... E-1
Bellechase ... E-1
Bermuda ... E-7
Bertrand ... G-3
Bienville ... F-3,F-5
Bolivar ... G-3
Bouny ... E-7
Bourbon ... E-5
Bradish ... G-2
Brainard ... J-6
Broad Ave., N. ... E-2
Broad AVe., S. ... G-2
Brooklyn ... F-8
Bruxelles ... B-1
Burgundy ... B-7,D-5,F-5
Cadiz ... K-2
Calhoun ... K-1
Calliope ... H-7
Callipest ... H-5
Camp ... K-6,G-6
Canal Blvd. ... F-4
Carondelet ... H-5,H-6,K-5
Castiglione ... C-1
Celeste ... J-8
Chartres ... C-7,D-6,F-5
Chestnut ... K-6
Chippewa ... K-7
Claiborne, N. ... A-6
Clairborne Ave. ... C-4
Claiborne Ave., S. ... H-4,J-3
Clara ... I-4
Clay ... F-6
Cleveland ... G-3
Clio ... I-4
Clio Pl. ... I-2
Clouet ... A-6
Coliseum ... K-6
Colombus ... D-3
Commerce ... G-6
Common ... G-5
Conery ... K-6
Congress ... A-7
Conti ... F-3,F-5
Crete ... C-1
Crossman ... F-6
Croza ... F-4
Dabadie ... C-2
Danneel ... J-5
Dauphine ... C-7,D-5,E-5
De Armas ... F-8
Decatur ... D-5,D-6
DeLachaise ... J-2
DeLaronde ... D-7,E-7
Delta ... G-6
Derbigny,N. ... A-6,C-4,F-3
Derbigny,S ... G-3,I-3,K-2
Diamond,N. ... H-6
Diamond,S. ... H-6
De Soto ... D-1
Diana ... F-8
Division ... K-8
Dixon ... H-1
Dorgenois,N. ... B-3,F-2
Dorgenois,S. ... J-2
Dryades ... I-5
Dugue ... B-1
Dumaine ... E-3,E-4
Dupre,N. ... C-1,E-1
Dupre,S. ... G-1
Earhart Blvd. ... I-3
Eden ... J-1
Elba ... J-1
Elk Pl. ... G-4
Elysian Fields Ave. ... C-5
Elza ... E-8
Erato ... H-7,I-4
Esplanade Ave. ... D-4
Euterre Ave. ... I-5,I-7
Euphbosine ... I-1
Eve ... J-1
Evelina ... E-8
Exchange Pl. ... F-5
Felciana ... A-6
Felicity ... J-6
First ... J-5
Florida AVe. ... B-1
Fontaineblau Dr. ... J-1
Fortin ... D-1
Foucher ... K-4
Fourth ... K-5
France ... A-8
Franklin Ave. ... A-4,C-6
Frenchmen ... C-4
Freret ... G-4
Front, N. ... F-6
Front, S. ... G-6
Fulton ... G-6
Gaiennie ... H-7
Gallier ... A-7
Galvez, N. ... C-3,F-3
Galvez, S. ... H-3,I-3,K-2
Gayoso, N. ... C-1,E-1
Gayoso, S. ... G-1
Gen. Pershing ... J-1,J-2
Gen. Taylor ... K-2
Gentilly Blvd. ... A-1
Girod ... H-5
Gov. Nicholls ... E-2,E-4
Grand Route St. John ... D-1
Gravier ... G-2,G-4
Hagan ... F-1
Harmony ... K-4
Hastings ... J-7
Havana ... B-1
Henderson ... I-8
Hewes ... J-1
Homer ... E-8
Howard Ave. ... H-6
Humanity ... A-2
Iberville ... F-5
Industry ... B-2
Independence ... A-7
Jackson Ave. ... I-4,J-6
Jane Pl. ... G-2
Japonia ... A-8
Jeff Davis Pkwy. ... I-1
Jefferson ... K-1
Jena ... J-1
Johnson, N. ... B-3,F-3
Johnson, S. ... H-3,K-2
Joseph ... K-1
Josephine ... J-6
Julia ... H-3,H-5
Kentucky ... A-8
Kerlerac ... D-4,D-5
LaFayette ... G-5,H-2
Laharpe ... D-3
Lamaroue ... F-8
Lapeyrouse ... D-3
Lasalle ... G-4,K-4
Laurel ... K-7
Lavergne ... E-7
Lefreniere ... A-1
Lesseps ... A-8
Liberty, N. ... E-4
Liberty, S. ... H-4,J-5
London Ave. ... C-3
Lopez, N. ... E-1
Lopez, S. ... H-1
Louisa ... A-6
Louisiana Ave. Pkwy. ... J-2
Loyola ... J-5
McKenna ... K-1
Madison St. ... E-5
Magazine ... G-6
Man Pl. ... G-2
Mandeville ... C-5
Manuel ... A-8
Marais ... B-7,C-5,E-4
Marengo ... K-3
Marigny ... C-5
Market ... J-7
Maurepas ... D-1
Mazant ... A-8
Melpomene ... I-5
Milan ... K-3
Miro, N. ... B-3,F-3
Miro, S. ... G-3,K-2
Mississippi River Bridge ... H-8
Morgan ... E-7
Montegut ... A-6
Mujsic ... A-4
Napoleon Ave. ... K-2
Nashville ... K-1
Natchez ... G-6
Newton ... F-8
New Orleans ... B-2
Notre Dame ... G-6
Nuns ... J-8
Octavia ... K-1
O'Keefe ... G-5
Oliver ... E-7
Onzaga ... C-3
Opelousas Ave. ... E-8
Orange ... I-7
Orchid ... E-1
O'Reilly ... C-1
Orleans Ave. ... E-3,E-5
Painters ... A-4
Palmetto ... H-1
Palmyra ... G-3
Paris AVe. ... B-1
Patterson ... E-7
Pauger ... C-4
Pauline ... A-7
Paulmorphy ... C-1
Pelican Ave. ... E-7
Peniston ... K-3
Perdido ... G-4,H-2
Peters ... F-6
Peters, N. ... D-6
Peters, S. ... G-6,I-8
Philip ... J-5,J-6
Piety ... A-6
Pleasure ... A-1
Poeyfarre ... H-6
Poland ... A-8
Ponce De Leon ... D-1
Pontchartrain Expy. ... H-1
Port ... C-6
Powder ... F-7
Poydas ... G-4
Prieur Pl. ... K-2
Prieur, N. ... C-3,F-3
Prieur, S. ... H-3,I-3
Prytania ... H-6,K-6
Ptolemy ... G-8
Race ... I-7
Rampart, N. ... B-7, D-5,E-4
Rampart, S. ... G-5,I-5
Religious ... I-8
Rendon, N. ... E-1
Rendon, S. ... H-1
Republic ... B-1
Richard ... J-7
River ... F-8
Robert ... K-2
Robertson, N. ... A-7, C-4,E-4
Robertson, S. ... G-4,I-4
Rocheblave, N. ... B-3,F-2
Rocheblave, S. ... K-2
Romain, N. ... C-4,F-3
Romain, S. ... G-3,I-3,K-2
Rosiere ... C-1
Rousseau ... J-8
Rousselin ... C-2
Royal ... C-7,D-5,E-5
St. Andrews ... I-5,J-6
St. Ann ... E-3,E-4
St. Bernard Ave. ... D-4
St. Charles Ave. ... G-5, I-6,K-6
St. Claude ... B-7,C-5
St. Ferdinand ... B-6
St. James ... J-8
St. Joseph ... H-5
St. Louis ... F-5
St. Mary ... J-6
St. Peter ... E-1,E-5
St. Philip ... E-5
St. Roch Ave. ... C-5
St. Thomas ... J-8
Salcedo, N. ... E-1
Salcedo, S. ... G-1
Saratoga ... G-4
Saratoga, S. ... I-5,K-5
Scraparu ... K-8
Second ... J-5
Seguin ... E-7
Serantine ... B-1
Sere ... A-1
Seventh ... K-4
Simon ... I-5
Sixth ... K-5
Slidell ... E-8
Socrates ... G-8
Spain ... C-5
State St. Dr. ... K-1
Tchoupitoulas ... G-6,I-8,K-8
Teche ... F-8
Terpsichore ... I-4,I-7
Thalia ... H-7,I-4
Third ... J-5
Toledano ... J-3,K-4
Tonti, N. ... B-3,F-2
Tonti, S. ... K-2
Toulouse ... F-1,F-5
Touro ... C-4
Treasure ... A-2
Tulane Ave. ... G-3
Union ... G-5
University Pl. ... G-5
Upper Line ... K-2
Urquhart ... B-7,C-4
Ursulines Ave. ... E-5
Vallette ... F-8
Vendome Pl. ... J-1
Verret ... E-8
Villere, N. ... B-7,C-4,E-4
Villere, S. ... G-4
Vincennes Pl. ... J-1
Washington ... K-5
Washington Ave. ... I-1
Water ... G-7
Wells ... F-6
White, N. ... E-1
White, S. ... G-1
Willow ... I-4
Wilkinson St. ... E-5
Wright ... J-7
York ... K-1

POINTS OF INTEREST

Annunciation Sq. ... I-7
Beauregard Sq. ... E-4
Canal St. Ferry ... F-6
Clay Park ... K-7
Coliseum Sq. ... I-6
Jackson Sq. ... E-5
Lafayette Sq. ... G-5
Mississippi River Bridge ... G-8
St. Roch Park ... B-5
Shakespere Park ... J-4
Taylor Park ... J-3
Washington Park ... D-5

NEW YORK

Adams St. ... A-1
Albany ... I-1
Allen ... H-3
Amsterdam Ave. ... B-4,C-3
Ann ... H-2
Anslie St. ... H-6
Ash ... F-5
Ashland Pl. ... J-4
Astor ... G-3
Astoria Blvd. ... C-7,C-8
Atlantic Ave. ... J-2,K-4,K-6
Attorney ... H-3
Auburn Pl. ... J-4
Avenue of the Americas ... D-3
Ave. A ... G-3
Ave. B ... G-3
Ave. C ... G-3
Ave. D ... G-4
Bainbridge St. ... K-7
Baltic St. ... K-3
Bank St. ... F-2
Banker St. ... G-5
Barclay St. ... H-1
Barrow ... G-2
Baruch ... H-4
Bayard St. ... H-6
Baxter ... H-2
Beach ... H-1
Beadle St. ... H-6
Beaver ... I-1,I-6
Bedford Ave. ... H-5,I-4, I-5,J-5
Beekman ... E-4,I-2
Bergen St. ... K-3
Bergenline Ave. ... A-1
Berginine ... A-1
Bergenwood ... A-1
Berry ... I-4
Bethune St. ... F-2
Bleecker St. ... G-2,J-7
Bonn ... C-1
Borden Ave. ... F-5
Bowery ... H-2
Bridge St. ... J-3
Broad ... I-1
Broadway ... A-2,A-4, B-1,D-3,D-7,E-3,E-8, H-3,I-4,I-6,J-7,K-8
Broadway St. ... G-2
Bromme ... G-2
Brooklyn Bridge ... I-2
Brooklyn Queens Connecting Hwy. ... J-4
Broome ... G-2
Buchanan ... B-1
Bushwick Ave. ... J-7,I-6
Butler St. ... K-3
Calyer ... G-5
Cambridge ... K-5
Canal ... H-2
Cardinal ... H-2
Carlisle ... I-1
Carlton Ave. ... J-4
Carmine ... G-2
Carroll St. ... K-2
Cedar ... I-1
Central ... C-3,J-8
Centre ... H-2
Central Park South ... D-3
Central Park West ... C-4
Chambers St. ... H-1
Charles ... F-2
Charlton ... G-2
Chauncey ... K-7,K-8
Cherry ... H-3,I-2
Christopher St. ... F-2
Chrystie ... H-2
Clark St. ... J-2
Clarkson ... G-2
Classon Ave. ... J-5
Clay St. ... F-5
Clermont Ave. ... J-4
Clifton ... C-1
Clinton ... H-3,I-4
Clinton Ave. ... J-4
Clinton St. ... K-2
Clifton Pl. ... J-5
Clymer ... I-4
Coenties ... I-1
Columbia ... C-1,H-3
Columbus ... B-4,C-3
Commercial ... F-5
Conimer St. ... G-5
Conselyea St. ... H-6
Cook St. ... I-6
Cooper ... C-1
Cooper St. ... K-8
Cornelia ... G-2
Cornelia St. ... J-8
Cortlandt ... H-1,I-1
Cour St. ... K-2
Covert St. ... K-8
Cranberry St. ... I-2
Crescent St. ... C-7,E-6
Crosby St. ... G-2
Cuylers ... I-1
Dean St. ... K-4
De Bevoise St. ... I-6
Decatur St. ... K-6,K-8
Degraw St. ... K-2,K-3
De Kalb St. ... J-5,J-7
Delancey St. ... H-3
Des Brosses ... G-2
Devoe St. ... H-6
Dey ... H-1
Diamond St. ... G-6
Ditmars Blvd. ... B-8
Division ... H-2,I-4
Division Pl. ... H-6
Dobbin St. ... G-5
Dominick ... G-2
Douglass St. ... K-3
Doughty ... I-2
Downing ... G-2
Driggs Ave. ... G-6, H-5,I-5
Duane ... H-1,H-2
Duer Pl. ... C-1
Durham ... A-1
Eckford St. ... G-6
Eldert St. ... K-8
Elizabeth ... H-2
Eldorado ... C-1
Eldridge ... H-3
Emerson ... J-5
Entrance St. ... E-4
Engert Ave. ... H-6
Essex St. ... H-3
Evergreen St. ... J-7
Fairview ... I-8
Flatbush Ave. ... J-3
Fletcher ... I-2
Forsyth ... H-2
Franklin ... H-1,H-2
Franklin Ave. ... J-5
Franklin St. ... F-5
Franklin Roosevelt Dr. ... F-4,H-4
Freedom Pl. ... C-3
Front ... I-2
Front St. ... I-3
Frost ... H-6
Frost St. ... H-5
Fulton ... C-1
Fulton St. ... H-1, I-2,J-3,K-5
Gansevoort St. ... F-2
Gardner ... G-7
Gates Ave. ... J-6,J-8,K-4
George ... I-7
Gerry ... I-6
Gould ... I-2
Gouveneur ... H-3
Graham Ave. ... H-6
Grand ... G-2
Grand Ave. ... K-5
Grand St. ... H-5,H-6,H-7
Grandview ... I-8
Green St. ... K-4
Greene ... G-2
Greene Ave. ... J-7,K-7
Greenpoint Ave. ... F-6,G-5
Greenwich ... F-2,G-1
Grove ... G-2
Grove St. ... J-7
Guernsey St. ... G-5
Hall St. ... J-4
Halsey St. ... J-8,K-5,K-7
Hamill ... H-2
Hamilton ... C-1
Hancock St. ... J-8, K-5,K-7
Hanson Pl. ... K-4
Hansman ... G-6
Harman St. ... J-7
Harrison ... A-1,H-1
Harrison Ave. ... I-5
Hart St. ... I-7,J-5
Havemeyer ... H-5
Henry ... H-2
Henry St. ... J-2,K-2
Henry Hudson ... C-3
Hester ... H-3
Hewes ... I-5
Hewes St. ... I-5
Heyward St. ... I-5
Hicks St. ... J-2
Highland ... C-1
Himrod St. ... J-7
Hobart Ave. ... D-8
Hooper St. ... I-5
Hope St. ... H-5
Hopkinson Ave. ... K-8
Honeywell St. ... E-7
Horatio St. ... F-2
Houston St. ... G-2,H-3
Howard ... H-2
Howard Ave. ... K-7
Hoyte Ave. ... C-7
Hubert ... H-1
Hudson ... C-1
Hudson Ave. ... A-2,B-1
Hudson Blvd. ... B-1
Hudson Blvd. E. ... B-1
Hull St. ... K-8
Humboldt St. ... G-6,H-6
Hunter St. ... E-6
Huron St. ... G-5
Imlay St. ... K-1
India St. ... G-5
Irving ... K-5
Irving Ave. ... I-7
Irving St. ... K-2
Jackson ... H-3
Jackson Ave. ... E-6
Jackson St. ... H-6
James ... H-2
Jane St. ... F-2
Java St. ... G-5
Jay St. ... H-1
Jefferson ... H-3
Jefferson Ave. ... I-7,J-8,K-5,K-7
Jefferson St. ... A-1
Jewel St. ... G-6
John ... I-2
Johnson Ave. ... I-6,I-7
John St. ... I-3
Jones ... G-2
Kane St. ... J-2
Keap St. ... I-5
Kent ... I-4
Kent Ave. ... H-4,J-5
Kent St. ... G-5
King ... C-1
King St. ... G-2,K-1
Kings Island Ave. ... G-6
Knickerbocker Ave. ... I-7,J-7
Kosciusko St. ... J-5
Lafayette ... H-2
Lafayette Ave. ... J-6,K-4
Laight ... G-1
Lawrence ... J-3
Lee Ave. ... I-5
Leonard ... H-2
Leonard St. ... G-5,H-6
LeRoy St. ... G-2
Lewis ... H-3
Lewis Ave. ... J-5
Lexington Ave. ... C-5,F-3,J-6,K-5
Liberty ... C-1,I-1
Lincoln Tunnel ... D-1
Linden St. ... J-7
Lispenard ... H-2
Livingston St. ... J-3
Lombardy St. ... G-6
Lonimer St. ... I-5,I-6
Ludlow St. ... H-3
Lynch St. ... I-5
Macon St. ... K-6
MacDougal St. ... G-2,K-8
Madison ... H-2,I-8
Madison Ave. ... C-5,F-3,K-7
Madison St. ... J-8,K-5
Mangin ... H-4
Manhatten Ave. ... F-5,H-6
Manhattan Bridge ... I-3
Marcy ... H-5
Marcy Ave. ... I-5,J-5
Marion St. ... K-7
Marshall ... I-3
Maspeth Ave. ... H-6
Mavjer St. ... I-6
McKibbin St. ... I-6
Meadowview ... A-1
Meeker Ave. ... G-6
Melrose St. ... I-7
Menahan St. ... J-7
Mercer St. ... G-2
Messerole ... H-7,I-6
Messerole Ave. ... G-6
Metropolitan Ave. ... H-4,H-6,H-8
Middagh ... I-3
Miller Hwy. ... D-2,G-1
Milton St. ... G-5
Mitchell ... E-4
Monitor St. ... G-6
Montague St. ... J-2
Montgomery ... H-3
Mt. Guiness Blvd. ... F-5
Monroe ... B-1,H-2
Monroe St. ... K-5,K-7
Montrose Ave. ... I-6
Moore St., N. ... H-1
Moore St. ... I-6,I-7
Morgan Ave. ... G-6,H-6
Morgan ... I-7
Morton ... G-2,I-4
Mott ... H-2
Moultrie ... G-6
Mulberry ... H-2
Murray St. ... H-1
Myrtle Ave. ... J-5,J-6,J-7
Nassau ... I-1
Nassau Ave. ... G-5
Navy St. ... J-3
New ... I-1
Newel St. ... G-6
Newkirk ... A-1
Newton Ave. ... C-7
Noble St. ... G-5
Norfolk St. ... H-3
Norman Ave. ... G-5
North Henry St. ... G-6
Northern Blvd. ... E-7
Nostrand Ave. ... J-5
Oak St. ... G-5
Old ... I-2
Onderdonk ... I-8
Pacific St. ... J-3,K-4
Page Pl ... H-8
Paidge Ave. ... F-5
Palisade Ave. ... A-2,B-1
Palmetto St. ... J-8
Park ... H-3
Park Ave. ... A-2,B-1, C-5,D-4,F-3
Park St. ... H-1
Park Row ... H-2
Park Row East ... H-2
Patchen Ave. ... J-7
Pearl ... H-2,I-2
Peck ... I-2
Pell ... H-2
Penn St. ... I-5
Perry St. ... F-2
Pierrpont St. ... J-2
Pilling ... K-8
Pitt St. ... H-3
Platt ... I-2
Pleasent ... C-1
Pleasant Ave. ... A-7
Plymouth St. ... I-3
Poplar ... I-3
Porter ... G-6,I-7
Powers St. ... H-6
President St. ... K-2
Prince St. ... G-2
Prospect ... I-3
Provost St. ... F-6
Pulaski St. ... J-5,J-6
Putman Ave. ... J-8,K-5
Putnam Ave. ... K-7
Quay St. ... G-5
Queens Blvd. ... E-6,E-7
Queens Midtown Tunnel ... E-5
Quincy St. ... J-6,K-5
Ralph Ave. ... J-7
Randolph St. ... I-7
Rector St. ... I-1
Reid Ave. ... J-7
Remsen St. ... J-2
Renwick ... G-2
Review Ave. ... F-6
Richardson St. ... H-6
Ridge ... H-3
River ... H-4
Riverside Dr. ... A-4,B-3
Rivington ... H-3
Roebling ... H-5
Rockaway ... K-8
Ross St. ... I-5
Rutgers ... H-3
Rutledge St. ... I-5
Russell St. ... G-6
Sackett St. ... K-2,K-3
St. James Pl. ... J-4
St. Marks Ave. ... K-4
St. Nicholas Ave. ... I-8
Sanford ... J-5
Sands ... I-3
Saratoga Ave. ... K-8
Seigel St. ... I-6
Seneca Ave. ... I-8
Schermephorne St. ... J-3
Scholes ... H-7,I-6
Shaefer St. ... K-8
Skillman Ave. ... E-7, F-6,H-6
Skillman St. ... J-5
Slip ... H-3
Smith Ave. ... A-1,K-2
Somers ST. ... K-8
South ... I-2
South Ave. ... E-4
Spencer St. ... J-5
Spring ... G-2
Spruce ... H-2
Stagg St. ... H-7,I-6
Stanhope St. ... J-7
Stanton ... H-3
Starr St. ... I-7
Sterling ... C-1
Stewart Ave. ... I-7
Stockholm St. ... I-7
Stone ... K-8
Stuyvesant Ave. ... J-7
Suffolk ... H-3
Sullivan St. ... G-2,K-1
Summitt St. ... K-2
Sumner Ave. ... J-6,J-7
Sumpter St. ... K-8
Sutton Pl. ... D-5
Sutton St. ... G-6
Suydam St. ... I-7
Taaffe Ave. ... J-5
Taylor St. ... I-4
Thomas St. ... H-2
Thompson St. ... G-2
Thomson Ave. ... E-6
Throop Ave. ... I-6,J-6,K-6
Tillary ... J-3
Tompkins Ave. ... J-6
Tonsor ... H-8
Trinity ... I-1
Troutman St. ... I-7,I-8
Tudor City Pl. ... E-4
Tunnel Exit St. ... E-4
Union ... I-5
Union St. ... K-2
University ... G-2
Van Buren ... J-6
Vandam ... G-2
Van Dam St. ... F-7
Vanderbilt ... E-4
Vanderbilt Ave. ... J-4
Van Brunt St. ... K-1
Vandervoort ... H-6
Varet St. ... I-6
Varick ... H-2
Varick Ave. ... H-7
Vernon Blvd. ... D-6,E-5
Vernon Ave. ... J-5
Vestry ... G-2
Vessey St. ... H-1
Vine ... I-2
Wall ... I-1
Walker ... H-2
Wallabout ... I-5,I-6
Walton St. ... I-5
Walworth Pl. ... J-5
Warren St. ... H-1,K-3
Warsoff Pl. ... J-5
Washington ... G-1,J-3
Washington Ave. ... J-4
Water ... I-2
Water St. ... I-3
Watts ... G-2
Waverly ... J-4
Weirfield St. ... J-8
West ... A-1
West St. ... F-4,G-2
Westevd ... C-3
White St. ... H-2
White Hall ... I-1
Willoughby St. ... I-7
Willett ... H-3
William ... I-2
Willoughby Ave. ... J-4
Williamsburg Bridge ... H-4
Wilson Ave. ... J-8
Wolcott ... K-1
Woodbine ... I-8
Woodbine St. ... J-8
Woodside ... E-8
Wooster St. ... G-2
Woodward Ave. ... I-8
Worth St. ... H-2
Wyckoff Ave. ... I-7
Wyckoff St. ... K-3
Wythe ... H-4
York ... I-3
York Ave. ... C-6,D-5
Zold Pl., S. ... G-4
1st Ave. ... C-5,F-4,G-3
1st Pl. ... K-2
1st St. ... C-6,H-6
1st St. ... H-5
2nd Ave. ... C-5,F-3,G-3
2nd Pl. ... K-2
2nd St. ... C-6,F-5,H-5
2nd St., E. ... G-3
3rd Ave. ... C-5,E-4,G-3
3rd Pl. ... K-2
3rd St. ... C-7,H-5
3rd St., E. ... G-3
3rd St., W. ... G-2
4th Ave. ... G-3
4th Pl. ... K-2
4th St. ... H-4,H-5
4th St., E. ... G-3
5th Ave. ... B-5
5th St. ... E-5,H-4,H-5
5th St., E. ... G-3
6th Ave. ... K-4
6th St. ... H-5
6th St., E. ... G-3
7th Ave. ... F-2,K-2
7th St. ... H-5
7th St., E. ... G-3
8th ... I-4
8th Ave. ... D-3,F-2
8th St. ... H-5
8th St., E. ... G-3
8th St., W. ... F-2
9th Ave. ... E-2
9th St. ... C-7,D-6,H-5
9th St., E. ... G-3
9th St., W. ... F-2
10th Ave. ... E-2
10th St. ... D-6,E-5,E-6,H-5
10th St., E. ... G-3
10th St., W. ... F-2
11th Ave. ... E-2
11th St. ... D-6,E-5,E-6,H-5
11th St., E. ... G-3
11th St., W. ... F-2
12th St. ... D-6,E-5,G-6
12th St., E. ... G-3
12th St., W. ... F-2
13th St. ... E-6
13th St., W. ... F-2
14th St. ... C-7,D-6
14th St., E. ... F-3
14th St., W. ... F-2
15th St. ... H-5
15th St., E. ... F-3
15th St., W. ... F-2
16th St., E. ... F-3
16th St., W. ... F-2
17th St., E. ... F-3
17th St., W. ... F-2
18th St., E. ... G-3
18th St., W. ... F-2
19th St. ... C-7
19th St., E. ... F-3
20th Ave. ... B-8
20th St. ... B-8
20th St., E. ... F-3
20th St., W. ... F-2
21st Ave. ... B-8
21st St. ... B-8,C-7, D-7,E-6,F-6
21st St., E. ... F-3
21st St. W. ... F-2
22nd St. ... E-6
22nd Rd. ... B-8
22nd St., E. ... F-3
23rd St. ... C-7,D-7,E-6
23rd St., E. ... F-3
23rd St., W. ... E-2
24th St. ... C-7,E-6
25th Ave. ... D-8
25th Rd. ... C-7
25th Rd., W. ... E-2
25th St., E. ... F-3
26th Ave. ... C-7
26th St. ... C-8
26th St., E. ... F-3
26th St., W. ... E-2
27th Ave. ... C-7
27th St. ... C-8,E-6
27th St., E. ... F-3
27th St., W. ... E-2
28th St. ... C-8,E-6
28th St., W. ... E-2
29th Ave. ... C-7,D-8
29th St. ... C-8,E-6
29th St., W. ... E-2
30th Ave. ... D-8
30th Dr. ... C-7
30th Pl. ... F-6
30th Rd. ... C-7
30th St. ... C-7,D-7,E-6,F-6
30th St., E. ... F-3
30th St., W. ... E-2
31st Ave. ... C-7
31st Dr. ... D-7
31st Pl. ... F-6
31st St. ... F-6
31st St., E. ... E-3
31st St., W. ... E-2
32nd St. ... D-7,E-7
32nd Pl. ... F-7
32nd St., E. ... E-3
32nd St., W. ... E-3
33rd St. ... C-8,D-7,E-6,F-7
33rd St., E. ... E-3
33rd St., W. ... E-2
34th Ave. ... D-7
34th St. ... F-7
34th St., E. ... E-4
34th St. W. ... E-2
35th Ave. ... D-6
35th St. ... C-1,C-8,E-7,F-7
35th St., E. ... E-4
35th St., W. ... E-2
36th Ave. ... D-6
36th St. ... C-1,C-8,E-7,F-7
36th St., E. ... E-4
36th St., W. ... E-2
37th Ave. ... D-6,E-8
37th St. ... C-1,C-8,E-8, F-7,G-6
37th St., E. ... E-4
37th St., W. ... E-3
38th ... E-8
38th Ave. ... D-6
38th St. ... C-8,E-8,F-7
38th St., E. ... E-4
38th St., W. ... E-3
39th Ave. ... E-6,E-8
39th Pl. ... F-7
39th St. ... C-1,F-7
39th St., E. ... E-4
39th St., W. ... D-3
40th Ave. ... E-6
40th St. ... F-7
40th St., E. ... E-4
40th St., W. ... D-3
41st Dr. ... E-8
41st St. ... C-1,C-8,E-7,F-7
41st St., E. ... E-4
41st St., W. ... D-3
42nd Pl. ... E-7
42nd St. ... C-8,E-7,F-7
42nd St., E. ... F-4
42nd St., W. ... D-3
43rd Ave. ... E-5,E-7
43rd Rd. ... E-5
43rd St. ... C-1,E-8,F-7,G-7
43rd St., E. ... F-4
43rd St., W. ... D-3
44th Ave. ... E-5
44th Dr. ... E-5
44th Rd. ... E-5
44th St. ... E-8,F-7,G-7
44th St, E. ... E-4
44th St., W. ... D-3
45th ... B-1
45th Ave. ... E-5
45th Rd. ... E-5
45th St. ... E-8,F-7
45th St., E. ... E-4
45th St., W. ... D-7
46th Ave. ... E-5
46th Rd. ... E-5
46th St. ... C-1,E-8,F-7
46th St., E. ... E-4
46th St., W. ... D-3
47th Ave. ... E-5,F-6
47th St. ... C-1,E-8,F-8,H-7
47th Rd. ... E-5
47th St., E. ... E-4
47th St., W. ... D-3
48th Ave. ... F-5,F-6
48th St. ... B-1,E-8,F-8,G-7
48th St., E. ... E-4
48th St., W. ... D-3
49th Ave. ... F-5
49th St. ... B-1,D-8,E-8,F-8
49th St., E. ... D-4
49th St., W. ... D-3
50th ... B-1
50th Ave. ... D-8,E-8,F-5
50th St. ... B-1,E-8,F-8,G-8
50th St., E. ... D-4
50th St., W. ... D-3
51st ... B-1
51st Ave. ... F-5
51st St. ... B-1,F-8
51st St., E. ... D-4
51st St., W. ... D-3
52nd Ave. ... F-8
52nd Rd. ... F-8
52nd St. ... B-1,E-8
52nd St., E. ... D-4
52nd St., W. ... D-3
53rd ... H-8
53rd St. ... B-1,F-8
53rd St., E. ... D-4
53rd St., W. ... D-3
54th Ave. ... F-5,G-7,G-8
54th Dr. ... G-7
54th Pl. ... H-8
54th Rd. ... G-7
54th St. ... B-1,E-8,F-8,H-8
54th St., E. ... D-4
54th St., W. ... D-3
55th Ave. ... F-5,G-7
55th Dr. ... G-7
55th St. ... B-1,E-8,F-8,H-8
55th St., E. ... D-4
55th St., W. ... D-3
56th Rd. ... G-7,G-8
56th St. ... B-1,E-8,F-8,H-8
56th St., E. ... D-4
56th St., W. ... D-3
57th Ave. ... G-7
57th Dr. ... H-8
57th St. ... B-1,E-8,F-8
57th Rd. ... G-8
57th St., E. ... D-4
57th St., W. ... C-3
58th Ave. ... H-8
58th Ln. ... F-8
58th Rd. ... H-8
58th St. ... B-1,E-8,F-8
58th St., E. ... D-4
58th St., W. ... C-3
59th St. ... A-1,G-8
59th Dr. ... H-8
59th Pl. ... H-8
59th St., E. ... D-4
59th St., W. ... C-3
60th St. ... A-1
60th St., E. ... D-4
60th St., W. ... C-3
61st St. ... A-1
61st St., E. ... D-4
61st St., W. ... C-3
62nd St. ... A-1
62nd St., E. ... D-4
62nd St., W. ... C-3
63rd St. ... A-1
63rd St., E. ... D-4
63rd St., W. ... C-3
64th St. ... A-1
64th St., E. ... D-4
64th St., W. ... C-3
65th St. ... A-1
65th St., E. ... D-4
65th St., W. ... C-3
66th St. ... A-1
66th St., E. ... D-4
66th St., W. ... C-3
67th St. ... A-1
67th St., E. ... C-4
67th St., W. ... C-3
68th St., E. ... C-4
68th St., W. ... C-3
69th St. ... A-1,C-4
69th St., E. ... C-4
69th St., W. ... C-4
70th St. ... A-1
70th St., E. ... C-4
71st St. ... A-2,C-3
71st St., E. ... C-4
72nd St. ... A-2,B-3
72nd St., E. ... C-5
73rd St. ... A-2,B-3
73rd St., E. ... C-5
74th St. ... A-2,B-3
74th St., E. ... C-5
75th St., ... A-2,B-3
75th St., E. ... C-5
76th St. ... A-2
76th St., E. ... C-5
76th St., W. ... B-4
77th St. ... A-2,B-3
78th St. ... A-2,B-3,C-5
79th St. ... A-2,B-3,C-5
80th St. ... B-3,C-5
81st St. ... B-3,C-5
82nd St. ... B-3,C-5
83rd St. ... B-3,C-5
84th St. ... B-4,C-5
85th St. ... C-4,C-5
86th St. ... B-4,B-5
87th St. ... A-4,B-4,B-5
89th St. ... A-4,B-5
90th St. ... A-4,B-5
91st St. ... A-4,B-5
92nd St. ... A-4,B-5
93rd St. ... A-4,B-5
94th St. ... A-4,B-5
95th St. ... A-4,B-4
96th St. ... A-4,B-5
97th St. ... A-4,B-5
98th St. ... A-4,B-5
99th St. ... A-4,B-6
100th St. ... A-4,B-6
101st St. ... B-6
102nd St. ... A-4,A-5,B-6
103rd St. ... A-4,A-6
104th St. ... A-4,A-6
105th St. ... A-4,A-6
106th St. ... A-6
107th St. ... A-6
108th St. ... A-6
109th St. ... A-6
110th St. ... A-6
111th St. ... A-6
112th St. ... A-6
113th St. ... A-6
114th St. ... A-6
115th St. ... A-6
116th St. ... A-6
117th St. ... A-6
118th ... A-6
119th St. ... A-6

New York City, NY

Scale of Miles

0 .2 .4 .6 .8

N

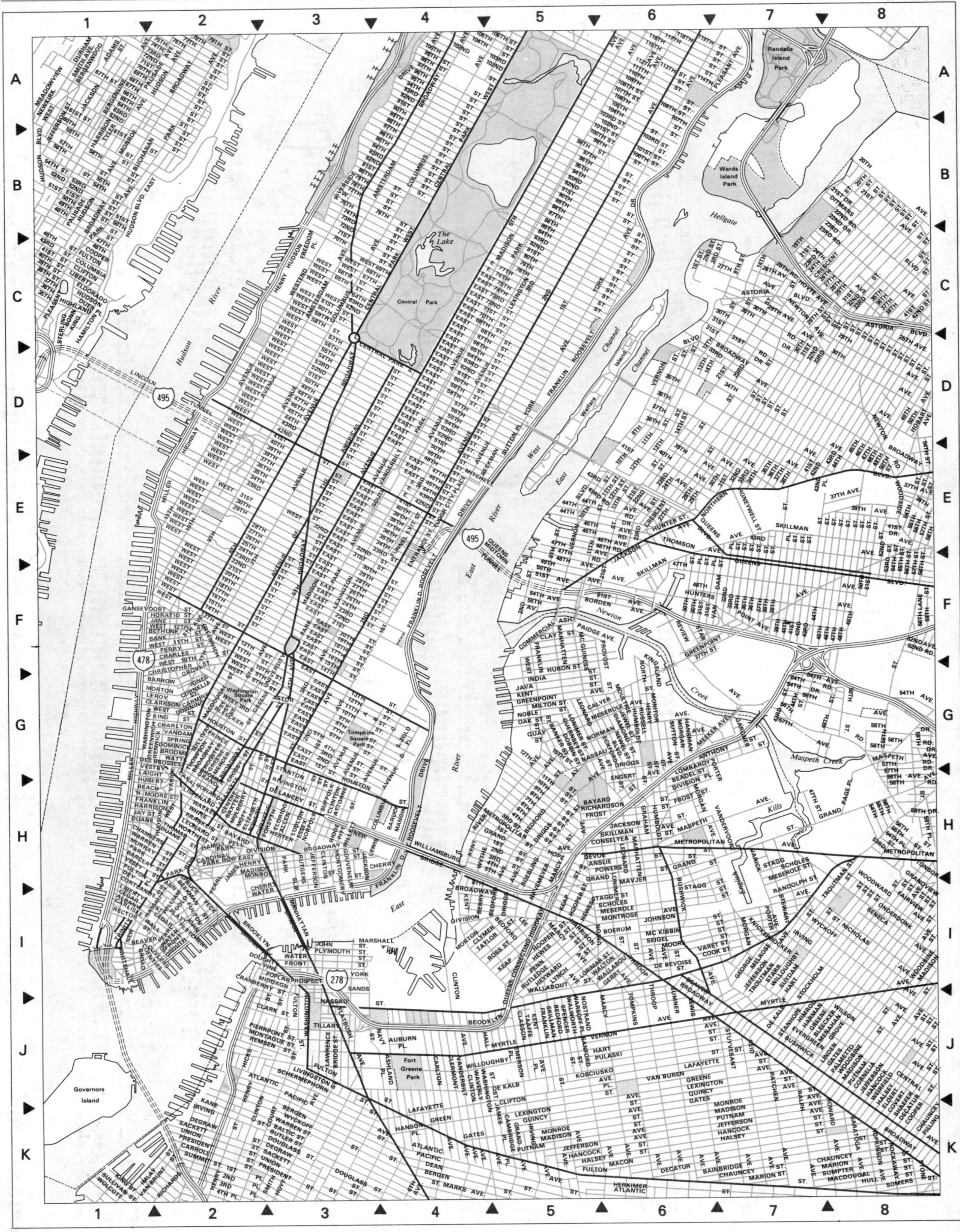